Hart Publishing
Oxford and Portland, Oregon

[illegible]
Hart Publishing c/o
International Specialized Book Services
5804 NE Hassalo Street
Portland, Oregon
97213-3644
USA

Hart Publishing is a specialist legal publisher based in Oxford,
England.
To order further copies of this book or to request a list of other
publications please write to:
Hart Publishing, Salter's Boatyard, Folly Bridge,
[illegible]
Telephone: +44 (0)1865 245533 or Fax: +44 (0)1865 794882
e-mail: mail@hartpub.co.uk
WEBSITE: http://www.hartpub.co.uk

British Library Cataloguing in Publication Data
Data Available
ISBN 1-84113-482-1 (hardback)

Typeset by Hope Services (Abingdon) Ltd
Printed and bound in Great Britain on acid-free paper by
MPG Books, Bodmin, Cornwall

Acknowledgements

This book is a modified version of a doctoral thesis defended in May 2003. Thanks are due to the following people for helpful discussions and comments: my supervisors, Vaughan Lowe and Derrick Wyatt, my examiners, Stephen Weatherill and Joanne Scott, as well as Elizabeth Fisher, Joost Pauwelyn, Gretchen Stanton, Doaa Abdel Motaal, Gabrielle Marceau, Nicolas Lockhart, Matthew Stilwell, Ulrich Hoffmann, Richard Blackhurst and David Morgan. Thanks are also due to the Rhodes Trust, Magdalen College, and the Europaeum for financial support and research grants.

Abbreviations

AB	Appellate Body
ADI	Acceptable daily intake
AdminLRev	Administrative Law Review
AFL-CIO	American Federation of Labor and Congress of Industrial Organizations
AJIL	American Journal of International Law
APA	Administrative Procedure Act
ArizJIntlCompL	Arizona Journal of International and Comparative Law
ArizStLJ	Arizona State Law Journal
AUIntlLRev	American University International Law Review
Berkeley JIntlL	Berkeley Journal of International Law
BSE	bovine spongiform encephalopathy
CAC	Codex Alimentarius Commission
CCGP	Codex Committee on General Principles
CFI	Court of First Instance
ChiJIntlL	Chicago Journal of International Law
CLC	Central Labor Councils
Codex	Codex Alimentarius Commission
ColumJTransL	Columbia Journal of Transnational Law
ColumLRev	Columbia Law Review
Cornell ILJ	Cornell International Law Journal
DC	District of Columbia
DSB	Dispute Settlement Body
DSU	Dispute Settlement Understanding
DukeJComp&IntlL	Duke Journal of Comparative and International Law
EBusLRev	European Business Law Review
EC	European Communities
ECJ	European Court of Justice
EHRLR	European Human Rights Law Review
EHRR	European Human Rights Reports
EJIL	European Journal of International Law
EPA	Environmental Protection Agency
EU	European Union
ff	and following
Fordham IntlLJ	Fordham International Law Journal
GATT	General Agreement on Tariffs and Trade

GMO	Genetically modified organism
HarvLRev	Harvard Law Review
HarvIntlLJ	Harvard International Law Journal
HRLJ	Human Rights Law Journal
ICJ	International Court of Justice
ICLQ	International and Comparative Law Quarterly
IntlTradeL&Reg	International Trade Law and Regulation
ITR	International Trade Reporter
JECFA	Joint FAO/WHO Expert Committee on Food Additives
JEnvtlL	Journal of Environmental Law
JIEL	Journal of International Economic Law
JIntlLBus	Journal of International Law and Business
JMPR	Joint FAO/WHO Meeting on Pesticide Residues
JWT	Journal of World Trade
Law&Pol'yIntlBus	Law and Policy in International Business
MichLRev	Michigan Law Review
MLR	Modern Law Review
NILR	Netherlands International Law Review
NLRB	National Labor Relations Board
NorthwesternJILBus	Northwestern Journal of International Law and Business
NRC	National Research Council (US)
NRDC	Natural Resources Defense Council
NYU Env'tlLJ	New York University Environmental Law Journal
OECD	Organisation for Economic Co-operation and Development
OIE	International Office of Epizootics
OJLS	Oxford Journal of Legal Studies
OSHA	Occupational Safety and Health Administration
ppm	part (or parts) per million
RECIEL	Review of European Community and International Environmental Law
SC	US Supreme Court
SciTechRev	Scientific and Technical Review
SPS	Sanitary and Phytosanitary
TBT	Technical Barriers to Trade
Tulane EnvtlLJ	Tulane Environmental Law Journal
UChiLRev	University of Chicago Law Review
US	United States
VaLRev	Virginia Law Review
VandJTransL	Vanderbilt Journal of Transnational Law
VandLRev	Vanderbilt Law Review
WashLeeLRev	Washington and Lee Law Review

WTO	World Trade Organization
YaleJReg	Yale Journal on Regulation
YEL	Yearbook of European Law

Table of Contents

Table of Cases

GATT AND WTO

UNITED STATES

EUROPEAN CASES (ECJ, CFI AND EFTA COURT)

UNITED KINGDOM

Table of Documents and Statutes

GATT/WTO DOCUMENTS

OTHER INTERNATIONAL DOCUMENTS

US STATUTES AND CONSTITUTION

EUROPEAN DOCUMENTS

1

Introduction

IN THE DEVELOPED world, we are preoccupied with safety. We insist that the food we eat, the toys we give our children and the products we use are all safe, but few actually stop to contemplate the workings of the vast regulatory machinery that supports our safety-conscious ways. Protecting the health and safety of people, plants and animals has come to be regarded as one of the core responsibilities of national governments.[1] While such health regulations were once regarded as principally of national concern, with the growth of international trade, many areas of national policy previously seen as primarily domestic have become of international concern.[2] This is especially true of health regulations.

Health regulations have appreciable direct and indirect effects on trade ranging from increased information or production costs being imposed on overseas producers to the outright ban on the import of certain products. Even though health regulations constitute significant non-tariff barriers to trade, as the international trading system has developed, the essential right of countries to take action to protect domestic health has not been questioned. Since the General Agreement on Tariffs and Trade[3] (GATT) was concluded in 1947, it has been recognised that, in committing themselves to trade liberalisation, countries did not give up the right to limit trade in order to protect health. When the Uruguay Round negotiators gathered at Punta del Este, the reservation of this vital power was never up for negotiation. After all, in promulgating such regulations, states are fulfilling a basic duty to protect their citizens.[4]

The importance of this right to take action to protect health can hardly be overemphasised, yet the appreciable trade effects of health regulations and their susceptibility to protectionist abuse demand that some limits be

[1] It should be noted that, in this work, 'health' refers to the health of humans and plants and animals, not only that of humans.

[2] AB Zampetti and P Sauvé 'New Dimensions of Market Access: An Overview' in OECD *New Dimensions of Market Access in a Globalising World Economy* (OECD Paris 1995) 13, 16.

[3] General Agreement on Tariffs and Trade (GATT) (Geneva 30 October 1947). Note that all WTO texts (including GATT 1947) are available from the WTO's website at <http:www.wto.org>.

[4] J Croome *Reshaping the World Trading System: A History of the Uruguay Round* (2nd edn WTO Geneva 1999) 201.

placed on recourse to health as a justification for trade-limiting measures. It is important to bear in mind that health regulations will *always* limit trade in some way—the protection of health is an essential and vitally important national prerogative. The challenge is one of formulating a set of constraints that will place some agreed limits on health regulations to ensure that the benefits of trade liberalisation are not unduly undermined by health regulations. In formulating the terms of GATT, negotiators understood that it should not be enough for a Contracting Party simply to claim that a trade-limiting rule is justified on the basis of health. Not only is health vulnerable to being used as a cloak for less laudable objectives, but health-based objectives can be achieved in a variety of ways with differing effects on trade. Moreover, it is not always clear what the demands of 'health' are, for example when it is not clear whether or in what quantities a particular substance is in fact harmful. GATT recognised these challenges by providing some constraints on the ability of Contracting Parties to cite health as a justification for trade-limiting rules. In particular, GATT provided in Article XX that nothing in the Agreement was to be construed so as to prevent Contracting Parties taking measures 'necessary to protect human, animal or plant life or health' provided that such measures were not applied so as to constitute a means of arbitrary or unjustifiable discrimination or a disguised restriction on international trade.

Despite the constraints imposed on health regulations in GATT, by the time the Tokyo Round was initiated in 1973, it was clear that non-tariff barriers (including health regulations) required further attention.[5] GATT had failed to control the exploitation of health and other regulations as non-tariff barriers because the dispute resolution system was weak and because the disciplines on health regulations were under-developed.[6] The consensus decision-making system in GATT allowed any Member to prevent a panel being established to hear a complaint against it or, following an adverse report, to prevent the panel report being adopted—a practice

[5] JH Jackson 'The Birth of the GATT–MTN System: A Constitutional Appraisal' in JH Jackson *The Jurisprudence of GATT and the WTO* (CUP Cambridge UK 2000) 34, 35; JH Jackson 'World Trade Rules and Environmental Policies: Congruence or Conflict?' in Jackson *Jurisprudence* (above in this note) 414, 419. By 1975, non-tariff barriers had been labelled 'the principal form of protectionism': MJ Marks and HB Malmgren 'Negotiating Nontariff Distortions to Trade' (1975) 7 Law&Pol'yIntlBus 327, 328.

[6] T Christoforou 'Settlement of Science-Based Trade Disputes in the WTO: A Critical Review of the Developing Case Law in the Face of Scientific Uncertainty' (2000) 8 NYUEnv'tlLJ 622, 622; DP Fidler *International Law and Infectious Diseases* (Clarendon Press Oxford 1999) 126; J Atik 'Science and International Regulatory Convergence' (1996–97) 17 Northwestern JILBus 736, 741; AO Sykes *Product Standards for Internationally Integrated Goods Markets* (Brookings Institution Washington DC 1995) 64; J Cromer 'Sanitary and Phytosanitary Measures: What They Could Mean for Health and Safety Regulations Under GATT' (1995) 36 HarvIntlLJ 557, 560; DA Wirth 'The Role of Science in the Uruguay Round and NAFTA Trade Disciplines' (1994) 27 Cornell IntlLJ 817, 822; H van Houtte 'Health and Safety Regulations in International Trade' in P Sarcevic and H van Houtte (eds) *Legal Issues in International Trade* (Graham & Trotman London 1990) 128, 130.

known as 'blocking'. Moreover, the substantive disciplines on health regulations were weak, which discouraged the Contracting Parties from bringing cases in the first place.[7] GATT's failure to provide the institutional dispute settlement system and substantive constraints necessary to tackle health-based non-tariff barriers became increasingly apparent as successive reductions in tariff levels focused attention on non-tariff barriers.[8]

When the Uruguay Round opened with the Ministerial meeting in Punta Del Este in September 1986, the negotiators were faced with a number of challenges. One challenge was to reform the dispute resolution system so that blocking would no longer be possible. Another challenge was to develop a set of disciplines to control the proliferation of health-based non-tariff barriers. With the basic right of states to regulate to protect health undisturbed, the question for negotiators was how to distinguish legitimate health regulations from illegitimate ones?[9] The answer that the Uruguay Round negotiators came up with was science. Their basic proposal—that only scientifically justified health regulations would be regarded as justified—was elegant in its simplicity, but concealed a host of difficulties that have taxed the WTO's credibility and legitimacy in the years since 1995. This is the story of those difficulties and efforts to resolve them.

Health regulations constitute non-tariff barriers to trade irrespective of whether they are disguised protectionism (and therefore 'sham' health regulations) or whether they are genuinely motivated by a concern to protect health.[10] In stipulating that only health regualtions backed by science could survive, the Uruguay Round negotiators were not only concerned with the abuse of health regulations to conceal protectionism, but also with trade barriers that resulted from misplaced, if genuine, concerns about health. According to the scientific justification rationale, if a health regulation is not based on a scientifically verified risk, it is not legitimate even if motivated by a bona fide concern about health.

With the WTO now an established institution operating since 1995, and with a number of major health cases having passed through the dispute resolution system, it is appropriate to take stock of the relationship between the national right to take action to protect health and WTO efforts to limit the trade impact of health regulations. Before the Uruguay Round, the concern was that the international system was ineffective in

[7] Fidler notes that, in several instances, formal dispute settlement under GATT was not pursued because there was no constraint requiring that the importing Member have a scientific basis for its trade-limiting health regulations: Fidler (n 6) 129–31.

[8] MJ Trebilcock and R Howse *The Regulation of International Trade* (2nd edn Routledge London 1999) 136, 145; EJ Ray 'The Political Economy of International Trade Law and Policy: Changing Patterns of Protectionism: The Fall in Tariffs and the Rise in Non-Tariff Barriers' (1987) 8 JIntlLBus 285.

[9] Legitimacy is used simply to identify those health regulations whose negative effects on trade must, according to the agreed norms of the international trade community, be tolerated.

[10] AO Sykes 'Regulatory Protectionism and the Law of International Trade' (1999) 66 UChiLRev 1, 17–18.

constraining health-based non-tariff barriers. Now, the concern is that the pendulum has swung too far in the opposite direction. Even before the Agreements negotiated during the Uruguay Round took effect on 1 January 1995, there was widespread concern, especially among civil society groups, that the new WTO would undermine national sovereignty. In particular, the fear (which has proved to be persistent), was that the WTO would establish itself as a quasi global government, undermining democratically legitimised sovereign choices regarding local priorities—particularly those ensuring high environmental, consumer and public health standards—and would prevent the Members from taking protective action in circumstances of scientific uncertainty.[11] The Appellate Body's first four decisions under the SPS Agreement did little to dispel such concerns.

In the first four cases decided under the SPS Agreement, the Appellate Body found that the defending Member's health regulations were inconsistent with the SPS Agreement. The first case was the *Hormones* case.[12] In that case, the US and Canada successfully argued that EC measures prohibiting the import of hormone-treated beef were inconsistent with the SPS Agreement. While the Appellate Body overturned a number of the panel's findings, it ultimately upheld the panel's conclusion that the EC measure failed the SPS Agreement's requirements on risk assessment. Australia was the next defendant facing a claim of inconsistency with the SPS Agreement. This time, the claim related to Australia's quarantine regulations, which prevented the import of fresh, chilled or frozen salmon. Again, the claim was successful.[13]

[11] On these concerns, see, eg: RA Cass and JR Haring 'Domestic Regulation and International Trade: Where's the Race?' in DLM Kennedy and JD Southwick (eds) *The Political Economy of International Trade Law* (CUP Cambridge UK 2002) 111, 111; GC Shaffer '"If Only We Were Elephants": The Political Economy of the WTO's Treatment of Trade and Environment Matters' in Kennedy and Southwick (eds) (above in this note) 349, 349, fn 1; MP Maduro 'Is There Any Such Thing As Free or Fair Trade? A Constitutional Analysis of the Impact of International Trade on the European Social Model' in G de Búrca and J Scott (eds) *The EU and the WTO: Legal and Constitutional Issues* (Hart Publishing Oxford 2001) 257, 261; R Howse 'Democracy, Science, and Free Trade: Risk Regulation on Trial at the World Trade Organization' (2000) 98 Michigan LRev 2329, 2330; JH Jackson 'The Great 1994 Sovereignty Debate: United States Acceptance and Implementation of the Uruguay Round Results' in Jackson *Jurisprudence* (n 5) 367, 381, 393; S Sassen *Losing Control? Sovereignty in an Age of Globalization* (Columbia UP New York 1996) 24–25. There are few who, like WJ Davey, think that, in general, the results of WTO dispute settlement do not show panels and the AB inappropriately limiting the discretion of Member governments' policy-making: WJ Davey 'Has the WTO Dispute Settlement System Exceeded Its Authority' in T Cottier and PC Mavroidis *The Role of the Judge in International Trade Regulation: Experience and Lessons for the WTO* (U Mich P Ann Arbor 2003) 43, 58.

[12] *EC–Measures Concerning Meat and Meat Products (Hormones)* WT/DS26/AB/R, WT/DS48/AB/R AB Report adopted 13 February 1998; *EC–Measures Concerning Meat and Meat Products (Hormones)* WT/DS26/R/USA modified US Panel Report adopted 13 February 1998 and WT/DS48/R/CAN modified Canada Panel Report adopted 13 February 1998.

[13] *Australia–Measures Affecting Importation of Salmon* WT/DS18/AB/R AB Report adopted 6 November 1998; *Australia–Measures Affecting Importation of Salmon* WT/DS18/R modified Panel Report adopted 6 November 1998.

After those two cases, it was hardly surprising when the third SPS case—the *Agricultural Products* case—was also decided in the complainant's favour.[14] According to the panel and the Appellate Body, the Japanese requirement that the efficacy of a particular quarantine treatment be established for each variety of certain agricultural products was inconsistent with the SPS Agreement. The immediate point is not whether those findings of inconsistency were justified, but that that string of losses set alarm bells ringing and re-ignited concerns that, in the longer term, WTO review of health regulations might unduly interfere with national health protection. After those three SPS cases came the *Asbestos* case, in which a challenged health regulation was finally upheld.[15] In that case, a French ban on asbestos and asbestos-containing products was upheld. While that case was not an SPS Agreement case, it was still the first WTO case in which the defending Member's health regulations were upheld. The *Asbestos* case was followed by another SPS case, the *Apples* case, in which the US successfully challenged various requirements imposed by Japan on the importation of US apples.[16] In that case, the Appellate Body upheld the panel's findings that the Japanese measure failed the scientific justification test (but did not qualify as a 'provisional measure') and also failed the risk assessment requirement of the SPS Agreement. With these five cases now decided, and several more working their way through the WTO dispute resolution system,[17] it is possible to consider what the advent of the WTO has meant for national health regulation.

In addressing the impact of the WTO on national regulatory autonomy, two questions have to be addressed. Firstly, how have the disciplines set out in GATT, the SPS Agreement and the TBT Agreement been interpreted

[14] *Japan–Measures Affecting Agricultural Products* WT/DS76/AB/R AB Report adopted 19 March 1999; *Japan–Measures Affecting Agricultural Products* WT/DS76/R modified Panel Report adopted 19 March 1999.

[15] *EC–Measures Affecting Asbestos and Asbestos-Containing Products* WT/DS135/AB/R AB Report adopted 6 April 2001; *EC–Measures Affecting Asbestos and Asbestos-Containing Products* WT/DS135/R modified Panel Report adopted 6 April 2001.

[16] *Japan–Meausres Affecting the Importation of Apples* WT/DS245/AB/R AB Report adopted 10 December 2003; *Japan–Meausres Affecting the Importation of Apples* WT/DS245/R Panel Report adopted 10 December 2003.

[17] The most prominent case currently in the WTO dispute resolution system is the case brought against the EU's approach to biotech products: *EC–Measures Affecting the Approval and Marketing of Biotech Products* WT/DS291 (US), WT/DS292 (Canada) and WT/DS293 (Argentina). In these cases, the US, Canada and Argentina allege that the EC has applied a de facto moratorium on the approval of biotechnology products and take issue with the refusal of specific EC Member States to allow the import of biotechnology products approved at the Community level. A single panel was established on 29 August 2003. Australia is also facing a number of challenges. In *Australia–Quarantine Regime for Imports* WT/DS287, the EC alleges that Australia's quarantine system as a whole (which it says prohibits the import of products without supporting risk assessments), as well as specific conditions applying to the import of pig meat, breach the SPS Agreement. A panel was established on 7 November 2003. Australia is also facing a case brought by the Philippines (*Australia–Certain Measures Affecting the Importation of Fresh Fruit and Vegetables* WT/DS270) in which similar issues are raised; a panel in this case was established on 29 August 2003.

and applied by the WTO's adjudicative arm? Secondly, do the constraints imposed by panels and the Appellate Body represent a realistic image of regulatory practice? The first question is addressed in Chapters 2 and 3, which offer a detailed (and necessarily technical) analysis of how the disciplines have been interpreted and applied by panels and the Appellate Body in order to assess the real impact of those Agreements on Members' regulatory autonomy. The second question is taken up in Chapter 4, which evaluates the basis of the scientific justification norm and the way in which it relates to regulatory practice on risk assessment and risk management. Through this process two essential points of tension are highlighted. The first point of tension relates to the ability of WTO Members to take protective action where the scientific evidence regarding the threat is uncertain. The second point of tension relates to the role of diverse social and cultural preferences in risk regulation. The SPS Agreement puts in place a model of regulation-making that emphasises the rational, scientific basis of regulatory decisions. Where in this model is the social dimension of regulation, which affects the regulatory process from beginning to end? These two points of tension constitute the twin focal points for anxiety about the WTO's impact on national sovereignty.

With these two points of tension in mind, Chapter 5 examines the precautionary principle. The precautionary principle is sometimes seen as a panacea for the anxieties surrounding the ability of countries to regulate in circumstances of uncertainty. This principle was raised in the *Hormones* case but, since that decision, the EC has sought to clarify its meaning and status. While the precautionary principle does overcome a fundamental challenge posed by the scientific justification criterion of the SPS Agreement, it is argued that the principle should not be embraced in the WTO. The value of the precautionary principle in the WTO is questioned because, in order to limit the negative trade effects of health-based non-tariff barriers, there must be meaningful and justiciable disciplines. In order to provide such disciplines, the precautionary principle would have to be accompanied either by a strict proportionality test or by a procedurally focused form of review but a comparative study of ECJ review of Community and Member State health measures as well as judicial review of agency rule-making in the US suggest that both of these options have significant drawbacks that render them of questionable utility in the WTO.

Chapter 6 proposes an alternative way to handle the tensions relating to scientific uncertainty and the use of social and cultural factors in regulation. In particular, it suggests that the standard of review being applied by WTO panels is an important component in determining how intense scrutiny of national health regulations will be. The intensity of scrutiny plays an important role in determining the extent to which scientific uncertainty will prevent a Member from taking protective action and the extent to which the social and cultural preferences implicated in a

Member's regulatory decisions will be interfered with. Chapter 6 sets out the Appellate Body's 'objective assessment' standard of review, and criticises it as incoherent. It is suggested that the WTO's standard of review need not languish in its unsatisfactory state but, rather, could be developed. The chapter looks at the Anti-Dumping Agreement's standard of review and notes that, outside the parameters of the Anti-Dumping Agreement, the objective assessment standard of review has been developed in a particular subset of cases (the safeguards cases).

In order to maximise the contribution that a proper standard of review can make to easing tensions in WTO review of national health regulations, it is necessary to have a clear idea of exactly what degree of deference is desirable. The essential difficulty is succinctly articulated by Sykes:

> To be politically acceptable within the international community, dispute resolution must remain reasonably deferential to the honest judgments of national regulators. But excessive deference makes dispute resolution ineffectual, and some 'intermediate' level of deference thus seems appropriate.[18]

The extent to which WTO Members' assessments should not be interfered with by WTO panels—ie, the degree of deference that is appropriate—should reflect the objectives of the organisation. In other words, review should not be more intrusive than is necessary to accomplish the aims for which the founding Member countries originally came together to form the WTO. In order to gain a clearer picture of the nature of the Members' commitment to one another and the type of review which is fitting, Chapter 7 considers the intensity of review applied in analogous circumstances in the US and EU. The chapter begins by taking up the standard of review applied to factual and legal questions in US judicial review cases. It then considers the rationales underlying close review of health arguments advanced where a commerce clause case is brought challenging state regulations limiting inter-state trade. The manifestly different levels of intensity of review applied by the ECJ to the health claims of the Community institutions and the Member States also help us to analyse the appropriate intensity of review in the WTO. The appropriate degree of deference is one question, the way in which to achieve it is another. Accordingly, the chapter goes on to consider how the standard of review might actually be developed in the WTO. To this end, it examines more closely whether the approach taken in the safeguards cases might show the way forward in health cases. It is suggested that the safeguards approach might be used to introduce a standard of review hinted at in the *Asbestos* panel report, the 'reasonable regulator' standard. The final chapter, Chapter 8, reviews the arguments made, draws some conclusions and reflects on the future trajectory of international supervision of national health regulation.

[18] Sykes *Product Standards* (n 6) 127.

2

Review of Health Measures under GATT

A THE ARCHITECTURE AND HISTORY OF THE PROVISIONS RELATING TO HEALTH

THE 'NATIONAL TREATMENT' discipline of Article III and the 'most favoured nation' (MFN) discipline of Article I are well known to those familiar with the constraints that the General Agreement on Tariffs and Trade[1] imposes on Members. Broadly speaking, national treatment requires that Members not discriminate against imports, and the MFN discipline requires that they accord each Member the same the benefits. Together, the national treatment and MFN disciplines constitute the foundation principles of GATT, but there is another discipline that is important for present purposes: Article XI's obligation not to impose quantitative restrictions on trade.[2] These disciplines are, of course, not absolute: GATT contains a number of exceptions including, in Article XX(b), an exception relating to health. According to Article XX(b), nothing in the General Agreement is to be construed to prevent the adoption or enforcement of measures 'necessary to protect human, animal or plant life or health' provided that 'such measures are not applied in a manner which would constitute a means of arbitrary or unjustifiable discrimination . . . or a disguised restriction on international trade'.

When the WTO came into being on 1 January 1995, the obligations and exceptions of GATT were retained: GATT 1994 incorporates the text of GATT as an annex.[3] The continuity of GATT is reinforced by treating panel reports adopted under the old GATT as part of the *acquis* that has

[1] General Agreement on Tariffs and Trade (GATT) (Geneva, 30 October 1947).
[2] GATT Art XI.
[3] General Agreement on Tariffs and Trade 1994 (GATT 1994) (Marrakesh, 15 April 1994). GATT 1994 incorporates the provisions of GATT 1947 as amended: GATT 1994 Art 1(a). References to GATT in this work are to the GATT annexed to GATT 1994.

been brought into the WTO.[4] Since 1995, however, two additional Agreements also apply to health regulations: the SPS Agreement and the TBT Agreement.[5] While the SPS Agreement expressly identifies itself as an elaboration of GATT Article XX(b),[6] the TBT Agreement does not. Nevertheless, both Agreements relate to the territory covered by GATT Article XX(b): the protection of human, animal or plant life or health.

It is important to have a clear idea of how the SPS Agreement, the TBT Agreement and GATT fit together in order to appreciate the continuing significance of the GATT disciplines. The SPS Agreement only applies to SPS measures. SPS measures are a subset of the health measures covered by Article XX(b). Where GATT Article XX(b) applies to *all* measures necessary to protect human, animal and plant life and health, the SPS Agreement only covers measures protecting against exposure to pests, disease-carrying or disease-causing organisms, disease-carrying animals or plants, and laws restricting additives, contaminants and toxins in food and feedstuffs.[7] The TBT Agreement applies to technical regulations (mandatory product standards) and standards (non-mandatory product standards), provided that the measure is not already covered by the SPS Agreement.[8] One of the 'legitimate objectives' for which technical regulations may be put in place is the 'protection of human health or safety, animal or plant life or health, or the environment.'[9] Accordingly, the TBT Agreement also covers some of the trade-limiting measures falling under GATT Article XX(b).

The diagram below shows that, of all the health measures covered by Article XX(b), some will fall within the SPS Agreement and some will fall within the TBT Agreement (which also covers some non-health measures). Others will not be covered by either Agreement and, if they fall foul of one GATT's impugning provisions (in health cases, typically either Article III or Article XI), will have to rely on GATT Article XX(b). The diagram also shows that, when a measure might otherwise fall within both the SPS and TBT Agreements, Article 1.5 of the TBT Agreement stipulates that it is the SPS Agreement that will apply. It should, however, be noted that the SPS Agreement is not conditional upon breach of a substantive GATT

[4] Although WTO panels may still find the reasoning of unadopted GATT panel reports useful: *Japan–Taxes on Alcoholic Beverages* WT/DS8/AB/R, WT/DS10/AB/R, WT/DS11/AB/R AB Report adopted 1 November 1996, DSR 1996:I 97, 106–8 ('*Japan–Alcohol II*').

[5] Agreement on the Application of Sanitary and Phytosanitary Measures (SPS Agreement) (Marrakesh, 15 April 1994); Agreement on Technical Barriers to Trade (TBT Agreement) (Marrakesh, 15 April 1994).

[6] SPS Agreement Preamble.

[7] SPS Agreement Annex A (summary of the detailed definition drawn from S Charnovitz 'The Supervision of Health and Biosafety Regulation by the World Trade Rules' (2000) Tulane EnvtlLJ 271, 176).

[8] TBT Agreement Annex 1 paras 1–2 (definitions), Art 1.5 (excluding SPS measures).

[9] TBT Agreement Art 2.2.

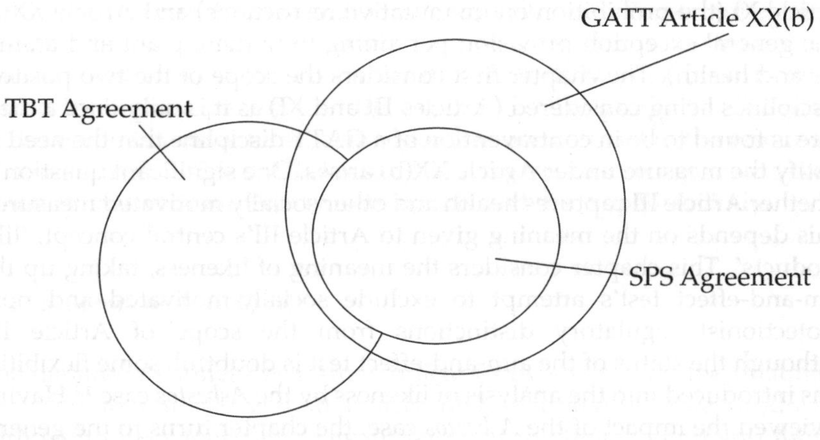

Coverage of health measures

provision; ie, a complaining Member need not show that GATT Article III or Article XI has been breached before the measure can be tested against the SPS Agreement.[10] Nevertheless, once a measure has been tested under the SPS Agreement and it has passed, there is little point trying to prove breach of a GATT provision because the measure will then be presumed to satisfy the requirements of GATT Article XX(b).[11] It is, however, customary for WTO Members to continue to mount arguments under both GATT and the SPS Agreement.[12] There is no equivalent provision stating that a measure which satisfies the TBT Agreement will satisfy the requirements of Article XX(b). Accordingly, one cannot conclude that a technical regulation which satisfies the TBT Agreement will *necessarily* satisfy GATT Article XX(b). In particular, as will be seen below, the interpretation of Article XX(b) is being developed so that the alleged risk must be demonstrated (almost certainly by scientific evidence) whereas the TBT Agreement does not contain any scientific justification discipline and no equivalent requirement has (as yet) been implied. Again, it seems to be the case that Members will still argue a full GATT case in addition to mounting arguments based on the TBT Agreement.[13]

This chapter will take up the GATT provisions that are most usually relevant to national health measures: Article III (national treatment),

[10] *EC Measures Concerning Meat and Meat Products (Hormones)* WT/DS26/R/USA modified US Panel Report adopted 13 February 1998 ('*Hormones*') para 8.36. Note also WT/DS48/R/CAN modified Canada Panel Report adopted 13 February 1998 para 8.39.

[11] SPS Agreement Art 2.4 (although the presumption is rebuttable).

[12] Eg, *Hormones* US Panel Report (n 10) paras 3.1–3.3.

[13] Eg, *EC–Measures Affecting Asbestos and Asbestos-Containing Products* WT/DS135/R modified Panel Report adopted 6 April 2001 ('*Asbestos*').

applying to like products, and the second sentence applying (through Note Ad Article III) to directly competitive or substitutable (DCS) products. Note Ad Article III:2 provides that a tax conforming to the requirements of the first sentence of Article III:2 will fall foul of the provisions of the second sentence 'only in cases where competition was involved between, on the one hand, the taxed product and, on the other hand, a directly competitive or substitutable product which was not similarly taxed.' It should also be noted that, although Article III is directed at *internal* taxation and regulations, taxes and regulations of the type referred to in Article III:1 that are collected or enforced at the time or point of importation are still to be regarded as subject to the provisions of Article III.[17]

In most cases, health measures are non-fiscal and so will fall under Article III:4. Health measures can, however, take a pecuniary form, and so may fall under Article III:2. For example, a WTO Member seeking to curb tobacco-related illness could levy a tax on cigarette consumption or it could use non-pecuniary means to achieve the same end, for example, by banning smoking in public places.[18] In either case, the measures would have to comply with Article III.

2 The Variable Concept of Likeness

Both Article III:4 and Article III:2 (first sentence) rely on the concept of likeness. The likeness or unlikeness of products is an ostensibly straightforward concept, but one which loses its clarity upon further scrutiny. The relativity and elusiveness of likeness has been recognised by GATT and WTO panels and by the Appellate Body. No hard and fast concept or articulation of the concept of likeness has been put forward against which likeness can be determined in every case.[19] Rather, a number of factors which are relevant to likeness have been identified, but the emphasis remains firmly on assessing likeness on a case-by-case basis. Not only does likeness depend heavily on the circumstances of the case, but the scope of likeness is also said to vary with the provision in which the expression occurs:

> The concept of 'likeness' is a relative one that evokes the image of an accordion. The accordion of 'likeness' stretches and squeezes in different places as different provisions of the *WTO Agreement* are applied. The width of the accordion in any one of those places must be determined by the particular provision in which

[17] Note Ad Article III.

[18] This example is drawn from JHH Weiler 'The Constitution of the Common Market Place: Text and Context in the Evolution of the Free Movement of Goods' in P Craig and G de Búrca (eds) *The Evolution of EU Law* (OUP Oxford 1999) 349, 357.

[19] For criticism of this lack of methodology, see Won-Mog Choi *'Like Products' in International Trade Law: Towards a Consistent GATT/WTO Jurisprudence* (OUP Oxford 2003) 154–55.

> the term 'like' is encountered as well as by the context and the circumstances that prevail in any given case to which that provision may apply.[20]

According to the Appellate Body, likeness is to be more broadly construed in respect of non-fiscal measures under Article III:4 than in respect of fiscal measures under Article III:2.[21]

3 Some Key Principles Applying to Fiscal and Non-Fiscal Measures

Although the scope of likeness varies with the paragraph of Article III that is being applied, there are some core ideas and principles that apply to the assessment of likeness throughout Article III. It is quite likely that these common principles will at least inform the interpretation of those provisions of the SPS and TBT Agreements that rely on the concept of likeness.[22] As noted above, Article III:1 articulates a non-protection principle that is implemented through the provisions of Articles III:2 and Article III:4. A general obligation to provide *equality of competitive opportunities* for imported products in relation to domestic products has been drawn from this overarching purpose and applies equally under both Article III:2 and Article III:4.[23] Another common theme is that likeness is to be assessed on a case-by-case basis. This principle was articulated by the *1970 Working Party on Border Tax Adjustments*[24] and a reference to it is part of the boilerplate in Article III likeness cases. A non-exhaustive list of the following

[20] *Japan–Alcohol II* AB Report (n 4) DSR 1996:I 97, 114. Note also the (actual and proposed) differences in likeness where it occurs in different Articles of GATT: RE Hudec '"Like Product". The Differences in GATT Articles I and III' in T Cottier and PC Mavroidis (eds) *Regulatory Barriers and the Principles of Non-Discrimination in World Trade Law* (U Michigan P Ann Arbor 2000) 101.

[21] *Asbestos* AB Report (n 14) para 99.

[22] The SPS Agreement imposes obligations directly by reference to the concept of like domestic products in Annex C, Arts 1(f) and 1(g). The jurisprudence of likeness is also relevant to when situations may be comparable under Arts 2.3 and 5.5 of the SPS Agreement. The TBT Agreement utilises the concept of like products in Arts 2.1, 5.1.1, 5.2.1, 5.2.5, Annex 3 para D. The AB has, however, cautioned against taking an overly casual attitude to importing analysis of GATT provisions to other Agreements: *EC Measures Concerning Meat and Meat Products (Hormones)* WT/DS26/AB/R, WT/DS48/AB/R AB Report adopted 13 February 1998 ('*Hormones*') para 239.

[23] *Section 337* (n 15) paras 5.11, 5.13; *Canada–Import, Distribution and Sale of Certain Alcoholic Drinks by Provincial Marketing Agencies* Report adopted 18 February 1992 BISD 39S/27 ('*Canada–Beer*') para 5.6; *Malt Beverages* (n 15) para 5.30; *Gasoline* Panel Report (n 16) para 6.10; *Korea–Measures Affecting Imports of Fresh, Chilled and Frozen Beef* WT/DS161/R, WT/DS169/R modified Panel Report adopted 10 January 2001 ('*Korea–Beef*') paras 623–24; *Korea–Measures Affecting Imports of Fresh, Chilled and Frozen Beef* WT/DS161/AB/R, WT/DS169/AB/R AB Report adopted 10 January 2001 ('*Korea–Beef*') para 135; *EC–Regime for the Importation, Sale and Distribution of Bananas* WT/DS27/AB/R AB Report adopted 25 September 1997 ('*Bananas*') para 213; *Asbestos* AB Report (n 14) para 97; *Japan–Alcohol II* AB Report (n 4) DSR 1996:1 97, 109–10.

[24] Report adopted 2 December 1970 BISD 18S/97 ('*Border Tax Adjustments*') para 18.

four criteria (originally identified in the same report) is widely used in analysing likeness under both Article III:2 and III:4: (i) the product's end uses in a given market; (ii) consumers' tastes and habits (which vary between countries); (iii) the product's properties, nature and quality; and (iv) the tariff classification of the product.[25] Although the working party in that case was, strictly speaking, referring to the expression 'like or similar products' and was suggesting criteria for determining similarity, subsequent panels and the Appellate Body have adopted the working party's statement as applying to the determination of likeness for both fiscal and non-fiscal measures.[26]

4 The Aim-and-Effect Test for the Assessment of Likeness

(a) Development of the aim-and-effect test

A core, non-exhaustive list of four criteria has been formulated for assessing the likeness of products. One critical issue that has arisen is whether the regulatory aims of a measure are relevant to the assessment of likeness under Article III. The 'aim-and-effect' test gives a prominent role to regulatory purposes in the assessment of likeness. According to the aim-and-effect test, products are not 'like' if the regulatory distinction between them was made on legitimate, non-protectionist policy grounds and does not have a protectionist effect. The test functions by effectively 'reading in' the non-protection purpose of Article III to the likeness requirement in Articles III:2 and III:4. The great appeal of the aim-and-effect test is that it protects Members pursuing legitimate social policies from facing the burden of justifying their measures under Article XX because no breach of Article III would be found.[27]

The prospect of Article III catching non-protectionist regulatory measures has generated concerns about regulatory autonomy. The aim-and-effect test responds to such concerns by confining the scope of

[25] *Border Tax Adjustments* (n 24) para 18. Note, though, that the fourth criterion was added after the *Border Tax Adjustments* case but has now become standard: *Asbestos* AB Report (n 14) para 101, fn 74.

[26] *Asbestos* AB Report (n 14) para 101 (re Art III:4); *Japan–Customs Duties, Taxes and Labelling Practices on Imported Wines and Alcoholic Beverages* Report adopted 10 November 1987 BISD 34S/83 ('*Japan–Alcohol I*') para 5.6 (re Art III:2); *Japan–Alcohol II* AB Report (n 4) DSR 1996:1 97, 113 (re Art III:2); *Gasoline* Panel Report (n 16) para 6.8 (re Art III:4); *Canada–Certain Measures Concerning Periodicals* WT/DS31/AB/R AB Report adopted 30 July 1997, DSR 1997:I 449, 466 ('*Canada–Periodicals*') (re Art III:2).

[27] On the history and development of the aim-and-effect test, see: R Hudec 'GATT/WTO Constraints on National Regulation: Requiem for an "Aim and Effects" Test' (1998) 32 International Lawyer 619 and R Howse and E Tuerk 'The WTO Impact on Internal Regulations—A Case Study of the Canada–EC Asbestos Dispute' in G de Búrca and J Scott (eds) *The EU and the WTO: Legal and Constitutional Issues* (Hart Publishing Oxford 2001) 283, 293ff.

Article III so that it only impugns protectionist measures and does not prevent differentiation between product categories for other policy purposes.[28] This desire to limit the impact of Article III on regulatory measures taken in pursuit of non-protectionist policy goals underpinned the panel's approach in the *Gas Guzzler* case.[29] In that case, the EC challenged, inter alia, a US law which distinguished between cars based on their fuel economy but did not distinguish between different trucks on the same basis. This gave rise to an issue about whether all cars are like products irrespective of their fuel economy and whether cars and trucks are like or DCS products. In the *Gas Guzzler* case, the panel reasoned that, because the purpose of Article III was to prohibit protectionism (and not to prohibit fiscal and regulatory distinctions designed to achieve other policy goals) and because the purpose of GATT was to lower trade barriers (and not to harmonise regulatory treatment), Article III simply *could not* be interpreted as prohibiting non-protectionist government policy initiatives.[30] According to the panel, 'issues of likeness under Article III should be analyzed primarily in terms of whether less favourable treatment was based on a regulatory distinction taken so as to afford protection to domestic production',[31] with the expression 'so as to afford protection' understood to refer to both aim and effect.[32]

(b) Rejection of the aim-and-effect test

Although popular with those keen to see the WTO stay away from national regulations put in place for environmental, ethical and other non-trade reasons, the status of the aim-and-effect test is now doubtful. The aim-and-effect test required that the non-protectionism purpose articulated in the first paragraph of the Article be read-in to Article III:2 (first sentence) and Article III:4 as a specific requirement, even though there is only an express mention of Article III:1 for the *second* sentence of Article III:2. What the Appellate Body has done (in *Japan–Alcohol II*) is to treat the express mention of Article III:1 in the second sentence of Article III:2 as disclosing a *specific criterion* (protectionism) for Article III:2 (second

[28] *Malt Beverages* (n 15) paras 5.25, 5.71.

[29] Note that a broad view of the scope of likeness puts more pressure on Article XX to avoid condemning legitimate policy initiatives. On this issue, see: DA Farber and RE Hudec 'GATT Legal Restraints on Domestic Environmental Regulations' in J Bhagwati and RE Hudec (eds) *Fair Trade and Harmonization* (Vol 2 MIT Press Cambridge MA 1996) 59, 72–73.

[30] *US–Taxes on Automobiles* DS31/R, 11 October 1994 (unadopted) paras 5.7–5.8 ('*Gas Guzzler*').

[31] *Gas Guzzler* (n 30) para 5.9.

[32] *Gas Guzzler* (n 30) para 5.10. Protection would be an aim where a change in competitive opportunities was a desired outcome and not merely incidental to the pursuit of the legitimate policy goal: para 5.10.

sentence) that is *implicitly* addressed by the terms of the first sentence of Article III:2.[33] Accordingly, the existence or non-existence of protectionism cannot be considered as part of the likeness analysis under the first sentence of Article III:2. That is not to say that the Appellate Body was totally impervious to concerns that the scope of Article III:2 (first sentence) would be too broad if the aim-and-effect test were rejected. Rather, the Appellate Body suggested that likeness should be construed narrowly 'so as not to condemn measures that its strict terms are not meant to condemn.'[34]

The aim-and-effect test is also unlikely to survive under Article III:4. In the *Bananas* case, the Appellate Body referred to its reasoning in the *Japan–Alcohol II* case, and stated that the same reasoning should be applied to Article III:4:

> Article III:4 does *not* specifically refer to Article III:1. Therefore, a determination of whether there has been a violation of Article III:4 does *not* require a separate consideration of whether a measure 'afford[s] protection to domestic production'.[35]

The Appellate Body followed up on this approach in the *Asbestos* case by finding that the requirement of 'less favourable treatment' of imports 'expresses the general principle, in Article III:1, that internal regulations "should not be applied . . . so as to afford protection to domestic production".'[36] By finding that the non-protection principle is incorporated within the terms of Article III:4, the Appellate Body implicitly rejected the consideration of regulatory purposes as part of the likeness analysis. This perception is reinforced by the Appellate Body's view that the determination of likeness under Article III:4 is 'fundamentally, a determination about the nature and extent of a competitive relationship between and among products.'[37]

(c) Non-market considerations outside the framework of the aim-and-effect test

Although a full-scale revival of the aim-and-effect test is now unlikely, in the *Asbestos* case, the Appellate Body did adopt a more flexible approach to likeness, which stands in contrast to its narrowly market-focused approach in *Japan Alcohol II*.[38] In the *Asbestos* case, Canada challenged a French ban on chrysotile asbestos. For reasons that do not presently concern us, the prohibition was considered under GATT Article III:4, rather than under the

33 *Japan–Alcohol II* AB Report (n 4) DSR 1996:I 97, 116.
34 *Japan–Alcohol II* AB Report (n 4) DSR 1996:I 97, 112.
35 *Bananas* AB Report (n 23) para 216 (emphasis in original).
36 *Asbestos* AB Report (n 14) para 100.
37 *Asbestos* AB Report (n 14) para 99.
38 *Japan–Alcohol II* AB Report (n 4) DSR 1996:1 97, 117 (endorsing a market focus).

TBT Agreement. When the Appellate Body came to consider the likeness of chrysotile fibres and substitutable fibres, it said that the list of criteria for likeness originally identified in the *Border Tax Adjustments* case is only indicative. As to what evidence will be relevant to likeness, the Appellate Body said that '[t]he kind of evidence to be examined in assessing the "likeness" of products will, necessarily, depend upon the particular products and the legal provision at issue.'[39] Most importantly, the Appellate Body found that evidence relating to the health risks associated with a product may be pertinent in an examination of 'likeness' under Article III:4 and could be accommodated under the existing criteria of physical properties and consumers' tastes and habits.[40] In the case at hand, the Appellate Body remarked that the carcinogenicity or toxicity of chrysotile asbestos constitutes a 'defining aspect' of its physical properties.[41] The significance of health effects is entrenched by two further findings by the Appellate Body: firstly, that the complaining party will face an extra burden in establishing likeness in the face of significant physical differences (which would include significantly different health risks);[42] and secondly, that where there are physical differences, a panel cannot conclude that the products are like without analysing consumers' tastes and habits.[43]

(d) Evaluation of the impact of the Asbestos *decision: what scope for consideration of regulatory aims?*

The prominence given to health risks by the Appellate Body will be pleasing for those concerned that the WTO not impinge unduly on the ability of Members to regulate to protect health. The *Asbestos* decision expanded the scope of considerations that are relevant to the assessment of whether the physical characteristics of the products and the attitudes of consumers are such that the products are 'like', but the impact of the decision on the broader issue of the leeway Members have to pursue non-protectionist regulatory policies without being called to account is limited.[44] The

[39] *Asbestos* AB Report (n 14) para 103.

[40] *Asbestos* AB Report (n 14) para 113.

[41] *Asbestos* AB Report (n 14) para 114.

[42] *Asbestos* AB Report (n 14) para 118.

[43] *Asbestos* AB Report (n 14) para 121. Note that, although the AB took a narrow approach to who the relevant consumers are by finding that manufacturers are the 'consumers' of chrysotile fibres, it did acknowledge that those manufacturers would be influenced by the opinions of their ultimate consumers: para 122.

[44] Cf Regan, who sees the decision as opening the way to consider regulatory purpose as an aspect of likeness: DH Regan 'Regulatory Purpose and "Like Products" in Article III:4 of GATT (With Additional Remarks on Article III:2' (2002) 36 JWT 443. Others, including Quick and Lau, prefer to retain the traditional approach whereby the purposes behind regulatory distinctions are considered under Art XX not as part of the like product analysis of Art III: R Quick and C Lau 'Environmentally Motivated Tax Distinctions and WTO Law' (2003) 6 JIEL 419, 431–33.

measure is dependent on government action or intervention.[48] While this finding has implications for any government health measures which operate on a technically voluntary basis, in most cases the legally binding character of health measures is not in doubt and the more pertinent issue will be the relationship between Article XI and Article III.

The question of the relationship between Articles III and XI arises because Note Ad Article III stipulates, *inter alia,* that regulations enforced at the time or point of importation are still to be regarded as internal regulations subject to the provisions of Article III. In theory at least, Article XI catches all restrictions barring market access (in which case they are illegal unless excused by an exception) and regulations which do not *bar* access to the market, but simply impede or hinder it, are subject to the non-discrimination test of Article III.[49] Where, however, a health measure is enforced at the border, there is still a real issue as to whether the measure is an import prohibition (and so subject to Article XI) or an internal regulation being enforced at the border (and so subject to Article III:4). If an argument arises as to whether Article III or Article XI applies to a health measure, the defending Member might well wish to argue that the measure is governed by Article III:4 because there is at least then an opportunity to argue that the imported product (which is injurious to health) is not 'like' another domestic product. Following the *Asbestos* case, a defending Member with a strong health case can feel optimistic about such an argument. By way of contrast, however, once it is determined that Article XI applies, there is little scope to argue that health-based distinctions are relevant[50]—the wording of the Article simply does not allow it because the concepts of 'import' and 'export' are clear, and the term 'prohibitions or restrictions' is broad and unqualified by any reference to protectionism. It is, then, not surprising that the analysis of measures under Article XI tends to be perfunctory. For example, in the *Thai Cigarettes* case, the US challenged Thai laws relating to tobacco control, which included a prohibition on the import of tobacco and tobacco products without an import licence. When the panel considered this ban under Article XI, it was content to note simply that, because Thailand had not granted licences for cigarette imports in the past 10 years, it had acted inconsistently with Article XI:1.[51]

[48] *Japan–Trade in Semi-Conductors* Report adopted 4 May 1988 BISD 35S/116 para 109 (government *requests* regarding export prices and production levels operated in a manner equivalent to mandatory requirements).

[49] Weiler 'The Constitution' (n 18) 356.

[50] Eg, note the panel's inability to consider the special historical, cultural and socio-economic circumstances (including the desire to protect the employment of a particular ethnic minority) behind Japan's maintenance of an import restrictions on leather: *Panel on Japanese Measures on Imports of Leather* Report adopted 15–16 May 1984 BISD 31S/94 para 44.

[51] *Thailand–Restrictions on Importation of and Internal Taxes on Cigarettes* Report adopted 7 November 1990 BISD 37S/200 ('*Thai Cigarettes*') para 67.

Panels dealing with the border between Articles III and XI appear not only to treat them as mutually exclusive,[52] but appear to treat them as having an 'either–or' relationship such that, if a regulatory measure excluding an import is not covered by one provision, it should be covered by the other. If the complaining Member raises Article III:4 and the claim fails, Article XI:1 may well be employed as a backstop. In this way, the scope of Article XI is, in practice, partially defined by the scope of Article III:4. For example, in the unadopted *Tuna–Dolphin I* report, the panel considered US measures excluding tuna not caught using dolphin-preserving practices. Having found that Article III:4 did not apply (on the basis that it only covers measures that are applied to 'products as such'[53]) the panel turned to Article XI:1 and found, without further analysis, that the direct import prohibition on certain tuna and tuna products was inconsistent with that Article.[54] The panel in *Tuna–Dolphin II* took a similar approach.[55] Likewise, in the *Canada–Beer* case, the panel disposed of a disagreement between the US and Canada on which Article covered the minimum price measures by simply noting that the minimum prices fell under the terms of the Note Ad Article III.[56] These cases suggest that panels are not interested in pursuing a theoretical discussion on the spheres of application of the two Articles, but will treat Article XI:1 as covering (within the limits of its terms) whatever product exclusions Article III:4 does not cover.[57]

In sum, while there has not been a great number of cases considering Article XI, when it has arisen, its substance has been treated as straightforward—measures are found to be inconsistent without protracted analysis—and it has been given a broad scope so that an exclusionary border measure which does not fall within Article III:4 may well be covered by Article XI:1. This is significant for WTO review of health regulations because it suggests that health regulations excluding a product from the import market that are not covered by Article III:4 will be considered under Article XI:1 and are almost certain to be inconsistent with it because the terms of Article XI:1 leave no room to consider the rationale for the exclusion and do not require that there be any discrimination

52 There does not seem to be any suggestion that the Articles may be co-extensive to any degree. Eg, in the *Canada–Beer* case, the panel repeatedly referred to deciding (or not having to decide) whether the measure was covered by Art III:4 *or* Art XI:1: *Canada–Beer* (n 23) paras 5.6, 5.27.

53 *US–Restrictions on Imports of Tuna* 3 September 1991 (unadopted) BISD 39S/155 ('*Tuna–Dolphin I*') para 5.14.

54 The panel did note, however, that the US had not presented any arguments on Art XI:1: *Tuna–Dolphin I* (n 53) para 5.18.

55 *US–Restrictions on Imports of* Tuna DS29/R, 16 June 1994 (unadopted) (reprinted in (1994) 33 ILM 839) ('*Tuna–Dolphin II*') paras 5.8–5.10.

56 *Canada–Beer* (n 23) para 5.28.

57 These are, however, 'old GATT' cases, and it is interesting to speculate whether WTO panels and the AB would be more inclined to theorise the distinction.

or protectionism.[58] Because Article XI does not require that there be protectionism, it would seem irrelevant that the defending Member does not itself produce a similar product. In this respect, Article XI represents a potentially far-reaching market access guarantee that can only be avoided in the name of health by recourse to Article XX.[59]

D THE HEALTH EXCEPTION: ARTICLE XX(b)

GATT Article XX(b), together with the introductory paragraph (or *chapeau*) provides:

> Subject to the requirement that such measures are not applied in a manner which would constitute a means of arbitrary or unjustifiable discrimination between countries where the same conditions prevail, or a disguised restriction on international trade, nothing in this Agreement shall be construed to prevent the adoption or enforcement by any contracting party of measures:
> . . .
> (b) necessary to protect human, animal or plant life or health;

By providing that Members can put in place trade-limiting measures and justify them as health measures, Article XX(b) raises the possibility of non-tariff barriers undermining the liberalisation gains achieved by diminishing tariff levels. Such concerns led to earlier cases emphasising that, as an exceptions clause, Article XX was to be interpreted narrowly, with the burden of proof being imposed on the party relying on it to exempt otherwise GATT-inconsistent measures.[60] More recently, the emphasis on interpreting Article XX narrowly as an exceptions clause has dropped away: exceptions, like other provisions, are to be interpreted according to the ordinary rules of treaty interpretation and do not, simply by virtue of their character as exceptions, warrant a stricter or narrower interpretation.[61] Nevertheless, when one examines Article XX(b) with a

[58] R Howse and D Regan 'The Product/Process Distinction—An Illusory Basis for Disciplining "Unilateralism" in Trade Policy' (2000) 11 EJIL 249, 251. Note also: MP Maduro 'Is There Any Such Thing As Free or Fair Trade? A Constitutional Analysis of the Impact of International Trade on the European Social Model' in G de Búrca and J Scott (eds) *The EU and the WTO: Legal and Constitutional Issues* (Hart Publishing Oxford 2001) 257, 261; and Weiler 'The Constitution' (n 18) 355ff.

[59] Thereby disappointing those, such as Howse, who believe that no legitimate regulatory action should be found to infringe a GATT provision in the first place: Howse and Regan (n 58).

[60] *Canada–Administration of the Foreign Investment Review Act* Report adopted 7 February 1984 BISD 30S/140 para 5.20; *Section 337* (n 15) para 5.27; *Tuna–Dolphin I* (n 53) para 5.22; *Malt Beverages* (n 15) para 5.41. Note also: GATT *Analytical Index: Guide to GATT Law and Practice* (6th edn GATT Geneva 1994) 519.

[61] *Hormones* AB Report (n 22) para 104 ('*Hormones*'). This approach is more in keeping with the principle that the terms of a treaty be given their natural and ordinary meaning: first principle of Article 31 of the Vienna Convention on the Law of Treaties (Vienna Convention) (Vienna, 23 May 1969). Art 3.2 of the DSU (Understanding on Rules and

view to gauging the intensity of the scrutiny and control over national health regulations that has been (and may in the future be) exerted by panels and the Appellate Body, it is clear that invoking Article XX(b) is no shortcut to a finding of conformity with GATT.[62] Rather, the following examination of the cases shows a significant emphasis on measures being the least trade-restrictive measures reasonably available, an expectation of regulatory conformity, an emphasis on scientifically certain health risks and even hints of a strict proportionality test. While the SPS Agreement was designed to overcome the potential for abuse of Article XX(b), the way in which Article XX(b) has been developed since 1995 suggests that the gulf between it and the SPS Agreement is not as great as might originally have been supposed.

In order to justify an otherwise GATT-inconsistent health measure under Article XX(b), the WTO Member must show: firstly, that the policy goal it is seeking to further falls within the range specified by paragraph (b) (ie, the protection of human, animal or plant life or health); secondly, that the measure is 'necessary' to effect that policy goal; and thirdly, that the conditions in the *chapeau* are satisfied (ie, that the measure is not applied so as to amount to arbitrary or unjustifiable discrimination, and is not a disguised restriction on international trade).[63] This section will proceed by considering the three aspects of a successful Article XX(b) claim set out above.

1 The Protection of Human, Animal or Plant Life or Health

The exact scope of the expression 'human, animal or plant life or health' has not been considered in any GATT or WTO cases. Nevertheless, policy and precedent suggest that a broad interpretation will be adopted, should a case arise where there is a real issue as to whether a particular policy objective is to be characterised as being concerned with human, animal or plant life or health. When a WTO Member is justifying a regulatory measure under Article XX(b), it has reached the end of the road: if the

Procedures Governing the Settlement of Disputes (Marrakesh, 15 April 1994)) refers to the 'customary rules of interpretation of public international law', a reference which has been taken to refer to Arts 31 and 32 of the Vienna Convention: *Gasoline* Panel Report (n 16) para 6.7; EU Petersmann *The GATT/WTO Dispute Settlement System: International Law, International Organizations and Dispute Settlement* (Kluwer London 1997) 111–12.

[62] Cf Bloche, who argues that, in the WTO era, panels and the AB have been so deferential to Members' health concerns that the protection of health has come to be an interpretive principle: MG Bloche 'WTO Deference to National Health Policy: Toward an Interpretive Principle' (2002) 5 JIEL 825, 831–835, 845.

[63] In respect of any paragraph of Art XX, the approach is the same—the defending Member must bring the measure within the scope of the paragraph being invoked before turning to the *chapeau*: *Gasoline* Panel Report (n 16) para 6.20.

justification fails, the measure will be inconsistent with GATT and will, in all likelihood, have to be withdrawn or modified. Panels and the Appellate Body will, no doubt, be acutely aware of the need not to condemn Members' measures unnecessarily by adopting an unduly narrow interpretation of that expression. The prediction of a broad interpretation under Article XX(b) is supported by the notably broad approach taken to the scope of 'exhaustible natural resources' under Article XX(g), which has seen clean air and turtles classified as exhaustible natural resources.[64] The Appellate Body's approach in the *Shrimp–Turtle* case is particularly noteworthy as it stressed that a flexible, evolutionary approach should be taken to 'natural resources' and referred extensively to modern environmental conventions.[65] Were a case to come before the WTO in which the definition of health was an issue, the panel might, in following the Appellate Body's lead in the *Shrimp–Turtle* case, refer to relevant conventions. One such relevant international agreement is the Constitution of the World Health Organization, whose Preamble broadly defines human health as 'a state of complete physical, mental and social well-being and not merely the absence of disease or infirmity.'[66] This raises the possibility of Article XX(b) serving to justify trade-limiting measures on a much broader understanding of health than is employed in the expressly science-focused SPS Agreement. Of course, this would not assist a Member whose measure fell within the definition of 'SPS measure' (as, in that case, it would have to comply with the SPS Agreement), but the possibility of citing mental and social health may assist in bringing a measure within Article XX(b) where the scientific evidence showing negative effects on physical health is limited.

Article XX(b) only excuses measures necessary 'to protect' health. The notion of protection has not attracted particular comment in the cases touching on this paragraph in the past, perhaps because it was not regarded as particularly problematic. It is likely that, if the issue arose in a future case, it would be found that the entire purpose of a regulation need not be 'to protect' health. While this suggestion is necessarily speculative, the approach taken in the *Korea–Beef* case suggests that panels will not demand singularity of purpose when it comes to determining whether measures fall within the scope of Article XX. In that case, the words 'to secure compliance with' a GATT-consistent regulation (in Article XX(d)) were interpreted to cover the Korean dual retail system (which confined

64 *Gasoline* Panel Report (n 16) para 6.37; *US–Import Prohibition on Certain Shrimp and Shrimp Products* WT/DS58/AB/R AB Report adopted 6 November 1998 ('*Shrimp–Turtle*') para 134. Note also the finding that herring and salmon stocks are exhaustible natural resources: *Canada–Measures Affecting Exports of Herring and Salmon* adopted 22 March 1988 BISD 35S/98 para 4.4.

65 *Shrimp–Turtle* AB Report (n 64) paras 129–34.

66 Constitution of the World Health Organization (New York, 22 July 1946).

sales of imported beef to specialist stores) even though it was only partially motivated by the need to secure compliance with the Unfair Competition Act.[67] It is as well that panels should avoid demanding a unity of regulatory purpose because, as is discussed in Chapter 4, regulatory agencies do not act in a vacuum. On the contrary, their agendas and pronouncements are influenced by history and politics.[68] Many regulatory standards are the result of a confluence of factors such as politically motivated instructions to investigate a suspected hazard as well as concern born of scientific evidence regarding a hazard. The scope of Article XX(b) would be drastically reduced if it were confined to circumstances where the *only* motivating factor was health protection.

It was suggested above that the protection of health should not be narrowly construed, either as to what 'health' is, or as to whether the sole and demonstrable purpose of regulatory action must have been to protect health. There is another aspect of the protection of health that presents rather more scope for intrusive panel review of national regulations. In the *Asbestos* case, the panel found that the notion of protection implied the *existence of a health risk* which required examination by the panel.[69] While the panel was at pains to disavow any role as an arbiter of scientific debates,[70] it still engaged in an exhaustive review of the copious scientific evidence introduced by the parties. According to the panel, its job was just to 'determine whether there is sufficient scientific evidence to conclude that there exists a risk for human life or health and that the measures taken by France are necessary in relation to the objectives pursued.'[71] It might be suggested that, as the parties had introduced all that evidence, the panel had little choice but to deal with it. Be that as it may, the panel was not obliged to find that protection required the demonstration of a scientifically verifiable health risk. The Appellate Body's decision on appeal also suggests that panels should assess the nature and character of the risk along scientific lines, although the Appellate Body did say that, as is the case under the SPS Agreement, a risk can be evaluated in qualitative as well as quantitative terms.[72]

[67] *Korea–Beef* Panel Report (n 23) para 658. Implicitly, another purpose was to protect the higher price of domestic beef.

[68] S Breyer *Breaking the Vicious Circle: Toward Effective Risk Regulation* (Harvard UP Cambridge MA 1993) 19–20; E Fisher 'Drowning by Numbers: Standard Setting in Risk Regulation and the Pursuit of Accountable Public Administration' (2000) 20 OJLS 109, 113; A Ogus *Regulation: Legal Form and Economic Theory* (OUP Oxford 1994) 6–10.

[69] *Asbestos* Panel Report (n 13) para 8.170.

[70] *Asbestos* Panel Report (n 13) paras 8.180–8.181.

[71] *Asbestos* Panel Report (n 13) para 8.182.

[72] *Asbestos* AB Report (n 14) para 167. The AB discussed the panel's assessment of the health risks of chrysotile asbestos in rejecting Canada's contention that the panel had an obligation to quantify the risk for itself and that it could not rely on the 'hypotheses' of the French authorities: para 165. The AB found that quantification was not required, and rejected the suggestion that the panel had merely relied on the French authorities' hypotheses: para 167.

While it would be going too far to suggest that the panel in the *Asbestos* case conflated the requirements of the SPS Agreement and GATT Article XX(b) by reading the SPS Agreement's scientific justification requirement in to Article XX(b), the panel did at least take from its study of the SPS disciplines and cases an emphasis on the scientific verifiability of health risks. No longer will a Member's assertion that its regulations are aimed at ameliorating a health risk be taken at face value and abuses guarded against through the necessity discipline and the *chapeau*. Now, Members will have to advance scientific proof—or at least would be unwise to neglect to advance such evidence—that the health risk in question really does exist. Given its confirmation that the panel did indeed have enough evidence to conclude that chrysotile-cement products do pose a risk to health,[73] it would appear that the Appellate Body agreed with the panel that, to take advantage of Article XX(b), the health risk must be approved. Requiring proof of the alleged health risk constitutes a definite development in the interpretation of Article XX(b), and is one which opens the door to more expansive panel review. Although scientific justification is already required under the SPS Agreement, requiring scientific proof of health risks under Article XX(b) is even more onerous because the defending Member bears the entire onus of proving the risk whereas, under the SPS Agreement, the complaining Member at least bears the burden of making out a prima facie case that the measure is not scientifically justified.

In addition, requiring that a health risk be proven to some scientific standard to exist before a measure can qualify under Article XX(b) would raise some awkward questions where the scientific evidence supporting the risk is uncertain. Whereas, in the SPS Agreement, there is at least *some* provision for measures to be taken in respect of uncertain risks (Article 5.7), Article XX does not contain a similar safety valve. It might be suggested that the precautionary principle will accommodate health concerns arising in circumstances of uncertainty but, as Chapter 5 argues, the status of the precautionary principle is not clear and its introduction into the WTO could be counterproductive. Given that there is no equivalent of the SPS Agreement's Article 5.7 and given that large question marks still hang over the precautionary principle, it would be unwise for WTO panels and the Appellate Body to set the scientific bar for proving a health risk too high. While some suggest that any measure broadly directed at health, including holistic health, should be accepted under Article XX(b),[74] it would be preferable to stay on the course charted by the *Asbestos* case and

[73] *Asbestos* AB Report (n 14) paras 155–63.

[74] R Howse and E Tuerk 'The WTO Impact on Internal Regulations—A Case Study of the Canada–EC Asbestos Dispute' in de Búrca and Scott (eds) (n 58) 283, 322 (Howse and Tuerk suggest that panels should defer to the Member where it is clear that the measure was directed to health (including holistic health) and not some other policy purpose).

see health measures as directed to actual risks to health. That said, some flexibility on the amount of evidence required to demonstrate the existence of a health risk is required given that there is no equivalent of Article 5.7's provisional measures in GATT. This is an area in which the standard of review, as discussed in Chapter 6, can be particularly helpful.

2 Necessity under Article XX(b)

Article XX(b) applies to measures that are 'necessary' to protect the life or health of humans, plants or animals. Although, in the drafting of Article XX(b), it was originally envisaged that the provisions of the *chapeau* would protect exporting countries against misuse of sanitary regulations,[75] the reference to necessity has been interpreted so as to provide significant constraints on regulatory autonomy. As is discussed below, to be 'necessary', the health measure must be the least trade-restrictive (LTR) measure available. This LTR discipline has given rise to concerns that it—or, more precisely its application by panels—unduly limits national regulatory autonomy.[76]

(a) Least trade-restrictive measure

The LTR test can be simply put: a measure will not be regarded as 'necessary' to protect life or health under Article XX(b) if the Member's objective can be achieved by another GATT-consistent or less inconsistent measure that is *reasonably available*. The LTR test has its origins in the *Section 337* case,[77] and was extended to necessity under Article XX(b) by the *Thai Cigarettes* case.[78] The LTR test is a form of proportionality analysis; it asks whether the measure is disproportionate because a less trade-restrictive measure would be equally effective in achieving the health goal. This type of proportionality analysis should not be confused with strict proportionality analysis, where there is a more extensive enquiry into whether the measure is disproportionate, either because the benefits it delivers to the Member instituting it are outweighed by the costs (in trade terms) imposed on other WTO Members, or because the risk is so small or uncertain that it does not warrant the measure deployed. While it is argued below that some instances of this more extensive concept of proportionality are emerging in the necessity analysis, for now the focus is on the simple LTR test.

75 GATT *Analytical Index* (n 60) 521.

76 See, eg: DM McRae 'The Contribution of International Trade Law to the Development of International Law' (1996) 260 Recueil des Cours 99, 198; MJ Trebilcock and R Howse *The Regulation of International Trade* (2nd edn Routledge London 1999) 153.

77 *Section 337* (n 15) para 5.26.

78 *Thai Cigarettes* (n 51) paras 74–75.

lower level of protection? Care needs to be taken to ensure that the WTO's LTR test is not allowed to slip any further towards a form of review in which panels second-guess the chosen level of protection.

(b) The reasonable availability of less trade-restrictive alternatives

As stated above, the LTR test does not require Members to implement a less trade-restrictive measure unless it is a *reasonably available* alternative. In the *Asbestos* case, Canada argued that it was unreasonable for France to ban asbestos rather than to protect its population by adopting controlled use practices. The Appellate Body took the opportunity to clarify what is meant by less trade-restrictive measures being 'reasonably available'. The Appellate Body stated that 'several factors must be taken into account, besides the difficulty of implementation.'[91] Drawing on its decision in the *Korea–Beef* case, the Appellate Body stated that the extent to which the alternative measure contributes to the realisation of the end pursued, and how vital or important the common interests or values being pursued are, should both be considered as additional factors.[92] Having noted that the objective being pursued by France was the preservation of human life and that asbestos posed a well-known health risk, the Appellate Body confirmed that France could not reasonably be expected to adopt any alternative measure if it would involve a continuation of the very risk that the French measure sought to halt.[93] Because the efficacy of the controlled use practices advocated by Canada remained to be demonstrated, the Appellate Body found that those practices did not constitute a reasonably available less trade-restrictive measure.[94]

In the *Asbestos* case, the Appellate Body refused to allow Canada to pressure France into adopting alternative regulatory practices whose efficacy had not been proved. A more interesting question would, however, have arisen if Canada had been able to establish that controlled use practices were effective. In that case, the Appellate Body would have had to determine the extent to which WTO Members are free to choose different regulatory strategies. If this were to happen, it would be interesting to see whether the Appellate Body would extend its implicit SPS Agreement analogy and qualify the LTR discipline by requiring that the measures be 'significantly' less trade-restrictive.[95] A reasonable and sustainable balance between the rights and interests of WTO Members and between the regulatory autonomy of Members and the supervisory jurisdiction of

91 *Asbestos* AB Report (n 14) para 170.

92 *Asbestos* AB Report (n 14) paras 171–72 (citing *Korea–Beef* AB Report (n 23) paras 162–63, 166).

93 *Asbestos* AB Report (n 14) paras 172, 174.

94 *Asbestos* AB Report (n 14) para 174.

95 A note to Art 5.6 of the SPS Agreement requires that the alternative measure be *reasonably* available and *significantly* less restrictive to trade.

the WTO suggests that this qualification be extended to the LTR analysis under Article XX(b). The preservation of life and health is a vital and important interest and a violation of GATT should not be found where the gains to trade in implementing an alternative measure would be minor.

(c) Consistency analysis

Where a Member's health regulations disclose inconsistencies—either in the level of protection sought, or in the means employed to achieve similar regulatory ends—those inconsistencies may indicate that there is a problem with a particular regulation. For example, where a regulation seeks to achieve a higher level of protection than the Member seeks in other situations, the choice of a higher standard may have been motivated by protectionism. Similarly, questions may be asked when a Member departs from its usual approach to a particular type of regulatory problem (such as consumer protection) and applies a more restrictive regulatory solution. The SPS Agreement explicitly encourages examination of any inconsistencies relating to the desired level of protection.[96] GATT, however, does not contain any similar invitation. Nevertheless, inconsistencies in regulatory strategies will attract attention as relevant to the LTR analysis. It seems that, if a Member departs from its usual regulatory practices, it will bear a particularly heavy burden in convincing the panel that the impugned measure is in fact necessary to protect health. In the *Korea–Beef* case, Korea argued on appeal that the panel had imported an illegitimate consistency test into Article XX(d).[97] What the panel had done was to rely, as one of two reasons for finding that Korea had not proved necessity, on the absence of a dual retail system in other sectors of the Korean economy in which there was a risk of misrepresentation of origin.[98] The panel found that Korea's approach to tackling misrepresentation in other sectors demonstrated that that problem could in fact be dealt with by GATT-consistent measures, such as normal policing under the Korean Unfair Competition Act.[99] The Appellate Body found that the panel was entitled to look to examples of Korea's approach in other areas where misrepresentation of origin was a problem:

> The application by a Member of WTO-*compatible* enforcement measures to the same kind of illegal behaviour—the passing off of one product for another—for like or at least similar products, provides a suggestive indication that an

[96] See Art 5.5 of the SPS Agreement, which aims at achieving consistency in the levels of protection sought by requiring that Members avoid arbitrary or unjustifiable distinctions in the levels of protection they consider appropriate in different situations.

[97] *Korea–Beef* AB Report (n 23) para 169 (quoting Korea's appellant's submission, para 167).

[98] *Korea–Beef* Panel Report (n 23) paras 659–64.

[99] *Korea–Beef* Panel Report (n 23) para 664.

alternative measure which could 'reasonably be expected' to be employed may well be available.[100]

In assessing the necessity of measures under Article XX(d), the *Malt Beverages* panel went beyond even regulatory consistency within a single law-making jurisdiction, and found that the fact that not all of the 50 states in the US maintained discriminatory distribution systems indicated that alternative measures for enforcement of state excise laws did indeed exist.[101]

These two cases suggest that there is at least a risk that an indirect expectation of regulatory consistency or conformity will be imposed, placing an additional burden on Members to justify departures from their regulatory approach in other areas. Relying too heavily on consistency to demonstrate that measures are not necessary risks imposing a further constraint on Members' regulatory autonomy. If consistency analysis is taken too far, unrealistic expectations of legislative and regulatory organisation and coherence will be imposed on Members, notwithstanding that the practical reality is such that high standards of coherence and organisation are lacking without that lack signifying protectionism. This is especially true where that Member consists of multiple states (such as the EC), is a federal state, or is a vast state with greatly varying conditions and levels of development within it (such as China). Panels should bear in mind that, while consistency might be a goal, it is certainly not a requirement at this point. Consistency, as illustrative of necessity, should be used carefully so that other considerations which might dictate a different approach—such as a desire to achieve a higher level of protection in a particular area—are not squeezed out. Particular care is required because the LTR interpretation of necessity is already fairly intrusive (recall the intrusion evident in the *Thai Cigarettes* case and the *Korea–Beef* panel decision) and the Appellate Body has already signalled that arguments relating to the higher cost of less trade-restrictive regulatory alternatives are unlikely to assist a defending Member.[102]

[100] *Korea–Beef* AB Report (n 23) para 172 (emphasis in original).

[101] *Malt Beverages* (n 15) para 5.43.

[102] *Korea Beef* Panel Report (n 23) para 673 ('with the WTO Agreement, the Members have made a bargain and compliance with the WTO Agreement may sometimes require (costly) adjustments to domestic policies and laws'); *Korea Beef* AB Report (n 23) para 180 (Korea could achieve its desired level of enforcement using WTO-consistent enforcement measures if it would devote more resources to enforcement). Note also the panel in the *Asbestos* case, which said that, as a country with advanced labour legislation and specialised administrative services, France should be expected to deploy administrative resources proportionate to its public health objectives and should be prepared to incur the necessary expenditure: *Asbestos* Panel Report (n 13) para 8.207.

(d) Weighing and balancing and the beginnings of proportionality reasoning

In some cases, panels and the Appellate Body are using the language of proportionality analysis and referring to their task in terms of 'weighing and balancing'. The use of this language suggests that panels and the Appellate Body are taking an expansionist view of their authority to evaluate Members' regulatory measures under Article XX.[103] As was discussed above, the original formulation of the LTR test does import a proportionality test, but it is a limited one. What is at stake here is a strict proportionality test that would allow panels to adjudicate on whether the Member is overreacting to a small or uncertain health risk, and to determine whether the trade costs outweigh the health benefits of the measure. The language of Article XX does not formally require that panels undertake any proportionality analysis of this kind, and such proportionality analysis is not naturally consistent with the preservation of Members' rights to set the level of health protection that they wish to achieve as high as they like. As soon as a panel or the Appellate Body is able to dismiss an Article XX(b) argument on the basis that the Member's action constitutes a disproportionate response to a health threat because the costs in trade terms outweigh the health benefits, Members' regulatory autonomy will be curtailed in a way that GATT in no way authorises. While panels and the Appellate Body have not gone this far, some specific cases under GATT and under the SPS Agreement[104] give cause for concern by hinting that this is the way WTO law is being developed.[105]

In the *Korea–Beef* case, the Appellate Body considered the meaning of necessity and identified a spectrum of meaning which might cover not only measures that are 'indispensable' to the attaining of a goal, but also those that merely 'make a contribution to' the attaining of a particular goal.[106] While the Appellate Body indicated that, at least for Article XX(d), necessity lay closer to the 'indispensable' pole, it stated that the necessity criterion should be informed by a contextual analysis.[107] According to the Appellate Body, unless a measure is necessary because it is 'indispensable',

[103] Note Axel Desmedt's consideration of the use of proportionality in WTO law generally. Desmedt concludes that, although aspects of proportionality analysis occur, these occurrences depend on the actual language found and do not indicate that proportionality has been accepted as a unwritten principle: A Desmedt 'Proportionality in WTO Law' (2001) 4 JIEL 441, 441.

[104] The beginnings of strict proportionality review under the SPS Agreement are addressed in the analysis of Article 2.2 of that Agreement.

[105] Note that Marceau predicted that the WTO would develop criteria that would allow panels to engage in some balancing: G Marceau, 'The Dispute Settlement Rules of the North American Free Trade Agreement: A Thematic Comparison with the Dispute Settlement Rules of the World Trade Organization' in EU Petersmann (ed) *International Trade Law and the GATT/WTO Dispute Settlement System* (Kluwer London 1997) 487, 513.

[106] *Korea–Beef* AB Report (n 23) para 161.

[107] *Korea–Beef* AB Report (n 23) para 161.

which Members just have to accept that their trade opportunities will be limited by other Members' health regulations. In sum, in introducing the additional factors outlined above and in seeing its task as one of 'weighing and balancing', the Appellate Body has re-characterised the WTO's adjudicative jurisdiction in a much more expansive way.

3 Limitations in the *Chapeau*

The *chapeau* to Article XX provides that:

> Subject to the requirement that such measures are not applied in a manner which would constitute a means of arbitrary or unjustifiable discrimination between countries where the same conditions prevail, or a disguised restriction on international trade, nothing in this Agreement shall be construed to prevent the adoption or enforcement by any contracting party of measures . . .

According to its terms, the *chapeau* addresses the *manner of application* of the measures, not the substance of the measures themselves.[114] The purpose of the *chapeau* is to prevent abuse of the exceptions and it does this by articulating three standards: measures must not (i) constitute arbitrary discrimination or (ii) unjustifiable discrimination, and must not (iii) be a disguised restriction on trade.[115] Although three separable standards have been identified, the approach of the Appellate Body in the *Gasoline* case suggests that the same considerations will be relevant to all three, by virtue of their shared purpose in avoiding abuse of the Article XX exceptions.[116] The cases do not present a neat approach to be followed in assessing whether any one of those three standards has been breached, but it is possible to derive some general principles about how the *chapeau* is to be applied. Firstly, a natural interpretation of the *chapeau*'s terms should be adopted: it is not to be applied as a catch-all provision so as to condemn any measure that undermines the multilateral trading system. As the Appellate Body said in the *Shrimp–Turtle* case:

> Maintaining, rather than undermining, the multilateral trading system is necessarily a fundamental and pervasive premise underlying the *WTO Agreement*; but it is not a right or an obligation, nor is it an interpretative rule which can be employed in the appraisal of a given measure under the chapeau of Article XX.[117]

[114] Cases confirm that the measure is the proper subject of enquiry under the *chapeau*: *US–Standards for Reformulated and Conventional Gasoline* WT/DS2/AB/R AB Report adopted on 20 May 1996, DSR 1996:I 3, 20 ('*Gasoline*') (citing *US–Imports of Certain Automotive Spring Assemblies* Report adopted 26 May 1983 BISD 30S/107 para 56); *Shrimp–Turtle* AB Report (n 64) paras 115, 147.

[115] *Gasoline* AB Report (n 114) DSR 1996:I 3, 21; *Shrimp–Turtle* AB Report (n 64) para 150.

[116] *Gasoline* AB Report (n 114) DSR 1996:I 3, 23.

[117] *Shrimp–Turtle* AB Report (n 64) para 116.

The second general principle applying to interpretation of the *chapeau* is that its terms should be interpreted so that the *chapeau* does not merely duplicate analysis undertaken under another provision. This means that the policy goal in question is considered under the specific paragraph of Article XX being relied on and cannot be examined again under the *chapeau*.[118] For example, the health-protection policy goal behind a measure will be relevant to the assessment of whether the measure satisfies the terms of paragraph (b) of Article XX. That health goal cannot, then, also be advanced in an argument over whether the application of the measure constitutes arbitrary discrimination, unjustifiable discrimination or a disguised restriction on trade.

The third general principle relating to the *chapeau* is its expression of the principle of good faith.[119] Seeing the *chapeau* as primarily concerned with good faith has a number of consequences for Members' regulatory autonomy. On the one hand, discussion of health regulations in terms of good faith constitutes a welcome departure from other aspects of WTO scrutiny of national health regulations which are more concerned with whether particular measures respond to provable risks and whether the least trade-restrictive measure was adopted. By focusing, for a change, on whether the regulations constitute good faith regulatory measures, this interpretation of the *chapeau* offers Members the opportunity to show their *bona fides*. On the other hand, though, the good faith assessment comes too late. If a Member has a health regulation which has been found to be inconsistent with Article III, for example, and has failed to satisfy the panel under Article XX(b) because the risk it purports to respond to has not been properly proved, or because the measure is not particularly well suited to achieving the policy objectives set, that Member will never have the opportunity to show the panel its good faith because it will never get as far as the *chapeau*. Moreover, as was discussed earlier, regulatory standards are often forged through the interaction of various interests and it may be difficult for a defending Member to show its purity of intent.

Although the exact content and scope of the three standards in the *chapeau* have still not been fully articulated in the cases, panels and the Appellate Body have steadily been taking steps to enhance the ability of the *chapeau* to serve its original purpose—preventing abuses of the Article XX exceptions. The days of a measure of being found not to be a 'disguised' restriction simply because it has been publicly announced are long gone.[120] Now a much more fluid and flexible approach prevails and

[118] *Shrimp–Turtle* AB Report (n 64) para 149.
[119] *Shrimp–Turtle* AB Report (n 64) para 158.
[120] This view was expressed in: *US–Prohibition of Imports of Tuna and Tuna Products from Canada* Report adopted 22 February 1982 BISD 29S/91 para 4.8 and was rejected in: *US–Imports of Certain Automotive Spring Assemblies* Report adopted 26 May 1983 BISD 30S/107 para 56.

one that is fully cognisant of the need to balance the rights and interests of the numerous WTO Members:

> The task of interpreting and applying the chapeau is, hence, essentially the delicate one of locating and marking out a line of equilibrium between the right of a Member to invoke an exception under Article XX and the rights of the other Members under varying substantive provisions . . . The location of the line of equilibrium, as expressed in the chapeau, is not fixed and unchanging; the line moves as the kind and the shape of the measures at stake vary and as the facts making up specific cases differ.[121]

It is to be hoped that panels and the Appellate Body exercise the enhanced authority that this flexibility gives them with an eye on the need to retain a balanced approach which accommodates the Members' need to remain free to regulate to protect the health of their populations and does not expand the trading rights of other Members beyond their agreed extent. It would be a regressive step if the ever more expansive approach taken toward necessity were matched with an overly zealous application of the *chapeau*.

E REVIEW OF GATT DISCIPLINES APPLYING TO HEALTH REGULATIONS

The basic structure of GATT relies on inculpatory and exculpatory provisions. Health measures may fall foul of Article III (national treatment) or Article XI (quantitative restrictions) and, if they do, must be justified by relying on Article XX(b). This basic structure has, however, caused some anxiety becauses it is thought that national measures that respond to legitimate regulatory goals should not fall foul of any inculpatory provision in the first place. In this sense, Article III has been criticised as being over-inclusive. While it may be preferable that health measures are never condemned as contravening a GATT provision (and so requiring rescue by Article XX(b)), concern over the scope of Article III is more intense where the social goal being pursued is not listed in Article XX (for example, prevention of child or sweated labour)—where there is no possibility of rescue, there is additional pressure to confine the inclupatory provision.

The aim-and-effect test for Article III is a manifestation of this desire to prevent legitimate regulatory action being impugned in the first place. Nevertheless, the status of that test appears to be very doubtful, meaning that Article III will continue to impugn non-protectionist national health measures. The *Asbestos* case does, however, suggest that where health risks are reflected in the physical characteristics of products or in the attitudes of consumers, products will not be regarded as 'like'. Two

[121] *Shrimp–Turtle* AB Report (n 64) para 159.

question marks do, however, hang over this approach: (i) what will happen when the health risks do not have the same level of scientific support as did the risks associated with chrysotile asbestos? and (ii) how far will the Appellate Body take the differences in consumer attitudes criterion? For example, will this mean that products are not like even if the scientific evidence of the health risk is very uncertain? The scope of Article III:4 is particularly important because exclusionary measures not caught by Article III:4 may well be picked up by Article XI. Article XI tends to be applied in a very straightforward manner, with little jurisprudence having developed around its terms. Although, when applied, Article XI tends not to be particularly troublesome, it can be unclear whether a border measure that excludes a product is to be considered under Article III or Article XI.

The terms of Article XX(b) have been subject to extensive development by panels and the Appellate Body. The most notable interpretation, which curtails Members' discretion, is the LTR interpretation of the necessity discipline. Although of long standing, the LTR discipline has been the subject of further development by the Appellate Body in the *Korea–Beef* and *Asbestos* cases where the language of strict proportionality and weighing and balancing has crept in without any real consideration having been given to whether there is a sound basis for this expanded review. Although references to proportionality and balancing have not imported a strict proportionality test, the concept of necessity has been modified so that it will more easily be satisfied if the trade costs are small or the interest being protected is particularly important. This modification should not pass unremarked. In addition, we may be seeing something of a narrowing of the gaps between Article XX(b) and the SPS Agreement in the finding that, in order to protect health, there must be a proven health risk.

These aspects of review under GATT show a general tendency to interpret the disciplines in a way that expands WTO review at the cost of Members' regulatory autonomy. This finding stands in contrast to what will be shown in the following chapter where it is argued that, notwithstanding some aggressive interpretations, a number of the SPS Agreement disciplines have been interpreted in a more sensitive manner. In working with the SPS disciplines, the Appellate Body has demonstrated a greater awareness of the need to balance WTO and Member state authority over domestic regulations than is evident in their interpretation of the GATT disciplines.

3

Review of Health Measures under the SPS and TBT Agreements

A REVIEW UNDER THE SPS AGREEMENT

TRADE DOES NOT trump health; that is a basic feature of the WTO system. The Preamble to the SPS Agreement[1] stipulates that 'no Member should be prevented from adopting or enforcing measures necessary to protect human, animal or plant life or health'. Article 2.1 entrenches this right, declaring that 'Members have the right to take sanitary and phytosanitary measures necessary for the protection of human, animal or plant life or health, provided that such measures are not inconsistent with the provisions of this Agreement.'[2] As that passage indicates, the right to take trade-limiting action on health grounds is qualified: in acting to protect health, WTO Members must still comply with the significant constraints imposed by the SPS Agreement. So significant are the constraints on regulatory action that all of the major SPS cases to date—the *Hormones*, *Salmon*, *Agricultural Products* and *Apples* cases[3]—have been lost by the defending Member.

[1] Agreement on the Application of Sanitary and Phytosanitary Measures (the SPS Agreement) (Marrakesh, 15 April 1994).

[2] Sanitary and phytosanitary measures (SPS measures) are, according to the Annex A definition, measures protecting against exposure to pests, disease-carrying or disease-causing organisms, disease-carrying animals or plants, and laws restricting additives, contaminants and toxins in food and feedstuffs (summary of definition drawn from S Charnovitz, 'The Supervision of Health and Biosafety Regulation by the World Trade Rules' (2000) Tulane EnvtlLJ 271, 176).

[3] *EC Measures Concerning Meat and Meat Products (Hormones)* WT/DS26/AB/R, WT/DS48/AB/R AB Report adopted 13 February 1998 ('*Hormones*'); *EC Measures Concerning Meat and Meat Products (Hormones)* WT/DS26/R/USA modified US Panel Report adopted 13 February 1998 and WT/DS48/R/CAN modified Canada Panel Report adopted 13 February 1998 ('*Hormones*'); *Australia–Measures Affecting Importation of Salmon* WT/DS18/AB/R AB Report adopted 6 November 1998, ('*Salmon*'); *Australia–Measures Affecting Importation of Salmon* WT/DS18/R modified Panel Report adopted 6 November 1998 ('*Salmon*'); *Japan–Measures Affecting Agricultural Products* WT/DS76/AB/R AB Report adopted 19 March 1999 ('*Agricultural Products*'); *Japan–Measures Affecting Agricultural Products* WT/DS76/R modified Panel Report adopted 19 March 1999 ('*Agricultural Products*'); *Japan–Measures Affecting the Importation of Apples* WT/DS245/AB/R AB Report adopted 10 December 2003 ('*Apples*'); *Japan–Measures Affecting the Importation of Apples* WT/DS245/R Panel Report adopted 10 December 2003 ('*Apples*').

Although, in the Preamble, the SPS Agreement is presented as an *elaboration* of the rules for the application of the provisions of GATT 1994[4] which relate to SPS measures, and in particular GATT Article XX(b), the SPS Agreement's obligations are independent of GATT.[5] In other words, Members are obliged to comply with the SPS Agreement irrespective of whether their SPS measures are otherwise inconsistent with a provision of GATT. If, however, a Member's SPS measures do conform to the SPS Agreement, they are presumed to be consistent with GATT.[6] The independence of the SPS Agreement from GATT is reinforced by the Appellate Body's confirmation that the complaining party bears the initial burden of proof of showing a *prima facie* case of inconsistency with the SPS Agreement[7] whereas, under GATT, the defending Member bears the entire burden of bringing a measure within Article XX(b). In other words, under GATT, the complaining Member will have to show an inconsistency with a GATT obligation, after which, the defending Member will attempt to prove that the otherwise GATT-inconsistent measure is protected by Article XX(b). Under the SPS Agreement, however, the complaining Member does not have to show an inconsistency with a GATT provision, but it does have to raise a *prima facie* case showing breach of the SPS Agreement before the burden falls on the defending Member to show that its measures are, in fact, consistent with the SPS Agreement. Given that the SPS Agreement has to be examined whether or not a GATT violation is found, panel practice has been to proceed directly to assessing the compatibility of the measures with the SPS Agreement.[8]

1 Scientific Justification

For a WTO Member's health measure to survive review under the SPS Agreement, it must have a proper scientific justification. The scientific justification requirement constitutes the most vital discipline in the SPS Agreement. By requiring that SPS measures be grounded in science, the SPS Agreement is taking a decisive step beyond the non-discrimination norms that form the core of GATT. It is no longer enough to be even-handed; now Members can be called to account for scientifically flawed SPS measures even if they are not discriminatory. In considering the role

[4] General Agreement on Tariffs and Trade 1994 (GATT 1994) (Marrakesh, 15 April 1994). GATT 1994 incorporates the provisions of GATT 1947 as amended: GATT 1994 Art 1(a).

[5] *Hormones* US Panel Report (n 3) para 8.36.

[6] SPS Agreement Art 2.4.

[7] *Hormones* AB Report (n 3) paras 98, 109; *Salmon* AB Report (n 3) paras 257–59. On the burden of proof, see, generally: J Pauwelyn 'Evidence, Proof and Persuasion in WTO Dispute Settlement: Who Bears the Burden?' (1998) 1 JIEL 227; and DP Fidler *International Law and Infectious Diseases* (OUP Oxford 1999) 137 (on the burden of proof according deference).

[8] *Hormones* US Panel Report (n 3) para 8.42; *Salmon* Panel Report (n 3) para 8.39.

of the scientific justification discipline, there are two important points to be made. The first point is that scientific justification is not a litmus test for protectionism. In other words, the existence or non-existence of a scientific justification is not determinative of protectionism. Some measures without a scientific basis will be protectionist and others will not. Conversely, some regulations motivated by protectionist impulses may nevertheless be scientifically justifiable. The second point is that, while the SPS Agreement aims to eliminate sham health measures, its aim is also broader than this. By impugning SPS measures without a proper scientific basis, the SPS Agreement not only identifies instances of protectionism parading as health protection, it also identifies instances in which markets are *unnecessarily* closed by scientifically unsupported health measures.[9] The SPS Agreement seeks to eliminate a whole set of trade barriers that do not result from protectionism per se, but may exist simply because of domestic regulatory resource limitations, or because consumer fears gave rise to demands for regulation. By seeking to limit health-based barriers to trade on a scientific basis, the SPS Agreement has a distinct (if limited) market-opening agenda.

The primary scientific justification requirements are to be found in Article 2.2. That Article provides that:

> Members shall ensure that any sanitary or phytosantiary measure is applied only to the extent necessary to protect human, animal or plant life or health, is based on scientific principles and is not maintained without sufficient scientific evidence, except as provided for in paragraph 7 of Article 5.

The scientific justification discipline is also enshrined in Article 3.3, which allows Members to introduce or maintain SPS measures which result in a higher level of protection than that provided for by measures based on international standards if there is a 'scientific justification'.

(a) *Interpretation of Article 2.2*

The scientific justification discipline has only been the subject of sustained analysis in the *Agricultural Products* and *Apples* cases. The first case involved a challenge to a Japanese requirement that, in order to have an import prohibition lifted, the efficacy of the quarantine treatment—which was fumigation—had to be tested and confirmed for each variety of certain agricultural products. The panel found, inter alia, that this requirement (known as the varietal testing requirement) breached Article 2.2 as it was maintained 'without sufficient scientific evidence'.[10] On appeal, Japan

[9] Of course, where a protectionist measure is scientifically supportable, it may nevertheless fall foul of other disciplines in the SPS Agreement, such as the consistency or least trade-restrictive measure disciplines (which are discussed below).

[10] *Agricultural Products* Panel Report (n 3) paras 8.43, 9.1.

argued that the panel had erred in its interpretation of the term 'sufficient scientific evidence.' As can be seen from the *Agricultural Products* case, the meaning attributed to this phrase will have a significant impact on the scope of WTO Members' retained authority to protect health.

In the *Apples* case, the US challenged the restrictions imposed by Japan on the importation of US apples. The panel identified 10 requirements[11] (including disease-free orchard status, buffer zone requirements, inspection requirements, chlorine treatment of fruit and packing facilities and certification requirements), which it treated as one 'measure' for the purposes of determining whether the Japanese requirements were consistent with the SPS Agreement.[12] As was the case in the *Agricultural Products* case, the panel in the *Apples* case found that the Japanese measure was maintained without sufficient scientific evidence, a finding which was upheld by the Appellate Body on appeal.[13]

(i) The 'rational relationship' criterion Article 2.2 requires that SPS measures not be maintained 'without sufficient scientific evidence'. While there is considerable scope for dispute about the meaning of 'sufficient scientific evidence', it is at least clear that the Appellate Body regards a risk assessment as a crucial element of a scientific justification under Article 2.2: according to the Appellate Body, Article 2.2 (scientific justification) is to be read together with the risk assessment discipline in Article 5.1.[14] The Appellate Body has, however, gone further than this in fleshing-out its conception of the requirements of Article 2.2.

In the *Agricultural Products* case, the panel held that the requirement that SPS measures be supported by 'sufficient scientific evidence' meant that there must be an 'objective or rational relationship' between the SPS measure and the scientific evidence.[15] The Appellate Body upheld the panel's interpretation, but offered some further hints as to the meaning of that expression:

> Whether there is a rational relationship between an SPS measure and the scientific evidence is to be determined on a case-by-case basis and will depend upon the particular circumstances of the case, including the characteristics of the measure at issue and the quality and quantity of the scientific evidence.[16]

By itself, the rational relationship interpretation of the 'sufficient scientific evidence' criterion is not necessarily intrusive. With the focus on the existence of a logical *relationship* between the evidence and the measure, it might, following the *Agricultural Products* case, have been thought

[11] For a full list, see *Apples* Panel Report (n 3) para 8.25.
[12] *Apples* Panel Report (n 3) paras 8.17–8.18.
[13] *Apples* Panel Report (n 3) paras 8.199, 8.222; *Apples* AB Report (n 3) paras 160, 168.
[14] *Agricultural Products* AB Report (n 3) para 76; *Hormones* AB Report (n 3) para 193.
[15] *Agricultural Products* Panel Report (n 3) paras 8.29, 8.42.
[16] *Agricultural Products* AB Report (n 3) para 84.

that strict requirements relating to the quantity or quality of scientific evidence would not be introduced through Article 2.2. By focusing on the logical relationship between the evidence and the measure, so the reasoning goes, Members would remain free to make regulations based on what they considered to be sufficient evidence, provided that there was a rational relationship between that evidence and the measure. The Appellate Body's elaboration of the rational relationship test in the *Agricultural Products* case does, however, hint at more intrusive scrutiny by listing the 'quality and quantity of the scientific evidence' as factors that are relevant to whether there is the requisite 'rational relationship'. The Appellate Body did not go on, in the *Agricultural Products* case, to explain its expectations of the quality and quantity of scientific evidence under Article 2.2, although it did acknowledge, in another context, that responsible and representative governments may act in good faith on the basis of what may be a divergent opinion coming from qualified and respected sources.[17] This suggests that the Appellate Body expects that a flexible attitude will at least be taken to the *quantity* of the scientific evidence, provided that the quality is good (scientific evidence from 'qualified and respected' sources).

(ii) The first Apples *heresy: the minimum risk threshold* Prior to the *Apples* case, it was thought that, provided that a Member can point to scientific evidence establishing that there is *some* risk, however small, a WTO panel cannot condemn the measure as lacking 'sufficient scientific evidence'. This traditional wisdom is exemplified by Pauwelyn's confident (pre-*Apples*) assertion that each Member has 'complete freedom to decide on the *level of risk* it can accept' and that a WTO panel 'cannot therfore, strike down a measure simply because it considers the risk involved to be "minimal"'.[18] The basis for this thinking, which was previously not even questioned by WTO panels, is that it is for the Members to set their appropriate level of protection and that this choice cannot be impugned, except perhaps on the basis of inconsistency under Article 5.5. Implicit in all of this is that there is no minimum risk threshold in order to establish that a measure is supported by sufficient scientific evidence under Article 2.2. The approach of the panel in the *Apples* case has called this long and dearly held view into question.

In the *Apples* case, the panel condemned Japan's measure as contrary to Article 2.2 on the basis that it was not supported by sufficient scientific evidence. The panel arrived at this finding even though it observed that:

17 *Hormones* AB Report (n 3) para 194.

18 J Pauwelyn 'Does the WTO Stand for "Deference to" or "Interference with" National Health Authorities When Applying the Agreement on Santiary and Phytosanitary Measures (SPS Agreement)?' in T Cottier and PC Mavroidis *The Role of the Judge in International Trade Regulation: Experience and Lessons for the WTO* (U Mich P Ann Arbor 2003) 175, 175 (emphasis in original).

> [E]ven if the scientific evidence before us demonstrates that apple fruit is highly unlikely to be a pathway for the entry, establishment and spread of fire blight within Japan, it does suggest that some slight risk of contamination cannot be totally excluded. The experts all categorized the risk as 'negligible'.[19]

The panel also observed that none of the experts was comfortable with their negligible risk conclusion leading to the immediate elimination of all of Japan's fire blight protection measures.[20]

While the panel in the *Apples* case stopped short of expressly stipulating that there is some minimum threshold of risk that is greater than 'negligible' risk (which at least one expert defined as a risk between zero and one in a million), its implicit finding that such a low level of risk is not sufficient does call into question the accepted view that WTO Members can take action to protect against such negligible risks, provided that they can be shown to exist. In so doing, the *Apples* panel has also implicitly contradicted the Appellate Body's finding in the *Salmon* case that a Member can choose 'zero risk' as its appropriate level of protection.[21]

The panel did not explicitly acknowledge that it was introducing any minimum risk criterion (and Japan did not assert that it had on appeal), but saw itself as guarding the rigours of the scientific justification criterion. If one looks at the way in which the panel analysed the scientific evidence, it was looking for studies that expressly established the various components of the pathway by which apples might introduce fire blight into Japan. In this quest, the panel refused to allow the small *possibility* of the introduction of fire blight through the import of apples to stand in for positive evidence that transmisison *would* occur. In and of itself, this approach may be of some concern to cautious importing WTO Members because it suggests that Article 2.2 requires positive evidence of that the exact risk in question *will* materialise without the measure in question rather than scientific evidence supporting a chain of reasoning according to which the risk in question *may* materialise.

(iii) The second Apples *heresy: strict proportionality analysis* The *Apples* panel's suggestion that there may, in fact, be a minimum risk threshold required in order for WTO Members to take action carries with it the clear implication that WTO panels may engage in strict proportionality review of Members' regulatory measures. As will be recalled from Chapter 2, strict proportionality review allows the reviewer to condemn a measure as disproportionate to the risk identified or to the costs imposed on other Members (thus allowing the panel indirectly to review that Member's chosen level of protection). Loose proportionality on the other hand, is less

[19] *Apples* Panel Report (n 3) para 8.173.
[20] *Apples* Panel Report (n 3) para 8.173.
[21] *Salmon* AB Report (n 3) para 125.

intrusive because it is confined to ensuring that, in achieving its chosen level of protection, the Member's measures are not more restrictive than required *to achieve that level of protection*. In short, the basic difference is that, whereas loose proportionality review leaves the chosen level of protection intact, strict proportionality review exposes it.

In the *Apples* case, the panel found that '[g]iven the negligible risk identified on the basis of the scientific evidence and the nature of the elements composing the phytosanitary measure at issue, the measure on the face of it is disproportionate to that risk.'[22] What the panel appears to have done is taken the 'rational relationship' criterion and, perhaps unintentionally, expanded it to the extent that it encompasses review of the proportionality of the measure and the risk. Recalling that the Article in question is Article 2.2 (which requires 'sufficient scientific evidence'), the rational relationship criterion permits an enquiry as to whether the scientific evidence supports the existence of the risk in question and the efficacy of the Member's measures in addressing it. If there is no real risk or the measures are ineffective in addressing that risk, then there will be no 'rational relationship' between the measure and the evidence.

The rational relationship enquiry does not authorise an enquiry into whether the Member's measure is *disproportionate* to the gravity of the risk. Nevertheless, this is precisely the type of enquiry that the *Apples* panel appears to engage in when it says that because the risk is 'negligible', the measure is disproportionate. In that case, nothing turned on this strict proportionality enquiry—the panel had already found that there was not sufficient scientific evidence to conclude that apple fruit were likely to serve as a pathway for the entry, establishment and spread of fire blight within Japan.[23]

While Japan did not specifically raise the panel's proportionality analysis on appeal, the Appellate Body did touch on it in considering Japan's argument that the panel erred in interpreting Article 2.2 of the SPS Agreement because it failed to accord a 'certain degree of discretion' to the importing Member. In considering this argument, the Appellate Body referred to the panel's conclusion that the measure was 'clearly disproportionate to the risk identified'.[24] While the Appellate Body did not criticise the panel's reasoning directly, it say that the 'clear disproportion' to which the panel referred 'relates to the application in this case of the requirement of a "rational or objective relationship between an SPS measure and the scientific evidence".'[25] It may be that, in making it clear that the panel's proportionality analysis was confined to the rational relationship enquiry, the Appellate Body was conscious of the fact that a broader

22 *Apples* Panel Report (n 3) para 8.181.
23 *Apples* Panel Report (n 3) para 8.176.
24 *Apples* AB Report (n 3) para 163.
25 *Apples* AB Report (n 3) para 163.

proportionality enquiry should not be encouraged. If this is the case, a clearer statement to that effect should have been made. If Members choose to impose tough restrictions in response to small risks, the present balance struck in the WTO system permits them to do this, provided that the risks are scientifically verified, the measures are effective in addressing the risks and the risks could not reasonably be addressed by less restrictive measures. Strict proportionality analysis constitutes a direct challenge to this delicate balance and it is to be hoped that future panels do not pursue the approach foreshadowed by the *Apples* panel.

(b) Entering the scientific fray and the use of experts

A broader question that arises in connection with Article 2.2 and the use of scientific criteria in adjudication more generally is the extent to which adjudicators are to engage with scientific controversies. For example, in the WTO, should panellists remain aloof from any scientific controversy, or should they engage with the substance of the scientific evidence at a more detailed level.

In determining whether Japan had complied with Article 2.2, the panel deciding the *Agricultural Products* case pointed to the absence of proof of a causal link between the test results which Japan said supported its measure and the existence of varietal differences.[26] This approach suggests that panels will engage in close scrutiny of the conclusions drawn from the scientific evidence by national regulators.[27] It seems that panels will find it difficult to avoid miring themselves in scientific controversies, particularly when they have experts available to help them assess and understand the scientific evidence and debate. The approach taken by the panel hearing the *Apples* case further supports this conclusion. In that case, there was no direct scientific controversy requiring resolution by the panel in order to determine the case. Nevertheless, the panel clearly engaged closely with the scientific evidence to the extent that it relied on flaws in studies cited by Japan to support its findings.[28]

Such engagement with scientific evidence raises the question of whether WTO panellists are equipped to make such scientific judgments. One would not expect WTO panellists hearing health cases to have any particular scientific or regulatory expertise, or any specific knowledge of the local conditions of the defending Member. But the question is, do they

[26] *Agricultural Products* Panel Report (n 3) para 8.42.

[27] Note that Charnovitz predicts that, if a scientific study is challenged as poorly conducted, future panels will seek to weigh competing scientific positions in the manner that many national courts do: S Charnovitz 'Improving the Agreement on Sanitary and Phytosanitary Standards' in GP Sampson and WB Chambers (eds) *Trade, Environment and the Millennium* (UN UP Tokyo 1999) 171, 177.

[28] *Apples* Panel Report (n 3) para 8.127.

need any particular expertise? Some think not,[29] but adjudication of claims under the SPS Agreement *does* entail engagement with scientific evidence and concepts. For example, the level of specificity at which a suspected risk must be studied in order for there to be a 'risk assessment' under the terms of Article 5.1 requires a scientific judgment on the validity and significance of generalised studies.[30] Similarly, assessments of scientific sufficiency are implicated in the requirement that panels determine whether there is a rational relationship between the measure and the risk assessment.[31] Even if panels are not directly being asked to determine for themselves whether a certain risk exists or to act as the arbiter in a scientific debate,[32] they are being asked to evaluate the competing claims being made by the two sides, even if the scientific questions are not abstract but are couched in terms of the relationship between the evidence and the scientific conclusion.

Pursuant to the Dispute Settlement Understanding[33] (DSU) (and with specific encouragement in the SPS Agreement and the TBT Agreement[34]), WTO panels can call on experts for help, either individually, or by convening a group.[35] Article 13.2 provides that panels 'may seek information from any relevant source and may consult experts to obtain their opinion on certain aspects of the matter'. That Article goes on to provide that, with respect to a scientific or technical matter, a panel may request a written advisory report from an expert review group. The SPS Agreement contains additional provisions relating to experts. Article 11.2 provides that a panel *should* seek advice from experts chosen by the panel in consultation with parties. The Article goes on to stipulate that, when it deems it appropriate, the panel may establish an advisory technical expert group or consult relevant international organisations. The TBT Agreement stipulates, in Article 14.2, that, at the request of a party to a dispute or at its own initiative, the panel may establish a technical expert group. In sum, by virtue of the provisions of the DSU and the SPS and TBT Agreements, panels enjoy a wide discretion to seek expert assistance.

[29] Eg, R Neugebauer 'Fine-Tuning WTO Jurisprudence and the SPS Agreement: Lessons From the Beef Hormones Case' (2000) 31 Law&Pol'yIntlBus 1255, 1274.

[30] Note that, in the *Hormones* case, the study was rejected as insufficiently specific to qualify as a risk assessment: *Hormones* AB Report (n 3) paras 200–201.

[31] *Hormones* AB Report (n 3) para 193; SPS Agreement Art 5.1 requires that the measure be 'based on' a risk assessment.

[32] Note the panel's admission of its lack of expertise in the *Asbestos* case and eagerness to emphasise that it was not its function to settle a scientific debate: *EC–Measures Affecting Asbestos and Asbestos-Containing Products* WT/DS135/R modified Panel Report adopted 6 April 2001 ('*Asbestos*') para 8.181.

[33] Understanding on Rules and Procedures Governing the Settlement of Disputes (Marrakesh 15 April 1994).

[34] Agreement on Technical Barriers to Trade (the TBT Agreement) (Marrakesh 15 April 1994).

[35] SPS Agreement Art 11.2; DSU Art 13.2 and Annex 4, TBT Agreement Art 14.2 and Annex 2.

In all of the health cases decided to date—the *Hormones, Salmon, Agricultural Product, Asbestos* and *Apples* cases—the panels have consulted experts individually.[36] While this preference for individual experts is understandable—an expert group would take time to generate a written report and panels may find that their hands are tied when an expert group provides a written report presenting a unified position—Pauwelyn suggests that, by using individual experts, panels then have to assess the various opinions of the experts to determine if there is common ground on particular issues, a task for which they are not well equipped.[37]

Several points of concern relating to the use of experts have arisen. One concern relates to the risk that, because of their lack of expertise, panels will ultimately delegate responsibility for assessing issues like whether there is a scientific basis for a health measure to experts.[38] For example, in the *Agricultural Products* case, the panel's reliance on experts is reflected in the way in which it phrased its question to the experts. The panel directly asked its experts to answer the very same question that the panel itself had to answer, viz, whether there was any objective or rational relationship between the varietal testing requirement and the evidence submitted by the parties.[39] In asking its experts this question, the panel risked giving the impression that it was delegating its adjudicatory responsibility to its experts. On occasion, this type of questioning has caused discomfort among the scientific experts themselves. For example, when the panel deciding the *Hormones* case held a meeting with the experts advising it, Dr Ritter expressed concern that, for him to answer the question posed—whether the residual hormones in beef would have a biological effect on consumers—would 'really be to pre-empt the outcome of this Panel.'[40] A related concern is that the panel will prefer to focus on the scientific evidence of the experts advising it, rather than the evidence of the parties. This is what appears to have happened in the *Asbestos* case, where, in supporting the panel's findings, the Appellate Body relied on the concurrence of the experts consulted by the panel and not on the evidence adduced by the parties.[41]

[36] Note in particular, J Pauwelyn 'The Use of Experts in WTO Dispute Settlement' (2002) 51 ICLQ 325, 325, 328. The readiness of WTO panels to call on experts contrasts with the reluctance of the ICJ to take expert advice: TM Franck *Fairness in International Law* (Clarendon Press Oxford 1995) 338ff.

[37] Pauwelyn (n 36) 328–29.

[38] JO McGinnis and ML Movsesian 'The World Trade Constitution' (2000) 114 HarvLRev 511, 594 (noting that, in the *Asbestos* case, the panel relied heavily on the comments of the experts in determining whether sufficient scientific evidence existed); TP Stewart and AA Karpel 'Review of the Dispute Settlement Understanding: Operation of Panels' (2000) 31 Law&Pol'yIntlBus 593, 634–36 (noting the influence of the experts consulted in the *Salmon* case).

[39] *Agricultural Products* Panel Report (n 3) para 8.35.

[40] *Hormones* US Panel Report and Canada Panel Report (n 3) Annex: Joint Meeting with Experts para 64.

[41] *EC–Measures Affecting Asbestos and Asbestos-Containing Products* WT/DS135/AB/R AB Report adopted 6 April 2001 para 162 ('*Asbestos*').

The approach of the panel in the *Apples* case should also be noted in this context. In that case, the panel members appeared to proceed by adopting the opinions of the experts as the *basis* from which it assessed the arguments of the parties. Upon reading the lengthy panel decision, the strong impression that emerges is that, having formed a view based on the advice it received form the experts it consulted, the panel effectively required Japan to adduce evidence sufficient to change the panel's mind. If nothing else, such an approach would be inconsistent with the burden of proof that applies in WTO cases, according to which the complaining member has to establish a *prima facie* case of inconsistency with a particular Article[42] and calls into question the conclusion that, where the scientific evidence on each side is equal, the defending Member will prevail.[43]

Another risk that attends the use of individual experts is that the opinion of any one expert may be unduly influential. Vern Walker provides an example where this happened in the *Hormones* case.[44] The panel had to consider whether, in light of the use of carbadox as a growth promotion agent in pig food in the EC, the ban on hormones in beef production meant that there was an arbitrary or unjustifiable difference in the level of sanitary protection the EC deemed appropriate in different situations. One of the EC's arguments was that there were no alternatives to carbadox with the same therapeutic action. In dismissing this argument, the panel relied solely on the opinion of *one* of the experts, who had suggested that oxytetracycline was a readily available alternative.[45] In general, however, it is not even possible really to grasp from panel reports what relative weight was accorded to any particular expert opinion, which leads to a worrying lack of transparency in panel decision-making.[46] A final concern relates to the scope of the expert consultation. Given the breadth of panels' discretion to seek information, there is little to constrain the questions they ask of the experts. One drawback of this lack of constraint has already been mentioned: panellists can ask the experts to, in effect, answer the question that the panel has to determine. Another drawback is that, in an SPS dispute, panels can ask the experts not only questions relating to scientific evidence and concepts, but also questions relating to risk management issues such as the cost-effectiveness of different regulatory responses and

[42] *Hormones* AB Report (n 3) paras 98, 109; *Salmon* AB Report (n 3) paras 257–59.

[43] This logical conclusion of the formal burden of proof is articulated by Pauwelyn amongst others (Pauwelyn (n 18) 177) but does not sit comfortably with the panel's approach in the *Apples* case.

[44] VR Walker 'Keeping the WTO from Becoming the "World Trans-science Organization": Scientific Uncertainty, Science Policy, and Factfinding in the Growth Hormones Dispute' (1998) 31 Cornell IntLJ 251, 311 n 282.

[45] *Hormones* US Panel Report (n 3) para 8.234; *Hormones* Canada Panel Report (n 3) para 8.237.

[46] Stewart and Karpel (n 38) 634.

compliance.[47] Such questions may go beyond the experts' areas of expertise (for example by asking risk management questions of scientists), and may also go beyond what the panel should really be enquiring into.[48]

The use of experts also raises a broader question about the nature of panel review of national health regulations. If one accepts that, in general, a non-expert judicial body should not engage in close review of technical matters, should the ready availability of expert advice be taken to ameliorate the panels' lack of expertise (relative to that of the national regulators), such that close review is justifiable? A defending Member justifies measures which: firstly, were taken in response to domestic problems, needs and priorities; secondly, were drawn up by its own regulators to fit in with the regulatory machinery of the state; and, thirdly, were based on its own experts' assessment of the scientific evidence (domestic and foreign) regarding a suspected hazard. In other words, the defending Member's perspective is holistic, drawing in both scientific and regulatory expertise. WTO panellists, on the other hand, do not necessarily offer either of those perspectives (scientific or regulatory), but generally offer a trade perspective.[49] Although panels' enjoy vicarious scientific expertise, one should hesitate before declaring the expertise gap between national regulator and panel to be bridged.

The first reason for hesitation is that the panels have to hand *scientific* expertise whereas, as we have seen, science does not dictate particular regulatory outcomes. When regulations are made, a great deal of *regulatory* expertise is also required. When WTO panels review health measures under the SPS Agreement, they are not only dealing with underlying scientific questions, such as whether the particular substance is harmful, but also with hybrid questions which draw in other kinds of expertise that are relevant to questions such as whether the least trade-restrictive measure has been employed. As Howse observes, the expertise that WTO panels need is situated at the intersection of science and regulation.[50] Panels have

[47] For example, in the *Hormones* case, the transcript of the meeting with the experts shows repeated reference (often at the initiation of the Chairman) to risk management issues such as the relative efficacy of regulatory responses, cost effectiveness and compliance: *Hormones* US Panel Report and Canada Panel Report (n 3) Annex: Joint Meeting with Experts paras 24, 172, 236, 268, 828, 838–48.

[48] The extent to which risk management decisions are reviewable by panels is considered in Chapter 4.

[49] The DSU provides that '[p]anels shall be composed of well-qualified governmental and/or non-governmental individuals' including those who have had experience with panel proceedings in the past (as panellists or advocates), those who have served as a Member's representative or in the Secretariat, those with academic credentials in trade law or policy and those who have served as a senior trade policy official of a Member: DSU Art 8.1.

[50] R Howse 'Democracy, Science, and Free Trade: Risk Regulation on Trial at the World Trade Organization' (2000) 98 Mich LRev 2329, 2345 (Howse's observation related specifically to the *Salmon* case). Trebilcock and Soloway also note that a single set of experts is not sufficient to handle the issues arising from risk assessment and risk management: M Trebilcock and J Soloway 'International Trade Policy and Domestic Food Safety

a wide power to seek information, which means that they need not be confined to seeking assistance from scientific experts in the future. Panels tend, however, to seek scientific expertise and, in so doing, only address *one* aspect of their lack of expertise (relative to that of the Members)—scientific expertise. In having scientific experts to hand, WTO panel members will be better placed to understand and to evaluate critically the scientific evidence advanced by the parties. The availability of scientific experts will not, however, put panellists in a better position to assess the many other considerations and forces that shape regulatory outcomes. These non-scientific factors are particularly important in determining the level of protection and the regulatory means for achieving that level, decisions which are open to examination under the least trade-restrictive measure discipline and the consistency discipline under Article 5.5 of the SPS Agreement.

The second reason to hesitate before endorsing close review by relying on the availability of expert assistance is that the experts are there to *help* the panel discharge *its* functions. Panel-appointed experts are not themselves an institution of the WTO dispute resolution machinery (notwithstanding explicit authorisation of their use), so the fact that panels can call on experts should not be allowed to affect the definition of the panel's authority vis-à-vis that of the Members.[51] While the availability of experts undoubtedly can increase the ability of panels to understand and deliberate on scientific questions, there is no guarantee that appropriate experts will always be used and, more importantly, there is no real oversight on the use that is made of their advice.[52] For these reasons, and because the availability of scientific expertise cannot address the regulatory expertise deficit of panels, we should be cautious in finding that the availability of expert assistance means that a more aggressive approach to review is appropriate.

Regulation: the Case for Substantial Deference by the WTO Dispute Settlement Body under the SPS Agreement' in DLM Kennedy and JD Southwick (eds) *The Political Economy of International Trade Law* (CUP Cambridge UK 2002) 537, 572.

51 Note also that the panel in the *Asbestos* case emphasised its lack of expertise, notwithstanding the fact that it consulted experts: *EC–Measures Affecting Asbestos and Asbestos-Containing Products* WT/DS135/R modified Panel Report adopted 6 April 2001 para 8.181.

52 The AB is unlikely to review a panel's decision whether to establish a review group: KJ Joergens 'True Appellate Review Or Only A Two-Stage Process? A Comparative View of the Appellate Body Under the WTO Dispute Settlement Understanding' (1999) 30 Law&Pol'yIntlBus 193, 223. As to the use panels may make of expert opinion, recall Walker's note about the extraordinary reliance by the panel in the *Hormones* case on the opinion of a single expert to dismiss a line of reasoning advanced by the EC: Walker (n 44) 311.

2 Discrimination, Consistency and Disguised Restrictions on International Trade

Not surprisingly, the SPS Agreement reiterates the core non-discrimination norm of GATT. Article 2.3 provides that:

> Members shall ensure that their sanitary and phytosanitary measures do not arbitrarily or unjustifiably discriminate between Members where identical or similar conditions prevail, including between their own territory and that of other Members. Sanitary and phytosanitary measures shall not be applied in a manner which would constitute a disguised restriction on international trade.

Article 5.5 also imposes a non-discrimination discipline:

> [W]ith the objective of achieving consistency in the application of the concept of appropriate level of sanitary or phytosanitary protection . . . each Member shall avoid arbitrary or unjustifiable distinctions in the levels it considers to be appropriate in different situations, if such distinctions result in discrimination or a disguised restriction on trade.

In the *Hormones* case, the Appellate Body suggested that 'Article 5.5 may be seen to be marking out and elaborating a particular route leading to the same destination set out in Article 2.3.'[53] The panel in the *Salmon* case went further, holding that a breach of Article 5.5 implies a breach of the more general obligations in Article 2.3.[54] Although it seems that a panel might find a breach of Article 2.3 without relying on Article 5.5, it is the latter Article that has been used in the cases and so provides the basis on which to assess the impact of the discrimination and disguised restriction norms, although the interpretation of the *chapeau* to GATT Article XX will also be relevant (particularly to the second part of Article 2.3 of the SPS Agreement) because both refer to whether measures are *applied* so as to result in a disguised restriction on international trade.

In the *Hormones* case, the Appellate Body determined that three elements must be proved before there will be a violation of Article 5.5.[55] First, it must be shown that the Member imposing the measure adopted its own appropriate levels of sanitary protection against risks to human life or health in several different situations. Secondly, it must be shown that those levels of protection exhibit arbitrary or unjustifiable differences (or distinctions in the language of Article 5.5). Thirdly, it must be shown that the arbitrary or unjustifiable differences result in discrimination or a disguised restriction on international trade.

[53] *Hormones* AB Report (n 3) para 212.

[54] *Salmon* Panel Report (n 3) paras 8.109, 8.160 and 8.184; *Salmon* AB Report (n 3) paras 243–50.

[55] *Hormones* AB Report (n 3) para 214.

Pursuant to Article 5.5, WTO panels may enquire into the validity of a Member's decisions on the level of risk it is prepared to accept in different situations. This power carries with it the distinct prospect of highly intrusive review and it is therefore not surprising that WTO supervision of regulatory consistency has raised concern.[56] These concerns should, however, be considered in light of the fact that the Appellate Body has recognised that, at present, consistency is a goal and not an obligation.[57] Moreover, there are some indications that, in reviewing SPS measures under Article 5.5, allowances will be made for the imperfections of real-world regulatory processes.

In the *Hormones* case, the Appellate Body stressed that Article 5.5 only aims to catch *arbitrary or unjustifiable* inconsistencies and continued, 'the goal set is not absolute or prefect consistency, since governments establish their appropriate levels of protection frequently on an *ad hoc* basis and over time, as different risks present themselves at different times.'[58] In that case, the Appellate Body lived up to its promise of sensitivity to national regulatory preferences and rejected the panel's conclusion that the difference between the EC's unlimited tolerance for naturally occurring hormones and its zero-tolerance for natural and synthetic hormones used for growth promotion was arbitrary and unjustifiable. According to the Appellate Body, there is a fundamental distinction between added hormones and naturally occurring hormones.[59]

Notwithstanding the Appellate Body's balanced approach in the *Hormones* case, there are some signs that a stricter regime is on the horizon. In the *Salmon* case, Canada challenged an Australian quarantine law that prohibited the import of fresh, chilled or frozen salmon. When the measure's compliance with the non-discrimination norm of Article 5.5 was considered, the Appellate Body accepted that 'warning signals' and 'additional factors' may be used to identify inconsistency with Article 5.5. The use of such warning signals and additional factors suggests a rather more heavy-handed approach than was evident in the *Hormones* case. For example, in the *Salmon* case, the Appellate Body was prepared to accept that breach of the risk assessment requirements (under Article 5.1) was 'a strong indication' that the measure was not really concerned with health

[56] Charnovitz ' Improving the Agreement' (n 27) 189–90; Charnovitz 'The Supervision of Health and Biosafety Regulation' (n 2) 283. Note also Chapter 2 above, where the increasing importance of consistency in assessing necessity was noted.

[57] *Hormones* AB Report (n 3) para 213.

[58] *Hormones* AB Report (n 3) para 213.

[59] *Hormones* AB Report (n 3) para 221. Note also the AB's concern with whether distinctions were motivated by protectionism in assessing the EC's acceptance of higher risks in respect of two substances used in pig-rearing than it was prepared to accept in respect of beef: *Hormones* AB Report (n 3) para 245.

protection, but was really a protectionist measure taken 'in the guise of' an SPS measure.[60]

Both Articles 2.3 and 5.5 bring into focus the regulatory distinctions that Members draw. Article 2.3 relates to differences between the situations of the regulating Member and other Members and between the situations of the various other Members. Article 5.5 relates to differences in the level of protection chosen in different situations. In its decisions on Article 5.5, the Appellate Body initially put in place a realistic model for review which allowed for factors of domestic importance and accepted that, under the gaze of the retrospective microscope, disorganisation or incoherence in regulation-making does not necessarily signal protectionism.[61] Such an approach promised to help preserve what the Appellate Body described as the 'delicate and carefully negotiated balance in the *SPS Agreement* between the shared, but sometimes competing interests of promoting international trade and of protecting the life and health of human beings'.[62] The Appellate Body's approach in the *Salmon* case does, however, threaten the achievements of the *Hormones* case. In particular, the Appellate Body's endorsement of the panel's use of warning signals and questionable additional factors risks imposing unrealistic expectations of regulatory coherence. It remains to be seen whether the Appellate Body's endorsement of warning signals and additional factors will be carried through into a generally stricter attitude to regulatory distinctions. If this does happen, we can expect that Members will find that, if they attempt to explain regulatory distinctions (either in the way they view the situation prevailing in different Members under Article 2.3 or in the level of protection chosen under Article 5.5) by reference to social or cultural preferences, their arguments will not be as sympathetically received as the *Hormones* decision may have led them to believe.

[60] *Salmon* AB Report (n 3) para 166. The other warning signals used were: the 'arbitrary or unjustifiable character of differences in levels of protection'; and the 'rather substantial difference in levels of protection': *Salmon* AB Report (n 3) paras 162–63. It is interesting to note, following the suspicion surrounding Australia's high SPS standards that, in Australia's WTO trade policy review, the WTO Secretariat defended Australia against accusations that its SPS standards are so stringent as to be protectionist. The Secretariat drew attention to the fact that Australia is highly dependent on agriculture, which receives little government assistance, and that Australia's viability as a reliable exporter depends on its exports not being disrupted by pests and diseases: WTO Secretariat *Trade Policy Review: Australia* (WT/TPR/S/104 26 August 2002) para 21. Notwithstanding the Secretariat's defence of Australia's policies, the EC has brought a case against Australia impugning its quarantine system: *Australia–Quarantine Regime for Imports* WT/DS287. For further criticism of the use of 'warning signals' and 'additional factors', see WJ Davey 'Has the WTO Dispute Settlement System Exceeded Its Authority' in T Cottier and PC Mavroidis *The Role of the Judge in International Trade Regulation: Experience and Lessons for the WTO* (U Mich P Ann Arbor 2003) 43, 54.

[61] On this misplaced equation between incoherence and protectionism, see: Charnovitz 'The Supervision of Health and Biosafety Regulation' (n 2) 284.

[62] *Hormones* AB Report (n 3) para 177.

3 Harmonisation

(a) Background

At the beginning of the Uruguay Round negotiations there was widespread agreement that harmonisation would deliver significant benefits in reducing the significant trade barriers that result from multiple and varying regulatory regimes.[63] Harmonisation by reference to the international standards of the Codex Alimentarius Commission (Codex), the International Office of Epizootics (OIE) and the International Plant Protection Convention (IPPC)[64] is strongly promoted in the SPS Agreement. Harmonisation is covered by Article 3, which comprises an obligation, an incentive and a countervailing right.

Article 3.1 obliges Members to base their SPS measures on international standards, guidelines or recommendations where they exist. Article 3.2 provides an incentive—if the measures 'conform' to the international standards, they are presumed to be consistent with the SPS Agreement and GATT. In response to pressure from the EC and outside consumer interests, however, Article 3.3 makes it clear that Members remain free to introduce or maintain measures resulting in a higher level of protection in certain circumstances.[65] Given the wide diversity of attitudes to risk and the level of protection that should be provided, the way in which the permission to deviate from international harmonised standards is interpreted is very important. A narrow reading of the permission to deviate and put in place more stringent standards would promote trade by strengthening the harmonised system. Such a narrow reading would, however, also aggravate WTO Members concerned that their ability to protect health will be compromised if they are so constrained by insufficiently rigorous international standards.

As its language is somewhat obscure and has given rise to interpretative difficulties, it is worth setting out Article 3.3 in full.

> Members may introduce or maintain sanitary or phytosanitary measures which result in a higher level of sanitary or phytosanitary protection than would be achieved by measures based on the relevant international standards, guidelines or recommendations, if there is a scientific justification, or as a consequence of the level of sanitary or phytosanitary protection a Member determines to be appropriate in accordance with the relevant provisions of paragraphs 1 through 8 of Article 5. Notwithstanding the above, all measures which result in a level of

[63] South Centre, *WTO Agreement on Sanitary and Phytosanitary Measures: Issues for Developing Countries* (South Centre Geneva 1999) 3–4.

[64] SPS Agreement Annex A Art 3.

[65] J Croome *Reshaping the World Trading System: A History of the Uruguay Round* (2nd edn WTO Geneva 1999) 203, 327.

sanitary or phytosanitary protection different from that which would be achieved by measures based on international standards, guidelines or recommendations shall not be inconsistent with any other provision of this Agreement.

A note to Article 3.3 provides that there will be a scientific justification if, based on an examination and evaluation of available scientific information in conformity with the Agreement, a Member determines that the international standard is not sufficient to achieve its appropriate level of SPS protection.

It is immediately apparent on reading Article 3 that the nature of Members' obligations vis-à-vis international standards is not clear. What does it mean to 'base' measures on international standards, as opposed to 'conforming' to them, and when exactly can a Member depart from international standards to achieve a higher level of protection? These issues were considered at length in the *Hormones* case.

(b) Article 3.1 and measures 'based on' international standards

The *Hormones* case saw a remarkable about-face on the meaning of the requirement that Members 'base' their SPS measures on international standards. The panel determined that measures would be *based* on international standards where they *conformed* to those standards, thereby conflating the two expressions—'base on' and 'conform to'—used in paragraphs 1 and 2 of Article 3.[66] One consequence of the panel's approach was that, in order to be 'based on' an international standard, the national standard would have to reflect the same level of protection.[67] The Appellate Body rejected the panel's conflation of 'base on' and 'conform to' and, more significantly, provided a much looser interpretation of what it means to 'base' one's SPS measures on an international standard. According to the Appellate Body, a measure may be based on an international standard where some but not all elements of the standard are incorporated into the measure.[68] While clearly much more lenient than the panel's interpretation, the limits of the Appellate Body's permissiveness are not clear. Just how far can a measure deviate from an international standard before it is not 'based on' that standard any more?

(c) The requirements of Article 3.3

Article 3.3 governs the circumstances in which a Member can depart from the level of protection set by an international standard. A casual reading

[66] *Hormones* US Panel Report (n 3) para 8.72; *Hormones* Canada Panel Report (n 3) para 8.75.
[67] *Hormones* US Panel Report (n 3) paras 8.72–8.73; *Hormones* Canada Panel Report (n 3) paras 8.75–8.76.
[68] *Hormones* AB Report (n 3) paras 163–66.

of Article 3.3 suggests that there are *two* situations in which a higher than international level of protection can be implemented: if there is a scientific justification, *or* if a higher level of protection than that provided by the international standard is determined to be appropriate in accordance with Articles 5.1–5.8. The Appellate Body has, however, found that there is in fact only one circumstance in which a Member can implement a higher level of protection: when it has complied with *all* the SPS disciplines including risk assessment.[69] The effect of the Appellate Body's decision is that, if a measure is not 'based on' an international standard, it must comply with all other aspects of the SPS Agreement.

(d) Relationship between Articles 3.1 and 3.3: burden of proof

In determining the burden of proof to prevail where a Member departs from an international standard under Article 3.3, in the *Hormones* case the Appellate Body again overturned the panel and offered an interpretation more generous to defending Members. The panel had described Article 3.3 as an exception to the general obligation contained in Article 3.1 and had accordingly determined that the entire burden of proof was on the defending Member to justify the measure under Article 3.3.[70] The Appellate Body disagreed with this rule-exception characterisation. Instead, the Appellate Body regarded Article 3.3 as recognising the 'autonomous right' of a Member to establish a higher level of protection, provided it complies with certain requirements.[71] The Appellate Body was not prepared to see the general rule—that a complaining party has to establish a *prima facie* case of inconsistency before the burden switches to the responding party—displaced by labelling Article 3.3 as an exception. Similarly, the Appellate Body stressed that Article 3.3 was to be interpreted by applying the normal rules of treaty interpretation, and not some narrower interpretation justified only by characterising the provision as an 'exception'.[72]

The Appellate Body's conclusion that Article 3.3 is a provision setting out the parameters of an autonomous right to set higher levels of protection (not an exception) is valuable as an emphatic confirmation that WTO Members have not foregone their right to determine the appropriate level of protection. For WTO Members concerned to protect their ability to respond to local health concerns, there is an important practical and symbolic difference between having the right to set a high level of protection (subject to the observation of stipulated disciplines) and having to justify that level itself. By reserving to themselves the right to set the desired level

69 *Hormones* AB Report (n 3) paras 175–76.
70 *Hormones* US Panel Report (n 3) para 8.86; *Hormones* Canada Panel Report (n 3) para 8.89.
71 *Hormones* AB Report (n 3) para 104.
72 *Hormones* AB Report (n 3) para 104.

of protection, the Members ensured that other Members and WTO panels could not second-guess a society's level of risk-aversion or say that it is overreacting to a particular threat. The Appellate Body's interpretation of Article 3.3 as an autonomous right confirms the sanctity of Members' rights to set their own levels of protection.

(e) Concerns attaching to harmonisation by reference to international standards

For countries with high SPS standards, there is a real fear that international harmonisation tends to lower standards. For example, the US has many standards that are higher than international standards, leading to fears, particularly among consumer and environmental groups, of a pressure to harmonise standards downwards.[73] Article 3.3 was inserted in order to allay fears over downward harmonisation, but, as was shown above, the scope of this Article (and, consequently, of Members' ability to depart from international standards) is still far from clear.[74] It does, however, seem fair to say that a defending Member is in no worse a position if it departs from an international standard than if no relevant international standard exists: in either case, the Member has to comply with the remaining disciplines, including those in Articles 2 (scientific justification) and Article 5 (risk assessment) of the SPS Agreement. It can, then, be seen that although the SPS Agreement provides a carrot encouraging Members to have their measures conform to international standards (the presumption of consistency with the SPS Agreement and GATT in Article 3.2), it does not provide any real stick punishing Members for ignoring such standards altogether.[75]

If international standards are going to fulfil their promise to provide neutral benchmarks that protect health but do not pander to protectionist lobby groups or irrational consumer paranoia, concerns at the way in which international standards are set will have to be addressed. Far from working in a rarefied atmosphere removed from politics and parochial and commercial interests, Codex is perceived as suffering from the influence of the numerous commercial NGOs that participate in its processes and the absence of developing country voices.[76] Moreover,

[73] DA Farber and RE Hudec 'GATT Legal Restraints on Domestic Environmental Regulations' in J Bhagwati and RE Hudec (eds) *Fair Trade and Harmonization* (Vol 2 MIT Press Cambridge MA 1996) 59, 62.

[74] Although some seem confident that states will be given a substantial amount of discretion in evaluating the level of protection needed: eg, AR Ziegler 'WTO Rules Supporting Environmental Protection' in F Weiss, E Denters and P de Waart (eds) *International Economic Law with a Human Face* (Kluwer Law International The Hague 1998) 203, 217.

[75] Note, though, the high transaction costs imposed on Members wishing to implement different or more stringent measures: MJ Trebilcock and R Howse *The Regulation of International Trade* (2nd edn Routledge London 1999) 146–47 .

[76] For statistics on corporate participation in Codex, see: J Braithwaite and P Drahos *Global Business Regulation* (CUP Cambridge UK 2000) 401, 407; and on developing country participation, see: South Centre (n 63) 13.

because Codex does, on occasion, determine standards by majority voting, its standards cannot always claim to reflect an international scientific consensus. For example, in the *Hormones* case, the EC was being held to account for deviating from Codex standards that were passed by the barest majority (33 to 29 votes, split along national lines) with 7 abstentions and which were adopted only after previous attempts by the US in 1986 and 1991 to have Codex declare hormone use safe had failed.[77] In such circumstances, it is not really clear why an international standard which does not reflect a scientific consensus should be privileged over a national scientific determination.[78] The controversy surrounding the use of Codex standards in the *Hormones* case also points to a more general question relating to how bodies like Codex function. There is a risk that their standard setting powers may be highjacked by Members keen to see their view adopted as *the* view of the international scientific community. After all, if a Member can have its standards adopted in Codex, it will not have to defend them under the SPS Agreement and the strength of the evidence supporting a particular standard is unreviewable even though it may do real harm to the trading opportunities of other Members. Moreover, there will be no real opportunity for other Members to challenge the regulation on the basis that a less restrictive measure would have sufficed. It might also be questioned whether, in respect of specific scientific issues, the international body necessarily has greater expertise than the Member being challenged.[79]

At a broader level, there seems to be a lack of real clarity on the nature of the system that the SPS Agreement's harmonisation provisions envisage. There is no indication of how the world trading system is to move beyond the disharmony of a formal obligation to 'base' measures on international standards coupled with an autonomous right to enact higher standards to full harmonisation. This lack of clarity and vision contributes to the tension between international supervision and national regulatory power. A far-reaching examination of the harmonisation project is in order. Such an examination should address the broader question of where decision-making power over health standards should be located—with

[77] For angry reactions to this, see: M Wynter 'The Agreement on Sanitary and Phytosanitary Measures in the Light of the WTO Decisions on EC Measures Concerning Meat and Meat Products (Hormones)' in P Mengozzi (ed) *International Trade Law on the 50th Anniversary of the Multilateral Trade System* (A Giuffrè Editore Milano 1999) 471, 482; Neugebauer (n 29) 1262.

[78] Indeed, it has even been (unsuccessfully) argued in a TBT case that only international standards adopted by consensus should qualify under that Agreement's harmonisation provisions: *EC–Trade Description of Sardines* WT/DS231/AB/R AB Report adopted 23 October 2002 ('*EC–Sardines*') paras 36, 108, 122.

[79] In the *Salmon* case, Australia complained that the OIE standards were not based on a risk assessment and that, compared to terrestrial animals, the OIE's work on aquatic diseases was in its infancy: *Salmon* Panel Report (n 3) para 4.107; Fidler (n 7) 143.

Members, with international bodies or with WTO adjudicators?[80]—as well as the more specific concerns attaching to the process by which international standards are set.

4 Risk Assessment

Article 5.1 requires that Members ensure that their SPS measures are 'based on' risk assessments. This requirement should be viewed in the context of the SPS Agreement's attempt to impose some common structure on the way in which WTO Members arrive at and impose SPS measures. The risk assessment requirement is designed to ensure that Members respond to *identified risks* and not *unsubstantiated fears*. Annex A defines risk assessment as follows (emphasis added):

> The *evaluation* of the *likelihood of entry, establishment or spread* of a pest or disease within the territory of an importing Member according to the sanitary or phytosanitary measures which might be applied, and of the associated potential biological and economic consequences; or the *evaluation* of the *potential for adverse effects* on human or animal health arising from the presence of additives, contaminants, toxins or disease-causing organisms in food, beverages or feedstuffs.

The remaining parts of Article 5 go on to prescribe various matters that Members must take into account in the assessment of risks. These include available scientific evidence, relevant economic facts, and the objective of minimising negative trade effects.[81]

The risk assessment discipline in Article 5 has proved central to the operation of the SPS Agreement. In all four of the SPS cases to date, the national measures have been found to be inconsistent with the risk assessment requirements. In the *Hormones* case, the Appellate Body upheld the panel's finding that the EC's risk assessment did not satisfy the requirements of Article 5.[82] In particular, the Appellate Body found that the studies referred to by the EC were not specific enough to constitute risk assessments.[83] Similarly, in the *Salmon* case, the Appellate Body supported

[80] JH Jackson *The World Trading System: Law and Policy of International Economic Relations* (2nd edn MIT Press Cambridge UK 1997) 346 (questioning whether 'a gradual drift of decision-making authority upward to international institutions is always best for the world'). See also: DC Esty *Greening the GATT: Trade, Environment, and the Future* (Institute for International Economics Washington DC 1994) 173 (on decentralised decision-making giving scope to local preferences).

[81] SPS Agreement Arts 5.2–5.4.

[82] The panel found that the EC measures did not conform to any of the scientific conclusions reached in the scientific studies referred to: *Hormones* US Panel Report (n 3) para 8.137; *Hormones* Canada Panel Report (n 3) para 8.140. The AB rejected the 'conform to' analysis, but still found that Art 5 was breached.

[83] *Hormones* AB Report (n 3) paras 200–1.

the panel's finding that Australia's risk assessment failed Article 5, but did so on the basis that the risk analysis itself did not meet the requirements of Annex A paragraph 4, whereas the panel found that the risk assessment did not reasonably support Australia's measures.[84] In the *Agricultural Products* case, the Appellate Body found that Japan had failed to conduct a risk assessment in respect of the varietal testing requirement.[85] In the *Apples* case, the problem identified by the panel was that the risk assessment did not focus sufficiently on the risks associated with transmission of fire blight through apple fruit (as opposed to other possible means of transmission). It should, however, be born in mind that these may not have been particularly difficult cases: as McGinnis and Movsesian noted regarding the *Hormones* and *Salmon* cases, '[i]t was not that national authorities had wrongly assessed the risks, but rather that they had failed to make genuine attempts to support their regulations with objective evidence.'[86] Harder cases will surely confront panels and the Appellate Body in years to come.[87]

The interpretative problems thrown up by risk assessment pose a particularly stern test for panels and the Appellate Body because, as Trebilcock and Howse put it, '[c]entral SPS issues such as scientific justification and allowable risk are difficult to arbitrate and lie at the heart of a country's sovereignty.'[88] Without the ability to act to protect domestic health in a timely and effective manner, WTO Members may feel that something very close to the core of their sovereignty is being tampered with. The following section suggests that, while the Appellate Body has, in general, been careful not to interpret the risk assessment discipline in a way that would stymie the ability of WTO Members to act effectively to protect health, some aspects of its interpretations are rather alarming in their preparedness to stipulate, in fairly detailed terms, what is and is not a 'risk assessment' for the purposes of Article 5.1.

84 *Salmon* Panel Report (n 3) para 8.99; *Salmon* AB Report (n 3) para 128. But note that the AB and the panel differed over what the measure at issue was.

85 *Agricultural Products* AB Report (n 3) para 113.

86 McGinnis and Movsesian (n 38) 601.

87 Canada, the US and Argentina have all requested consultations with the EC regarding the approval and marketing of biotech products: *EC–Measures Affecting the Approval and Marketing of Biotech Products* WT/DS291/1 (US request for consultations dated 20 May 2003), WT/DS292/1 (Canada's request for consultations dated 20 May 2003), WT/DS293/1 (Argentina's request for consultations dated 21 May 2003). Another case (with a lower profile) that raises some difficult questions is the EC's challenge to Australia's quarantine system. Australia is widely acknowledged as taking a very conservative approach to quarantine matters, an approach which the EC condemns as protectionist: *Australia–Quarantine Regime for Imports* WT/DS287/1 (Request for consultations dated 9 April 2003).

88 Trebilcock and Howse (n 75) 145.

(a) The meaning of risk assessment

In approaching the question of what an acceptable risk assessment will be, the Appellate Body has been careful not to tie the SPS system to any particular model of risk assessment. Rather, the Appellate Body has been concerned to stress that its main focus will be to see that governments are responding to real, identified and evaluated risks and are not engaging in knee-jerk reactions to purely hypothetical risks. In line with this approach, risks may be assessed qualitatively *or* quantitatively,[89] but Members will not be able to rely on the kind of risk that always remains because science can never prove the absolute safety of any substance.[90] The Appellate Body's willingness to accept qualitative as well as quantitative risk assessments is particularly notable when one considers that for some, including international bodies like the OIE, only quantitative risk assessment provides a properly objective basis for regulation-setting.[91]

Although the Appellate Body showed notable flexibility in accepting qualitative risk assessment, it has prescribed some demanding criteria for risk assessments. In particular, risk assessments must be sufficiently *specific* to satisfy Article 5.1. In the *Hormones* case, for example, the Appellate Body rejected general studies of the carcinogenic risk of hormones and suggested that a proper risk assessment would have assessed the hormones on an individual basis, and would have paid particular attention to their use for growth promotion purposes and the potential risk arising from residues in food.[92] In the *Apples* case, the panel rejected Japan's 1999 risk assessment because it did not focus sufficiently on the risks of transmission of fire blight through apple fruit, as opposed to other modes of transmission.[93] The Appellate Body upheld this finding on appeal.[94]

With this focus on detailed and context-specific risk assessments, the Appellate Body's emphasis is clearly on positive evidence of harm. What the Appellate Body's specificity criteria require is a highly specialised risk assessment that addresses the narrow circumstances of the eventual measure (as well as other measures that might have been applied).[95] Whether

[89] *Hormones* AB Report (n 3) para 186.

[90] *Hormones* AB Report (n 3) para 186. Note that the precautionary principle is discussed in Chapter 5.

[91] JA Kellar 'The Application of Risk Analysis to International Trade in Animals and Animal Products' (1993) 12 SciTechRev (OIE) 1023, 1028 (condemning qualitative assessments as intuitive and bias-prone).

[92] *Hormones* AB Report (n 3) para 199.

[93] *Apples* Panel Report (n 3) paras 8.277–8.280.

[94] *Apples* AB Report (n 3) para 206.

[95] Walker suggests this means that all measures not based on focused studies will fail (Walker (n 44) 298) and Sykes suggests that this means that regulators will be unable to eliminate low level risks that are not susceptible to rigorous demonstration (AO Sykes 'Exploring the Need for International Harmonization: Domestic Regulation, Sovereignty, and Scientific

or not this is a reasonable demand for wealthy countries (who might still feel that it is unduly prescriptive), it is undoubtedly highly impractical for poorer countries. In any event, the demand for specificity puts a limit on the extent to which WTO Members will be able to rely on risk assessments conducted by other countries or international bodies. The Appellate Body had found that Members need not conduct their own risk assessments and then base measures on them but, rather, that they can draw on risk assessments and other scientific evidence from any quarter produced at any time.[96] The latitude that this gave Members to beg and borrow from various sources is significantly curtailed by the level of specificity that the Appellate Body appears to be demanding. Add to this the Appellate Body's desire for comprehensive risk assessment—it failed the risk assessment in the *Salmon* case on the basis that '*some* evaluation' of the likelihood of entry, establishment or spread of the disease was 'not enough'[97]—and one comes to doubt claims that the risk assessment discipline is elastic and easily satisfied.[98]

(b) *The meaning of measures being 'based on' a risk assessment*

As set out above, a Member need not carry out its own risk assessment. Rather, it can rely on a risk assessment carried out by any other Member or international organisation and need not have that risk assessment to hand before it takes action.[99] In making these findings, the Appellate Body stressed that the words 'based on' referred to the objective and observable relationship between a risk assessment and a measure and did not import a chronological relationship.[100] Although several expressions have been used to describe this relationship, the Appellate Body appears to have settled on requiring a 'rational relationship between the measure and the risk assessment.'[101] In focusing on the *relationship* between the measure and the risk assessment, the Appellate Body rejected the panel's more narrow view that the measures must *conform* to the scientific conclusions reached

Evidence Requirements: A Pessimistic View' (2002) 3 ChiJIntlL 353, 364); cf Davey, who suggests that the AB's decisions on risk assessment have been reasonable and not too restrictive of Member governments' decision-making: Davey (n 60) 53.

96 *Hormones* AB Report (n 3) paras 189–90.

97 *Salmon* AB Report (n 3) paras 124, 128 (emphasis in original). The AB also found that the third requirement was not made out because, again, '*some* evaluation' of likelihood is not enough: para 134.

98 J Atik 'Science and Regulatory Convergence' (1996–7) 17 Northwestern JILBus 736, 745.

99 The AB in the *Hormones* case overturned the panel's suggestion that Art 5.1 requires that the risk assessment must actually have been taken into account when the measures were enacted or maintained: *Hormones* AB Report (n 3) paras 189–90.

100 *Hormones* AB Report (n 3) para 189. The AB also said (at para 193) that there must be a 'rational relationship' between the risk assessment and the measure.

101 *Hormones* AB Report (n 3) para 193. The others are: 'sufficiently supported or reasonably warranted by the risk assessment' and 'sufficiently warrant—that is to say, reasonably support—the SPS measure at stake': *Hormones* AB Report (n 3) paras 186, 193.

in the risk assessments.[102] It is not, however, clear to what extent a measure and a risk assessment can enjoy a 'rational relationship' if the measure departs from the scientific conclusions reached in the risk assessment. Rather than approving of measures which depart from the scientific conclusions of their underlying risk assessments, perhaps what the Appellate Body had in mind was allowing risk assessments to incorporate a *range* of scientific views whose conclusions may not be consistent. Indeed, the possibility of divergent scientific views does appear to have been of concern to the Appellate Body as it went on to find that risk assessments can set out mainstream and divergent scientific views.[103] According to the Appellate Body, while governments will normally base their regulations on mainstream scientific opinion, '[i]n other cases, equally responsible and representative governments may act in good faith on the basis of what, at a given time, may be a divergent opinion coming from qualified and respected sources.'[104] Even so, the Appellate Body was not prepared to allow the EC to base its measures on the opinion of the sole expert asserting that a cancer risk existed, saying that 'the single divergent opinion expressed by Dr Lucier is not reasonably sufficient to overturn the contrary conclusions reached in the scientific studies referred to by the European Communities'.[105] The treatment of Dr Lucier's evidence has led some commentators to suggest that the Appellate Body was only paying lip-service to minority science.[106]

(c) Risk assessment does not authorise a balancing exercise

The SPS Agreement does not authorise panels or the Appellate Body to conduct fresh risk assessments or to weigh up whether the cost of the measures is justified when set against the magnitude of the risk guarded against, or the trade costs to other Members. Article 5.4 requires that Members 'take into account the objective of minimizing negative trade effects' when determining the appropriate level of protection, but it does not actually limit Members' freedom to choose a high level of protection by reference to the negative trade effects to be suffered by other Members. Within the confines of Article 5.1, if Members are able to identify a real and

[102] *Hormones* US Panel Report (n 3) para 8.117; *Hormones* Canada Panel Report (n 3) para 8.120.

[103] *Hormones* AB Report (n 3) para 194.

[104] *Hormones* AB Report (n 3) para 194.

[105] *Hormones* AB Report (n 3) para 198.

[106] JM Wagner 'The WTO's Interpretation of the SPS Agreement has Undermined the Right of Governments to Establish Appropriate Levels of Protection Against Risk' (2000) 31 Law&Pol'yIntlBus 855. Compare others who suggest that, with the AB's reference to divergent scientific opinion, it will always be possible to generate a risk assessment: C Thorn and M Carlson 'The Agreement on the Application of Sanitary and Phytosanitary Measures and the Agreement on Technical Barriers to Trade' (2000) 31 Law&Pol'yIntlBus 841, 846.

discernible (not merely hypothetical) risk, they are free to adopt measures to combat that risk even though a cost–benefit analysis might suggest that the regulatory response is inappropriate: only the Members can decide on the level of acceptable risk. The integrity of this division of decision-making power lies at the heart of the balance negotiated by the SPS Agreement: in exchange for accepting onerous disciplines, such as the scientific justification requirement, the Members retained the right to determine just how risk averse their health policies should be.[107]

In sum, the decisions of the panels and Appellate Body in these cases have fleshed out the risk assessment discipline. There are, however, widely varying views on how much latitude the WTO rules on risk assessment leave Members to apply their own (as opposed to international) SPS standards. For many, the rational relationship interpretation, together with (i) the Appellate Body's overruling of the *Hormones* panel's procedural requirement, (ii) its willingness to accept divergent scientific opinion and (iii) its acceptance of regulation in response to minute risks, means that Article 5 has not been allowed to be too restrictive.[108] Moreover, others point out that the Appellate Body has not presumed to make independent judgments about the necessity of protective measures.[109] For some, however, the interpretations offered by the Appellate Body are so generous to national regulation that they might even be accused of failing to uphold the substantive scientific disciplines envisaged by the SPS Agreement.[110] Given that a number of questions still await determination, final judgment on whether the Appellate Body has struck the right balance between ensuring that Article 5.1 is sufficiently robust and not imposing excessive constraints on national regulation would be premature.

5 Least Trade-Restrictive Measure

As will be recalled from Chapter 2, the least trade-restrictive (LTR) measure discipline—which requires that Members utilise the least restrictive means by which to achieve their regulatory goals—is potentially a very powerful discipline. In GATT, the LTR discipline was found within the Article XX(b) requirement that measures be 'necessary' to protect health. In the SPS Agreement, the LTR discipline is express: Article 5.6 provides that, in establishing or maintaining SPS measures to achieve the appropriate level

[107] Recall, however, that the panel's approach to Art 2.2 in the *Apples* case implicitly calls this balance into question.

[108] Fidler (n 7) 140; S Charnovitz 'Environment and Health Under WTO Dispute Settlement' (1998) 32 The International Lawyer 901, 915.

[109] McGinnis and Movsesian (n 38) 594; Stewart and Karpel (n 38) 601.

[110] RD Thomas 'Where's the Beef? Mad Cows and the Blight of the SPS Agreement' (1999) VandJTransL 487, 490; note also Atik (n 98) 740 (science-based standards represent a swing back towards national discretion).

of protection, Members must ensure that such measures are not more trade-restrictive than required, taking into account technical and economic feasibility. The LTR discipline is also expressly qualified in two significant respects by a note to Article 5.6, which states that a measure is not more trade-restrictive than required 'unless there is another measure, *reasonably available* taking into account technical and economic feasibility, that achieves the appropriate level of sanitary or phytosanitary protection and is *significantly less restrictive* to trade.'[111]

The note to Article 5.6 is particularly important for three reasons. Firstly, the three components of the note have been taken to constitute the test for breach of Article 5.6.[112] The less restrictive alternative (i) must be reasonably available, (ii) must achieve the appropriate level of protection, and (iii) must be significantly less restrictive to trade. Secondly, the terms of the note should be sufficient to ensure that Article 5.6 is not subjected to the general critique attaching to LTR requirements. According to that critique, it is always possible for those observing from the sidelines to come up with some less restrictive alternative.[113] By emphasising that the alternative must provide *significant* trade gains, the note to Article 5.6 should help the SPS Agreement's LTR discipline avoid this criticism. Thirdly, the existence of the note's express qualifications to the LTR discipline mean that we can expect the understanding of the LTR discipline in the SPS Agreement and GATT to diverge because those qualifications apply only to the SPS Agreement. Although the necessity discipline in GATT has been interpreted only to require the use of *reasonably available* alternatives[114]—which may amount to much the same thing as the SPS Agreement's reference to the technical and economic feasibility of alternatives—there is no definite GATT equivalent of the SPS Agreement's additional requirement that the measure be significantly less restrictive to trade.

It seems that the Appellate Body has taken heed of the disquiet expressed at the handling of the LTR discipline under GATT (where it was feared that panels might find that alternatives exist without proper evidence of their likely efficacy in the defending Member's territory). When applying the LTR discipline under the SPS Agreement, the Appellate Body has, on two occasions, refused to find that less trade-restrictive alternatives existed because of a lack of evidence. For example, in the *Salmon* case, the Appellate Body found that, although there were alternative measures (as identified in the 1996 Final Report submitted by Australia), there was not sufficient evidence to determine whether they would achieve

[111] Emphasis added.
[112] *Salmon* Panel Report (n 3) para 8.167; *Salmon* AB Report (n 3) para 194.
[113] Esty (n 80) 48.
[114] *Section 337* (n 15) para 5.26.

Australia's appropriate level of protection.[115] The *Salmon* case also raises the question of the appropriate source of the alternative measures to be assessed. Whereas, in the *Salmon* case, the alternatives were drawn from Australia's own report, in the *Agricultural Products* case, the Appellate Body stipulated that it is for the complaining party to suggest alternatives and to make a *prima facie* case of inconsistency with Article 5.6.[116] Moreover, panels have been cautioned not to construct that *prima facie* case for the complaining party by using information provided to it by its expert advisers.[117]

Just how panels and the Appellate Body assess whether alternative measures will achieve the country's appropriate level of protection will affect the balance between regulatory autonomy and international supervision. The Appellate Body's firm hand in placing the burden of proof on the complaining party and unwillingness to find a violation of Article 5.6 in the absence of sufficient evidence suggest that it is keeping the appropriate scope of its review under this Article in mind. It will also be relevant to enquire how much detail of alternative measures must be presented, when measures will be 'reasonably available', and how much less restrictive a measure must be to be 'significantly' less restrictive to trade. It is also still unclear what panels will make of the note's reference to alternatives being reasonably available 'taking into account technical and economic feasibility'. In particular, that express reference would seem to be an open invitation to panels to pursue vigorously the position taken (without the benefit of an express reference to economic feasibility) by the panel in the *Asbestos* case. In that case, the panel was of the view that, as a developed country, France could be expected to adopt expensive but less trade-restrictive alternatives: 'it is legitimate to expect a country such as France with advanced labour legislation and specialized administrative services to deploy administrative resources proportionate to its public health objectives and to be prepared to incur the necessary expenditure.'[118] If panels begin to meddle in questions of domestic resource allocation and the structure of a Member's regulatory administration, accusations that the WTO is intruding into areas of national sovereignty are sure to follow.[119] Panels must remain aware that, in any case before them, they are

[115] *Salmon* AB Report (n 3) paras 210–13 (note, by way of contrast, the charge that the panel pointed to 'a menu of options from which it asserted that Australia could have fashioned an alternative policy': Charnovitz 'The Supervision of Health and Biosafety Regulation' (n 2) 285). Note also the lack of evidence on the efficacy of testing by product in the *Agricultural Products* case: *Agricultural Products* Panel Report (n 3) para 8.84 (upheld by the AB: *Agricultural Products* AB Report (n 3) paras 98–100).

[116] *Agricultural Products* AB Report (n 3) paras 126, 130.

[117] *Agricultural Products* AB Report (n 3) para 130.

[118] *Asbestos* Panel Report (n 32) para 8.207.

[119] One concern is that the WTO may adopt the ECJ's more intrusive approach in which it takes it upon itself to balance trade and environmental values: Trebilcock and Howse (n 75) 153, 164.

considering only a small portion of the defending Member's regulatory apparatus. While it may be tempting to enforce *the* most efficient solution to a particular regulatory problem, panels should take care not to distort inadvertently the balance of resource allocations within national regulatory systems. Only an infinitesimal proportion of regulations come before the WTO. If panels dictate the level of resources to be allocated to those few, high profile, cases, they risk distorting the vast majority of regulations which never come to light in the WTO.

The balance struck by the SPS Agreement leaves it to Members to determine their appropriate level of protection. It is true that that balance limits the ability of the SPS Agreement to address trade barriers arising out of disparate national policies,[120] but it is the balance which was struck and it must be respected. That allocation of decision-making power could be upset if the WTO 'slip[s] into developing a jurisprudence of "preferred" solutions'.[121] The Appellate Body has emphasised that Article 5.6 is not to be used as a vehicle for second-guessing the desired level of protection and that expert advisers are not to be used as substitutes for the presentation of a *prima facie* case by the complaining party. Against these interpretations (which are favourable to defending countries), the Appellate Body has suggested norms of good regulatory decision-making and required that Members distinguish between their appropriate and actual levels of protection.

6 Provisional Measures

In order to survive review under the SPS Agreement, the measure must have a scientific justification (Article 2.2) and must be based on a risk assessment (Article 5). Where the state of scientific knowledge is such that a risk assessment cannot be completed or a scientific justification advanced, a Member may still act to protect health by relying on Article 5.7. Article 5.7 permits the provisional adoption of SPS measures where the 'relevant scientific information is insufficient'. This provision is crucial as it constitutes the only way in which measures which do not meet the scientific justification requirements of Article 2.2 can survive review under the SPS Agreement. Because scientific understanding can lag behind the need to take protective action, the SPS Agreement's provisional-measures Article recognises the need to protect the ability of governments to respond to perceived health threats without waiting idly until the scientific jury delivers its verdict. While Article 5.7 recognises that

[120] AO Sykes *Product Standards for Internationally Integrated Goods Markets* (The Brookings Institution Washington DC 1995) 118–19.

[121] McGinnis and Movsesian (n 38) 580.

responsible governments may adopt a cautious approach and regulate in conditions of scientific uncertainty, the constraints that Article imposes may limit the ability of Members to continue to protect against risks in circumstances where the scientific uncertainty is enduring, or where the Member is unwilling or unable to devote the necessary resources to conducting further scientific research. Australia, in particular, will be interested to see a broad approach taken to this aspect of Article 5.7 as it is currently facing a number of challenges to its quarantine system.[122] One of the novel issues raised in those challenges is the extent to which Australia can justify its quarantine system, which its opponents say bans the import of a product until a risk assessment is undertaken and supports access being given to that product. What this means is that the importation of a specific product may well be banned even though no risk assessment has been undertaken, leaving Australia apparently in breach of the SPS Agreement. Even if the attack on the basic approach of Australia's quarantine system is dropped,[123] the question will arise as to whether Australia can rely on Article 5.7 to support an import ban simply because, due to resource constraints and the ordering of domestic priorities, it has not yet conducted a risk assessment of that product. The resource implications of the approach taken in answering this question are clear.

(a) Interpretation of the terms of Article 5.7

Article 5.7 provides as follows:

> In cases where relevant scientific evidence is insufficient, a Member may provisionally adopt sanitary or phytosanitary measures on the basis of available pertinent information, including that from the relevant international organizations as well as from sanitary or phytosanitary measures applied by other Members. In such circumstances, Members shall seek to obtain the additional information necessary for a more objective assessment of risk and review the sanitary or phytosanitary measure accordingly within a reasonable period of time.

The meaning of this Article was considered at length in the *Agricultural Products* and *Apples* cases. In the *Agricultural Products* case, the panel found that Japan's varietal testing rule—requiring that, in respect of specified fruits, the efficacy of quarantine treatments be established on a varietal basis—was inconsistent with Article 2.2 and did not qualify as a provisional measure under Article 5.7 because there was no evidence that Japan

[122] *Australia–Quarantine Regime for Imports* WT/DS287 (case brought by the EC); *Australia–Certain Measures Affecting the Importation of Fresh Fruit and Vegetables* WT/DS270 (case brought by the Philippines).

[123] The panel may, however, decide that the SPS Agreement can only be used to review a specific measure and does not allow a Member to challenge the entire quarantine system of another Member.

was taking steps to obtain the necessary additional information.[124] Japan challenged these findings on appeal. The Appellate Body upheld the panel's finding that Article 5.7 disclosed four requirements, all of which had to be met.[125] The four requirements are: (i) measures are to be imposed in a situation where the relevant scientific information is insufficient; (ii) measures are to be adopted on the basis of pertinent information; (iii) the Member must seek to obtain the additional information necessary for a more objective assessment of risk; and (iv) the Member must review the measure within a reasonable period of time.

(i) The insufficiency of scientific information The question of when scientific information is 'insufficient' is, on its face, somewhat esoteric. Scientific information is never full and never perfect: as is discussed in Chapter 4, all risk assessments and scientific studies incorporate various assumptions and uncertainties. When addressing the question of the sufficiency of scientific information in the context of the SPS Agreement, however, the real issue is how the concept of sufficiency affects the treatment of SPS measures. More particularly, the pertinent question is whether the concept of sufficiency is applied in such a way as to avoid creating a *gap* between the areas occupied by Article 2.2 and Article 5.7. If there is such a gap, a measure may be found to be contrary to the SPS Agreement because there is not sufficient scientific evidence to support the measure under Article 2.2, but there is too much scientific evidence available for the measure to qualify as a 'provisional' measure under Article 5.7. The decision of the panel in the *Apples* case suggested that there may indeed be such a gap between the sufficiency required for Article 2.2 and the insufficiency required to qualify under Article 5.7.

In the *Apples* case, the panel found that Japan could not rely on Article 5.7 because, as regards fire blight, the situation was not one where there was insufficient scientific information. According to the panel, 'Article 5.7 was obviously designed to be invoked in situations where little, or no, reliable evidence was available on the subject matter at issue.'[126] As the panel found that, with regard to fire blight, 'not only a large quantity but a high quality of scientific evidence has been produced over the years', Japan could not rely on Article 5.7 by pointing to specific aspects of the dissemenation of fire blight to which uncertainties still attached. According to the panel's approach, Article 5.7 can only be invoked when a WTO Member is regulating to protect against potential harm at the fringes of scientific knowledge. By fixing Article 5.7's reference to 'insufficiency' to a subject matter in general (such as fire blight), rather than to specific questions (such as questions regarding the dissemenation of fire blight bacteria), the panel adopted a fairly restrictive approach to Article 5.7.

[124] *Agricultural Products* Panel Report (n 3) paras 5.58–5.61.
[125] *Agricultural Products* AB Report (n 3) para 89 (on the four requirements).
[126] *Apples* Panel Report (n 3) para 8.129.

On appeal, the Appellate Body did not expressly reject the panel's approach, but did qualify it in such a way as to ameliorate concerns that, by simultaneously confining Article 5.7 to the fringes of scientific knowledge and imposing onerous requirements to satisfy Article 2.2, there would be a gap into which otherwise legitimate national health regulations may fall. The Appellate Body sought to avoid the distinction, which Japan and the panel had drawn, between uncertainty or lack of information regarding a situation (such as fire blight in general) and uncertainty or lack of information regarding specific questions. The Appellate Body found that the question to be addressed in applying the first criterion of Article 5.7 (relevant scientific evidence is insufficient) is whether the available scientific evidence is sufficient, in quantitative or qualitative terms, to permit an assessment of the risks as required by Article 5.1.[127] In other words, where the panel saw Article 5.7 as relevant only to subjects in respect of which very little information exists, the Appellate Body found that Article 5.7 can apply whenever the available scientific evidence is insufficient to permit a Member to conduct a risk assessment that will satisfy the requirements of Article 5.1.

In linking Articles 5.1 and 5.7 in this way, the Appellate Body has gone a long way towards guarding against a potential gap between the scientific evidence required of regular and provisional SPS measures. Although the Appellate Body did not relate the quantity of scientific evidence to be required under Article 5.7 to that which will be required under Article 2.2 (but instead referred to the information required to conduct a risk assessment), it is likely that the Appellate Body's finding will be treated as applicable to the relationship between those two Articles as well, so that what is insufficient for the purposes of Article 2.2 will be insufficient for the purposes of Article 5.7 too. The Appellate Body's linking of Articles 5.1 and 5.7 is a positive development as it emphasises the need to maintain a reasonable balance between protecting the rigours of the scientific assessment criteria (including Article 5.1) and ensuring that Article 5.7 is not marginalised by overly narrow interpretations. In theory at least, the Appellate Body's approach in the *Apples* case means that, the more rigorous the requirements imposed under Article 5.1, the broader the range of measures that will be covered by Article 5.7. At the very least, this link should limit the extent to which future panels and the Appellate Body will be ready to adopt more restrictive interpretations of Article 5.1.

(ii) Insufficiency and uncertainty Besides raising the possibility of a 'gap' between Articles 2.2 and 5.7, the panel's statement that Article 5.7 was only intended to address situations where little or no reliable evidence was available indicated that the panel thought that its focus, in applying

[127] *Apples* AB Report (n 3) para 179.

Article 5.7, should be on the availability of scientific *evidence* not scientific *uncertainty*. Japan sought to challenge the panel's statement on the grounds that its conception of Article 5.7 does not provide for what Japan called situations of 'unresolved uncertainty'.[128] Japan's concern was that, while the panel's focus on the availability of reliable evidence on a subject matter allowed for situations of 'new' uncertainty (where a new risk is identified), it did not allow for situations of 'unresolved' uncertainty (where uncertainties remain unresolved despite accumulated scientific evidence). According to Japan, the panel's approach restricted Article 5.7 to situations of 'new' uncertainty.

In answering Japan's contention, the Appellate Body focused on the wording of Article 5.7 and rightly observed that that Article is triggered by the insufficiency of scientific evidence, rather than by scientific uncertainty.[129] While, as the Appellate Body observed, the concepts of insufficiency of evidence and scientific uncertainty are not interchangeable, it should not be supposed that the distinction means that Article 5.7 does not accommodate situations of scientific uncertainty. Where a potential hazard has been identified but is poorly understood, it might be said that there is a significant degree of scientific uncertainty, but, in such a situation, it is also likely to be the case that there will be insufficient scientific information to conduct a risk assessment under Article 5.1 and arrive at a measure that will be supported by sufficient scientific evidence for the purposes of Article 2.2. In this situation, Article 5.7 would apply. In short, where such broad uncertainties exist, there is unlikely to be 'sufficient scientific information' and Article 5.7 will be available.

As Japan observed, however, the more difficult issue arises where there is a hazard that is, in general, quite well understood (such as fire blight) but uncertainties persist regarding specific questions (such as the risk of transmission through apple fruit). On its face, the Appellate Body's answer to Japan's concern appears unsatisfactory as it implicitly confirms Japan's fear that Article 5.7 cannot be used where uncertainty attaches to a specific question in circumstances where the hazard is otherwise well understood and plenty of reliable scientific evidence exists. However, when one considers the Appellate Body's response on this point in the context of its earlier findings on the relationship between Articles 5.1 and 5.7, it seems that Japan's concerns may be answered. It will be recalled that, in the *Apples* case, the Appellate Body found that Article 5.7 will take over when the scientifc evidence is insufficient to conduct a risk assessment for the purposes of Article 5.1. It follows, then, that Article 5.7 will be available if, in order to conduct a proper risk assessment that will satisfy

[128] *Apples* AB Report (n 3) para 183, referring to para 101 of Japan's appellant's submission.
[129] *Apples* AB Report (n 3) para 184.

Article 5.1, a specific question needs to be addressed but (notwithstanding that the hazard in question is *generally* well understood) there is insufficient scientific evidence on that *particular* question with the result that a particular step of the risk assessment cannot be completed.

(iii) Obtaining additional information and reviewing provisional measures It is clear from the *Agricultural Products* case that the obligation to 'seek to obtain' additional information will not be satisfied by half-hearted attempts to collect further information as it comes to hand. Rather, Members must take targeted action to collect further information that will be germane to conducting a risk assessment.[130] As the information collected by Japan did not address the core issue—whether varietal characteristics cause a divergence in the efficacy of quarantine measures—it failed to abide by its obligation to 'seek to obtain the additional information necessary for a more objective assessment of risk'.[131]

According to the second sentence of Article 5.7, Members must review provisional SPS measures within a reasonable period of time. In the *Agricultural Products* case, it was determined that Japan had not reviewed the measure within a reasonable period of time, even though the obligation to review provisional measures came into effect on 1 January 1995 and the dispute settlement proceedings were begun barely two years later (the US requested consultations on 7 April 1997).[132] Most WTO Members will still have huge numbers of health measures on the books that pre-date the coming into force of the SPS Agreement. If any of these measures cannot be supported as scientifically justified, Members will have to rely on Article 5.7. In light of the attitude taken to review in the *Agricultural Products* case, however, such claims may well fail if the Member has not reviewed the measure since the SPS Agreement came into force in 1995. According to the *Agricultural Products* case, the assessment of whether the measure has been reviewed within a reasonable period of time will take into account the difficulty of obtaining the additional information (said to be relatively easy by the panel in the *Agricultural Products* case) and the characteristics of the provisional SPS measure.[133] Nevertheless, the message from the *Agricultural Products* case is that Members cannot afford to be complacent in reviewing their regulations; they must actively seek further information and must keep the provisional measures under review.

130 *Agricultural Products* AB Report (n 3) para 92.

131 *Agricultural Products* Panel Report (n 3) para 8.56. Japan cited two studies and the information it acquired when exporting countries applied for access.

132 *Agricultural Products* Panel Report (n 3) para 5.85; *Agricultural Products* AB Report (n 3) para 93.

133 *Agricultural Products* Panel Report (n 3) para 5.86; *Agricultural Products* AB Report (n 3) para 93.

Collecting further information and reviewing measures clearly requires the dedication of resources. Accordingly, the approach taken by panels and the Appellate Body to these obligations (in terms of how vigorously Members are to be required to seek additional information and how frequently they must review measures) has significant implications for the allocation of regulatory and scientific resources. In other areas, panels and the Appellate Body have not shied away from taking a tough stance on the costs of complying with GATT and other WTO obligations. While the Members may not object in principle to accepting that, in some instances, meeting their WTO obligations will require the devotion of additional resources, there is greater potential for resentment if panels and the Appellate Body start to direct resource allocation on specific regulatory issues.

(b) Problems with provisional measures

There is a growing body of literature pointing out that some degree of uncertainty is inherent even in scientific enquiries and that 'science policy' is used to bridge gaps and make assumptions.[134] Aside from such inherent uncertainty, scientific knowledge does not always keep pace with the need to respond to health threats. Article 5.7 appears to proceed from the premise that any gaps in scientific evidence can be filled by obtaining additional information. Even if one accepts that Members should be obliged to expend resources seeking to eliminate any scientific gaps that prevent them undertaking a full risk assessment, what if that uncertainty is enduring? As was stressed by the Appellate Body in the *Agricultural Products* case, Article 5.7 only requires that Members '*seek* to obtain' additional information.[135] Perhaps, then, panels and the Appellate Body will be prepared to allow Members to keep reviewing and maintaining provisional measures for long periods of time if it appears that a genuine effort is being made to gather more scientific information. It is, however, unlikely that Members will be permitted to keep looking for evidence of harm where other evidence exists to suggest that the harm does not exist.

Panels and the Appellate Body should tread carefully in applying Article 5.7. The scientific justification discipline in the SPS Agreement is strong, and Article 5.7 constitutes the only means by which protective action can be taken without a scientific justification. Given the domestic importance of being able to act in such circumstances, a wide reading should be given to this provision. In applying Article 5.7, panels and the Appellate Body should also keep in mind that not all uncertainties consist

[134] On uncertainty and science policy, see two leading commentators: DA Wirth 'The Role of Science in the Uruguay Round and NAFTA Trade Disciplines' (1994) 27 Cornell IntLJ 817; Walker (n 44). The issue of uncertainty is taken up in Chapter 4.

[135] *Agricultural Products* AB Report (n 3) para 92.

of data gaps that can be filled with more work completed to meet a deadline. Accordingly, provided that a defending Member demonstrates its commitment to science-based regulation by striving to enhance its scientific knowledge, the fact that the provisional measures have been in existence for a number of years should not mean that they have not been reviewed within a 'reasonable' period of time.

Another troublesome aspect of Article 5.7 is the nature of the 'available pertinent information' on which provisional measures can be based. The Appellate Body has not made it clear whether such information may include consumer fears or cultural preferences (such as an aversion to genetic modification) or whether the information must be of the same type as would be relevant to a risk assessment (such as scientific information and estimates of the population's exposure). It is suggested that, while some leeway to respond to consumer concerns should be allowed, Article 5.7 should not be allowed to subvert the scientific focus of the SPS Agreement by being used to authorise long-term measures which were put in place to respond to consumer fears when there is no credible evidence of harm.

7 Additional Disciplines

The SPS Agreement contains a number of additional provisions which do not warrant lengthy analysis here but should be mentioned for the sake of completeness.

(a) Equivalence

The first of these additional disciplines is the attempt, in Article 4, to encourage recognition of the equivalence of other Members' SPS measures. Article 4 requires Members to accept the SPS measures of another Member as equivalent if the exporting Member 'objectively demonstrates' to the importing Member that its measures achieve the same level of SPS protection. Although not the subject of any reports to date, there is obvious scope for disagreement over whether the equivalence of measures has been objectively demonstrated. This provision should be contrasted with the equivalence provisions in the TBT Agreement which suggest a more limited scope for review by referring to the importing Member being 'satisfied' on the question of equivalence.[136] There is, then, the possibility of WTO Members effectively being required to acknowledge the equivalence of another Member's SPS measures by virtue of Article 4 and its reference to equivalence being 'objectively demonstrated'.

[136] TBT Agreement Arts 2.7 and 6.1.

(b) Procedural requirements

The SPS Agreement contains a number of provisions that shape the domestic regulatory process, its execution and the provision of information. Article 6 imposes substantive requirements on national regulatory processes by requiring Members to analyse exporting countries at a regional level and recognise the concept of pest- or disease-free areas as well as low pest areas. Article 7 provides for transparency by requiring Members to notify changes in their SPS measures.[137] Control, inspection and approval procedures are governed by Article 8 and Annex C, which seeks, *inter alia*, to limit delay, includes a like treatment obligation, limits information requirements, protects confidentiality and limits requirements in respect of individual specimens to those that are 'reasonable and necessary'. Finally, Article 9 provides for technical assistance and Article 10 covers developing country needs.

8 Overview of the SPS Agreement's Disciplines

As can be seen from the foregoing discussion, the SPS Agreement imposes a number of significant constraints on the ability of Members to regulate to protect domestic health.[138] There are two points to be stressed. Firstly (and a point which is often overlooked), the SPS Agreement seeks to eradicate not only *deliberately* protectionist SPS measures (ie those SPS measures put in place to protect a domestic industry), but also those SPS measures that respond to genuine health concerns[139] but are *unnecessary* because they are not based on scientific evidence or because they are more trade-restrictive than they need to be. Other provisions support this objective by encouraging the use of international standards, requiring that the Member conduct a risk assessment and ensuring that the Member adopts a coherent approach to regulating risks by imposing a consistent level of protection in comparable situations. Secondly, the SPS Agreement does

[137] Notifications can be viewed on the WTO's internet site <http://www.wto.org>. SPS Agreement Annex B provides further detail on publication, enquiry points and notification procedures.

[138] Cf Bloche, who sees the AB's findings on issues like minority science, the 'rational relationship' interpretation of the requirement that measures be 'based on' a risk assessment and the absence of a procedural requirement to take the cited risk assessment into account *before* regulating as demonstrating a far-reaching posture of deference to Members' regulators: MG Bloche 'WTO Deference to National Health Policy: Toward an Interpretive Principle' (2002) 5 JIEL 825, 836–37. While the benefit of these findings for national regulatory autonomy are not disputed, arguably Bloche focuses rather narrowly on these positives and fails to consider the more restrictive aspects of the AB's approach.

[139] Note, TR Reid 'What's Eating the Europeans? Killer Cornflakes' *International Herald Tribune* (London) 2 March 2001, 1 (suggesting that Europeans are more worried about unfounded health risks than their American counterparts).

not purport to supervise the level of risk that each Member is prepared to accept. Members are free to be as risk averse or as casual about risk as they please. The Agreement simply requires that a Member's response to a risk (even if it implements a low risk acceptance policy) has a scientific justification, is based on a risk assessment and meets the Agreement's other requirements.

B REVIEW UNDER THE TBT AGREEMENT

Not all health measures will be covered by the SPS Agreement. Many of the health measures that are not covered by the SPS Agreement will be covered by the TBT Agreement.[140] Like SPS measures, technical regulations constitute a significant source of non-tariff barriers to trade. Almost without exception, any product which is to be exported into another market will have to comply with the technical specifications of the importing market.[141] Complying with foreign technical regulations imposes considerable costs on exporters. Exporters must not only expend considerable resources just finding out what those requirements are, but they must also make the necessary modifications to production processes and plant, and must also prove that their products comply with the relevant specifications of the importing country. The TBT Agreement seeks to minimise these costs by imposing a number of substantive and procedural obligations on WTO Members which, like the SPS Agreement's disciplines, apply concurrently with GATT.[142] These disciplines are set out below and, where appropriate, their application by panels and the Appellate Body is considered, although it should be noted at the outset that the TBT Agreement has only really been considered in two cases, the *Asbestos* case (which concerned a French ban on chrysotile asbestos) and the *Sardines* case (which concerned EC rules restricting use of the name 'sardines' to fish of the *sardina pilchardus* species).

1 Scope of Application

The TBT Agreement distinguishes between technical regulations and standards, and imposes different sets of obligations in respect of the two categories. Technical regulations are *mandatory* requirements relating to

140 The TBT Agreement does not cover SPS measures as defined by the SPS Agreement: TBT Agreement Art 1.5.

141 Unless there is a mutual recognition or equivalence agreement between the exporting and importing countries, in which case the exporter will have to comply with the standards of the exporting country.

142 *Asbestos* AB Report (n 41) para 80.

'product characteristics or their related processes and production methods' and 'may also include or deal exclusively with terminology, symbols, packaging, marking or labelling requirements as they apply to a product, process or production method.'[143] A standard, by contrast, is a document (approved by a 'recognized body') providing for 'common and repeated use, rules, guidelines or characteristics for products or related processes and production methods'[144] with which compliance is *not mandatory*. Standards may also include or deal exclusively with terminology, symbols etc. As can be seen from the definitions, the scope of technical regulations and standards is very broad, as is fitting given the ubiquity of such regulations and standards. Although the TBT Agreement applies to both standards and regulations, the focus here will be on the way in which WTO Members are constrained in their choice of *mandatory* product specifications (ie, technical regulations).

(a) The test for technical regulations

In considering the application of the TBT Agreement, it must first be determined whether the measure is a technical regulation. Following the *Asbestos* and *Sardines* cases, it can be confidently stated that the TBT Agreement will enjoy a wide scope through the interpretation given to the definition of 'technical regulation'. In the *Asbestos* case, the Appellate Body found that three criteria must be met.[145] Firstly, the document must apply to an identifiable product or group of products. Secondly, the document must lay down one or more characteristics of the product. Thirdly, compliance with the product characteristics must be mandatory.

(i) Identifiable product The *Asbestos* case concerned a French Decree which contained a general ban on asbestos but also provided for some limited exceptions. In considering the case, the panel had to determine whether the measure was a technical regulation. It split the Decree into two parts and decided that the general ban was not a technical regulation because it did not relate to the characteristics of *identifiable products*, but that the exceptions to the ban did fall under the TBT Agreement.[146] The Appellate Body determined that the panel should not have split the

143 TBT Agreement Annex 1, para 1.

144 TBT Agreement Annex 1, para 2. Note that the TBT Agreement's reference to processing and production methods has generated discussion on the application of the TBT Agreement to process-based distinctions: RJ Zedalis 'The Environment and the Technical Barriers to Trade Agreement: Did the *Reformulated Gasoline* Panel Miss a Golden Opportunity?' (1997) 44 NILR 186; H Ward 'Trade and Environmental Issues in Voluntary Eco-Labelling and Life Cycle Analysis' (1997) 6(2) RECIEL 139, 143ff; SW Chang 'GATTing a Green Trade Barrier: Eco-Labelling and the WTO Agreement on Technical Barriers to Trade' (1997) 31(1) JWT 137.

145 *Asbestos* AB Report (n 41) paras 66–70.

146 *Asbestos* Panel Report (n 32) paras 8.58, 8.70–8.71.

Decree but should have considered it as a single measure.[147] Because products need not be expressly identified[148] and because product characteristics can take a positive or negative form,[149] the Appellate Body was able to find that, in effect, the French Decree imposed a mandatory characteristic on an identifiable group of products: *all* products must be asbestos free.[150]

A similar issue arose in the *EC–Sardines* case. In that case, Peru challenged an EC regulation which stipulated that that only fish of the species *sardina pilchardus* could be described as 'sardines'. Peru was successful before the panel, which agreed that the EC rule was not based on a relevant international standard, as required by Article 2.4. The relevant standard was a Codex standard, which provided that, while only *sardina pilchardus* could be described simply as 'sardines', another 20 fish species could be described as sardines provided that that description was accompanied by a reference to (i) the country of origin (eg 'Peruvian sardines'), (ii) the geographic area of origin, (iii) the species or (iv) the common name of the species.

On appeal before the Appellate Body, the EC admitted that its regulation was a technical regulation under the TBT Agreement, but argued that its regulation only applied to *sardina pilchardus*. According to the EC, the preserved fish of the species *sardinops sagax* (found along the Chilean and Peruvian coasts) was not an 'identifiable product' under that regulation.[151] The Appellate Body dismissed this argument on the basis that, by virtue of the EC Regulation, preserved *sardinops sagax* are prohibited from being identified and marketed using the word 'sardines'.[152] The Appellate Body reiterated that the 'identifiable product' requirement was concerned mainly with compliance and enforcement, and noted that the EC regulation had in fact been enforced against preserved *sardinops sagax* in Germany, thus demonstrating its status as an identifiable product under that regulation.[153]

In both the *Asbestos* and *Sardines* cases, the Appellate Body took a broad but pragmatic approach to the requirement that there be an identifiable product. If a regulation clearly *affects* a product, for example by blocking its access to the market or prescribing the way in which it must be described or labelled, that product will be treated as an identifiable product and the first test will be satisfied. Clever arguments that the regulation only applies to that which it directly regulates and not to that which it, by

147 *Asbestos* AB Report (n 41) para 64.
148 *Asbestos* AB Report (n 41) para 70.
149 *Asbestos* AB Report (n 41) para 69.
150 *Asbestos* AB Report (n 41) para 72.
151 *EC–Sardines* AB Report (n 78) para 27.
152 *EC–Sardines* AB Report (n 78) paras 182–84.
153 *EC–Sardines* AB Report (n 78) para 185.

necessary implication excludes from the market, will get short shrift from the Appellate Body. The status of general bans is, however, still somewhat unsettled. Because there is no real use for asbestos fibres that are not incorporated into a product, the Appellate Body was able to conclude that there was something more than a simple prohibition on asbestos fibres—there was a ban on *products containing* asbestos fibres. In fact, the Appellate Body in the *Asbestos* case acknowledged that 'if this measure consisted *only* of a prohibition on asbestos *fibres*, it might not constitute a "technical regulation".'[154] It is difficult to predict how panels and the Appellate Body will treat general bans in the future. While the *Asbestos* decision suggests that they may be excluded from the TBT Agreement, a panel, following on the reasoning of the *Sardines* case,[155] may well decide that a general ban includes an implicit ban on an identifiable group of products, namely *all* products.

(ii) Product characteristics The second requirement for application of the TBT Agreement is that the regulation must impose at least one product characteristic. In the *Sardines* case, the EC argued that its regulation did not set out product characteristics, but merely constituted a naming rule.[156] Not surprisingly, the Appellate Body was not impressed by this argument and dismissed it, reasoning that being prepared exclusively from *sardinas pilchardus* was a product characteristic of sardines laid down by the EC regulation.[157] Moreover, the Appellate Body reiterated that product characteristics include the means of identification, a concept that clearly includes the naming of a product.[158] Accordingly, the EC regulation was found to be a technical regulation because (i) preserved *sardinops sagax* was an identifiable product under the regulation, (ii) the regulation imposed a product characteristic (sardines must be made exclusively from *sardinas pilchardus*) and (iii) compliance with the regulation was mandatory.

2 TBT Agreement Disciplines

Following the *Asbestos* and *Sardines* cases, it seems that panels will, with the Appellate Body's blessing, take a wide view of the scope of the TBT Agreement. This will help to ensure that the residual category of health regulations, subject only to GATT, will be minimised. Like the SPS Agreement, the TBT Agreement recognises that Members vary in their levels of conservatism when it comes to health, environmental and consumer

[154] *Asbestos* AB Report (n 41) para 71 (emphasis in original).
[155] Essentially that reserving the name 'sardines' for *sardina pilchardus* imposes requirements applicable to other fish, such as *sardinops sagax*.
[156] *EC–Sardines* AB Report (n 78) para 28.
[157] *EC–Sardines* AB Report (n 78) para 190.
[158] *EC–Sardines* AB Report (n 78) para 191.

protection standards.[159] In other words, the TBT Agreement does not purport to legislate a maximum level of protection that WTO Members may adopt. While it is true that the substantive disciplines of the TBT Agreement are much more limited than those of the SPS Agreement and that the TBT Agreement focuses on procedural guarantees, the TBT Agreement does still provide exporting Members with additional guarantees not provided for in GATT. In particular, the TBT Agreement applies a least trade-restrictive (LTR) measure discipline to *all* technical regulations (not just those that have failed MFN or national treatment tests) and includes harmonisation provisions. These substantive disciplines, together with the TBT Agreement's detailed procedural requirements relating to the preparation, adoption and application of technical regulations and conformity assessment procedures means that defending Members are still likely to argue that their measures are not technical regulations covered by the TBT Agreement. The *Asbestos* and *Sardines* cases suggest, however, that in any borderline cases, panels will incline to find that the measure is a technical regulation and so within the scope of the TBT Agreement.

The remainder of this section takes up some of the more significant disciplines in the TBT Agreement, leaving out the multitude of procedural protections and transparency provisions which minimise the trade costs of technical regulations and standards and conformity assessment procedures by seeking to ensure that they are developed and applied with appropriate consultation and provision of information. The disciplines taken up below are those that have the potential to impose more *substantive* limits on the specific standards and regulations that a Member can adopt, rather than those procedural requirements that govern how they must be adopted and applied.

(a) Unnecessary obstacles to trade

One of the most valuable ways in which the TBT Agreement seeks to minimise the negative trade effects of technical regulations and standards is by ensuring that they do not create unnecessary obstacles to international trade.[160] The Preamble applies this aim to both technical regulations and standards, but only technical regulations are subject to a specific least trade-restrictive obligation in Article 2.2:

> Members shall ensure that technical regulations are not prepared, adopted or applied with a view to or with the effect of creating unnecessary obstacles to

[159] The Preamble provides that 'no country should be prevented from taking measures necessary to ensure the quality of its exports, or for the protection of human, animal or plant life or health, of the environment, or for the prevention of deceptive practices, at the levels it considers appropriate' subject to various requirements.

[160] TBT Agreement Preamble.

international trade. For this purpose, technical regulations shall not be more trade-restrictive than necessary to fulfil a legitimate objective, taking account of the risks non-fulfilment would create.

Importantly, the list of 'legitimate objectives' in Article 2.2 (which includes health) is not exhaustive, raising the possibility that additional social priorities may, in time, be included. While this means that technical regulations can be put in place to serve a wide range of policy goals, it does also mean that a complaining Member may challenge the legitimate objective advanced by the defending Member.[161] Article 2.2 also specifies that, in assessing such risks (presumably the previously mentioned risks of non-fulfilment), consideration must be given to, *inter alia*, 'available scientific and technical information, related processing technology or intended end-uses of products.' Thus, it can be seen that, within the procedural focus on the preparation, adoption or application of technical regulations by a central government body, there is a specific substantive LTR obligation which itself specifies certain relevant considerations (available scientific and technical information etc).

It is not clear whether, in reviewing compliance with the LTR obligation, panels and the Appellate Body would be tempted to read-in the qualifications to that obligation in the SPS Agreement (which bring in consideration of whether the alternative measures are reasonably available taking into account technical and economic feasibility and require that the alternatives be 'significantly less restrictive to trade').[162] Without these qualifications, the LTR discipline in the TBT Agreement has the potential to be far more intrusive than its SPS Agreement cousin, which is presumably not what was intended. Another point that remains obscure is the extent to which the LTR discipline is confined to the regulatory process—the preparation, adoption and application of the technical regulation—rather than the substantive measure itself. Some commentators argue that the TBT Agreement is generally about the regulatory process and so choose to minimise its substantive aspects. For example, Howse and Tuerk suggest that the LTR discipline is directed more to evaluating the regulatory *process* behind measures than the measures themselves.[163] While it is true that the TBT Agreement undoubtedly chooses to focus on procedural guarantees, it does include certain substantive disciplines and it is hard to see how a panel could possibly assess whether the technical regulation is 'more trade-restrictive than necessary' without addressing the substantive terms of the regulation.

161 A Desmedt 'Proportionality in WTO Law' (2001) 4 JIEL 441, 458.

162 SPS Agreement, fn to Art 5.6. On this, see Desmedt (n 161) 459.

163 R Howse and E Tuerk 'The WTO Impact on Internal Regulations—A Case Study of the Canada–EC Asbestos Dispute' in G de Búrca and J Scott (eds) *The EU and the WTO: Legal and Constitutional Issues* (Hart Publishing Oxford 2001) 283, 313–14.

The TBT Agreement also seeks to ensure that conformity assessment procedures do not implement unnecessary barriers to trade. Article 5.1.2 provides that such procedures 'shall not be more strict or be applied more strictly than is necessary to give the importing Member adequate confidence that products conform with the applicable technical regulations or standards, taking account of the risks non-conformity would create.' The potential of this provision to authorise intrusive review hinges on whether panels will regard an importing Member's lack of confidence that products conform as reviewable. Given the inherent subjectivity of notions such as confidence, it is unlikely that this provision will be interpreted as authorising review going much beyond non-discrimination.

(b) Non-discrimination and national treatment

Pursuant to Article 2.1, Members must ensure that imported products are accorded treatment 'no less favourable than that accorded to like products of national origin and to like products originating in any other country.' Conformity assessment procedures must also be prepared, adopted and applied so as to grant access to conformity assessment procedures on a non-discriminatory basis (both in MFN and national treatment terms).[164] In applying Article 2.1, panels may well turn to the extensive case law on likeness developed under GATT Article III.[165]

(c) Harmonisation

The TBT Agreement encourages the use of international standards for both technical regulations and standards. Article 2.4 obliges Members to use relevant international standards (or parts thereof) 'as a basis' for technical regulations except when those standards would be an 'ineffective or inappropriate means for the fulfilment of the legitimate objectives pursued, for instance because of fundamental climatic or geographical factors or fundamental technological problems.' Where a technical regulation is 'in accordance with relevant international standards', it is rebuttably presumed not to create an unnecessary obstacle to international trade.[166] Article 2.4 of the TBT Agreement can be usefully contrasted with the harmonisation provisions of the SPS Agreement.[167] It will be recalled that Article 3.1 of the SPS Agreement obliges Members to 'base' their SPS

[164] TBT Agreement Art 5.1.1.
[165] This case law was discussed in Chapter 2.
[166] TBT Agreement Art 2.5.
[167] Note that there is an additional (and similarly drafted) harmonisation provision in Art 5.4, which relates to the use of 'relevant guides or recommendations' issued by international standardising bodies in conformity assessment procedures. Arts 2.6 and 5.5 also encourage harmonisation by requiring Members to participate as fully as possible in the work of international standardising bodies.

measures on international standards and that the Appellate Body held in the *Hormones* case that to be 'based' on an international standard, only some elements of the standard need to be incorporated in the measure.[168] In the case of the SPS Agreement, this interpretation was adopted in order to distinguish measures 'based' on international standards from those that 'conform to' such standards. Although the TBT Agreement does not draw the same distinction between measures that are 'based' on international standards and those that 'conform to' international standards, it might nevertheless be supposed that the Appellate Body would prefer to adopt an interpretation of 'as a basis' in Article 2.4 of the TBT Agreement that would make the harmonisation obligations of the two Agreements consistent. It seems, though, that the Appellate Body in the *Sardines* case imposed a slightly more demanding standard than would have been expected following its permissive interpretation of what is required for an SPS measure to be 'based on' an international standard.

In the *Sardines* case, the EC appealed the panel's finding that the Codex standard was not used 'as a basis' for the EC regulation. In its appeal, the EC argued, *inter alia*, that the test should not be whether the international standard was the principal constituent or fundamental principle of the regulation, but rather, whether there is a 'rational relationship' between the standard and the technical regulation.[169] It is true that the Appellate Body did find that the words 'based on' refer to the existence of a rational relationship, but it will be recalled that the Appellate Body adopted that interpretation in relation to the requirement that an SPS measure be 'based on' a risk assessment and not in relation to the harmonisation provisions of the SPS Agreement. Accordingly, while the EC's argument highlighted an inconsistency in the Appellate Body's approach to the meaning of 'based on' in the SPS Agreement,[170] it was on shaky ground when promoting the adoption of the rational relationship interpretation in the TBT Agreement's harmonisation provisions. The Appellate Body agreed that its analysis of the meaning of the words 'based on' in the harmonisation provisions of the SPS Agreement was relevant to the meaning of the words 'as a basis' in the TBT Agreement. The Appellate Body then highlighted its reference in the *Hormones* case to the dictionary definition of the expression 'based on', which emphasises whether one thing stands, is founded, is built, or is supported by another.[171] Accordingly, the Appellate Body upheld the panel's conclusion that, for an international standard to serve

[168] *Hormones* AB Report (n 3) para 163.

[169] *EC–Sardines* AB Report (n 78) paras 42, 243.

[170] 'Based on' does not mean the same thing for Article 3.1 (harmonisation) as it does for Article 5.1 (risk assessment).

[171] *EC–Sardines* AB Report (n 78) paras 242–43 (referring to *Hormones* AB Report (n 3) para 163).

'as a basis' for a technical regulation, it must be used as the principal constituent or fundamental principle of the regulation.[172]

Following the *Sardines* case, one must expect a greater focus on replicating the basic content of the international standard than might have been expected following the *Hormones* case. In the *Sardines* case, the Appellate Body stressed that Members will not be able to fulfil their harmonisation obligations by cherry-picking the agreeable aspects of the applicable international standard.[173] Rather, they must implement all relevant parts of the international standard. This suggests that defending Members should perhaps not expect a great deal of latitude when implementing international standards, both under the SPS and TBT Agreements.

Like the harmonisation provisions of the SPS Agreement, the TBT Agreement includes provisions allowing Members to depart from international standards. In particular, the second half of Article 2.4 provides that Members need not use international standards as a basis for their technical regulations when such standards 'would be an ineffective or inappropriate means for the fulfilment of the legitimate objectives pursued, for instance because of fundamental climatic or geographical factors or fundamental technological problems.' In the *Sardines* case, the panel had imposed the burden of proof for showing that the international standard was ineffective or inappropriate on the EC.[174] The Appellate Body rejected this allocation, finding instead that, as was the case for Article 3.3 of the SPS Agreement, Article 2.4 of the TBT Agreement is not an exception as such, meaning that it is for the complaining Member to raise a *prima facie* case that the international standard was effective and appropriate to fulfil the defending Member's legitimate objectives.[175] While the Appellate Body was confident that complaining Members will have adequate opportunity to find out what the defending Member's legitimates objectives are,[176] it remains to be seen whether they will really be in a position to mount an informed argument proving the efficacy of international standards in the defending Member's territory. What is likely to happen (and what appears to have happened in the *Sardines* case) is that the panel will not be especially demanding in the proof it will require before finding that a complaining Member has raised a *prima facie* case of adequacy and efficacy.

[172] *EC–Sardines* AB Report (n 78) paras 243–44.

[173] *EC–Sardines* AB Report (n 78) para 250.

[174] *EC–Trade Description of Sardines* WT/DS231/R modified Panel Report adopted 23 October 2002 ('*EC–Sardines*') paras 7.50–7.51.

[175] *EC–Sardines* AB Report (n 78) para 275.

[176] *EC–Sardines* AB Report (n 78) paras 277–80 (this information could be collected through the dispute settlement process and under the terms of the TBT Agreement).

(d) Recognition of equivalence and mutual recognition of conformity assessment procedures

Article 2.7 requires Members to 'give positive consideration' to accepting another Member's technical regulations as equivalent to its own if satisfied that they fulfil the objectives behind that Member's own technical regulations. There is no equivalent provision applying to standards, although Article 6.1 does encourage mutual recognition of conformity assessment procedures in respect of both technical regulations and standards. Article 6.2 provides that Members 'shall ensure' that their conformity assessment procedures permit 'as far as practicable' the implementation of the Article 6.1 mutual recognition of conformity assessment procedures.

With its focus on the satisfaction of the importing Member that the technical regulations or conformity assessment procedures are equivalent and reliable, the drafting of the Articles concerned with mutual recognition does not suggest very much scope for panel review of a Member's refusal to accept another Member's regulations or procedures as equivalent.[177]

C CONCLUSION

The TBT Agreement will apply to some health measures not covered by the SPS Agreement. Its substantive disciplines are, however, much more limited than those imposed by the SPS Agreement. In fact, the TBT Agreement's substantive obligations do not extend far beyond those already embodied in the GATT national treatment and MFN obligations (Articles III:4 and I:1), although it should be remembered that, under the TBT Agreement, even non-discriminatory regulations must meet the least trade-restrictive discipline. The principal contribution of the TBT Agreement lies in its promotion of transparency and information exchange.[178]

The TBT Agreement is not an easy agreement to apply. The obligations depend, variously, on whether the measure is a technical regulation, or simply a non-mandatory standard, and also on whether the regulation or standard is being adopted and administered by a central government body, some other level of government or a non-governmental body. Of the substantive disciplines to be found in the TBT Agreement, the least

177 On mutual recognition in the TBT Agreement, see JH Mathis 'Mutual Recognition Agreements: Transatlantic Parties and the Limits to Non-tariff Barrier Regionalism in the WTO' (1998) 32(6) JWT 5.

178 C Thorn and M Carlson 'The Agreement on the Application of Sanitary and Phytosanitary Measures and the Agreement on Technical Barriers to Trade' (2000) 31 Law&Pol'yIntlBus 841, 842.

trade-restrictive alternative is the most significant, although a number of question marks hang over its meaning given the proliferation of different versions of the LTR test in GATT, the SPS Agreement and the TBT Agreement. The harmonisation provisions have, however, emerged from the *Sardines* case showing rather more bite than might have been anticipated.

It is plain that the SPS Agreement is also not an easy Agreement to apply. It imposes a number of disciplines, but the relationships between them and the meaning of the terms they employ is not always clear. Perhaps the difficulties presented by the text of the SPS Agreement reflect the difficulty of the task it sets itself: to identify protectionist and ill-founded SPS measures through the scientific justification, consistency and least trade-restrictive requirements. This task is particularly difficult because Members are, in principle, perfectly entitled to protect their populations by health regulations; there is no supranational regulatory authority. Moreover, this aspect of regulatory sovereignty is jealously guarded and politically sensitive. The world of national regulatory decision-making is not a perfect one. Budgetary constraints, political pressures and the institutional framework for studying regulatory questions all mean that national regulations may not always reflect world best practice. SPS measures should not be struck down for imperfections that simply reflect limitations endemic to the reality of regulatory decision-making.

The lack of clarity of the SPS Agreement has presented panels and the Appellate Body with a wealth of interpretative opportunities, and no doubt there are more to come. Some interpretations suggest a close review of national regulatory decision-making while others give greater scope to Members to accommodate local priorities and structure regulatory decision-making in different ways. Current areas of concern include: the prescriptiveness of the risk assessment requirements; the use of advisory experts to answer the question before the panel (rather than merely advise and help the panel to understand the evidence presented by the parties); the readiness of some panels to leap to protectionist conclusions when national regulatory procedures are somewhat incoherent; the use of international standards when serious concerns have been raised about the internal procedures of such organisations; and over-confident panel assessments of the viability of regulatory alternatives under the least trade-restrictive measure test. There are also a great many areas of uncertainty. The scope of Article 5.7's provisional measures in particular will be important in achieving the appropriate level of WTO review of national regulations.

While some interpretations may ring alarm bells for regulatory sovereignty, two points should be borne in mind. Firstly, and most importantly, the SPS Agreement does not authorise the WTO to second-guess regulatory priorities. Members are free to impose measures whose cost to the international trading system may be quite disproportionate to their benefits. The WTO can only require that those measures be scientifically justified and comply with the other SPS disciplines. The second point is that it should be remembered that the obligations imposed by the SPS Agreement are interconnected—a strict approach in one area may allow for a more generous approach in another. For example, the WTO's approach to risk assessment was criticised as being overly prescriptive when it comes to the specificity required of risk assessment studies. While not disavowing this criticism, it should be acknowledged that imposing strict requirements on what a risk assessment must study does allow more latitude to be given to Members by only requiring a rational relationship between the scientific evidence and the measures, and allowing reliance on divergent scientific opinion. The process is one of give and take and no doubt further fine-tuning will take place in the years to come.

4

Risk Regulation, Culture and Uncertainty

A THE IMPORTANCE OF UNDERSTANDING REGULATORY PRACTICE

REGULATIONS TO PROTECT health are made all around the world. In some countries, enormous resources are devoted to regulation-making, whereas in others, resources are more limited. For international review of national health regulations to be successful, it must be built on an awareness of real and achievable regulatory practices. If the system of review posits a model of regulation-making that is divorced from reality, it risks being either over-inclusive (by condemning practices which form part of generally accepted regulatory practice) or under-inclusive (by failing to identify lapses which should result in a regulation being identified as illegitimate). That is not to say that international benchmarks should merely *reflect* existing regulatory practice and should never demand improvements. For example, in agreeing provisions requiring that the Members base their SPS measures on risk assessments, and ensure that SPS regulations are easily available to interested parties, negotiators of the SPS Agreement[1] may well have wished to raise the overall standard of regulatory practice among WTO Members. There is nothing inherently wrong with agreeing disciplines based on such aspirational objectives, but it is important that, in applying those disciplines, panels and the Appellate Body bear in mind the importance of not putting in place an unrealistic and unachievable model of regulatory practice. In other words, a reasonable degree of resonance is required between the WTO's model of the regulatory practice demanded by the SPS Agreement and achievable regulatory good practice.

This chapter begins by exploring the nature of risk regulation. Where the previous two chapters provided an in-depth analysis of the disciplines of GATT and the SPS and TBT Agreements (which focused on the extent to which the interpretations adopted by the Appellate Body have constrained WTO Members), this chapter expands on that analysis by

[1] Agreement on the Application of Sanitary and Phytosanitary Measures (SPS Agreement) (Marrakesh, 15 April 1994).

examining how the model of regulation-making constructed by the WTO measures up to regulatory practice. In particular, this chapter examines expectations concerning the nature of science and its role in the development of health regulations. Regulations have a strong normative element; embedded within their prescriptions is a picture of how, as a society, we wish to live.[2] Two major aspects of how a society defines itself and responds to risk are addressed in this chapter: how uncertainty is approached; and what factors are considered relevant in regulation-making. The attitude that is adopted towards uncertainty is important because it determines whether a particular society will privilege innovation by being reluctant to regulate without compelling evidence of harm, or whether it will be more circumspect, preferring the status quo. How one conceives of the factors that are relevant to regulation-making is also important. For example, is consumer apprehension about perceived hazards relevant to regulatory decision-making, or should regulators seek to act on a narrowly 'rational' basis? These are serious questions because the apprehension that WTO rules do not permit Members sufficient leeway to respond to uncertainty and local preferences destabilises support for WTO review of national health regulations.[3]

B RISK REGULATION

Although comparatively young, the study of regulation is an established and extensive field of academic study in its own right.[4] What follows is not an attempt to present an exhaustive review of this field, but to provide a snapshot of the regulation of health hazards which will highlight particular points of interest for this study of the WTO. When the SPS Agreement was negotiated, the WTO Members stipulated that SPS measures must have a scientific justification and be based on a risk assessment. In so doing, the WTO Members nailed their colours to a particular mast. Rather than rely only on discrimination to identify illegitimate health regulations, they chose

[2] E Fisher 'Drowning by Numbers: Standard Setting in Risk Regulation and the Pursuit of Accountable Public Administration' (2000) 20 OJLS 109, 114 (referring to NRC *Understanding Risk: Informing Decisions in a Democratic Society* (National Academy Press Washington DC 1996)).

[3] Trebilcock and Soloway provide an overview of these concerns: M Trebilcock and J Soloway 'International Trade Policy and Domestic Food Safety Regulation: The Case for Substantial Deference by the WTO Dispute Settlement Body under the SPS Agreement' in DLM Kennedy and JD Southwick (eds) *The Political Economy of International Trade Law* (CUP Cambridge UK 2002) 537, 537–43.

[4] General studies include: R Baldwin and M Cave *Understanding Regulation: Theory, Strategy and Practice* (OUP Oxford 1999); R Baldwin et al *A Reader on Regulation* (OUP Oxford 1998); A Ogus *Regulation: Legal Form and Economic Theory* (OUP Oxford 1994); C Sunstein *After the Rights Revolution: Reconceiving the Regulatory State* (Harvard UP Cambridge MA 1990). On regulation of health risks particularly see: VR Walker 'Keeping the WTO from Becoming the "World Trance-Science Organization": Scientific Uncertainty, Science Policy, and Factfinding in the Growth Hormones Dispute' (1998) 31 Cornell ILJ 251.

to place their faith in a formal method of regulation-making that emphasises the value-neutrality and positivism of science as a basis for regulation.[5] While science may not have proved as uncontroversial a means for distinguishing legitimate and illegitimate health measures as those negotiating the SPS Agreement may have hoped, and while some would argue that the focus on science subjugates all other interests,[6] regulation based on scientific risk assessment *is* what the Members agreed to. In evaluating the WTO's approach to its chosen touchstone—scientific risk assessment—it is important to bear in mind that formalised risk assessment is a relatively new phenomenon. Formal risk assessment, and particularly the emphasis on quantitative risk assessment, dates from the late 1960s.[7] That is not to say that risk assessment emerged fully formed and ready to be employed as an international benchmark at that time. Rather, methods of risk assessment developed significantly during the 1970s and 1980s. In fact, when the International Office of Epizootics (OIE) learned that its standards would occupy a privileged position in the SPS regime—OIE standards attract the harmonisation obligations of Article 3—it had to develop a working model of risk assessment quickly, even though it had long been committed to sound science.[8] As the Codex Alimentarius Commission (CAC) has stressed, methods of risk assessment continue to evolve.[9] Nevertheless, the basic terrain which concerns us here is reasonably settled.

1 Risk Assessment, Risk Management and Risk Communication

In risk regulation, 'risk analysis' is an umbrella term comprising three aspects: risk assessment, risk management and risk communication.[10]

[5] As such, the WTO may be accused of adopting a mechanistic or positivistic review of science: G Little 'BSE and the Regulation of Risks' (2001) 64 MLR 730, 733; K Barrett and C Raffensperger 'Precautionary Science' in C Raffensperger and JA Tickner (eds) *Protecting Public Health and the Environment: Implementing the Precautionary Principle* (Island Press Washington DC 1999) 105, 108–13.

[6] J Scott 'On Kith, Kine (and Crustaceans): Trade and Environment in the EU and WTO' in JHH Weiler (ed) *The EU, the WTO, and the NAFTA: Towards a Common Law of International Trade?* (OUP Oxford 2000) 125, 157 (the SPS Agreement is a technocratic zone in which the values entering law through science are obscured and culture and context are silenced); M Echols *Food Safety and the WTO: The Interplay of Culture, Science and Technology* (Kluwer Law International The Hague 2001) ch 1, 5.

[7] NRC *Science and Judgment in Risk Assessment* (National Academy Press Washington DC 1994) 2; JA Kellar 'The Application of Risk Analysis to International Trade in Animals and Animal Products' (1993) 12 SciTechRev (OIE) 1023, 1025.

[8] Kellar (n 7) 1024.

[9] CAC *Report* (24th Session 2001 ALINORM 01/41) (Appendix II) 83.

[10] CAC *Procedural Manual* (13th edn FAO/WHO Rome 2003) 42. Note, though, that the NRC has attempted to move towards a more fluid model of the way in which risks are regulated by employing a model which eschews formal distinctions between aspects of risk analysis and focuses on multiple inputs to the decision-making process, communication and participation: NRC *Understanding Risk* (n 2) ch 1 (see the diagram at 28).

Risk assessment has been described as a 'systematic approach to organizing and analyzing scientific knowledge and information for potentially hazardous activities or for substances that might pose risks under specified conditions.'[11] Risk assessment is typically divided into the four stages established by the National Research Council (NRC) in its 1983 *Red Book*: hazard identification, dose-response assessment, exposure assessment and risk characterisation.[12] In its own work, Codex draws the boundaries slightly differently—dividing risk assessment into hazard identification, hazard characterisation (including dose-response assessment), exposure assessment and risk characterisation[13]—although it seems that the distinction between hazard characterisation and the NRC's dose-response stage is not significant for present purposes. Hazard identification is the first stage of risk assessment, and, as its name suggests, entails the identification of known or potential health hazards. In the hazard identification stage, the regulatory authorities determine which potential hazards to investigate and determine whether exposure to an agent can cause an adverse health effect. Thus, hazard identification has both agenda-setting and scientific aspects. Dose-response assessment refers to the study of how differing dosages affect health (for example, does double the dose result in double the risk of suffering an adverse outcome?), and exposure assessment refers to the examination of the levels at which, for example, people are exposed to the substance in question in various walks of life. Risk characterisation refers to the stage in which the primary conclusions about hazard, dose-response and exposure are integrated into an assessment of risk which is presented in a form which is useful to decision-makers and risk managers.[14]

Risk assessment is the first component of risk analysis, and tends to be seen as a technical or scientific phase in which experts analyse information and, if necessary, conduct further studies to provide the underlying factual information required by decision-makers. Risk management, the second component of risk analysis, is seen as the overtly political or value-laden stage in which risk managers consider scientific, political, economic and engineering information in order to decide what the acceptable level of risk

[11] NRC *Science and Judgment* (n 7) 4. For a similar emphasis on risk assessment as a method for organising and analysing information, see also: Joint FAO/WHO Expert Consultation *Application of Risk Analysis to Food Standards Issues* (WHO/FNU/FOS/95.3 Geneva 1995) 6.

[12] NRC *Risk Assessment in the Federal Government: Managing the Process* (National Academy Press Washington DC 1983) (the *Red Book*) 19–20; Walker (n 4) 256–57; NRC *Science and Judgment* (n 7) 25–27.

[13] CAC *Procedural Manual* (n 10) 44. See also: FAO/WHO *Application of Risk Analysis to Food Standards Issues* (n 11) 24.

[14] In its 1996 Report, the NRC stressed that risk characterisation should not merely summarise the conclusions of scientific risk assessment, but should integrate and synthesise all relevant information: NRC *Understanding Risk* (n 2).

is and how it should be achieved.[15] Although, as will be seen below, a strict division between the scientific and political elements of regulation-making is not altogether unproblematic, the guiding aspiration is to provide decision-makers with scientifically determined *facts* on which to base regulatory choices; this goal underpins the legitimacy claims of science-based risk regulation. The third component, risk communication, refers to the interactive process in which information and opinions are exchanged among risk assessors, risk managers and other interested parties throughout the process.[16]

(a) Science policy in risk assessment

Risk assessment is a heavily scientific activity which is supposed to provide the objectively determined and value-neutral factual basis on which risk managers act. Risk assessment's claim to objectivity and neutrality is, however, complicated by the extensive use of science policies and assumptions. Scientific enquiries are challenged by uncertainties of various kinds and of varying degrees of severity. In some circumstances, the uncertainties will be such that good scientific methods will not permit the presentation of any factual conclusions because a properly scientific study cannot be conducted. Scientists do, however, use a range of assumptions and techniques to overcome other uncertainties, such as those related to gauging the significance of results observed in animals for human health. These assumptions and techniques are known as 'science policies' and form part of mainstream scientific method. A typical menu of policies employed in a risk assessment might include: the use of animal data drawn from the most sensitive species to predict human responses; the use of body weight scaling for interspecies comparisons; the assumption that absorption in animals and humans is approximately the same; the use of a linear dose-response model; and the use of a 100-fold safety factor to account for interspecies and intraspecies differences in susceptibility.[17]

[15] NRC *Science and Judgment* (n 7) 5; FAO/WHO *Application of Risk Analysis to Food Standards Issues* (n 11) 6.

[16] CAC *Procedural Manual* (n 10) 47–48.

[17] For an account of the risk assessment policies used by JECFA and JMPR (the bodies which conduct many of the risk assessments behind Codex standards) see: Joint FAO/WHO Consultation *Risk Management and Food Safety* (FAO Food and Nutrition Paper 65 Rome 1997) 8–9.

On the use of safety factors, see: S Breyer *Breaking the Vicious Circle: Toward Effective Risk Regulation* (Harvard UP Cambridge MA 1993) 43; FAO/WHO *Application of Risk Analysis to Food Standards Issues* (n 11) 8, 17; FB Cross 'Paradoxical Perils of the Precautionary Principle' (1996) 53 WashLeeLRev 851, 857.

On the use of animal data for humans, see: Breyer (above in this note) 45–46; FAO/WHO *Application of Risk Analysis to Food Standards Issues* (n 11) 12, 15–16; Walker (n 4) 263–65; Cross (above in this note) 857; JD Fraiberg and MJ Trebilcock 'Risk Regulation: Technocratic and Democratic Tools for Regulatory Reform' (1998) 43 McGill LJ 835, 853.

On the dose-response models, see: Breyer (above in this note) 44; FAO/WHO *Application of Risk Analysis to Food Standards Issues* (n 11) 15.

Because there are inevitable gaps in the science of risk assessment, default assumptions and policies must be used in order to be able to conduct a risk assessment in the first place.[18] While different regulatory agencies employ different assumptions and policies—meaning that risk assessments of the same hazard can generate results varying by several orders of magnitude[19]—such assumptions and policies tend to be chosen in order to arrive at the most conservative risk estimations. For example, a review of the evidence of the scientific experts advising the panel which decided the *Hormones* case shows repeated reference to the way in which ADI (acceptable daily intake) figures were established using very sensitive end points from non-human primates, with the vulnerability of sensitive members of the population taken into account when establishing safety factors.[20] Although these policies and assumptions are scientifically informed, they are, ultimately, policy-driven,[21] and some, such as the use of a safety factor of 100, have been described as little more than arbitrary.[22] Extrapolations from animal studies to humans, and from high to low doses, rely on assumptions and models which tend to be conservative. Conservative assumptions also feature prominently in exposure assessment, where risk assessors sometimes postulate far-fetched exposure scenarios in order to arrive at a risk estimate that would not underestimate the risk even for the most exposed person in the population.[23]

Does the use of such policies and assumptions mean that scientific risk assessment does not provide a useful basis for regulatory action? Some would undoubtedly argue that it does.[24] Ulrich Beck, for example, condemns science as based on a house of cards of speculative assumptions, and dismisses its claim to value-neutrality as a chimera.[25] While some,

[18] Joint FAO/WHO Consultation *Risk Management and Food Safety* (n 17) 9.

[19] A Stirling *On Science and Precaution in the Management of Technological Risk* (Institute for Prospective Technological Studies Seville 1999) 2 (also 'The Precautionary Principle in Science and Technology' in T O'Riordan, J Cameron and A Jordan (eds) *Reinterpreting the Precautionary Principle* (Cameron May London 2002) 61); P Slovic 'Beyond Numbers: A Broader Perspective on Risk Perception and Risk Communication' in DG Mayo and RD Hollander (eds) *Acceptable Evidence: Science and Risk Values in Risk Management* (OUP Oxford 1991) 48, 49.

[20] *EC Measures Concerning Meat and Meat Products (Hormones)* WT/DS26/R/USA modified US Panel Report adopted 13 February 1998 and WT/DS48/R/CAN modified Canada Panel Report adopted 13 February 1998, Annex: Transcript of the Joint Meeting with Experts, para 65 ('*Hormones*'). On conservatism within risk assessment, see also paras 24, 163, 286.

[21] NRC *Red Book* (n 12) 36; Walker (n 4) 260–61.

[22] Fraiberg and Trebilcock (n 17) 845.

[23] On exposure estimates, see: Breyer (n 17) 46; Walker (n 4) 266; Cross (n17) 858.

[24] See, eg: M Angell *Science on Trial: The Clash of Medical Evidence and the Law in the Breast Implant Case* (WW Norton & Co New York 1996) 178–80 (describing the rejection of science by humanists, and by some feminist and multicultural scholarship); Stirling 'The Precautionary Principle' (n 19) 61; J Atik 'Science and International Regulatory Convergence' (1996–97) 17 Northwestern JILBus' 736, 737–38, 748 (expecting scientific consensus to be split along national lines).

[25] U Beck *Risk Society: Towards a New Modernity* (M Ritter (trans) Sage Publications London 1992) 29, 174.

such as Beck, reject science as a basis for regulatory action, the role of value judgments in science should not be overemphasised.[26] Ultimately, the question must be whether the use of policy in scientific risk assessment robs science of its promise as an organising principle in risk regulation. When used consistently and explicitly, science policies and default assumptions at least ensure consistency in approach.[27] Moreover, the use of such policies and assumptions is accepted as a part of mainstream science. The real dialogue now concerns methods by which the extent of the conservatism that is built into risk estimates can be made clear to risk managers and the development of principles upon which science policies should be chosen.[28] Unless the assumptions and policies that have been employed to overcome data gaps and uncertainties in risk assessment are made explicit, risk managers may apply their own 'safety factors' and ultimately add an additional layer of conservatism which, because of the conservatism built-in to risk assessment, is not necessary. Policies and assumptions are not 'extra-scientific'. Rather, they constitute an indispensable part of the practice of scientific risk assessment.

(b) The boundary between risk assessment and risk management

The integration of policies and assumptions into mainstream scientific risk assessment highlights the fact that the division between risk assessment and risk management is permeable. The elaboration of these policies and assumptions is, in itself, a risk management responsibility.[29] In an effort to preserve, to the greatest extent possible, the scientific purity of risk assessment and to reserve the political decisions to risk management, the NRC's *Red Book* recommended a fairly strict separation between risk assessment and risk management.[30] More recently, however, the NRC and others have seen more interaction between the two[31] although it is still customary to pursue a 'functional separation' between risk assessment and risk

[26] Shrader-Frechette criticises both cultural relativists (who overemphasise value judgments), and naïve positivists (who deny value judgments): KS Shrader-Frechette *Risk and Rationality: Philosophical Foundations for Populist Reforms* (U California Press Berkeley 1991) 29–30, 39.

[27] FAO/WHO *Application of Risk Analysis to Food Standards Issues* (n 11) 12; Walker (n 4) 261.

[28] NRC *Science and Judgment* (n 7) 7–8, 11; CAC *Working Principles for Risk Analysis in the Framework of the Codex Alimentarius* (26th Session 2003 ALINORM 03/41) (Appendix IV) paras 23, 41.

[29] CAC *Working Principles for Risk Analysis* (n 28) para 13; FAO/WHO *Risk Management and Food Safety* (n 17) 4.

[30] NRC *Red Book* (n 12) 15, 17–19, ch 3.

[31] NRC *Understanding Risk* (n 2) 33–35. In questioning the wisdom of the separation of risk assessment and risk management, the NRC was not questioning the value of insulating science from political pressure, but was concerned that the rigid separation tended to exclude other sources of information which are necessary for good decision-making from the risk characterization: 24–25, 34.

management.[32] While the role of policy in risk assessment is now openly acknowledged, the functional separation between risk assessment and risk management reflects a continuing desire to minimise the role of policy in the heavily scientific phase of risk assessment and a continuing belief in the value of separating, as far as possible, the scientific and policy/political aspects of risk regulation.[33] While separation was typically advocated as a means to preserve the purity of scientific assessment, it has, more recently, been advocated by those committed to enhancing the democratic legitimacy of regulation-making by ensuring that decisions are ultimately taken by those who are politically accountable. As the European Commission put it in its White Paper on Food Safety, '[l]egislation implies a political decision and involves judgements not only based on science but on a wider appreciation of the wishes and needs of society. There must be a clear separation between risk management and risk assessment.'[34] According to the Commission's reasoning, the European Food Safety Authority should not be entrusted with risk management responsibilities because to do so would dilute democratic accountability and would deprive the Commission of the ability to fulfil its mandate to protect consumers.[35]

The WTO has, itself, been challenged by the distinction between risk assessment and risk management. The SPS Agreement requires that Members base their SPS measures on risk assessments, if they are choosing not to use international standards.[36] Although the definition of risk

[32] CAC *Criteria for the Consideration of the Other Factors Referred to in the Second Statement of Principle* (Decision of the 24th Session of the Commission 2001 ALINORM 01/41); CAC *Statements of Principle Relating to the Role of Food Safety Risk Assessment* (Decision of the 22nd Session of the Commission 1997 ALINORM 97/37); *Working Principles for Risk Analysis* (n 28) para 9; FAO/WHO *Risk Management and Food Safety* (n 18) 7; FAO/WHO *Application of Risk Analysis to Food Standards Issues* (n 11) 30; RE Löfstedt and D Vogel 'The Changing Character of Regulation: A Comparison of Europe and the United States' (2001) 21 Risk Analysis 399, 401–3; Fraiberg and Trebilcock (n 17) 848; Walker (n 4) 261.

[33] Note, for example, Codex's concern to ensure that the scientific integrity of risk assessment is protected by continuing to separate risk assessment and risk management: *Criteria for the Consideration of Other Factors* (n 32). Expert bodies such as JECFA and JMPR are the scientific risk assessors, and the CAC is the risk manager: CCGP *Report* (17th Session 2002 ALINORM 03/33) para 24.

[34] European Commission *White Paper on Food Safety* COM (1999) 719 final para 32. Note, however, that there seems to be some ambivalence about committing to a firm separation—the Commission's Scientific Steering Committee has also suggested that quality of life (including questions relating to risk perception and consumer fear) should form part of the scientific risk assessment: European Commission *The Future of Risk Assessment in the European Union: Second Report on the Harmonisation of Risk Assessment Procedures* (adopted by the Scientific Steering Committee 10–11 April 2003) 73. A rather unconvincing attempt was made in another document to justify this move by linking perception of risks with psychosomatically induced effects on health: European Commission *Final Report on Setting the Scientific Framework for the Inclusion of New Quality of Life Concerns in the Risk Assessment Process* (adopted by the Scientific Steering Committee 10–11 April 2003) 3.

[35] Commission *White Paper* (n 34) para 32. (The EFSA was subsequently established by the EFSA Regulation (n 50).)

[36] SPS Agreement Arts 3.3, 5.1.

assessment in Annex A of the SPS Agreement is one that is consistent with the understanding of risk assessment set out above, in the *Hormones* case, the Appellate Body refused to institute a strict separation between risk assessment and risk management as far as the provisions of the SPS Agreement were concerned.[37] In the *Hormones* case, the panel had strictly distinguished between risk assessment and risk management, on the basis that risk assessment is a scientific examination of data and facts, and not a policy exercise involving social value judgments made by political bodies.[38] For the panel, policy was purely the province of risk management. Observing that the SPS Agreement does not mention the term risk management, the Appellate Body rejected the panel's distinction as not based on the text of the agreement under examination.[39] The Appellate Body went on to discuss its conception of risk assessment, according to which risk assessment in the SPS Agreement may be qualitative as well as quantitative and may consider factors other than those mentioned in Article 5.2.[40]

In refusing to interpret the SPS Agreement's reference to risk assessment in a way that adopts a firm risk assessment—risk management distinction, the Appellate Body's concern seems to have been to avoid formally institutionalising a very narrow model of risk assessment which requires quantitative analysis and excludes considerations not susceptible to laboratory analysis.[41] The Appellate Body's intention does not appear to have been to reject the general scheme of risk regulation outlined above or to suggest that risk assessment may be overtly policy-driven at the expense of scientific risk assessment.[42] Rather, the Appellate Body indicated that risk assessment can and should extend beyond the laboratory, into evaluating 'risk in human societies as they *actually exist*'.[43]

In avoiding the risk assessment—risk management distinction, the Appellate Body may not have been motivated simply by its desire to avoid instituting a narrow version of laboratory-bound risk assessment. It may also have been motivated by a desire not to see risk management put beyond its jurisdiction by virtue of the fact that the term is not mentioned in the SPS Agreement. If the traditional distinction were transposed into

[37] *EC Measures Concerning Meat and Meat Products (Hormones)* WT/DS26/AB/R, WT/DS48/AB/R AB Report adopted 13 February 1998 ('*Hormones*') para 181.

[38] *Hormones* US Panel Report (n 20) paras 8.94–95 and *Hormones* Canada Panel Report (n 20) paras 8.97–98.

[39] *Hormones* AB Report (n 37) 181.

[40] *Hormones* AB Report (n 37) paras 186–87.

[41] *Hormones* AB Report (n 37) paras 186–87.

[42] Concerns have been voiced that the AB's elision of risk assessment and risk management allows more scope for policy decisions to creep into risk assessment processes: D Crawford-Brown, J Pauwelyn and K Smith 'Environmental Risk, Precaution and Scientific Rationality in the Context of WTO/NAFTA Trade Rules' (forthcoming in Risk Analysis, draft on file) 9–10. For further criticism, see: Trebilcock and Soloway (n 3) 561.

[43] *Hormones* AB Report (n 37) para 187 (emphasis added).

the SPS Agreement, it could be argued that, absent reference to risk management, risk management decisions not explicitly mentioned in the Agreement are beyond the WTO's jurisdiction. It is clear that some aspects of what would normally be understood as risk management are definitely covered by the SPS Agreement, notwithstanding the fact that that particular term is not used. For example, Article 5.6 requires that the SPS measure must not be more trade-restrictive than is required to achieve the appropriate level of protection. The choice among available measures to combat a health threat is a core risk management activity, and one which is reviewable by WTO panels. It is similarly clear that other aspects of risk management are not reviewable, principally the appropriate level of protection chosen by any particular Member. By refusing to confine references to risk assessment in the SPS Agreement to the activities which fall within risk assessment in regulatory practice, the Appellate Body has opened up the possibility of reviewing a wider range of risk management decisions. The extent to which the WTO may engage in review of the factors used in risk management is taken up below.

C OTHER LEGITIMATE FACTORS: SOCIAL AND CULTURAL PREFERENCES

Risk assessment is a process which provides decision-makers with *information*, not a regulatory prescription. In other words, risk assessment does not tell risk regulators what, if any, regulation is required. The information generated by a risk assessment is only one body of information considered by risk managers when deciding whether action is required and, if so, what action to take. Besides scientific findings, other factors such as economic feasibility, the desired level of protection, popular demands for regulation and the effect of regulation on investment patterns will influence the regulatory outcome. A number of interesting questions arises from the role of these 'other factors' in regulation-making. Firstly, how is reference to 'other factors' accommodated (if at all) into the SPS Agreement's model of regulation-making?[44] Can WTO panels and the Appellate Body review a Member's use of reliance on such factors? To what extent *should* the WTO recognise such factors as having a legitimate role in regulation-making?

[44] Wagner argues that the SPS limits governments' ability to choose levels of risk protection based on factors like local preference: JM Wagner 'The WTO's Interpretation of the SPS Agreement has Undermined the Right of Governments to Establish Appropriate Levels of Protection Against Risk' (2000) 31 Law&Pol'yIntlBus 855, 856–59.

1 'Other Factors' and the SPS Agreement

In an effort to eliminate protectionist and unnecessary non-tariff barriers, the SPS Agreement imposes strict scientific justification requirements. The SPS Agreement does not specify the extent to which social values and consumer preferences (including public fears) may be taken into account in national regulatory processes, but its structure and scientific focus suggests that a high priority will be placed on rational, scientifically-driven regulation.

There are three provisions of the SPS Agreement that raise the issue of how these 'other factors' are and should be treated in the WTO. Firstly, Article 5.1 requires that a Member's SPS measure be 'based on' a risk assessment. What does 'based on' mean in this situation, and to what extent can other factors intervene before the relationship between the risk assessment and the SPS measure is so attenuated that the measure is no longer 'based on' the risk assessment? Secondly, Article 5.2 specifies that WTO Members must, in their risk assessments, take into account a list of factors. Given that the Appellate Body has found that the list of factors in Article 5.2 is not closed,[45] to what extent can recourse be had to 'other factors' as part of a risk assessment under the SPS Agreement? Finally, the consistency discipline in Article 5.5 (which requires WTO Members to avoid distinctions in the levels of protection they consider appropriate in different situations) invites scrutiny of why a particular Member's population worries about one risk and not another. Can distinctions in the chosen level of protection (or, indeed, the decision to investigate one hazard and not another) be defended on the basis of social and cultural preferences?

(a) The use of 'other factors' and the requirement that measures be 'based on' a risk assessment

The Appellate Body has already made it clear that the requirement, in Article 5.1, that SPS measures be 'based on' risk assessments, is not a procedural requirement. In other words, the Member in question need not show that a risk assessment preceded the adoption of the measure. Instead, the Member can defend the measure by relying on a risk assessment conducted at any time and by any government or international organisation.[46] The issue is whether there is a 'rational relationship' between the risk assessment and the measure, or, as the Appellate Body has also put it, whether the measure is 'sufficiently supported or

[45] *Hormones* AB Report (n 37) para 187.
[46] *Hormones* AB Report (n 37) paras 189–90.

reasonably warranted' by the risk assessment.[47] Accordingly, there must be a substantive, direct and logical relationship between the measure and the risk assessment that is said to support it. In rejecting the procedural view of Article 5.1, the Appellate Body has, in one respect, made it easier for a Member to satisfy the requirements of that Article: it is not necessary that the measure have been procedurally based on a risk assessment (a risk assessment conducted years after the measure was put in place can be relied upon) and the risk assessment can come from any quarter (it need not have been conducted by the national authorities). The rejection of the procedural view does, however, also mean that it will not be enough that a Member conducted a risk assessment before instigating a measure if the conclusions of that risk assessment are clearly contradicted or dismissed by the measure put in place. The question, then, is just how close the measure must be to the risk assessment in order for it to be sufficiently supported or reasonably warranted by that risk assessment. In particular, can the role of 'other factors' be so important in structuring the measure and determining the level of protection chosen that the measure is not really 'based on' the risk assessment?[48]

Health regulations rely, for their logical coherence, on the existence of a causal relationship between a hazard (eg asbestos exposure) and a harm (eg cancer). The strength of the evidence supporting the causal relationship between the hazard and the harm varies from case to case. Some causal relationships are supported by a great deal of evidence; others are not, but attract regulatory action nonetheless. This variance serves to highlight the importance of non-factual considerations in shaping regulatory outcomes.[49] Where the scientific evidence of cause and effect is strong, other factors, such as consumer concerns, may not play an important role in the decision to take protective action. Where, however, the evidence of a causal relationship is weaker, consumer concerns (or other non-scientific factors) will play a more important role in the decision to take preventative action. The EU has gone to some trouble to make clear its attitude to the interaction of scientific and non-scientific factors in risk regulations. According to the EU, science should *inform* risk management decisions,[50] but its role is balanced by an explicit emphasis on consumer confidence, and factors such as social, ethical, traditional and environmental consid-

[47] *Hormones* AB Report (n 37) para 186.

[48] Note that, in this section, 'other factors' are presumed to constitute part of risk management, not risk assessment.

[49] M McGarvin 'Science, Precaution, Facts and Values' in O'Riordan et al (eds) (n 19) 35, 41.

[50] Regulation (EC) No 178/2002 of the European Parliament and of the Council (28 January 2002) laying down the general principles and requirements of food law, establishing the European Food Safety Authority and laying down procedures in matters of food safety ('EFSA Regulation') Preamble para 34, Art 22.5.

erations.[51] With its explicit acknowledgement of the importance of non-scientific factors, the EU's approach highlights the possibility that 'other factors' may play such an important role in directing the risk management decision that the SPS measure is no longer 'based on' the risk assessment in any meaningful sense.[52]

It would seem then, that, under Article 5.1, a Member's recourse to 'other factors' is not directly reviewable. While the panel is not directly empowered to determine whether reference to particular societal concerns or preferences is legitimate, in determining whether the measure is 'sufficiently supported' or 'reasonably warranted' by that risk assessment, reference to other factors may become indirectly reviewable. By determining whether the relationship between the measure and the risk assessment falls short of the mark, it is likely that panels will be influenced by their perception of the legitimacy of the supervening factors to which the national authorities have referred. For example, if a panel regarded reference to public fears as a legitimate approach in risk regulation, it would be more inclined to see the logical relationship between a measure and a risk assessment as preserved even if the measure adopted a more conservative attitude than the risk assessment suggested was warranted. On the other hand, if a panel were not so favourably disposed, it would be more inclined to regard a such a measure as no longer enjoying that logical relationship.

(b) The consideration of 'other factors' within risk assessment

The foregoing discussion has presumed that such 'other factors' belong in risk management and not risk assessment; that assumption is implicit in asking whether such factors can overshadow risk assessment to the extent that the required nexus between the risk assessment and the measure is lost. Two of the Appellate Body's findings do, however, raise another alternative. If the Article 5.2 list of factors to be considered in a risk assessment is not closed,[53] and if the traditional distinction between risk assessment and risk management is not to be read-in to the SPS Agreement,[54] then it might be possible for a WTO Member to argue that such other factors may legitimately be considered as part of a risk

[51] EFSA Regulation (n 50) Preamble paras 19, 23, Art 6.3. On consumer concern, see also: Case C–180/96 *UK v Commission* [1998] 4 ECR I–2265 ('*UK BSE*') and Case C–331/88 *R v The Minister for Agriculture, Fisheries and Food and the Secretary of State for Health, ex p Fedesa* [1990] ECR I–4023, 4047 (AG Mischo).

[52] Note that the EU even foresees that it may not always be possible to base a food law on a risk assessment: EFSA Regulation (n 50) Art 6.1 (cf Codex, which, following some debate, concluded that a measure must always be based on a risk assessment: CCGP *Report* (17th Session 2002 ALINORM 03/33) para 43.

[53] *Hormones* AB Report (n 37) para 187.

[54] *Hormones* AB Report (n 37) para 181.

assessment under Article 5.2.[55] Legitimising the role of other factors in risk regulation by bringing them in under Article 5.2 would, however, be counterproductive. By arguing that other factors form a legitimate part of risk assessment, one directly exposes them to review by WTO panels when it is by no means clear that they would otherwise have been reviewable. As was set out above, some risk management decisions are clearly reviewable and others are not. Subject to the following discussion of consistency, the use of other factors in risk regulation is not one of the clearly reviewable aspects of risk management. There is little to be gained by trying to reinvent such risk management considerations as risk assessment considerations simply to get them in under Article 5.2 because the SPS Agreement does not outlaw their use in the first place and is otherwise silent on the question of review. Reinventing other factors as components of risk assessment is also ill-advised because it would undermine efforts which have been made in Codex to agree upon the appropriate role of other factors' in risk regulation.

In 1995, Codex adopted the *Statements of Principle Concerning the Role of Science in the Codex Decision-Making Process and the Extent to Which Other Factors Are Taken into Account*. Principle 2 states that, when appropriate, Codex will have regard to other legitimate factors relevant for the health protection of consumers and for the promotion of fair practices in the food trade.[56] Six years later, this rather obscure provision was elaborated upon when Codex adopted a statement entitled, *Criteria for the Consideration of the Other Factors Referred to in the Second Statement of Principle*. These *Criteria* state, *inter alia*, that: other legitimate factors may be identified in the risk management process; consideration of other factors should not affect the scientific basis of risk analysis (the separation between risk assessment and risk management should be respected in order to ensure the scientific integrity of risk assessment); and the integration of other legitimate factors into risk management should not create unjustified barriers to trade (with particular attention being given to the impact of the inclusion of such other factors on developing countries).[57] While still not a model of clarity, the *Criteria* document clearly suggests that 'other factors' belong in risk management and should, as far as possible, not be allowed to interfere with the scientific integrity of risk assessment.

[55] This is something that the EC may find appealing given its ambivalence about firmly separating risk assessment and risk management; on the one hand, it sees separation as preserving the right of those who are politically accountable to pay due regard to public fears and perceptions through risk management, but, on the other hand, it has suggested introducing what it calls 'quality of life' factors into scientific risk assessment: compare Commission *White Paper* (n 34) para 32 with Commission *The Future of Risk Assessment* (n 34) 73 and Commission *Setting the Framework* (n 34) 3, 12.

[56] CAC *Statements of Principle Concerning the Role of Science in the Codex Decision-Making Process and the Extent to Which Other Factors Are Taken into Account* (Decision of the 21st Session of the Commission 1995 ALINORM 95/37).

[57] CAC *Criteria for the Consideration of Other Factors* (n 32).

It appears, however, that a level of disagreement persists, notwithstanding the adoption of the *Criteria* by Codex. When, in July 2002, the European Commission responded in the WTO to concerns voiced by other WTO Members regarding the EU's regulation of genetically modified organisms (GMOs), it rebuked Canada and the United States for having failed to support efforts to have the issue of 'other legitimate factors' thrashed out in Codex.[58] While the Codex *Criteria* and the European Commission's comments clearly regard the consideration of other legitimate factors as part of risk management, some of the WTO Members raising concerns about the European GMO rules thought that the consideration of other legitimate factors would take place under the risk assessment stage.[59] Despite this continuing debate over whether other factors fall under risk assessment or risk management, consideration of other factors should be seen as a risk management activity because, otherwise, the functional separation of risk assessment and risk management would be terminally compromised. As was shown above, limiting the role of policy and politics in risk assessment to the greatest extent possible constitutes an important foundation of risk regulation. If other factors are considered as part of risk assessment, it will lose its claim to be as free from politics and policy as is practicable. If this happens, even the ideal of scientific risk assessment will have been sacrificed and, as a consequence, the value of scientifically-based methods of risk regulation will be called into question.

(c) 'Other factors' and the consistency discipline

One area in which the controversy over the status of other factors in risk regulation is particularly prominent is in the consistency discipline. It will be recalled that Article 5.5 of the SPS Agreement requires consistency in the level of protection that WTO Members determine is appropriate in different situations. Consistency is a laudable aim, but is it an unrealistic expectation in light of the dynamic and haphazard way in which regulatory standards have developed?[60] The hazards that different societies deem worth worrying about vary: each society has its 'worry beads'.[61] To take a very well-known example, where Americans are said to be

[58] *Response from the European Commission to Comments Submitted by WTO Members under Either or Both G/TBT/N/EEC/6 and G/SPS/N/EEC/149* (G/SPS/GEN/337, G/TBT/W/179 26 July 2002) 15–16.

[59] Commission Response to GMO Comments (n 58) 15–16.

[60] On inconsistencies and incoherence, see: AO Sykes 'Exploring the Need for International Harmonization: Domestic Regulation, Sovereignty, and Scientific Evidence Requirements: A Pessimistic View' (2002) 3 ChiJIntlL 353, 367 (noting inconsistencies in the cost per life saved of various regulations); Breyer (n 17) 19–21; Fisher 'Drowning by Numbers' (n 2) 113.

[61] R and JX Kasperson 'Hidden Hazards' in Mayo and Hollander (eds) (n 19) 9, 9 (referring to RW Kates 'Managing Technological Hazards: Success, Strain, and Surprise' in National Academy of Engineering *Hazards: Technology and Fairness* (National Academy Press Washington DC 1985) 206).

preoccupied with cancer risks, Europeans fret about GMOs. Even within any particular regulatory jurisdiction, there are significant problems with consistency and the rationality of agenda selection. Many cultures have particular practices that may seem irrational to the outsider. Why, for example, should a natural-cheese loving country accept a higher level of risk in respect of a traditional cheese than it accepts in respect of other (probably imported) cheeses carrying the same type of risk? Being prepared to overlook some risks for cultural reasons (eg, natural cheeses) and taking aggressive action in respect of others (eg, a society's 'worry beads') are two sides of the same coin—in both cases, inconsistencies in the level of protection adopted are attributable to societal preferences.

It is difficult to predict how far the Appellate Body will be prepared to go in allowing Members to rely on such societal preferences in justifying what might otherwise appear to be arbitrary distinctions in the level of protection chosen in comparable situations—will the existence of a particular tradition mean that the distinction is not 'arbitrary'? Should the fact that imported cheeses have to meet safety standards that are not imposed on traditional cheeses put the Member in breach of the SPS Agreement's consistency discipline? Ostensibly, yes, because a different level of protection is being adopted in comparable situations with a clear trade barrier resulting. On the one hand, it might be pointed out that, while the Appellate Body has indicated (in the *Hormones* case) that Article 5.5 should not be applied rigidly, it was clearly referring to the inconsistencies that arise from the ad hoc nature of regulation-making and not inconsistencies that arise from deliberate distinctions between traditional and non-traditional foods.[62] On the other hand, it would be true to say that, in the *Hormones* case, the Appellate Body found that there was a fundamental distinction between added hormones and naturally-occurring hormones.[63] While that latter finding does suggest that there may be some room for distinctions based on perceptions about how food is produced, it is by no means clear that this would extend to what would amount to exemptions for traditional foods.

It is likely that, sooner or later, the WTO will have to decide to what extent it will be prepared to allow cultural or societal preferences and perceptions to shape national regulations. When the WTO does have to grapple with this question, what should it do? Should it acknowledge that these factors inevitably play a role in regulatory decicion-making, or should it attempt to reinforce the SPS Agreement's ideal of regulations as the products of scientific determinations? It is suggested below that, while a role should be established for societal preferences, we should be cautious before adding public fear to that list.

[62] *Hormones* AB Report (n 37) para 219.
[63] *Hormones* AB Report (n 37) para 221.

2 Distinguishing Between Various Societal Preferences

(a) Contextual distinctions and cultural traditions

It is well known that the public perceive risks differently from experts. Sunstein and Pildes write: '[t]he problem with expert approaches is that they ignore some distinctive features of citizen evaluations of risks that are far from irrational.'[64] Their argument is that ordinary citizens evaluate risks in a different way from experts. Experts conducting cost–benefit analyses or comparative risk assessments in order to choose between policy options typically refer to annual mortality rates. Ordinary people, on the other hand, tend not to rank risks according to annual mortality rates but refer to a number of contextual factors such as the nature of the risk, whether people subject themselves to it voluntarily, whether it is uncontrollable, whether it causes permanent loss, how the risk is distributed across society, and the social conditions under which the risk is generated. Sunstein and Pildes argue that it is fully rational to attend to contextual differences of this sort.[65] The domestic political importance of being able to regulate in a way that accommodates some of these concerns is evident in the US Administrative Action Statement, which sets out the US Administration's view of what the SPS Agreement means. That Statement stresses that, as understood by the US Administration, Article 5.5 would permit different levels of protection to be based on factors like whether exposure to the risk is voluntary.[66] This may well be true as Article 5.5 refers to the SPS Committee taking account of the 'exceptional character of human health risks to which people voluntarily expose themselves'.

A case can certainly be made to support a lasting role for popular contextual distinctions between risks based on factors like whether the risk is of a kind that people expose themselves to voluntarily. It is arguable that Members should be able to defend regulatory distinctions made on the basis of this kind of public perception about scientifically verified risks because reference to these kinds of factors would not undermine the SPS Agreement's fundamental commitment to fact-based regulation. Reference to such contextual factors is an entirely appropriate aspect of risk management that does not diminish the importance of the scientific aspects of risk assessment where the underlying risks have a credible scientific basis. Given that the WTO is already criticised for failing to allow Members sufficient scope to regulate to respond to public priorities, it would be as well for panels and the Appellate Body to accept reference to

64 CR Sunstein and R Pildes 'Experts, Economists, and Democrats' in CR Sunstein *Free Markets and Social Justice* (OUP New York 1997) 128, 128.

65 Sunstein and Pildes (n 64) 130–33.

66 (1994) 6 US Code Congressional and Administrative News 4040, 4107. On consistency and voluntariness, see also: Walker (n 4) 269.

public perceptions of various risks where to do so would not undermine the organising principle of the SPS Agreement: scientifically-verified risk.

The same might also be said in respct of allowing Members some leeway in respect of an apparent inconsistency in the level of protection adopted in comparable situations where the inconsistency has its roots in cultural practices. An example was given above, of a society that is prepared to accept a higher risk in repsect of a traditional food (natural cheese) than it is prepared to accept in respect of other products that do not have any cultural associations. It was suggested above that it is still not clear whether the Appellate Body would be prepared to endorse such distinctions. The WTO's choice of approach will, in part, depend on how it sees its role in the global trade regime. For example, will the WTO challenge existing social preferences which have significant implications for trade? Should it, like the ECJ, combat historically-based cultural preferences which have limited competition and trade,[67] or should its mission be more limited? On balance, it may be best for the WTO to accept that, where there is an established tradition associated with a particular food, the fact that a Member is prepared to accept a higher risk in connection with that food than it is prepared to accept in respect of non-traditional equivalents does not mean that its regulations are in breach of Article 5.5. It will, however, be important to ensure that any allowance for cultural or traditional distinctions is not abused to excuse protectionism.

(b) Public fear and public dread

What, then, of public fear? To what extent should the WTO allow leeway for Members to respond to public fears when, for example, determining whether a distinction between levels of protection is arbitrary for the purposes of Article 5.5 of the SPS Agreement. Public fear may be said to exist in two distinct situations. Firstly, when people in a society fear one risk more than another when experts regard the risks as comparable because they carry the same annual mortality rates, we might say that a particular public fear attaches to one of those risks. That type of public fear can be called 'dread'. The other kind of public fear occurs when the public (or a section of it) fear that something is harmful even though there is no credible scientific evidence to suggest that this is the case.[68] It is in this sense that the expression 'public fear' is used here.

[67] Eg, Case C–407/85 *Drei Glocken GmbH v USL Centro-Sud* [1988] ECR 4233 (in overturning a prohibition on marketing imported pasta not made purely of durum wheat, the ECJ was keen not to allow consumer preferences to be crystallised in this way). Note, though, that even within the EU it is felt by some that insufficient scope is given to the local traditions that enhance the EU: D Chalmers '"Food for Thought": Reconciling European Risks and Traditional Ways of Life' (2003) 66 MLR 532, 559–60.

[68] For example, in the UK, many parents are concerned that the triple MMR (measles, mumps and rubella) vaccine is linked to autism despite a lack of a credible scientific basis for this fear.

While adopting different levels of protection in relation to different risks because one is the focus of public dread may not fit naturally with the SPS Agreement's commitment to expert-led regulation—if the risks are comparable, Article 5.5 indicates that the same level of protection *should* be adopted—it may be that some leeway can be created to allow Members to respond to a public demand for tougher regulation of the dreaded risk. It may be that the WTO will be prepared to regard distinctions that respond to public dread as non-arbitrary and justifiable. To take this view would not necessarily undermine the basis of the SPS Agreement. In committing themselves to that Agreement, the Members may be said to have agreed only to use trade-limiting regulatory barriers in respect of scientifically-verified risks, but they did not commit themselves to a model of regulation-making that casts out public perceptions altogether. To the extent that public dread relates to risks that have a basic scientific basis—ie, the more and less dreaded risks both relate to proven hazards—responding to public dread does not undermine the SPS Agreement's bottom line: regulation only in respect of scientifically-verified risks.

The same cannot be said for regulation in response to public fear in the sense described above. The ability of Members to respond to public fears is regarded as particularly important by those concerned that regulation should respond to the public concerns irrespective of whether those concerns are justified.[69] Some commentators have even gone so far as to suggest that Members should be free to reject the outcomes of scientific risk assessments if the public demand for regulation is sufficiently strong.[70] However, where reference to public perceptions of risks based on different contextual factors and dread does not undermine the SPS Agreement, reference to completely unsubstantiated public fears would do precisely that. If a Member is able to regulate and restrict trade just because of public fears, there is no place for the scientific justification rationale and the whole scheme of the SPS Agreement is rendered nugatory. Without that scientific justification discipline, there is a very real possibility that the door will be opened to precisely the kind of protectionism that the SPS Agreement was developed to address. There is also the question of the methodological basis on which public opinion should be determined and how proof of public opinion might be adduced in proceedings.[71] One

[69] Walker's attitude is common. He asks what would be left of the sovereignty inherent in risk management decisions if consumer anxieties and other domestic concerns could not be weighed in the balance: Walker (n 4) 306.

[70] J Bohanes 'Risk Regulation in WTO Law: A Procedure-Based Approach to the Precautionary Principle' (2002) 40 Columbia JTransL 323, 329; and R Howse 'Democracy, Science, and Free Trade: Risk Regulation on Trial at the World Trade Organization' (2000) 98 MichLRev 2329, 2330, 2335, 2337, 2350.

[71] J Scott and E Vos 'The Juridification of Uncertainty: Observations on the Ambivalence of the Precautionary Principle within the EU and the WTO' in C Joerges and R Dehousse *Good Governance in Europe's Integrated Market* (OUP Oxford 2002) 253, 279, 285. Their suggestion is

might also query how public fear should be handled given that governments in liberal societies have very little control over the primary driving force behind public fear: the media. If efforts are being made to rationalise and organise health-based regulation to reduce trade barriers, it would seem regressive to legitimise a system where the trading opportunities of exporting countries depend on the fickle and unpredictable tides of public opinion. All of which is not to say that Members should ignore public fears about unsubstantiated hazards, but that it would be better for those fears to be addressed through efforts to educate the public and build trust in national regulatory decision-makers.[72]

(c) Conclusion on reference to social and cultural factors

There is, as Scott and Vos remark, an unresolved tension between non-arbitrary, rational decision-making on the one hand and transparency, participation and responsiveness to public opinion on the other.[73] It is important that the WTO recognise that social and cultural factors do have a legitimate role in risk regulation. But such a recognition still leaves open the question of how WTO panels are to approach social and cultural factors. Of course the limits that the WTO panels place on the use of social and cultural factors in health regulation will be contentious. If the Members are given little opportunity to rely on such factors to justify differences in the level of protection chosen in different situations, some WTO Members will feel that their regulatory autonomy is being stifled. If, on the other hand, Members are given greater leeway to rely on such factors, other WTO Members will feel that the collective commitment to science-based regulation is being diluted, with adverse consequences for trading opportunities.

It has been suggested here that the WTO could remain true to its mission of tackling gratuitous trade barriers by acknowledging that social and cultural factors are not necessarily irrational. Although the SPS Agreement undoubtedly embraces science-driven regulation, it should not be supposed that there is no scope in the Agreement for social and cultural factors[74]—

that, just as states must adduce evidence of the scientific basis of a risk, so too they should be required to adduce evidence of the strength of public opinion.

[72] The need for risk communication strategies to address public fears is widely recognised: see, eg, European Commission *Final Report on Setting the Scientific Framework for the Inclusion of New Quality of Life Concerns in the Risk Assessment Process* (adopted by the Scientific Steering Committee 10–11 April 2003) 12–15.

[73] Scott and Vos (n 71) 278.

[74] Some, like Howse, are quite optimistic and see the AB as having avoided the extremes of scientific/technocratic regulation and democratic regulation that is responsive to public perceptions by understanding science to play a role within democratically-justified regulation: R Howse 'Adjudicative Legitimacy and Treaty Interpretation in International Trade Law: The Early Years of WTO Jurisprudence' in JHH Weiler (ed) *The EU, the WTO and the NAFTA* (OUP Oxford 2000) 35, 65. Cf those, such as Scott, who see the SPS Agreement as silencing culture and context: Scott (n 6) 157.

with the exception of responding to unsubstantiated public fears, taking account of cultural traditions and public perceptions of risks need not signal a move away from the science-based discipline of the SPS Agreement. That said, the Appellate Body has not yet explored the role and limits of cultural and social factors, particularly in situations where such factors account for regulatory distinctions. Whatever stance the Appellate Body takes on this issue, it is sure to attract controversy.

D UNCERTAINTY AND SCIENCE-BASED REVIEW IN THE WTO

Perhaps the greatest anxiety attaching to WTO review of national health measures is that the science-based requirements of the SPS Agreement prevent Members taking action to protect health in circumstances of uncertainty.[75] If uncertainty prevents the provision of a 'scientific justification', precautionary action cannot be successfully defended in the WTO without relying on Article 5.7. This anxiety is fuelled by the perception that agricultural, industrial and food production practices are advancing at such a pace that the safety of the products generated through such mechanisms cannot be satisfactorily established.[76] In part, concerns about the SPS Agreement's scientific benchmark stem from an oversimplified view of scientific risk assessment and the nature of uncertainty. This section seeks to present a more reasoned view of uncertainty and to explore the extent to which uncertainty can be accommodated *within* the scientific norms of the SPS Agreement.

Article 2.2 of the SPS Agreement stipulates that SPS measures must be based on scientific principles and must not be maintained without sufficient scientific evidence. Article 5.1 requires that SPS measures be based on a risk assessment, which Article 5.2 states must take into account available scientific evidence, amongst other factors. In both the *Hormones* and *Agricultural Products* cases, the Appellate Body confirmed that the scientific justification discipline in Article 2.2 is to be read together with the risk assessment discipline in Article 5.1.[77] Article 5.7 allows provisional

[75] Here, the word 'uncertainty' is used in its lay sense to denote gaps in information or understanding which are relevant to regulatory action. For more technical taxonomies of uncertainty, see: NRC *Science and Judgment* (n 7) 165; FAO/WHO *Application of Risk Analysis to Food Standards Issues* (n 11) 12; McGarvin (n 49) 42; Kellar (n 7) 1031; T O'Riordan and J Cameron 'Editorial Introduction' in T O'Riordan and J Cameron (eds) *Interpreting the Precautionary Principle* (Cameron May London 1994) 62, 62–65; J Hunt 'The Social Construction of Precaution' in O'Riordan and Cameron (eds) (above in this note) 117, 117 (utilising Wynne's characterisation of uncertainty: B Wynne 'Uncertainty and Environmental Learning: Reconceiving Science and Policy in the Preventative Paradigm' (2000) Global Environmental Change 111).

[76] O'Riordan et al 'The Evolution of the Precautionary Principle' in O'Riordan et al (eds) (n 19) 9; McGarvin (n 49) 55.

[77] *Hormones* AB Report (n 37) para 193; *Japan–Measures Affecting Agricultural Products* WT/DS76/AB/R AB Report adopted 19 March 1999 para 76.

measures to be taken where relevant scientific evidence is insufficient, provided that: (i) the provisional measures are based on available pertinent information; (ii) continuing efforts are made to obtain the additional information necessary for a more objective assessment of risk; and (iii) the measure is reviewed within a reasonable period of time. The way in which the relationship between Articles 5.2 and 5.7 is constructed suggests that SPS measures can be divided into two neatly differentiated groups. In the first group are permanent[78] regulations, which are based on 'proper' scientific evidence and a risk assessment that satisfies the requirements of Article 5.1. The second group comprises regulations promulgated in circumstances where the scientific evidence is not sufficient for a qualifying risk assessment to be conducted.

This bifurcation of regulatory measures is problematic. The world is not neatly divided into areas of scientific clarity and scientific ignorance. As was shown above, the science behind all risk assessments utilises policies and assumptions in order to estimate risk in the face of uncertainties. The fact that most risk assessments have, buried within them, various uncertainties (which have been overcome by recourse to science policies) is easily obscured by the confidence and specificity of the risk estimates generated. This does not mean that a risk assessment that utilised science policies to overcome some types of uncertainty (regarding, for example, the significance for humans of results derived from animal studies) would fail under Articles 5.1 and 5.2 of the SPS Agreement. Such a risk assessment would be unlikely to fail because the use of such policies and assumptions is not anti- or extra-scientific but, rather, constitutes part of mainstream science.[79] In short, uncertainty is not anathema to risk assessment. On the contrary, risk assessment is a method of organising scientific and technical information *and* its associated uncertainties.[80] Rather than there being two clear categories of scientific evidence—sufficient and insufficient scientific evidence—there is a spectrum of knowledge.[81] Even in situations of uncertainty so severe that a permanent measure would not be appropriate, more limited or temporary action will still be based on whatever scientific evidence is available.[82] The point was captured well by

[78] Permanent only in the sense of not relying on the provisional measures exception of Article 5.7.

[79] Howse makes a similar point, suggesting that there will be a sufficient scientific basis even where there are inherent uncertainties due to the limits of scientific risk assessment: R Howse 'Democracy, Science, and Free Trade: Risk Regulation on Trial at the World Trade Organization' (2000) 98 MichLRev 2329, 2341–42. See also Walker (n 4) 258.

[80] FAO/WHO *Application of Risk Analysis to Food Standards Issues* (n 11) 12; NRC *Science and Judgment* (n 7) 161.

[81] For a diagram of the evidentiary spectrum, see: McGarvin (n 49) 40.

[82] According to Codex practice, where the scientific data are insufficient or incomplete, the CAC should not elaborate a standard, but should consider elaborating a related text, such as a code of practice, provided that such a text 'would be supported by the available scientific evidence': CAC *Report* (24th Session 2001 ALINORM 01/41) paras 80–81 (see also *Working*

one of the experts advising the *Hormones* panel, Dr Ritter, who said: 'I think it would be silly for any scientist to presume that the day will ever come, on this issue or on any other, where we could say we know enough and that there is no need to do any further work.'[83] Scientific knowledge constitutes a spectrum, and, while one would always like to know *more*,[84] whether or not one knows *enough* to regulate is a separate question. As Vern Walker notes, there is a 'continuum between a merely speculative risk and a conclusively demonstrated one' with 'a vast stretch of undemonstrated, unquantified but scientifically plausible risks' in between.[85]

The existence of a spectrum of evidence is not acknowledged by the SPS Agreement. Instead, that Agreement posits some invisible and unspecified borderline between sufficient and insufficient scientific evidence. WTO Members attempting to comply with the SPS Agreement may well be unsure as to how much scientific evidence is required for a proper risk assessment and how certain that evidence must be. Similarly, it is not clear how spare the 'available pertinent information' necessary to rely on Article 5.7 can be. For example, would a provisional measure prompted by citizens' concerns at an apparent cancer cluster satisfy the requirements of Article 5.7 where the connection between the observed effect (the cancer cluster) and the suspected cause is still entirely speculative? The issue of the degree of scientific certainty required also arises outside the SPS Agreement in at least two situations. Firstly, where a health measure is to be justified under GATT Article XX(b), how certain must the evidence be in order to justify regulatory action? Secondly, if a Member, inspired by the *Asbestos* case, wishes to argue that two products are not like because their health effects differ, how compelling must the evidence be? The Appellate Body has has little opportunity to clarify these issues, although it has suggested that a certain flexibility should be applied to the notion of the sufficiency of scientific evidence in the SPS Agreement. In the *Hormones* case, the Appellate Body said that, in assessing whether sufficient scientific evidence exists, panels should bear in mind that 'responsible, representative governments commonly act from perspectives of prudence and precaution where risks of irreversible, eg, life-terminating, damage to human health are concerned.'[86]

Principles for Risk Analysis (n 28) para 10). The Codex statement demonstrates that there are greater and lesser degrees of evidence, with different regulatory and responses being appropriate depending on the degree of information.

[83] *Hormones* US Panel Report (n 20) and *Hormones* Canada Panel Report (n 20) Annex: Transcript of the Joint Meeting with Experts para 423.

[84] Experimental science never claims full certainty: Q Balzano and AR Sheppard 'The Influence of the Precautionary Principle on Science-Based Decision-Making: Questionable Applications to Risks of Radiofrequency Fields' (2002) 5 J Risk Research 351, 354–55.

[85] Walker (n 4) 305.

[86] *Hormones* AB Report (n 37) para 124.

What is frightening to many about science-based regulation is that it is thought to prevent action being taken until the all the facts are in. Where significant harm may ensue, adopting a 'wait-and-see' approach may well be politically unacceptable. It might be asked why there is such concern, given that Article 5.7 does allow for provisional measures where the available scientific evidence is insufficient. Does this provision not accommodate the unwillingness to adopt a wait-and-see attitude? One potential problem with relying on Article 5.7 to appease concerns is that provisional measures must be based on 'available pertinent information'. Just what this available pertinent information should be is, at this point, obscure, as this requirement has not been fully elucidated in the cases decided to date. It does, however, seem fair to suggest that the Appellate Body would not allow WTO Members to take precautionary action based solely on wholly unsubstantiated concerns about possible negative health effects. An additional, and more significant, problem is that the structure of Article 5.7 supposes that all types of uncertainty can be remedied by further research. Uncertainty does not always take the form of a gap which can be filled at all, or within any predictable period of time.[87] By conditioning recourse to Article 5.7 on the obligation to 'seek to obtain the additional information necessary for a more objective assessment of risk and review the sanitary or phytosanitary measure accordingly within a reasonable period of time', the SPS Agreement does not provide an avenue for action in the face of enduring or irremediable uncertainty.[88] Members may also be unwilling to brand specific health measures as 'provisional', but may prefer to support their measures as fully-fledged legitimate health regulations notwithstanding that they were adopted in circumstances of uncertainty. Perhaps this is why the EC preferred to defend the hormones ban as satisfying the full requirements of the SPS Agreement rather than rely on Article 5.7. Had the EC relied on Article 5.7, it might have been seen to have undermined its own stance on hormones by conceding that a risk assessment had not been carried out and would also have condemned its measures as merely provisional.

E CONCLUSION

Since the late 1960s, risk regulation practices have been formalised. Three distinct aspects of risk analysis have been identified: risk assessment, risk management and risk communication. Regulation based on this model of

[87] There is not always a clear progression from incertitude to calculable risks: McGarvin (n 49) 43. On the likely progression of research on GMO safety, see: O'Riordan et al 'The Evolution of the Precautionary Principle' in O'Riordan et al (eds) (n 19) 29–30.

[88] Fisher 'Drowning by Numbers' (n 2) 115 (making the point that uncertainty is rarely due to a simple need to do more research).

risk analysis claims legitimacy through the promise that scientific risk assessment delivers the *facts* to risk managers who then consider what regulatory action to take in the light of other factors, including political considerations. Scientific risk assessment is not, however, entirely devoid of policy. Risk managers in fact set risk assessment policies, which are typically designed to arrive at very conservative risk estimates. This realisation should not destroy the legitimacy claims of science-based risk regulation. The appealing, but illusory, vision in which all policy factors are confined to risk management may be shattered, but an ordered way of regulating based on the facts—as far as they are discernible—remains. The use of policies and assumptions in risk assessment does not mean that the faith placed in it by the WTO Members was ill-advised. On the contrary, science-based regulation constitutes a viable constraint on protectionist non-tariff barriers. The trouble is, however, that it may go too far and limit the ability of WTO Members to regulate in a way that satisfies national priorities. This concern is evident in the vexed question of the role of other factors in risk regulation.

Despite some progress on the role of other factors having been made in Codex, the extent to which social and cultural factors may justify inconsistencies in the chosen level of protection is not clear. Nor is it obvious from the cases decided in the WTO to date how close the relationship between the risk assessment and the measure must be for the measure to be 'based on' the risk assessment. If being 'based on' a risk assessment is fundamentally about the rationality of the relationship between the measure and the risk assessment, will the required rational relationship be disturbed if the results of the risk assessment are overshadowed, in terms of the nature of the measure adopted or the level of protection chosen, by social and cultural factors? For example, if a risk assessment suggested that, taking local conditions into account, substance X is carcinogenic at residue level Y. Will a measure be based on the risk assessment if it sets a maximum residue level far below level Y because the local population has an especial dread of cancer or because the production processes involved in the production of substance X are deeply unpopular? Regulating in a way that promotes national priorities and values also encompasses adopting a particular attitude to the significance of certainty and the appropriate regulatory response to it. The SPS Agreement does provide for regulation in the face of uncertainty in two ways. A risk assessment that qualifies under Article 5.1 may utilise the assumptions and policies that have long been accepted as part of mainstream science in order to overcome some uncertainties that would otherwise prevent the completion of a risk assessment. The SPS Agreement also accommodates uncertainty by allowing provisional measures under Article 5.7, although the borderline between the level and type of uncertainty that can be accommodated within a risk assessment under Article 5.1 and that which necessitates recourse to Article 5.7 is not clear. In response to this lack of clarity and the onerous requirements of Article 5.7 (gap-filling research and review within a reasonable period of time), the value of the precautionary principle should be considered. It is to this topic that the next chapter now turns.

5

The Precautionary Principle, Proportionality and Procedure

ONE OF THE MOST significant points of tension between national regulatory autonomy and international supervision relates to the treatment of scientific uncertainty. In a trade regime whose linchpin is scientific justification, are Members able to take protective action 'just in case'? With national decision-makers wary of being criticised for failing to act in a precautionary manner[1] and with fears that the WTO disciplines restrict such preventative action in circumstances of uncertainty, is the precautionary principle the answer?[2] The precautionary principle promises that uncertainty *need not*—in some formulations, *should not*—lead to inaction in the face of a possible threat. The precautionary principle is an intensely politicised concept,[3] situated as it is at the heart of the debate on how to resolve the tension between expert-led regulation and the desire of elected officials to respond to widespread popular concerns about unverified hazards. This debate is conducted on both national and international stages, but nowhere is it more fiercely contested than in the WTO.[4] Concerns about the WTO's impact on national sovereignty extend to all aspects of its remit, but, to an extent the WTO's response to the precautionary principle is likely to be seen (at least in some quarters) as indicative of its response to a broader challenge to its legitimacy. To this extent, the fate of the precautionary principle has come to be perceived by some, particularly in civil society, as the decisive skirmish in the on-going battle to defend national sovereignty against the depredations of the WTO. This chapter suggests that the WTO should exercise caution before adopting the precautionary principle but that, even if that principle is not accepted as a justification for regulatory action, all is not lost: Members can

[1] Note, for example, the conclusions of the *The BSE Inquiry* (known as the 'Phillips Report') into BSE in the United Kingdom. The Report, released in October 2000, can be downloaded at <http://www.bseinquiry.gov.uk/report/index.htm>.

[2] The precautionary principle is referred to as the 'PP' in the footnotes.

[3] T O'Riordan et al 'The Evolution of the Precautionary Principle' in T O'Riordan, A Jordan and J Cameron (eds) *Reinterpreting the Precautionary Principle* (Cameron May London 2002) 9, 9.

[4] See, particularly, J Scott and E Vos 'The Juridification of Uncertainty: Observations on the Ambivalence of the Precautionary Principle within the EU and the WTO' in C Joerges and R Dehousse *Good Governance in Europe's Integrated Market* (OUP Oxford 2002) 253.

still regulate in circumstances of uncertainty and take action in responding to local social preferences.

This chapter takes up the European Commission's 'Communication on the Precautionary Principle' (the Communication) and explores the implications of its blend of science-based risk regulation and precaution for the WTO. The central argument of the chapter is that, however it is presented, the precautionary principle weakens science as the yardstick by which legitimate and illegitimate health regulations are to be distinguished. If the precautionary principle is to be embraced in the WTO, it must be complemented by another basis of review that will prevent the principle being used to undermine the progress made by the SPS Agreement[5] in curtailing health-based non-tariff barriers. Two alternative additional bases of review are considered: proportionality and procedural review. The prospects of strict proportionality review in the WTO are addressed through an examination of proportionality review in the ECJ, and it is rejected as leading to a degree and type of scrutiny that is not suited to the WTO. While procedural review's promise of deference to regulators may seem appealing, experience in the EU suggests that procedural review needs to be backed up by substantive benchmarks in any case, and experience in the US shows that procedural review's promise of deference can conceal quite intensive scrutiny. Moreover, the logic of procedural review is grounded in an accountability and transparency rationale that does not translate easily to the WTO.

A THE PRECAUTIONARY PRINCIPLE

1 Precaution in the WTO

In the *Hormones* case, the EC argued that the precautionary principle is a general customary rule of international law, or at least a general principle of law.[6] Noting that the status of the precautionary principle in international law is a subject of continuing academic debate, the Appellate Body declined to take a position on the status of the principle in international law.[7] Nevertheless, the Appellate Body suggested that the precautionary principle 'finds reflection' in Articles 5.7 and 3.3 of the SPS Agreement, although it need not be assumed that Article 5.7 exhausts the relevance of the precautionary principle.[8] Despite the fairly sympathetic

[5] Agreement on the Application of Sanitary and Phytosanitary Measures (the SPS Agreement) (Marrakesh, 15 April 1994).

[6] *EC Measures Concerning Meat and Meat Products (Hormones)* WT/DS26/AB/R, WT/DS48/AB/R AB Report adopted 13 February 1998 para 121 ('*Hormones*').

[7] *Hormones* AB Report (n 6) para 123.

[8] *Hormones* AB Report (n 6) para 124.

hearing given to the EC's precautionary principle submission, the Appellate Body ultimately stressed that the precautionary principle does not override the specific provisions of the SPS Agreement.[9]

Japan took a different approach in raising the precautionary principle before the Appellate Body in the *Apples* case.[10] In its appeal against the panel decision, Japan argued that the panel had failed in its duty (under Article 11 of the DSU) to make an 'objective assessment' of the facts of the case by, *inter alia,* failing to take into account the precautionary principle or the caution emphasised by the panel's experts.[11] What it interesting about Japan's approach is that, rather than raising the precautionary principle under Article 5.7, or even under Article 2.2, Japan relied on it in attacking the panel's evaluation of the scientific evidence before it. Japan argued that the precautionary principle ought to have *informed* the panel's consideration of the evidence before it and that the experts' statements cautioning against removing contols over the importation of apples in a single step should have been given greater weight by the panel in its conclusions on whether the fire blight pathway could be completed.[12] Ultimately, the Appellate Body rejected Japan's argument on two bases. Firstly, it found that, by noting the experts' reservations about lifting all import controls at once, the panel had in fact taken the experts' statements of caution 'into account'.[13] Secondly, the Appellate Body observed that the weight to be attributed to particular evidence and the evaluation of facts was a matter that lay within the discretion of the panel as trier of fact. Accordingly, the weight to be attributed to the experts' statements of caution was a matter for the panel, not the Appellate Body.[14]

Following the *Hormones* and *Apples* cases, it can be observed that both direct and indirect attempts to integrate the precautionary principle into the WTO have failed. In the *Hormones* case, the Appellate Body rejected the argument that the precautionary principle effectively modifies the obligations imposed by the SPS Agreement. In the *Apples* case, the Appellate Body rejected Japan's attempt to use the precautionary principle to modify the Article 2.2 discipline indirectly by having that principle inform the panel's evaluation of whether the scientific evidence supports the measure. While it might be argued that Japan's approach did not extend far beyond the Appellate Body's finding in the *Hormones* case that, in considering whether a measure is supported by sufficient scientific evidence,

[9] *Hormones* AB Report (n 6) para 125.

[10] *Japan–Measures Affecting the Importation of Apples* WT/DS245/AB/R AB Report adopted 10 December 2003 (*'Apples'*); *Japan–Measures Affecting the Importation of Apples* WT/DS245/R Panel Report adopted 10 December 2003 (*'Apples'*).

[11] *Apples* AB Report (n 10) paras 218, 232–34.

[12] In other words, whether fire blight could be introduced and established in Japan through the importation of apples.

[13] *Apples* AB Report (n 10) para 237.

[14] *Apples* AB Report (n 10) para 238.

panels are to bear in mind that governments often act from perspectives of prudence and precaution where risks of irreversible damage to human health are concerned,[15] the Appellate Body's response in the *Apples* case confirms its continuing reluctance to accord the precautionary principle any official status in the WTO.

With the precautionary principle devoid of official status within the SPS Agreement, whatever precautionary action WTO Members wish to exercise must fit within one of two categories. Firstly, precautionary action may be justified as a provisional measure under Article 5.7. Secondly, precautionary action may, in some circumstances, still qualify as being based on sufficient scientific evidence because, as Chapter 4 showed, a certain amount of precaution and risk averseness is built-in to scientific risk assessment processes and, as the Appellate Body has recognised, the sufficient scientific evidence criterion should be applied flexibly where where risks of irreversible damage to human health are concerned.[16] Notwithstanding the Appellate Body's endorsement of flexibility in applying the scientific justification criterion and the existence of Article 5.7 (which allows provisional measures), fears persist that WTO rules prevent precautionary action in circumstances of uncertainty.

2 Introducing the European Communication

The EC, for one, was not placated by the Appellate Body's promise of flexibility in applying the scientific justification standard. In March 2000, the EC submitted its 'Communication on the Precautionary Principle' to the WTO.[17] In its Communication, the EC attempts to establish the status of the precautionary principle outside the narrow confines of international environmental law. While the origins of the precautionary principle in German law are widely acknowledged,[18] the international home of the principle is in international environmental law. A number of international environmental agreements implement the precautionary principle.[19] Most famously, the Rio Declaration provides that, '[w]here there are threats of serious or irreversible damage, lack of full scientific certainty shall not be used as a reason for postponing cost-effective measures to prevent

[15] *Hormones* AB Report (n 6) para 124.

[16] *Hormones* AB Report (n 6) para 124.

[17] European Commission *Communication from the Commission on the Precautionary Principle* (G/SPS/GEN/168 14 March 2000). The European document reference is: COM/2000/0001.

[18] J Cameron 'The Precautionary Principle' in G Sampson and WB Chambers (eds) *Trade, Environment and the Millennium* (UN UP Tokyo 1999) 239, 240–41; S Boehmer-Christiansen 'The Precautionary Principle in Germany—Enabling Government' in T O'Riordan and J Cameron (eds) *Interpreting the Precautionary Principle* (Cameron May London 1994) 31.

[19] For a review of the relevant environmental agreements, see: Commission *Communication on the Precautionary Principle* (n 17) point 4 and Annex II.

environmental degradation.'[20] The Rio Declaration's prohibition on using a lack of scientific certainty as a reason *not to act* is typical of the role which international environmental agreements ascribe to the precautionary principle. Rather than condemn *inaction*, the EC's Communication seeks to establish the precautionary principle as a means by which *action* taken in the absence of scientific certainty can be defended against a challenge brought by a trading partner. Positioning the precautionary principle as a principle capable of deployment to authorise contentious regulatory action in an international regime such as the WTO certainly constitutes a marked development in the principle's history. From functioning largely (if not exclusively) as a non-justiciable principle exhorting governments not to rely on uncertainty as an excuse for not taking protective action on the environment, the precautionary principle is being asked to function as a justiciable principle authorising trade-limiting action in circumstances where the feared harm to health has not been proved.[21]

Formulations of the precautionary principle in international agreements and academic writings vary.[22] Rather than being diverted by stronger versions of the precautionary principle—which are tied up with a political culture of protest and distrust of expert decision-makers[23]—the focus here will be on the European Commission's Communication and whether the model it proposes should be accepted in the WTO. The Communication attempts to contribute to the debate about the meaning of the precautionary principle by establishing a common understanding of the factors that might lead to that principle being invoked in decision-making and to establish guidelines for its application. The Communication acknowledges that there is a risk that unwarranted recourse to the precautionary principle might serve as a justification for disguised protectionism, and

[20] Rio Declaration on Environment and Development (UN Conference on Environment and Development) (Rio de Janeiro 3–14 June 1992 reprinted in 31 ILM 874 (1992)) principle 15.

[21] Note, though, that something of a bridge between these two uses of the precautionary principle is provided by the Biosafety Protocol, which states that lack of scientific certainty shall not prevent a party from 'taking a decision' with regard to living modified organisms: Cartagena Protocol on Biosafety to the Convention on Biological Diversity (Montreal 29 January 2000) Art 10 para 6.

[22] For accounts of more moderate and more extreme versions of the precautionary principle, see: JB Wiener and MD Rogers 'Comparing Precaution in the United States and Europe' (2002) 5 J Risk Research 317, 320–21; RB Stewart 'Environmental Regulatory Decisionmaking under Uncertainty' (preliminary discussion draft) (UCL Symposium on the Law & Economics of Environmental Policy 2001) (available at <http://www.cserge.ucl.ac.uk/Stewart.pdf> on 16 August 2002); J Morris 'Defining the Precautionary Principle' in J Morris (ed) *Rethinking Risk and the Precautionary Principle* (Butterworth-Heinemann Oxford 2000) 1, 1; J Bohanes 'Risk Regulation in WTO Law: A Procedure-Based Approach to the Precautionary Principle' (2002) 40 ColumJTransL 323, 331ff.

[23] O'Riordan et al 'The Evolution of the Precautionary Principle' (n 3) 9. (Note also the strong emphasis on participatory democracy that is associated with the precautionary principle: O'Riordan et al (as above) ch 1; E Fisher 'Is the Precautionary Principle Justiciable?' (2001) 13 JEnvtlL 315, 320.)

suggests that the development of international guidelines would facilitate the prevention of such protectionist abuse. The Communication goes on to set out the role of the precautionary principle in the EU, both in the legal texts and in the case law of the ECJ, as well as in Community policy. By drawing heavily on international environmental treaties, the Communication claims to demonstrate that the precautionary principle is an established rule of international law, which is sanctioned by the SPS Agreement. According to the Communication, recourse to the precautionary principle will be triggered when, following an evaluation of the available scientific data, cause–effect relationships cannot be established because scientific uncertainty cannot be overcome by recourse to prudential techniques such as relying on animal models to establish potential effects in humans, using body weight ranges to make inter-species comparisons etc. The Communication also provides a set of general principles which apply to all risk management measures, whether they are based on the precautionary principle or on a complete risk assessment: measures must be proportionate to the desired level of protection; measures must not be discriminatory in their application; measures should be consistent with other measures already adopted in similar circumstances; the benefits and costs of action versus those of inaction should be examined (including economic cost-benefit analysis, and an examination of the socio-economic impact of various options); and finally, measures must be re-evaluated in the light of scientific developments with a commitment to further research on the part of the regulating state. The last section of the Communication addresses the burden of proof, and determines that measures based on the precautionary principle *may* assign responsibility for the production of scientific evidence on the business community.

Since the Commission's Communication was published, it has been considered by both the European Parliament and the European Council. Both the Parliament and the Council have welcomed the Communication and endorsed its general thrust, although they have stressed the need for greater civil society involvement.[24] The reaction from other WTO Members has, however, been less uniformly positive. While most welcomed the attempt to clarify the meaning and use of the precautionary principle, significant reservations were voiced about: (i) the possibility of the principle being abused or used to override WTO obligations; and (ii) whether, in view of Article 5.7 of the SPS Agreement, the need for the principle has been demonstrated.[25]

[24] European Council *Presidency Conclusions: Nice European Council Meeting* (SN 400/00 December 2000) Annex III paras 1, 15; European Parliament *Resolution on the Commission Communication on the Precautionary Principle* (A5–0352/2000 December 2000) paras 1–2, 16, 32.

[25] WTO Committee on Sanitary and Phytosanitary Measures *Summary of the Meeting Held on 15–16 March 2000* (G/SPS/R/18 18 April 2000) paras 4–12.

3 Precaution and the Precautionary Principle

Precaution and the precautionary principle are not one and the same. The previous chapter showed that caution is exercised in many aspects of scientific risk assessment. For example, the most sensitive species of animal may be chosen, a linear dose-response model may be used, and safety factors may be applied in calculating the acceptable daily intake (ADI) figure. The way in which scientific data is interpreted also leaves room for more or less conservative approaches to risk. What this means is that, as the FAO puts it, 'precaution has been and should remain an essential element of risk analysis'.[26] Indeed, for most developed countries, precaution is an integral element of regulatory strategy.[27] A country can take a cautious attitude to health issues, for example, in the way it identifies potential hazards and conducts risk assessments, and in the level of protection it adopts, without having recourse to the precautionary principle as such.[28] While US regulations relating to health and the environment undoubtedly employ the notion of precaution,[29] the US remains sceptical of the 'precautionary principle' and has not endorsed the EU's attempts to integrate the principle into the WTO.[30] The precautionary principle goes beyond precaution in risk regulation because it rejects the scientific default position that, absent proof, a cause–effect relationship cannot be presumed.[31]

[26] FAO *Report of the Conference 'International Food Trade Beyond 2000: Science-Based Decisions, Harmonization, Equivalence and Mutual Recognition'* ALICOM 99 25 (FAO Rome 1999) Appendix I ('General Recommendations') para 5 (available from <http://www.fao.org>).

[27] OECD *Overview of National Food Safety Systems and Activities* (SG/ADHOC/FS(2000)5/FINAL) (available at <http://www.olis.oecd.org/olis/2000doc.nsf> on 14 August 2002) para 33.

[28] This distinction between the precautionary principle and the element of caution that scientists apply in their assessment of scientific data is recognised by the EC: Commission *Communication on the Precautionary Principle* (n 17) point 5 (referring to the distinction between the precautionary principle and the 'prudential approach' to risk assessment); by Codex (CAC *Report* (24th Session 2001 ALINORM 01/41) para 77) and by academics (Wiener and Rogers (n 22) 318; D Santillo et al 'The Precautionary Principle in Practice: A Mandate for Anticipatory Preventative Action' in C Raffensperger and JA Tickner (eds) *Protecting Public Health and the Environment: Implementing the Precautionary Principle* (Island Press Washington DC 1999) 36, 46; D Bodansky 'The Precautionary Principle in US Environmental Law' in O'Riordan and Cameron (eds) (n 18) 203, 204; cf FB Cross 'Paradoxical Perils of the Precautionary Principle' (1996) 53 WashLeeLRev 851, 856).

[29] US Food and Drug Administration *Precaution in US Food Safety Decisionmaking* (Annex II to the US's National Food Safety System Paper submitted to the OECD, SG/ADHOC/FS(2002)5/ANN/FINAL) (available at <http://www.foodsafety.gov/~fsg/fssystem.html> on 13 August 2002).

[30] SPS Committee *Summary* (n 25); CAC *US Government Submission to the Committee on General Principles of the CAC for the Committee's April 10–14, 2000 Meeting* (available at <http://www.fsis.usda.gov/OA/codex/confpaper.htm> on 7 August 2002). On the PP in the US, see J Tickner and C Raffensperger 'The American View on the Precautionary Principle' in O'Riordan et al (eds) (n 3) 183.

[31] M Angell *Science on Trial: The Clash of Medical Evidence and the Law in the Breast Implant Case* (WW Norton and Co New York 1996) 113.

Under the precautionary principle, even if not proved, a suspected cause–effect relationship can form the basis of regulatory action. By contrast, a regulatory regime which does not employ the precautionary principle as such may well use conservative assumptions and policies, but, at the end of the day, if the risk assessment does not support the suspected link, that link will not be presumed to exist.[32]

Discussion about the future of the precautionary principle in the WTO risks being side-tracked by a focus on perceived trans-Atlantic differences in risk averseness. While the US has not embraced the precautionary principle in the WTO, it would be wrong to assume that its domestic regulations are necessarily less protective than those of the EU. In fact, the level of protection afforded by regulations in both jurisdictions depends on the particular issue at stake.[33] In order to address the precautionary principle sensibly, it is necessary to move beyond the caricature of Europe as paranoid Luddites opposed to science and innovation, and the United States as forward-looking and risk-taking. Polarised visions of the precautionary principle must, as a close cousin of this caricature, also be jettisoned: it is neither a panacea for the problems generated by industrialisation and globalisation, nor is it simply the ruse of technophobic Europeans bent on undermining the scientific basis of risk regulation.[34] As the following examination of the European Commission's proposal shows, the precautionary principle is not 'anti-science' and does not herald a break with risk regulation based on scientific risk assessment. In this respect, the Communication can only have disappointed those who seek some kind of purity in a version of the precautionary principle that challenges the authority of science and restores what is perceived as the lost democratic control over risk.[35]

[32] Another way of putting it is that the PP prefers to minimise false negatives (eg, harmful substances identified as harmless) whereas the traditional scientific approach minimises false positives (eg, harmless substances identified as harmful): K Barrett and C Raffensperger 'Precautionary Science' in Raffensperger and Tickner (eds) (n 28) 105, 111–12; KS Shrader-Frechette *Risk and Rationality: Philosophical Foundations for Populist Reforms* (U California Press Berkeley 1991) 134.

[33] Wiener and Rogers (n 22) 319, 334; JB Wiener 'Whose Precaution After All? A Comment on the Comparison and Evolution of Risk Regulatory Systems' (2003) 13 DukeJComp&IntlL 207, 208–15; D Vogel *Ships Passing in the Night: The Changing Politics of Risk Regulation in Europe and the United States* (EUI Working Paper 2001/16 Florence 2001) 1 (if generalisations of risk averseness are possible, they do not suggest that the EU was always more conservative: in the 1960s to 1980s, regulation of environmental, health and safety risks in the US was generally stricter than in Europe).

[34] Wiener and Rogers (n 22) 319 (on the need to reject polarised views); B Durodié 'Plastic Panics: European Risk Regulation in the Aftermath of BSE' in J Morris (ed) (n 22) 140, 162 (sees the PP as departing from scientific rationality).

[35] On this 'spirit' of the PP, see: A Jordan and T O'Riordan 'The Precautionary Principle in Contemporary Environmental Policy and Politics' in Raffensperger and Tickner (eds) (n 28) 15, 16, 19.

4 The European Commission's Communication on the Precautionary Principle

The European Commission's Communication does not define the precautionary principle, as such, but focuses on the circumstances in which it may be used. According to the Communication, the precautionary principle may be invoked where 'scientific information is insufficient, inconclusive, or uncertain and where there are indications that the possible effects on the environment, or human, animal or plant health may be potentially dangerous and inconsistent with the chosen level of protection.'[36] A similar description is provided in the European Regulation establishing the European Food Safety Authority (EFSA Regulation), which provides that:

> [W]here, following an assessment of available information, the possibility of harmful effects on health is identified but scientific uncertainty persists, provisional risk management measures necessary to ensure the high level of health protection chosen in the Community may be adopted, pending further scientific information for a more comprehensive risk assessment.[37]

According to the Commission, the precautionary principle has become 'a full-fledged and general principle of international law', an observation which, it says, is confirmed by the WTO Agreements.[38] The Commission justifies its rather optimistic view of the status of the precautionary principle in international law and the WTO as follows. Having recounted the international environmental agreements in which the precautionary principle occurs, the Commission then finds that the precautionary principle has been consolidated in international environmental law and has now become a general principle of international law. The Commission notes that the Preamble to the WTO Agreement highlights the closer links between international trade and environmental protection, and then says that a consistent approach to the precautionary principle demands that it be taken into account in the SPS Agreement and TBT Agreement.[39] The Commission then states that Article 5.7 of the SPS Agreement indicates that that Agreement 'clearly sanctions the use of the precautionary principle'.[40] While one might take issue with the Commission's characterisation

[36] Commission *Communication on the Precautionary Principle* (n 17) point 1.

[37] Regulation (EC) No 178/2002 of the European Parliament and of the Council (28 January 2002) laying down the general principles and requirements of food law, establishing the European Food Safety Authority and laying down procedures in matters of food safety [2002] OJ L031/1–24 ('EFSA Regulation') Article 7.1.

[38] Commission *Communication on the Precautionary Principle* (n 17) point 4.

[39] Agreement on Technical Barriers to Trade (the TBT Agreement) (Marrakesh, 15 April 1994).

[40] Commission *Communication on the Precautionary Principle* (n 17) point 4.

of the status of the precautionary principle in international law[41] and the WTO—which, incidentally, was disputed by other WTO Members[42]—the point is not so much whether the Commission's characterisation was correct, but what effect adoption of the precautionary principle would have on review of health measures in the WTO. In particular, how would legitimate and illegitimate health regulations be distinguished if the precautionary principle were adopted in the WTO?

It might be suggested that the Commission's Communication is entirely consistent with the SPS Agreement because it sees Article 5.7 as an implementation of the precautionary principle. To the extent that the EC might be prepared to confine its reliance on the precautionary principle to circumstances falling within Article 5.7, there need be no difficulty. However, it seems that the EC's ambitions for the precautionary principle go beyond the confines of Article 5.7—note the attempt in the *Hormones* case to invoke the precautionary principle without justifying the measures in question under Article 5.7—and so its wider implications must be addressed.

The Commission's conception of the precautionary principle is not one that rejects science as socially constructed. Rather, it seeks to prevent scientific uncertainty undermining the achievement of the higher level of protection that the EC has chosen for itself. To this end, the Communication stresses that, before the precautionary principle is invoked, scientific data relevant to the risks in question must be evaluated. Every effort should be made to conduct a risk assessment, with the realisation that it is not always possible to complete a comprehensive assessment of risk. Nevertheless, the Communication envisages that a report should in all cases be made assessing the available knowledge and information.[43] It is only where the scientific data are seriously deficient and a risk assessment cannot be accomplished by using what the Communication calls 'prudential techniques' for overcoming uncertainty[44] that decision-makers need to rely on the precautionary principle to act. Thus, the Commission's Communication constitutes a reasonably moderate statement of the precautionary principle, which disappointed some groups who saw the Communication as providing an emasculated version of precaution.[45] The

[41] On this, see: J Cameron 'The Precautionary Principle in International Law' in O'Riordan et al (eds) (n 3) 113.

[42] SPS Committee *Summary* (n 25) paras 5 (Canada), 6 (the US), 10 (Argentina).

[43] Commission *Communication on the Precautionary Principle* (n 17) point 5.1.

[44] The Communication lists the following prudential aspects: the use of animal models to establish potential effects in man, the use of body weight ranges to make inter-species comparisons, the use of a safety factor in evaluating ADI (acceptable daily intake) figures, not adopting ADI figures for substances recognised as genotoxic carcinogenic, and adopting ALARA (as low as reasonably achievable) as a basis for certain toxic contaminants: Commission *Communication on the Precautionary Principle* (n 17) point 5.1.3.

[45] A Jordan 'The Precautionary Principle in the European Union' in O'Riordan et al (eds) (n 3) 143, 158.

Communication is moderate because it does not see the precautionary principle as an *alternative* model of regulation which departs from the normal model of risk analysis, comprising risk assessment, risk management and risk communication. Rather, the Communication retains a preference for scientifically-based action, but provides *an avenue for action* where a risk evaluation cannot be completed because of uncertainty.

The US has expressed concern that the precautionary principle could be used to justify trade-restricting action based on a (minimally plausible[46]) public fear alone.[47] In light of the Commission's commitment to utilising a 'less theoretical and more concrete' perception of risk, in which public participation should be encouraged (at least in deciding whether to conduct an examination of the scientific information on a perceived risk)[48] this concern is understandable. Indeed, since its publication in 2000, the Communication has been accused of failing to provide the necessary checks and balances to prevent the precautionary principle being used unwisely, particularly when politicians are under pressure to respond to public outrage.[49]

A great deal has been written about public risk perception and how it differs from so-called 'expert' risk perception. As was noted in Chapter 4, some aspects of public risk perception which are not fully accounted for in expert assessments of risk (such as voluntariness, social distribution and dread), should be regarded as legitimate bases for risk management decisions. Acknowledging that some factors that contribute to the generation and intensity of public fears should be recognised as legitimate components of risk regulation is one thing. Finding that public fears should always prompt regulation, irrespective of the fears' bases, is quite another. Some notable commentators have, however, supported regulation responding to public fears, even if those fears are groundless. For example, although Howse recognises that democracy is about more than just pandering to public demands, he would ultimately support bending to popular will even in the face of contradictory scientific evidence, provided

[46] Minimally plausible because discussion of the PP may become absurd if it is taken to respond to implausible risks: see, eg, CR Sunstein 'Beyond the Precautionary Principle' (preliminary draft) (John M Olin Law & Economics Working Paper No 149 Chicago 2002) (available at <http://www.law.uchicago.edu/Lawecon/index.html> on 9 August 2002) 7.

[47] US Government *Submission on the Commission's Communication* (n 30) paras 9, 24. Cf Bentley who does not see any potential for regulation based only on public fears on the basis that the PP's reference to 'lack of full scientific certainty' does not mean 'in the absence of any scientific evidence at all' (P Bentley 'A Re-Assessment of Article XX, Paragraphs (b) and (g), of GATT 1994 in the Light of Growing Consumer and Environmental Concern about Biotechnology' (2000) 24 Fordham IntlLJ 107, 111–12), although the Communication does not make clear the minimum scientific data necessary to trigger the PP: JD Graham and S Hsia 'Europe's Precautionary Principle: Promise and Pitfalls' (2002) 5 J Risk Research 371, 381.

[48] Commission *Communication on the Precautionary Principle* (n 17) points 5.1.1, 6.2.

[49] Graham and Hsia (n 47) 384–85; Q Balzano and AR Sheppard 'The Influence of the Precautionary Principle on Science-Based Decision-Making: Questionable Applications to Risks of Radiofrequency Fields' (2002) 5 J Risk Research 351, 356, 358.

that that evidence had been 'considered'.[50] While it is true that regulations responding to public fear may well not have a protectionist intent, the SPS Agreement is not just concerned with eliminating protectionism masquerading as health protection. In stating that only health regulations with a scientific basis can justify limits on market access, the SPS Agreement goes well beyond simply uncovering covert protectionism: it opens markets that, according to scientific analysis of risks, are unnecessarily closed. If public fear is legitimated as a basis for regulation,[51] it must be acknowledged that this would curtail the SPS Agreement's trade liberalising potential. Whether one applauds[52] or decries this is another question; the point here is simply that the market-opening agenda would be restricted.

B THE PRECAUTIONARY PRINCIPLE AND THE WTO

The main reason why the WTO should not rush to embrace the precautionary principle with open arms is that, by itself, the precautionary principle does not provide a viable basis for distinguishing legitimate and illegitimate health regulations.[53] If one takes the view that trade-restricting regulatory action should be permitted, even though it has not been shown that the substance in question is harmful (or would be harmful at the levels of exposure that would be experienced), the basis on which the SPS Agreement currently distinguishes between legitimate and illegitimate health regulations is fatally undermined. If the work done since the Tokyo Round on reining-in non-tariff barriers is not to be unravelled, the

[50] See, eg: R Howse 'Democracy, Science, and Free Trade: Risk Regulation on Trial at the World Trade Organization' (2000) 98 MichLRev 2329, 2330, 2335, 2337, 2350. See also Bohanes (n 22) 329, 361; JD Fraiberg and MJ Trebilcock 'Risk Regulation: Technocratic and Democratic Tools for Regulatory Reform' (1998) 43 McGill LJ 835, 886. Such an attitude goes even beyond the importance given to public fears within the EU. While the ECJ views public fear as a legitimate *contributing* basis for regulatory action, it appears to be hesitant to endorse regulation based only on public concern: Case C–180/96 *UK v Commission* [1998] 4 ECR I–2265 ('*UK BSE*') and Case C–157/96 *R v MAFF, ex p The National Farmers' Union* [1998] ECR I–2211 ('*MAFF (BSE)*' paras 42–44) (where the ECJ played down the relative role of consumer concerns as a motivating factor).

[51] Note that governments commonly do not rely on public estimates of risk where they *underestimate* (rather than overestimate) risks (T Kuran and CR Sunstein 'Availability Cascades and Risk Regulation' (1999) Stanford LRev 683, 707) which raises the question of why governments should necessarily respond to public *overestimations* of risk.

[52] One would expect applause from those who object to the scientific justification criterion as limiting the ability of governments to respond to citizens' cultural or religious beliefs about food: eg, M Echols *Food Safety and the WTO: The Interplay of Culture, Science and Technology* (Kluwer Law International The Hague 2001) ch 1.

[53] Other commentators have other reasons for querying the PP: Sunstein 'Beyond the Precautionary Principle' (n 46) (the strong form of the PP is paralysing); Stewart (n 22) (strong versions of the PP do not provide a sound or desirable prescription for regulation); Cross (n 28) 859–60 (regulation imposed on the basis of the PP will often cause more health harm than good); Bohanes (n 22) 338 (noting that the precautionary principle makes the application of the least trade-restrictive discipline problematic).

precautionary principle would have to be accompanied by some other basis of review. Two obvious candidates present themselves: proportionality and procedural review. Each of these options has significant drawbacks, which should only be accepted if a very real need is demonstrated, but it is not clear that we really do need the precautionary principle in order to cope with scientific uncertainty.

1 Do We Need the Precautionary Principle?

The *raison d'être* of the precautionary principle is its status as a principle which permits (or, in stronger versions, mandates) protective action in circumstances of uncertainty. It should, however, be acknowledged that scientific risk assessment already provides a number of mechanisms to manage uncertainty. As the National Research Council's 1994 Report argued, 'uncertainty is always with us and . . . it is crucial to learn how to conduct risk assessment in the face of it.'[54] Because mainstream science and risk assessment techniques incorporate a fair degree of flexibility on the framing assumptions, techniques and policies that may be utilised, WTO Members already enjoy a degree of latitude on how they arrive at the 'facts' on which regulations are based.[55] The fact that the data set underlying a risk assessment is incomplete does not necessarily mean that the inquiry is no longer 'scientific'; rather, the appropriate handling of uncertainties is *part* of the scientific process of risk assessment.[56] In responding to the Commission's Communication in the WTO, Canada and the US questioned the need for the precautionary principle and stressed the fact that precaution has long been a feature of science-based approaches to regulation.[57] When the Communication was discussed in Codex, the US again queried the need for the precautionary principle, asking a number of questions seeking clarification of the distinction between what the Commission refers to as the 'prudential' aspects of risk assessment, and the precautionary principle.[58] According to the Commission, the prevailing uncertainties

[54] NRC *Science and Judgment in Risk Assessment* (National Academy Press Washington DC 1994) 161.

[55] Recall that risk estimates can vary by orders of magnitude, and that it is widely acknowledged that 'actual or probable human risks are not being predicted' (Joint FAO/WHO Expert Consultation *Application of Risk Analysis to Food Standards Issues* (WHO/FNU/FOS/95.3 Geneva 1995) 18); a water-tight representation of 'reality' is not expected in risk assessment.

[56] DA Wirth 'The Rule of Science in the Uruguay Round and NAFTA Trade Disciplines' (1994) 27 Cornell IntlLJ 817, 837. Note that the use of policy assumptions in risk assessment, and the role of precaution as part of risk assessment in circumstances of uncertainty is acknowledged by Codex: CAC *Working Principles for Risk Analysis in the Framework of the Codex Alimentarius* (26th Session 2003 ALINORM 03/41) (Appendix IV) para 11.

[57] SPS Committee *Summary* (n 25) paras 5 (Canada), 6 (the US).

[58] US Government *Submission on the Commission's Communication* (n 30).

may be such that a risk assessment cannot be completed at all, even using 'prudential' approaches.[59] It is this eventuality that, in the Commission's view, warrants recourse to the precautionary principle. It should, however, be recalled that, in addition to the techniques that scientific risk assessment offers for coping with uncertainty, Article 5.7 provides a clear and explicit avenue for regulating in such circumstances. It will be recalled that Article 5.7 provides that:

> [WTO Members may] provisionally adopt sanitary or phytosanitary measures on the basis of available pertinent information . . .. In such circumstances, Members shall seek to obtain the additional information necessary for a more objective assessment of risk and review the sanitary or phytosanitary measure accordingly within a reasonable period of time.

Why, then, is Article 5.7 not enough?

The Commission's position on Article 5.7 is not clear. Its model of the precautionary principle is, in many ways, consistent with Article 5.7. Like Article 5.7, the Communication also envisages measures adopted in the absence of proper scientific proof as being subject to review as scientific knowledge develops. However, where Article 5.7 actually imposes an obligation on the Member in question actively to seek out the additional information necessary for a more objective assessment of risk, the Communication merely encourages further scientific research and re-evaluation of measures as scientific information develops;[60] Article 5.7 is, in this respect, more demanding than the Commission's precautionary principle. The Communication does not, however, state that Article 5.7 and its model of the precautionary principle are coterminous. Rather, the Communication leaves open the possibility that the precautionary principle may lead to measures being adopted which would not be defended as Article 5.7 provisional measures in the WTO. This is precisely what happened in the *Hormones* case, when the EC relied on the precautionary principle while attempting to justify its regulations as 'non-provisional' measures complying with Articles 2.2 and 5.1 of the SPS Agreement. An unwillingness to defend measures as provisional measures under Article 5.7 is one reason why the existence of Article 5.7 may not allay concerns relating to the ability of Members to regulate in circumstances of uncertainty.[61] This reluctance to brand measures as provisional may, in turn, be related to some of the shortcomings of Article 5.7. Article 5.7 and Article 2.2 posit an identifiable dividing line between sufficient and

[59] Commission *Communication on the Precautionary Principle* (n 17) point 5.1.3.

[60] Commission *Communication on the Precautionary Principle* (n 17) point 6.3.5.

[61] Note that it has been suggested that the benchmark of scientific risk assessment applies to provisional measures as a certain level of objective evidence will be needed to show that they do not constitute a disguised restriction on trade (N Salmon 'A European Perspective on the Precautionary Principle, Food Safety and the Free Trade Imperative of the WTO' (2002) 27 European LRev 138, 147–48) although the argument is not wholly convincing.

insufficient scientific evidence, which is problematic. Moreover, Article 5.7 takes the view that uncertainty is always remediable by further work but the time limits set on provisional measures may mean that they cannot accommodate measures taken in circumstances of enduring uncertainty (although the EC is promoting the view that the Article's reference to review 'within a reasonable period of time' relates to the state of scientific knowledge and not the passage of time as such[62]). It should also be noted that, with the spread of science-based assessment in the WTO, a Member may be expected to provide a scientific justification in circumstances where Article 5.7 does not apply to assist in justifying action taken in circumstances of uncertainty (such as under GATT Article XX(b)).

Despite these limitations on Article 5.7, the significance of the provision should not be overlooked.[63] Nor should the ability of scientific risk assessment to handle significant areas of uncertainty be discounted. Moreover, because the meaning of the terms of Article 5.7 is not settled, it remains possible that the Appellate Body will interpret Article 5.7 in a way that minimises some of its potential shortcomings. In addition, the Appellate Body has indicated that a flexible view may be taken of the sufficiency of the scientific justification advanced where the consequences to human health may be dire.[64] As such, while the WTO system's approach to regulatory action taken in circumstances of uncertainty is not altogether clear, the absolute need for the precautionary principle, particularly within the SPS Agreement, has not been demonstrated.

The fact that a pressing need for the precautionary principle has not been demonstrated is one justification for questioning the wisdom of introducing that principle into the WTO. The other, more pressing, reason to hesitate relates to the additional bases of review that would be required to accompany the precautionary principle if it is to avoid functioning as an invitation to abuse or expand health-based non-tariff barriers.

2 Problems Associated with Reviewing Health Measures Based on the Precautionary Principle

The precautionary principle is not a substantive principle—it does not direct a particular outcome.[65] Rather, when it is used internationally to

62 Commission *Communication on the Precautionary Principle* (n 17) point 4.

63 Note that even some commentators firmly in the environmental camp have questioned the need for the precautionary principle, given the existence of Article 5.7: eg, S Charnovitz 'The Supervision of Health and Biosafety Regulation by World Trade Rules' (2000) 13 Tulane EnvtlLJ 271, 292.

64 *Hormones* AB Report (n 6) para 124. Note also the suggestion that scientific justification is relative to the available scientific information: Wirth (n 56) 826.

65 Fisher 'Is the Precautionary Principle Justiciable?' (n 23) 319.

permit otherwise unlawful action, it gives regulators permission to act without supporting scientific evidence by privileging the avoidance of possible harm. Because the precautionary principle is not concerned with the actual decision reached, substantive review (such as that provided for by the SPS Agreement where the actual decision reached is reviewed) becomes much more difficult. The precautionary principle cannot function as a principle upon which to distinguish legitimate from illegitimate health regulations. This is because the only measures which the precautionary principle might condemn are those that do not go far enough—such as a failure to act—rather than those that go too far. In other words, the precautionary principle cannot tell us that trade-limiting action should not have been taken, and this raises significant problems for a trade regime committed to minimising health-based non-tariff barriers.

(a) Uncertainty and the precautionary principle within Europe

Underlying the Commission's Communication is a subtle message: the precautionary principle is nothing new and is not a wholesale challenge to understandings of scientific rationality or to the prevailing model of risk analysis. Those curious about how the type of review that the Commission's blend of science-based and precautionary risk regulation might generate would do well to look at the ECJ's own jurisprudence as the ECJ has had a long experience with reviewing health-based measures. Moreover, since 1993, the EC Treaty has included an explicit reference to the precautionary principle.[66] Article 174(1) (ex Article 130r(1)) of the EC Treaty (which was introduced by the Maastrict Treaty in 1993) states, *inter alia,* that Community policy on the environment shall contribute to protecting health, and Article 174(2) (ex Article 130r(2)) states that Community policy on the environment should aim at a high level of protection, that Community policy should be based on the precautionary principle and on the principle that preventative action should be taken, and that the polluter should pay. Here we see the bridge from the precautionary principle as a purely environmental principle to one relevant to health protection being built. The Commission's later Communication represents the consolidation of the effort begun in Article 174 to extend the precautionary principle outside the environment and to apply it to health protection.

[66] Consolidated Version of the Treaty Establishing the European Community (available at <http://europa.eu.int/eur-lex/en/treaties/dat/ec_cons_treaty_en.pdf>) (the EC Treaty). The consolidated version incorporates amendments since the treaty was originally signed (Treaty Establishing the European Economic Community (Treaty of Rome) (25 March 1957)). The reference to the PP was introduced by the Treaty on European Union (Maastrict 7 February 1992, entered into force 1 November 1993).

Given the importance of the precautionary principle, it is somewhat surprising that it has not attracted more discussion in the ECJ.[67] Until recently, the most sustained discussion of the precautionary principle within the ECJ has been connected with the cases arising from the bovine spongiform encephalopathy (BSE) outbreak and its aftermath, especially the French government's refusal to comply with the Community authorities' decision to lift the ban on British beef.[68] Not surprisingly, then, it is to the BSE cases that the Commission turned when it responded to the US's concerns that the Commission's Communication had not defined the precautionary principle. The Commission pointed to the *MAFF (BSE)* case, in which the National Farmers' Union and others challenged various measures adopted by the UK's Ministry of Agriculture, Fisheries and Food pursuant to a Commission Decision on emergency measures to protect against BSE. In that case, the court explained the conditions for the application of the precautionary principle as follows:

> When there is uncertainty as to the existence or extent of risks to human health, the institutions may take protective measures without having to wait until the reality and seriousness of those risks becomes fully apparent.[69]

This description of the circumstances in which the principle may be invoked does not, however, reveal a great deal about how the ECJ will conduct its review of measures taken in reliance on the precautionary principle. Other cases do expand on the type of review that can be expected.

In his Opinion in the *NFU (BSE)* case, in which the National Farmers' Union challenged the French government's refusal to lift the French ban on the import of beef, veal and bovine products from the UK, AG Mischo made the following statements:

> Judicial review of the observance of the precautionary principle must be exercised with caution.

[67] The PP is, however, frequently mentioned in a great many cases without attracting any real analysis; see, eg: Case C–9/00 *Palin Granit Oy* (ECJ 18 April 2002) para 23 and AG Jacobs (17 January 2002) para 25 (PP relevant to the interpretation of the word 'waste'); Case T–326/99 R *Olivieri v Commission* [2000] ECR II–1985 para 77; Case C–248/99 P *France v Monsanto* (ECJ 8 January 2002) para 66 and AG Alber (29 May 2001) paras 92, 120; Case C–514/99 *France v Commission* [2000] ECR I–4705 para 22; Case C–6/99 *Greenpeace (France) v Ministère de l'Agriculture et de la Pêche* [2000] ECR I–1651 paras 19, 40, 44; Case C–318/98 *Criminal Proceedings against Giancarlo Fornasar and ors* [2000] ECR I–4785 para 37 and AG Cosmas para 33; Case C–352/98 *Laboratoires pharmaceutiques Bergaderm SA v Commission* [2000] I–5291 paras 23, 38; Case C–94/98 *R v The Licensing Authority* [1999] ECR I–8789 AG La Pergola para 29; Case C–67/97 *Criminal Proceedings against Bluhme* [1998] ECR I-8033.

[68] For a list of the measures lifting the ban, see AG Mischo's Opinion in Case C-241/01 *National Farmers' Union v Secrétariat général du gouvernement* (ECJ 2 July 2002) ('*NFU (BSE)*') para 2.

[69] *Comments from the European Commission Services to the Codex Secretariat* (available at <europa.int/comm/food/fs/ifsi/eupositions/ccgp/ccgp01_en.html> on 14 August 2002) referring to *MAFF (BSE)* (n 50) para 63.

> Since that principle is to be applied in situations of great uncertainty, we cannot expect the courts to impose their own convictions, the possible basis of which is difficult to discern, moreover, in the realm of scientific problems.[70]

AG Mischo added that the question was not one of removing the precautionary principle from the sphere of judicial review, but merely of recognising that the courts can only exercise minimal review 'since the political authorities must be granted a broad discretion.'[71] Encapsulated in these statements are a number of the central themes that define ECJ review of Community health regulations. The ECJ is concerned to protect the broad discretion of the Community institutions and has stressed that the Community legislature enjoys a wide discretionary power in matters concerning the common agricultural policy[72] and matters concerning social policy.[73] The ECJ is particularly conscious of only exercising light review when the Community institution has, in the process of forming its policy, had to evaluate complex technical or economic data.[74] In general, the ECJ has no desire to engage with the factual basis of Community action. As the court has remarked, 'where a Community authority is called upon, in the performance of its duties, to make complex assessments, it enjoys a wide measure of discretion, the exercise of which is subject to a limited judicial review in the course of which the Community judicature may not substitute its assessment of the facts for the assessment made by the authority concerned.'[75] This reticence is, as AG Mischo's comments show, compounded when the prevalence of uncertainty means that the action is based on the precautionary principle.

The Commission's Communication emphasises that regulation within Europe is not anti-science, but a closer examination of another case arising out of the French refusal to accept British beef shows just how limited the ECJ's oversight of scientific evidence is, especially when the precautionary principle is invoked. In the *UK BSE* case,[76] the UK sought annulment of the same Commission Decision (96/239/EC) that was challenged by the National Farmers' Union in the *MAFF (BSE)* case. In rejecting the UK's request for annulment, the court confirmed that science plays an important role in regulatory decision-making. It is, however, also clear from that

[70] *NFU (BSE)* (n 68) (AG Mischo) paras 73–74.On regulation in circumstances of uncertainty, see also Case C-180/96 R *UK v Commission* [1996] ECR II 1-3903.

[71] *NFU (BSE)* (n 68) (AG Mischo) para 75.

[72] Case C–331/88 *R v MAFF, ex p Fedesa* [1990] ECR I-4023 ('*Fedesa*') paras 8, 14; Case C–189/2001 *Jippes v Minister van Landbouw, Natuurbeheer en Visserij* [2001] ECR I-5689 ('*Jippes*') para 80.

[73] Case C–84/94 *UK v Council* [1996] ECR I-5755 ('*UK–Working Time Directive*') para 58.

[74] Case 138/79 *SA Roquette Frères v Council* [1980] ECR 3333 ('*Roquette*') para 25; *UK–Working Time Directive* (n 73) para 58; *Fedesa* (n 72) para 11 (AG Mischo); Case C–120/97 *Upjohn Ltd v The Licensing Authority* [1999] ECR I-223 ('*Upjohn*') para 34.

[75] *Upjohn* (n 74) para 34.

[76] *UK BSE* (n 50).

case that the court does not expect the Community institutions coming before it always to be in a position to point to comprehensive scientific evidence demonstrating a health risk. According to the ECJ's vision, science is an integral part of Community regulatory decision-making, but regulatory decision-making can actively respond to the silences in scientific evidence—its uncertainties and developing suspicions—as well as to its positive findings of hazard.[77] In the *UK BSE* case, the UK challenged the Commission's decision to ban the export of beef and veal and derived products to other Member States and to non-Member countries. Even though transmissibility to humans had not been definitively established, the Commission's decision was supported on the basis that a risk of transmission *could not be excluded* and the resulting uncertainty created serious concern among consumers.[78] The UK challenged the decision on a number of grounds, including breach of the principle of proportionality (on the basis that the decision was inappropriate for the purpose of protecting public or animal health as adequate measures had already been adopted by the UK and the Community which had been shown to be effective).[79] What is striking about the way in which the Commission argued its case was its willingness to rely on *uncertainty* as supporting its decision. Rather than attempting to present its scientific evidence as disclosing positive evidence of risk, the Commission openly relied on uncertainty. For example, regarding the ban on live exports, the Commission argued that:

> [T]he contested decision is justified . . . on account of the reassessment of the significance of existing *doubts*, particularly in relation to the presence of the BSE agent in young animals, the *uncertainties* associated with the system for tracing animals and identifying those that were at risk, the *lack of certainty* regarding the age at which the animal will be slaughtered and the risk of vertical or horizontal transmission.[80]

The ECJ endorsed this reliance on uncertainty by regarding it as opening up a field of discretion which demands light review. Having noted that, when the contested decision was made, there was great uncertainty as to the risks posed by live animals, bovine meat and derived products, the court said that 'where there is uncertainty as to the existence or extent of risks to human health, the institutions may take protective measures without having to wait until the reality and seriousness of those risks

[77] Other cases also show that the ECJ regards science as a tool for regulation, not as its master: *UK–Working Time Directive* (n 73) paras 166–67 (AG Léger) (while Community action may be based on scientific data, 'scientific research cannot constitute the sole basis on which the Community legislature can take action and a measure cannot therefore be challenged, particularly in the field of social policy, for making no reference . . . to grounds justified by scientific evidence.'

[78] Preamble to Commission Decision (EC) 96/239 on emergency measures to protect against bovine spongiform encephalopathy [1996] OJ L78/47.

[79] The UK's fifth plea was summarised by the ECJ: *UK BSE* (n 50) para 76.

[80] *UK BSE* (n 50) para 85 (emphasis added).

become fully apparent.'[81] In order to support its approach, the court referred to Article 174 of the EC Treaty, which entrenches the precautionary principle as a basis for Community action on health and the environment.[82] In then reviewing the live animal export ban, the ECJ gave full effect to its promise and effectively found that, because the scientific evidence had not proved safety, the measure passed review:

> [T]he scientific uncertainty concerning the manner in which BSE is transmitted, particularly as regards its transmissibility through the mother, coupled with the lack of a system for tagging animals and controlling their movements, has meant that *there can be no certainty* that the mother of a calf is completely free from BSE or, even if she is, that the calf itself is completely unaffected by the disease.[83]

Accordingly, the court found that the ban on live exports could not be regarded as manifestly inappropriate (the standard by which the proportionality of Community action is judged).[84] Similarly, the court found that the ban on export of bovine meat could not be regarded as manifestly inappropriate because, on the basis of the statement of a *minority* member of the Community's own Scientific Veterinary Committee, it was not possible to *exclude* the risk of transmission through muscle meat.[85] One suspects that AG Tesauro was not exaggerating when he said that, in the absence of 'irrefutable scientific evidence', the court lacks any basis on which to assess the adequacy or otherwise of the measure at the time it was decided on.[86]

More recently, however, the Court of First Instance (CFI) has retreated somewhat from this high water mark of deference to Community action and has suggested that some very significant constraints may be imposed on Community regulators.[87] In *Pfizer Animal Health v Council*, Pfizer challenged the withdrawal of approval for certain antibiotics previously used

[81] *UK BSE* (n 50) paras 98–99. See also Case T–13/99 *Pfizer Animal Health v Council* [2002] ECR II-3305 (*'Pfizer'*) para 139.

[82] *UK BSE* (n 50) para 101.

[83] *UK BSE* (n 50) para 102 (emphasis added).

[84] *UK BSE* (n 50) para 103.

[85] *UK BSE* (n 50) paras 105–106.

[86] *UK BSE* (n 50) 2228 (AG Tesauro). Note that AG Tesauro's Opinion also applies to *MAFF (BSE)* (n 50) (where the court's judgment contains a number of similar points relating to the breadth of the Community's measure of discretion, especially in circumstances of uncertainty: paras 39, 41).

[87] The ECJ has also integrated much of the approach one sees in *Pfizer* in its case law on review of Member State health regulations. For example, in Case C–192/01 *Commission v Denmark* (ECJ 23 September 2003), we see much that is familiar from the European Commission's *Communication on the Precautionary Principle* (n 17): a Member State must show that there is a real risk to public health; a detailed assessment of risk is required; if, following such an assessment, scientific uncertainty persists, the precautionary principle permits the Member State to take protective measures; a purely hypothetical approach to risk is not permitted: paras 46–51.

as additives in animal feed.[88] Approval was withdrawn because there was thought to be a risk that antibiotic resistance might be transferred from animals to humans. It was conceded by the Council that, at the time the measure was adopted, the development of such transferred antibiotic resistance in humans had not been scientifically established.[89] Thus, the ability of the Community to regulate in circumstances of uncertainty was squarely before the CFI. The CFI sought to emphasise that recourse to the precautionary principle does not allow action to be taken where risks are 'purely hypothetical'.[90] According to the court, while the precautionary principle does allow action in respect of risks that have not been scientifically *confirmed* or *fully demonstrated*, those risks must still be 'adequately backed up by the scientific data available at the time when the measure was taken.'[91] The court was, however, not simply faced with a case of scientific uncertainty because, in regulating, the Council had rejected the advice of a Community scientific committee that the relevant antibiotics did not constitute an immediate risk to public health. In finding that the Council did not make an error in rejecting the committee's advice, the CFI said a Community institution is free to disregard the opinion of a Community scientific committee provided that it explains why it is disregarding that opinion and can point to other scientific evidence of commensurate probative value on which it relies.[92]

In the context of other decisions of the CFI and ECJ,[93] the *Pfizer* case can be seen as marking the maturation of the court's developing approach to reconciling the precautionary principle and scientific regulatory approaches, but care should be taken not to overstate the significance of the *Pfizer* decision. The CFI did reaffirm the essentially narrow scope of judical review of Community action and confirmed that the Community institutions enjoy a broad discretion when determining the level of acceptable risk and making complex factual assessments in the performance of its duties:

> It follows that, in this case, in which the Community institutions were required to undertake a scientific risk assessment and to evaluate highly complex scientific and technical facts, judicial review of the way in which they did so must be limited. The Community judicature is not entitled to substitute its assessment

[88] *Pfizer* (n 81). Note also the parallel case of Case T–70/99 *Alpharma Inc v Council* [2002] ECR–II 3495. The judgment in *Pfizer* is very long, but a summary of the CFI's conclusions is given in J Scott 'European Regulation of GMOs and the WTO' (2003) 9 Columbia JEurL 213, 220–23.

[89] *Pfizer* (n 81) para 41.

[90] *Pfizer* (n 81) para 143.

[91] *Pfizer* (n 81) paras 144, 146. Note, though, that it is not clear what this minimal scientific credibility criterion actually requires.

[92] *Pfizer* (n 81) para 199.

[93] Eg, Case C–236/01 *Monsanto Agricoltura & ors v Presidenza del Consiglio dei Ministri & ors* (ECJ 9 September 2003) (*'Monsanto') and* Case C–192/01 *Commission v Denmark* (ECJ 23 September 2003).

measure is proportionate to the level of protection sought (loose proportionality).[101] In discussing proportionality, the Communication states that '[m]easures based on the precautionary principle *must not be disproportionate to the desired level of protection* and must not aim at zero risk, something which rarely exists.'[102] By stressing the relationship between the measure and the desired level of protection, the Communication focuses on loose proportionality, not strict proportionality. Accordingly, if the promise of proportionality in the Commission's Communication is limited to this type of loose proportionality, it will not provide the necessary brake on the precautionary principle because such loose proportionality review does not enquire into the level of protection chosen when protective action is taken, notwithstanding a lack of knowledge about the supposed hazard. Only strict proportionality review can accomplish this.

While it is true to say that the Communication certainly focuses on loose proportionality review (ensuring that the measure is proportionate to the level of protection chosen), the regulation establishing the European Food Safety Authority (EFSA) raises the possibility that strict proportionality might still be envisaged as a limit on the use of the precautionary principle. Article 7.2 of that Regulation stipulates that measures adopted on the basis of the precautionary principle 'shall be proportionate *and* no more restrictive of trade than is required to achieve the higher level of health protection chosen in the Community.'[103] By using the word 'and', this passage implicitly distinguishes between proportionality and the least trade-restrictive-measure discipline (loose proportionality), thus raising the possibility that the envisaged proportionality might be strict proportionality. While this possibility is technically open on the face of the EFSA Regulation, some fairly active interpretation is required to derive a strict proportionality requirement, and so one should not leap to the conclusion that strict proportionality review is envisaged. The Communication does, however, definitely extend beyond loose proportionality review in one respect: it stipulates that measures must not aim at zero risk. Such a prohibition on zero risk policies would at least prevent the WTO Members from instituting extreme measures to achieve zero risk and, in so doing, would provide a limitation not currently provided for in the WTO—in the *Salmon* case, the Appellate Body made it clear that WTO Members were free to pursue a zero risk policy.[104] Just preventing the pursuit of zero risk is, however, not enough. Because the precautionary principle permits trade-limiting regulatory action where the anticipated causal chain of harm has not been established, without strict proportionality review there is nothing to

[101] McNelis (n 98) 550.

[102] Commission *Communication on the Precautionary Principle* (n 17) point 6.3.1 (emphasis added).

[103] EFSA Regulation (n 37) (emphasis added).

[104] *Australia–Measures Affecting Importation of Salmon* WT/DS18/AB/R AB Report adopted 6 November 1998 para 197.

prevent a country adopting exceedingly risk-averse policies which, whether or not deliberately protectionist, limit trading opportunities.

Loose proportionality review is useful, but cannot provide a sufficiently strong basis of review to prevent the precautionary principle leading to proliferation of health-based non-tariff barriers. If the price of the precautionary principle is to be *strict* proportionality review, should we accept it? In considering this question, it is worth taking an excursion into the jurisprudence of the ECJ as it has had some experience with proportionality review.

(b) Proportionality review in the EU

(i) Proportionality review of Community action Proportionality is a basic principle of EU law, and is one to which both the Member States and the Community are subject. But it means different things in different situations. In a detailed study of proportionality, Takis Tridimas writes, 'proportionality is a flexible principle which is used in different contexts to protect different interests and entails varying degrees of judicial scrutiny.'[105] In particular, when the ECJ is reviewing trade-limiting health measures put in place by a Member State, proportionality is applied aggressively as a 'market integration mechanism' in order to promote trade between the states. On the other hand, where the proportionality norm is applied to review of Community policy measures, the court is concerned to give full credit to the decisions of the Community, subject to the rights of the individual being respected, and a lighter version of proportionality prevails.[106] For present purposes, the significance of the ECJ's proportionality principle lies in the ECJ's reluctance to impose strict proportionality review even on Member States which are relying on Article 30 of the EC Treaty to defend regulations that detract from the single market, a circumstance in which one might have expected to see strict proportionality review in action.

According to the ECJ, in order to satisfy the proportionality principle, there are three tests to be applied.[107] Firstly, measures adopted by the Community must not 'exceed the limits of what is appropriate and necessary in order to attain the objectives legitimately pursued by the legislation in question'. Secondly, 'when there is a choice between several appropriate measures recourse must be had to the least onerous'. Thirdly, 'the disadvantages caused must not be disproportionate to the aims pursued.' Almost identical tripartite formulations of proportionality are

[105] T Tridimas *The General Principles of EC Law* (OUP Oxford 1999) 93.
[106] Tridimas (n 105) 90.
[107] *Jippes* (n 72) para 81. On the three elements of proportionality review of Community action, see: C Henkel 'The Allocation of Powers in the EU: A Closer Look at the Principle of Subsidiarity' (2002) 20 Berkeley JIntlL 359, 375–76.

found in other health-related cases.[108] Assessing whether the disadvantages of a measure are disproportionate to the aims it serves suggests a kind of strict proportionality review because it allows the reviewer to decide whether the regulator is overreacting to the health threat. If the threat is small or highly speculative, the disadvantages may be disproportionate to the limited or speculative gains. It is, however, exceedingly rare for the ECJ to dispute the Community's evaluation of whether the benefits of a measure outweigh its disadvantages.[109] The ECJ is reluctant to utilise the third limb of proportionality (strict proportionality) principally because this evaluation constitutes a political balance which falls squarely within the Community's discretion. Generally, when the proportionality of Community action is considered, the ECJ has limited its assessment to determining whether the action was 'manifestly inappropriate having regard to the objective which the competent institution is to pursue.'[110]

(ii) Proportionality review of Member State action Although the ECJ has been prepared to exert a more vigorous form of proportionality review over the Member States, it has still shied away from strict proportionality review. Article 30 (ex 36) of the EC Treaty gives the Member States the right to restrict trade on health grounds. The second sentence of Article 30 seeks to prevent protectionist abuse of the right to restrict trade by providing that prohibitions or restrictions must not 'constitute a means of arbitrary discrimination or a disguised restriction on trade'.[111] According to the ECJ, the principle of proportionality 'underlies' this second sentence of Article 30 and prevents the trade-limiting potential of Article 30 from abuse.[112] In a line of cases, beginning with *Sandoz*, proportionality is very

[108] *Alpharma* (n 88) para 324; *Pfizer* (n 81) para 411; *UK BSE* (n 50) para 96; Case 265/87 *Hermann Schräder HS Kraftfutter GmbH & Co KG v Hauptzollamt Gronau* [1989] ECR 2237 ('*Schräder*') para 21; *Fedesa* (n 72) para 13; Joined Cases C–133/93, C–300/93, C–362/93 *Crispoltoni v Fattoria Autonoma Tabacchi and Donatab Srl* [1994] I-4863 ('*Crispoltoni*') para 41. For a narrower statement of proportionality, see: *UK–Working Time Directive* (n 73) para 57.

[109] For an example of (limited and supportive) engagement, see: *MAFF (BSE)* (n 50) para 57 (the extension of the export ban to third countries was a 'relatively small price to pay'); Case 5/73 *Balkan-Import-Export GmbH v Hauptzollamt Berlin-Packhof* [1973] ECR 1091, para 23 (a non-health case finding that the burdens imposed by the Council on traders were not manifestly out of proportion to the object in view).

[110] *UK BSE* (n 50) para 97. The same 'manifestly inappropriate' formula is expressed, with minor variations in the text, elsewhere: *Jippes* (n 72) para 82; Case C-27/95 *Woodspring District Council v Bakers of Nailsea Ltd* [1998] ECR I-1847 para 38; *Crispoltoni* (n 108) para 42; *Fedesa* (n 72) para 14; *Schräder* (n 108) para 22.

[111] This purpose was confirmed by the ECJ in Case 40/82 *Commission v UK* [1982] ECR 2793 ('*UK Poultry I*') para 36.

[112] Case 174/82 *Criminal Proceedings against Sandoz BV* [1983] ECR 2445 para 18; confirmed in: Case 227/82 *Criminal Proceedings against van Bennekom* [1983] ECR 3883 para 39; Case 274/84 *The State v Leon Motte* [1985] ECR 3887 para 23; Case 304/84 *Ministère Public v Claude Müller* [1986] ECR 1511 para 23; Case 178/84 *Commission v Germany* [1987] ECR 1227 ('*German Beer*') para 44; Case C–42/90 *Criminal Proceedings against Jean-Claude Bellon* [1990] ECR I-4863 para 14; Case C–400/96 *Criminal Proceedings against Jean Harpegnies* [1998] ECR I-5121 para 34; Case C–55/99 *Commission v France* [2000] ECR I-11499 para 29.

closely tied to the concept of necessity. The court has said that the principle of proportionality means that only restrictions on trade that are *necessary* to achieve the legitimate objective need be tolerated.[113] As such, a form of loose proportionality review that addresses the relationship between the aim and the measure is the most prominent form of proportionality review of Member State action.[114]

It is clear from the ECJ's case law that the Member States are subject to the loose, necessity form of proportionality—a great many cases emphasise the least trade-restrictive alternative (LTA) test. It is, however, not entirely clear whether the Member States are ever subject to the strict form of proportionality analysis under Article 30. It seems that, while loose proportionality and strict proportionality can both be identified in the ECJ's case law,[115] the court has tended not to distinguish between the less restrictive alternative test (loose proportionality) and strict proportionality.[116] The reason why it matters whether Member States are subject to strict proportionality review is that it gives the reviewer a much more extensive platform from which to consider the merits of national regulatory strategies. If a reviewer can say that the national authorities are overreacting to a perceived threat, or that the burdens they are imposing on free movement are simply not justified by the health aims being pursued, the remaining national freedom to regulate is quite obviously much more constrained. In general, once the legitimacy of the health aim has been established, the court tends to focus on the least trade-restrictive alternative (LTA) review. But in cases where the court doubts the health aims, one does find remarks suggesting strict proportionality review. For example, in the first *UK Poultry* case, the ECJ did not credit the UK's measures to combat Newcastle disease with being a seriously considered health policy and went on to find that 'in the situation actually prevailing, . . . the possibility of infection by imported poultry products would be so much due to sheer hazard that it cannot justify a complete prohibition of imports from Member States which admit the use of vaccine.'[117] In that passage, the ECJ clearly indicates that it regards the UK's action as a disproportionate

[113] This statement is found in the cases cited in n 112 (above) at the same paras.

[114] Note, though, that the ECJ's vigorous approach in promoting labelling as a less restrictive alternative comes close to imposing strict proportionality review because, in promoting labelling, the court is treading a very fine line between telling a Member State that labelling will achieve the state's objectives and telling the state that, in order to facilitate trade, it should be satisfied with the level of protection afforded by labelling. On the ECJ's promotion of labelling, see: JHH Weiler 'The Constitution of the Common Market Place: Text and Context in the Evolution of the Free Movement of Goods' in P Craig and G de Búrca (eds) *The Evolution of EU Law* (OUP Oxford 1999) 349, 368.

[115] G de Búrca 'The Principle of Proportionality and its Application in EC Law' (1993) 13 YEL 105, 113.

[116] Tridimas (n 105) 92 referring to AG van Gerven in Case C–159/90 *SPUC v Grogan* [1991] ECR I-4685 and AG Mischo in *Fedesa* (n 72) as supporting the tripartite division.

[117] *UK Poultry I* (n 111) paras 38, 44.

response (an overreaction) to the threat. Similarly, in the follow up *UK Poultry* case on the equivalent Northern Ireland restrictions, the court simply found that the risk to the poultry flock of Northern Ireland was 'extremely slight' and could not justify a complete prohibition of imports from Member States permitting vaccination.[118] Other statements suggesting that full proportionality review in health cases might be possible can be found in *UK UHT I*,[119] the *France–Italian Wine* case,[120] *Denkavit II*,[121] the *German Beer* case,[122] and the *Greece–Butter* case.[123] The point about the possibility of strict proportionality review should not be laboured. Suffice it to note that, although in most cases proportionality review of Article 30 health cases amounts to LTA review—and is therefore akin to necessity review in the WTO—it seems that the European law does contain at least the prospect of strict proportionality review which carries with it far greater potential for merits review of the level of protection being sought.

(iii) Strict proportionality review and the WTO The precautionary principle raises the possibility that the regulatory authorities in particularly risk-averse societies will act quickly to restrict trade whenever there is a slight possibility of harm, irrespective of the damage done to other WTO Members. Strict proportionality review promises to short-circuit this scenario by giving the reviewer power to judge whether the actions of the regulator are disproportionate to the threat at hand. As such, strict proportionality review constitutes a significant incursion into the right of WTO Members to determine their own level of risk aversion through the 'appropriate level of protection' mechanism.

The sovereign right to determine one's own level of protection is a central tenet of the WTO's oversight of national health measures. It, more than any other provision, secures for WTO Members the right to determine their

[118] Case 40/82 *Commission v UK* [1984] ECR 283 ('*UK Poultry II*') para 16.

[119] Case 124/81 *Commission v UK* [1983] ECR 203 ('*UK UHT I*') para 33 (the ECJ concluded that the UK's dealer licensing requirements constituted an impediment to free movement that was disproportionate in relation to the objective pursued).

[120] Case 42/82 *Commission v France* [1983] ECR 1013 ('*France–Italian Wine*') para 54 (the ECJ expressed necessity and the proportionality of the objectives and the obstacles to trade as separate criteria).

[121] Case 73/84 *Denkavit Futtermittel GmbH v Land Nordrhein-Westfalen* [1985] ECR 1013 ('*Denkavit II*') para 14 (the ECJ stated that the health inspection measures must be reasonably proportionate to the aim pursued *and* satisfy the LTA test).

[122] *German Beer* (n 112) 1257 (AG Slynn said it was disproportionate to exclude the whole of society from beer other than nationally produced beer because some additives may constitute a risk for a person drinking in excess of 1000 litres of beer per year or for an alcoholic already suffering from cirrhosis of the liver).

[123] Case 205/89 *Commission v Greece* [1991] ECR I-1361 ('*Greek Butter*') (AG van Gerven stated that Greek laws requiring the production of a health certificate for imported pasteurised butter had to satisfy the necessity test and also had to be proportionate to the objective sought to be attained).

own health policies and priorities, without interference from the WTO. All of the other disciplines and obligations are secondary to this fundamental right. Strict proportionality review would make a Member's chosen level of protection reviewable and would, thereby, inevitably and drastically alter the current balance of rights and responsibilities. Given that Article 5.7 provides for provisional measures and science policies are an accepted feature of mainstream risk assessments, WTO Members should consider carefully whether the *additional* latitude that the precautionary principle may allow is worth sacrificing the hitherto inviolable right to set one's own level of protection. The reluctance of the ECJ to impose strict proportionality review highlights just how significant this step would be in the WTO. The constitutional structure of the European Union is such that, when the Member States limit intra-Community trade on health grounds, intrusive review is *prima facie* warranted. Unlike the Member States of the European Union, whose mutual commitment to market integration means that any market limiting action is to be greeted with suspicion, the extent of WTO Members' mutual commitments is more limited. The founding principle of the WTO is that liberalised trade is of mutual benefit. Thus, while WTO Members are engaged in efforts to liberalise trade, there is no overarching political and economic unification project of the kind that characterises the EU. Where the EU is engaged in building an economic and political community, WTO Members are only committed to liberalising trade by adhering to various disciplines and exchanging concessions. If the ECJ hesitates at the brink of strict proportionality review even when Member States' actions compromise the unification project, it is hard to imagine why the invasion into national choices that accompanies strict proportionality would be appropriate in the WTO.

4 The Precautionary Principle and Procedural Review

Strict proportionality review is not attractive in the WTO because it would open the door to *more* (not less) extensive review of national regulatory preferences. Utilising strict proportionality review would require WTO panels to engage in weighing the costs and benefits of regulatory action. It is the desire to avoid giving the WTO this responsibility that has contributed to efforts to develop a procedural model of review.[124] Procedural models of review focus on *how* the national regulation was formed, not its substantive content. Like proportionality review, procedural review offers

[124] See, eg: M Trebilcock and J Soloway 'International Trade Policy and Domestic Food Safety Regulation: The Case for Substantial Deference by the WTO Dispute Settlement Body under the SPS Agreement' in DLM Kennedy and JD Southwick (eds) *The Political Economy of International Trade Law* (CUP Cambridge UK 2002) 537, 556.

a justiciable limit to recourse to the precautionary principle. By ensuring that discretionary decision-making is transparent and accountable, procedural review promises an alternative means by which to constrain discretionary decision-making. Utilising procedural review as a means to constrain the precautionary principle requires careful consideration in the WTO context because it promises review which allows recourse to the precautionary principle, while preventing its abuse, but does not extend the scope of review in the way that strict proportionality review would.

This section begins by setting out some proposals for procedural review in the WTO and then considers some of the limitations of procedural review, particularly in relation to controlling recourse to the precautionary principle. In particular, it is suggested that procedural guarantees are, by themselves inadequate. The section then refers to US judicial review case law in order to show that the procedural review's promise of deference can be more apparent than real. It is further argued that, if a procedural approach to review were adopted in the WTO, there is a risk that diversity among WTO Members would be further eroded by the identification of a single 'correct' way to conduct a risk assessment. Finally, it is argued that the underpinning logic of procedural review, which was crafted in closed domestic system, does not necessarily retain its coherence when applied to the WTO.

(a) Proposals for procedural review in the WTO

Procedural review is attractive to those concerned that WTO rules unnecessarily limit the ability of Members to regulate as they see fit because it takes, as its point of departure, an explicit commitment to non-intrusive review. By refusing to second-guess the decisions and evaluations of regulators, procedural review is regarded as necessarily less intrusive than substantive review. While this claim is problematic, its basic logic does have some validity and proposals for procedural review in the WTO deserve further consideration.

In 1998, Fraiberg and Trebilcock proposed a proceduralised system for review of domestic risk regulation. Their proceduralised model comprised: mandatory risk assessment (with explicit articulation of uncertainties and provision for a notice and comment procedure);[125] mandatory cost–benefit analysis (also with explicit assumptions and provision for public comment);[126] and minimal judicial review, which, with some exceptions, would be confined to review of procedure.[127] Fraiberg and Trebilcock's model also included 'blue ribbon' peer review to break any

[125] Fraiberg and Trebilcock (n 50) 872–74.
[126] Fraiberg and Trebilcock (n 50) 875–76.
[127] Fraiberg and Trebilcock (n 50) 884–85.

deadlocks on the risk assessment and cost–benefit analysis. By focusing on procedure, judicial review would be deferential, although the court could overturn the regulation if it were patently unreasonable and could also depart from its procedural mandate in considering the equitable aspects of the measure (for example, risk distribution across different groups of society). Four years later, and this time writing with Julie Soloway, Trebilcock proposed a very similar procedural system for use in the WTO. This system also comprised mandatory scientific risk assessment, mandatory cost–benefit analysis, notice and comment procedures, blue ribbon peer review, and minimal judicial review.[128]

Another developed proposal for procedural review has been offered by Jan Bohanes. Bohanes was concerned that strictly scientific criteria are problematic from a welfare maximisation and public choice perspective. According to Bohanes, democratically legitimised decisions should be respected even if they are incompatible with scientific analysis.[129] Accordingly, Bohanes was sympathetic to the precautionary principle, but acknowledged that the margin of discretion it affords is inconsistent with the level of review required under the SPS Agreement. He proposed a compromise in which national regulators would be granted more discretion in determining the substance of regulations in exchange for more stringent procedural constraints to prevent protectionist abuse of their enhanced discretion.[130] Under Bohanes's model, national governments would be required to show that they had 'taken into account' scientific studies, cost–benefit analysis and the views of the private sector and civil society.[131] This focus on transparent and informed decision-making would not, however, prevent a regulatory authority responding to public demands for regulation. On the contrary, a regulatory authority would be able to overrule the conclusion of a risk assessment.[132]

Robert Howse also joined in the procedural jamboree. While not proposing a new model of procedural review, as Trebilcock and Soloway do, Howse focused on justifying respect for trade-offs made within the democratic process of a WTO Member on the grounds that those trade-offs were made explicitly, transparently, and in a manner consistent with democratic rationality.[133] For Howse, what is important is not the actual choice made, or the substantive basis for that choice, but the *manner* in which the choice was made. In this respect, Howse's work reinforces the recent emphasis on transparency and procedure in writings on the WTO's

[128] Trebilcock and Soloway (n 124).
[129] Bohanes (n 22) 329.
[130] Bohanes (n 22) 328–29.
[131] Bohanes (n 22) 365.
[132] Bohanes (n 22) 366.
[133] Howse (n 50) 2337.

review of health regulations.[134] Mention should also be made of Pauwelyn's suggestion that the applicable standard of review could be 'lowered' if the SPS Agreement were re-focused to set out the steps national authorities have to take when enacting health measures (such as what factors must be examined, what evidence must be gathered and from whom such evidence should be gathered).[135]

(b) The insufficiency of procedural guarantees

The model of regulation-making that the European Commission is promoting places a very high value on procedure. In its Communication, the Commission set out 'guidelines' for applying the precautionary principle. According to those guidelines, where decision-makers become aware of a risk they must first obtain 'through a structured approach, a scientific evaluation, as complete as possible, of the risk'.[136] Once this scientific evaluation has been performed, its conclusions should be evaluated to show that the desired level of protection could be jeopardised. A cost–benefit analysis should also be conducted before decisions are taken on what action (if any) is appropriate and consideration must be given to assigning responsibility for gathering further scientific data and putting in place mechanisms to ensure that the measures are reviewed as further data become available.[137] Throughout the process, procedures should be 'as transparent as possible and . . . involve all interested parties at the earliest possible stage.'[138] By stressing that the precautionary principle is only to be applied once scientific processes have been exhausted, the Commission's Communication emphasises the procedural apsects of regulation-making in circumstances of scientific uncertainty.[139]

[134] See also J Scott 'On Kith, Kine (and Crustaceans): Trade and Environment in the EU and WTO' in JHH Weiler (ed) *The EU, the WTO, and the NAFTA: Towards a Common Law of International Trade?* (OUP Oxford 2000) 125, 126 (noting that the difficulties of assessing domestic preferences militates in favour of procedural rather than substantive tests and notes a widespread procedural turn in Community law (at 164) including MP Maduro *We, the Court: The European Court of Justice & the European Economic Constitution* (Hart Publishing Oxford 1998) 169ff (Maduro's focus on ensuring representation of affected interests)). Note also S Zleptnig 'The Standard of Review in WTO Law: An Analysis of Law, Legitimacy and the Distribution of Legal and Political Authority' (2002) 13 EBusLRev 427 (promoting a standard of review that responds to the quality of the procedure by which the national rule was arrived at).

[135] J Paulwelyn 'Does the WTO Stand for "Deference to" or "Interference with" National Health Authorities When Applying the Agreement on Sanitary and Phytosanitary Measures (SPS Agreement)?' in T Cottier and PC Mavroidis *The Role of the Judge in International Trade Regulation: Experience and Lessons for the WTO* (U Mich P Ann Arbor 2003) 175, 185.

[136] Commission *Communication on the Precautionary Principle* (n 17) point 6.1.

[137] Commission *Communication on the Precautionary Principle* (n 17) point 6.3.5.

[138] Commission *Communication on the Precautionary Principle* (n 17) point 6.2. On transparency, see: McNelis (n 98) 547.

[139] On procedural understandings of the PP, see: Fisher 'Is the Precautionary Principle Justiciable?' (n 23).

Although, in describing its model of precautionary regulation-making, the Commission's commitment to procedural guarantees against abuse is manifest, even it shies away from taking the position that such procedural guarantees are, in and of themselves, sufficient. In particular, the Communication sets out a number of general principles that apply to measures based on the precautionary principle: they must be proportional, non-discriminatory and consistent with measures adopted in other circumstances. Thus, the procedural approach is shored up with a set of substantive constraints that would be justiciable if incorporated into any statement of the precautionary principle in the WTO. Indeed, these substantive constraints are already found in the SPS Agreement[140] and their inclusion in the Communication may be read as confirming that, in order to constrain recourse to the precautionary principle, procedural guarantees must be supplemented with substantive limits.

A similar model of regulation-making emerges from the ECJ's case law. While that case law also reveals a commitment to procedural constraints—measures may only be based on the precautionary principle once as full a scientific assessment as possible has been undertaken, a Community institution can only act without obtaining the opinion of a Community scientific committee in confined circumstances and can only disregard the opinion of a Community scientific committee if it explains why it is disregarding that opinion and points to other scientific evidence of commensurate probative value[141]—it also reveals substantive constraints designed to complement procedural guarantees. In addition to the usual proportionality requirement, it has been held that the precautionary principle does not allow action to be taken where risks are 'purely hypothetical'.[142] In other words, there must be some basic minimal level of scientific information required to prove that the fears have a credible basis. Another substantive limitation takes the form of the prohibition on Community

[140] Assuming, that the Communication's reference to proportionality refers to loose not strict proportionality as discussed earlier in this chapter.

[141] *Pfizer* (n 81) para 199.

[142] *Pfizer* (n 81) para 143; *Alpharma* (n 88) para 156. Although the CFI referred to the following judgments of the ECJ and CFI as supporting that finding—*UK BSE* (n 50) para 99; *MAFF (BSE)* (n 50) para 63; and Case T–199/96 *Laboratoires pharmaceutiques Bergaderm SA v Commission* [1998] ECR II-2805 para 66—it is difficult to agree that the paragraphs cited do in fact support that claim as they all simply confirm that, where there is uncertainty 'as to the *existence* or extent' of risks to human health, protective measures can be taken without waiting for the '*reality* and seriousness' of those risks to become fully apparent (emphasis added). By stating that protective measures may be taken when there is still doubt over the *existence* of a risk, the ECJ's pronouncements would seem to be notably more permissive than the CFI's statement that action may not be taken in respect of risks that are still 'purely hypothetical'. In *Pfizer* and *Alpharma*, the CFI also noted that the same conclusion about merely hypothetical risk was reached in Case E–3/00 *EFTA Surveillance Authority v Norway* [2001] 2 CMLR 47 paras 36–38. Note also, in the same vein: *Monsanto* (n 93) para 106; and Case C–192/01 *Commission v Denmark* (ECJ 23 September 2003) para 49.

measures aimed at achieving 'zero risk'.[143] While it is doubtful whether the ECJ would review the Community's compliance with these substantive limitations very vigorously, it is still telling that the ECJ has felt it necessary to complement procedural obligations with such substantive limitations.

It has been suggested above that the procedural review has some limitations that have been implicitly recognsied both in EU cases relating to the precautionary principle and in the Commission's Communication. Both of those sources suggest that, in controlling recourse to the precautionary principle, procedural guarantees alone are not enough. While a procedural approach can provide a good overall framework for using the precautionary principle in a responsible manner, basic minimum benchmarks and complementary substantive requirements are necessary—both the Communication and EU case law specify that regulators may not respond to 'mere hypotheses', and the Communication itself stipulates that measures based on the precautionary principle should be proportional, non-discriminatory, consistent with similar measures, and based on a cost–benefit analysis. In short, procedural approaches are only a partial solution; substantive limits are still required. Besides only being a partial solution, there is a risk that procedural review's promise of deference may be more apparent than real. As the following examination of US judicial review cases shows, far from being deferential, procedural review can be highly intrusive. These cases demonstrate just how permeable the boundary between substantive and procedural questions are and just how easily an ostensibly procedural enquiry can drift into review of very substantive questions.

(c) The false promise of deference

By enquiring into how a decision was reached, rather than what the decision is, procedural review promises a method of review suited to generalist adjudicators with no desire to second-guess the expert judgments of regulators.[144] The temptation, though, is to stray beyond ensuring, for example, that a risk assessment was carried out to addressing *how* the risk assessment was conducted. In both cases, the adjudicator is concerned with the processes behind the regulation (not the substantive regulation itself), thereby giving the appearance that an enquiry into how a risk

143 *Pfizer* (n 81) para 152; *Alpharma* (n 88) para 165. Note that the Communication also stipulates that measures must not aim at zero risk: Commission *Communication on the Precautionary Principle* (n 17) point 6.3.1.

144 On the thinking reinforcing procedural models of judicial review in the US, see generally, JH Ely *Democracy and Distrust: A Theory of Judicial Review* (Harvard UP Cambridge MA 1980) (judicial review should concern itself with questions of participation, not the substantive merits of the political choice made).

assessment was conducted still constitutes procedural not substantive review. It is, however, very easy to slip from procedural review into review of the procedural aspects of substantive questions. This assertion requires some explanation. It was suggested above that review of substantive issues such as scientific justification may engage the reviewer in some procedural issues. For example, in reviewing a scientific justification, one might well ask how an experiment giving rise to crucial scientific data was carried out. The same type of enquiry might also be conducted, having commenced on a procedural path, by addressing not only whether a risk assessment was conducted, but whether it was properly conducted. The point is that procedural enquiries can easily stray into questions of methodology.

Review of methodology has a rather more benign image than it deserves.[145] In a significant 1994 article on science and review of regulatory decision-making, Wirth argued that science is not well suited to adjudication and noted that domestic courts in GATT countries rarely scrutinise the fundamental correctness of scientific conclusions, but extend deferential review, focusing on processes or methodologies.[146] While this may be true of review for some WTO Members, it is not true of the US. Notwithstanding its focus on methodology, review of regulatory decision-making in the US is far from uniformly deferential.[147]

What we see when we enquire into the US judicial review experience is an apparently intractable tension between deference and scrutiny. This tension is apparent in the way in which the courts have attempted to reconcile what is, in practice, very close review of agencies' methodologies and data with a formal recognition that some deference is due to agency determinations. An amount of background information is required in order to illustrate the way in which US judicial review demonstrates how easily procedural review can find itself in substantive territory, and how intrusive review of methodology can be. Judicial review in the US is governed by the Administrative Procedure Act[148] (APA). If the particular statute under which the agency is operating is silent on the applicable standard of review, the APA sets out the standard of review. The APA draws a distinction between two kinds of rule-making: formal rule-making (with quasi-judicial hearings), and informal rule-making (conducted without quasi-judicial hearings, but usually with some kind of notice and comment procedure). Under the APA, a formal rule-making

145 Although it should be noted that, when the ECJ reviews the actions of the Community in circumstances of uncertainty, its procedural constraints have not resulted in intrusive review because of the ECJ's very strong commitment to deferential review of Community action.

146 Wirth (n 56) 841–43.

147 Fraiberg and Trebilcock (n 50) 884; DA Farber 'The Case Against Clarity' in Kennedy and Southwick (eds) (n 124) 575, 579.

148 5 USC § 551 ff (1994) ('APA').

will be overturned if the rule is 'unsupported by substantial evidence'.[149] Informal rule-making, on the other hand, will be overturned if it is 'arbitrary, capricious, an abuse of discretion, or otherwise not in accordance with law'.[150]

Ostensibly, substantial evidence review is more substantive, and arbitrary and capricious review more procedural. This distinction is reinforced by the common belief that the substantial evidence standard is more demanding than the arbitrary and capricious standard,[151] as one would expect based on the dogma that procedural review is less intrusive than substantive review. An examination of the cases shows, however, that both bases of review frequently result in the court engaging in intrusive review of the methodology and data underpinning the studies on which regulations are based.

The US courts have never shied away from acknowledging that some deference is due to agency determinations. What they have, however, done (under both the substantial evidence and arbitrary and capricious standards) is to attempt to reconcile deference and scrutiny by setting up formal limits to their decision-making powers: courts are not to substitute their judgments for those of the agencies and are not to arrive at their own factual conclusions on scientific controversies. These limits do not actually prevent the courts from engaging in intense scrutiny of agency decisions and imposing their own vision of proper regulatory practice. Consequently, the courts' claim to deference appears strained.

The 'arbitrary and capricious' standard is said to be deferential, and designed to 'ensure that the agency considered all of the relevant factors and that its decision contained no "clear error of judgment."'[152] Notwithstanding such promises of deference, more substantive and intrusive review takes place. In *Citizens to Preserve Overton Park Inc v Volpe*,[153] Justice Marshall famously described arbitrary and capricious review in the following terms:

[149] APA § 706(2)(E).

[150] APA § 706(2)(A). Although strictly 'arbitrary *or* capricious' review, the common shorthand is 'arbitrary *and* capricious'. *De novo* review is also provided for by the APA, but in circumstances that are not presently relevant.

[151] There is, however, some debate on this point: JL Mashaw, RA Merrill and PM Shane *Administrative Law: The American Public Law System: Cases and Materials* (4th edn West Group St Paul 1998) 821; M Shapiro *Integrating Scientific Expertise into Regulatory Decision-Making: The Frontiers of Science Doctrine: American Experiences with the Judicial Control of Science-Based Decision-Making* (EUI Working Paper No 96/11 EUI Florence 1996) 6; AC Aman and WT Mayton *Administrative Law* (West Publishing Co St Paul 1993) 457.

[152] Eg, *Pacific Coast Federation of Fishermen's Associations v National Marine Fisheries Service* 265 F 3d 1028, 1034 (US Ct of Apps (9th Cir), 2001) ('*Pacific Coast*') (referring to *Arizona v Thomas* 824 F 2d 745, 748 (US Ct of Apps (9th Cir), 1987), which quotes *Overton Park* (n 153) 416).

[153] 401 US 402, 91 S Ct 814 (1971) ('*Overton Park*').

> Although this inquiry into the facts is to be searching and careful, the ultimate standard of review is a narrow one. The court is not empowered to substitute its judgment for that of the agency.[154]

In the years that followed, the lower courts, and particularly the DC Circuit, took Justice Marshall's instruction that the inquiry into the facts was to be 'searching and careful' and that the Secretary's decision was to be subjected to 'probing, in-depth review'[155] as an invitation to engage in aggressive review.[156]

In engaging in this 'searching and careful' inquiry, the courts have frequently passed judgment on such matters as the methodology underlying experiments or data collection on which the agency relies, the sufficiency of the agency's criteria and what conclusions can, in fact, be drawn from the evidence.[157] The key point is that, by and large, judges have not regarded this intense examination of data and methodology as taking them beyond their competence as laymen or as straying into the forbidden realm of substituting the court's judgment for that of the agency. For example, in *South Terminal Corp v EPA*,[158] the First Circuit reviewed air quality achievement plans (issued by the Environmental Protection Agency (EPA)) for Boston and for the local airport. Judge Campbell referred to *Overton Park*'s instruction to engage in 'searching and careful' review and concluded that the court therefore had to assure itself that the EPA's technical conclusions were founded on supportable data and methodology and met minimal standards of rationality.[159] The court then considered such matters as the number of air readings taken, the operation of a single monitoring site and the placement of the reading device relative

[154] *Overton Park* (n 153) 416.

[155] *Overton Park* (n 153) 415.

[156] PM Wald 'Judicial Review in Midpassage: The Uneasy Partnership Between Courts and Agencies Plays On' (1996) 32 Tulsa LJ 221, 226; SA Shapiro and RE Levin 'Judicial Incentives and Indeterminacy in Substantive Review of Administrative Decisions' (1995) 44 Duke LJ 1051, 1066; TO McGarity 'Some Thoughts on "Deossifying" the Rulemaking Process' (1992) 41 Duke LJ 1385, 1410.

[157] Other notable cases include *International Harvester Co v Ruckelshaus* 478 F 2d 615 (US Ct of Apps (DC Cir), 1973) ('*International Harvester*') (where, having promised restraint and deference, Judge Leventhal dismantled the assumptions behind the EPA's determination on whether effective technology was available to meet an emissions standard); *Motor Vehicle Manufacturers Association of the US Inc v State Farm Mutual Automobile Insurance Co* 463 US 29, 103 S Ct 2865 (1983) (where the majority found that the agency had been too quick in dismissing the benefits of automatic belts and delved into the empirical evidence on seatbelt use, adding its own assumptions to arrive at a different conclusion on the significance of that evidence); *Ohio v EPA* 784 F 2d 224, 230 (US Ct of Apps (6th Cir), 1986) (the EPA's failure to validate the accuracy of the air pollution model in the vicinity of the plants was arbitrary); *AFL-CIO v OSHA* 965 F 2d 962 (US Ct of Apps (11th Cir), 1992) (requirement that the EPA separately assess health effects for over 400 substances); *Pacific Coast* (n 152) (the court rejected the choice of scale at which environmental effects were assessed, the choice of time scale and the logic of conclusions drawn from evidence regarding revegetation).

[158] 504 F 2d 646 (US Ct of Apps (1st Cir), 1974) ('*South Terminal*').

[159] *South Terminal* (n 158) 655.

to the street kerb. In effect, the court created and imposed substantive standards on the investigative methodology employed by the EPA and found the agency wanting. Although careful to stress that the court was not necessarily saying that the EPA's conclusions as to photochemical and carbon monoxide levels at the airport were incorrect, Judge Campbell still found that they were without reliable foundation and were, accordingly, arbitrary and capricious.[160]

When one turns to the case law on the substantial evidence standard of review, a similar picture emerges. On the one hand, the substantial evidence standard is said to be deferential,[161] but a number of cases show that, like the arbitrary and capricious standard of review, there is plenty of potential for intrusive review. One of the most notorious cases in American administrative law is *Industrial Union Department, AFL-CIO v American Petroleum Institute*,[162] which concerned the Secretary of Labor's decision to lower the exposure limit for benzene from 10 p.p.m to 1 p.p.m. In overturning the new exposure limit, the Supreme Court placed a heavy emphasis on quantitative methods,[163] showed disdain for regulatory assumptions such as the carcinogen policy[164] and showed no sensitivity to the uncertainty that is pervasive in risk assessment.[165] Even if one accepts Justice Stevens's claim that at no point did the court make factual determinations of its own or reject those of the agency,[166] the Supreme Court still imposed a particular vision of proper regulatory methods on American agencies at large and conducted an intrusive review. Even more striking was the decision of the Fifth Circuit in *Gulf South Insulation*[167] where the court condemned the agency's reliance on an animal study as the basis for its computerised risk assessment: 'it is not *good science* to rely

160 *South Terminal* (n 158) 665.

161 The substantial evidence standard is said to be satisfied where there is 'such relevant evidence as a reasonable mind might accept as adequate to support a conclusion': *Consolidated Edison Co v NLRB* 305 US 197, 229, 59 S Ct 206 (1938); *Aqua Slide 'N' Dive v CPSC* 569 F 2d 831 (US Ct of Apps (5th Cir), 1978); *Gulf South Insulation v Consumer Product Safety Commission* 701 F 2d 1137, 1143 (US Ct of Apps (5th Cir), 1983) ('*Gulf South Insulation*').

162 448 US 607, 100 S Ct 2844 (1980) ('*Benzene*').

163 The agency was criticised for not having come to *precise* conclusions about the risks of low level exposures: *Benzene* (n 162) 633. Compare *United Steelworkers* where the DC Circuit was impressed that, in respect of a lead standard, OSHA had not relied on assumptions, but had amassed voluminous evidence on the *specific* harmful effects of lead at particular blood lead levels, and was prepared to accord the agency some leeway in arriving at the specific numerical limit and on the complex issue of air-lead monitoring: *United Steelworkers of America, AFL-CIO-CLC v Marshall* 647 F 2d 1189 (US Ct of Apps (DC Cir), 1980) 1248, 1253, 1259.

164 The carcinogen policy stipulates that, absent proof of a safe level of exposure, it must be assumed that any level above zero represents some increased risk of cancer.

165 The agency had claimed that it was unable to construct a reliable dose-response curve at low exposures.

166 *Benzene* (n 162) 659 (note though that the dissentients took issue with this claim: *Benzene* (n 162) 695).

167 The case concerned a ban on urea-formaldehyde foam insulation in residences and schools. For reactions to this case, see: McGarity 'Some Thoughts' (n 156) 1417–18; and Mashaw, Merrill and Shane (n 151) 605.

on a single experiment, particularly one involving only 240 subjects, to make precise estimates of cancer risk.'[168] In effect, the court was not prepared to pass a standard based on a study it regarded as having been conducted on too small a scale to qualify as 'good' science. The court did not elaborate on where it derived the requirement of 'good' science from and why it departed from the minimum of 'reputable scientific thought' referred to in *Benzene*.[169]

While the practices described above constitute the mainstream approach to judicial review of scientifically based health and safety regulations, it should not be supposed that there have been no countervailing voices or that that intrusive approach to review is wholly unqualified. In a much publicised debate in the DC Circuit, the dominant approach—which advocates immersion in the technical detail of cases and sees any reluctance to grapple with scientific and technical intricacies as an abdication of judicial responsibility[170]—was fiercely resisted by Judge Bazelon, who preferred a narrowly procedural approach to review. Judge Bazelon was highly suspicious of the tendency of judges to make 'plausible-sounding, but simplistic, judgments of the relative weight to be afforded various pieces of technical data'[171] and once declared:

> Socrates said that wisdom is the recognition of how much one does not know. I may be wise if that is wisdom, because I recognize that I do not know enough about dynamometer extrapolations, deterioration factor adjustments, and the like to decide whether or not the government's approach to these matters was statistically valid.[172]

Although there are signs that, after the rationalist heyday of the late 1970s and 1980s, there is an increasing recognition of the limits of scientific methods and a shift towards deference, those signals remain mixed.[173] There are a number of cases indicating that the courts still have a lot of confidence in their ability to dismantle methodology and data sets, and still believe that this is a fitting practice in supposedly deferential judicial review.[174] By continuing to focus on methodology, the courts are

[168] *Gulf South Insulation* (n 161) 1146 (emphasis added).

[169] *Benzene* (n 162) 656.

[170] *Ethyl Corp v EPA* 541 F 2d 1 (US Ct of Apps (DC Cir), 1976) 36 (Judge White), 68 (Judge Leventhal).

[171] *Ethyl Corp* (n 170) 66 (Judge Bazelon quoting himself in *International Harvester* (n 157) 652).

[172] *International Harvester* (n 157) 650–51.

[173] McGarity 'Some Thoughts' (n 156) 1421–22; ER Morrison 'Judicial Review of Discount Rates Used in Regulatory Cost-Benefit Analysis' (1998) 65 UChiLRev 1333, 1356–58.

[174] Eg, *Corrosion Proof Fittings v EPA* 947 F 2d 1201, 1216, 1218–19 (US Ct of Apps (5th Cir), 1991) where the Fifth Circuit presumed to instruct the EPA on how to go about its inquiry and, on the basis of expertise gleaned from *The Economist*, faulted the agency for failing to discount benefits as well as costs, and also highlighted other methodological flaws. Note also *Appalachian Power Co v EPA* 249 F 3d 1032, 1053 (US Ct of Apps (DC Cir), 2001) where the DC Circuit was concerned to go behind the modelling of complex phenomena to scrutinise the veracity of the assumptions on which the model was based. Cf, though, *Custer County Action*

engaging in an intrusive search for rigour and accuracy[175] that formally observes a degree of deference by stopping short of substituting court judgments for those of agencies and not actually drawing factual conclusions. As the US judicial review case law shows, the line between direct analysis of the substantive scientific justification and procedural review which focuses on methodology is terribly uncertain, and review focusing on methodology is no guarantee of deference. Advocates of a proceduralised version of review in the WTO should bear these points in mind as they suggest that procedural review's promise of unintrusive review is rather more complicated than it may, at first sight, appear. Before leaving procedural review, two further potential disadvantages of procedural review must be considered: homogeniety and the curtailing of the WTO's trade-liberalising agenda.

(d) Homogeneity

A curious paradox attending procedural review is that, although it is a model of review that promises minimal intrusion into national regulatory preferences and priorities, it can be more intrusive than science-based review which ostensibly leaves less room for national preferences. One respect in which procedural review can be intrusive is in its imposition of a particular model of regulation-making procedure. Even within the OECD, countries differ in the extent to which regulatory decision-making is transparent and interested parties are consulted.[176] Countries also differ in their methods of regulatory analysis and methods for coping with scientific uncertainty. Such variation within the OECD reflects national cultural and political norms,[177] and that variation can only be greater across the entirety of the WTO Membership. Procedural review risks imposing a particular model of regulatory practice on all WTO Members, thereby overriding an additional set of national preferences. While some

Association v Garvey 256 F 3d 1024, 1035–36 (US Ct of Apps (10th Cir), 2001) where the court refused to be drawn into a debate about the merits of various ways of measuring noise levels and stressed that, where different expert opinions exist, it is for the agency and not the court to choose between them. Another less intrusive case is *City of Waukesha v EPA* 320 F 3d 228, 251–55 (US Ct of Apps (DC Cir), 2003) where the court adopted a reasonably deferential approach to the EPA's radiation standards, finding that it was for the EPA to resolve any contradictory evidence and that it was enough that there was a rational relationship between the EPA's model and the situation to which it was applied.

175 It should, however, be noted that even the rationalists have recognised that scientific methods do not always deliver definitive answers. This realisation has been formalised as the 'frontiers of science' doctrine, which distinguishes simple findings of fact from scientific determinations at the frontiers of science, in respect of which courts must be particularly deferential: *Baltimore Gas and Electric Co v NRDC Inc* 462 US 87, 103, 103 S Ct 2246 (1983). Note also *Ethyl Corp* (n 170) 28 and *Reserve Mining Co v EPA* 514 F 2d 492 (US Ct of Apps (8th Cir), 1975).

176 OECD *Overview* (n 27) para 41.

177 OECD *Overview* para 42; S Jasanoff 'Acceptable Evidence in a Pluralistic Society' in the DG Mayo and RD Hollander (eds) *Acceptable Evidence: Science and Risk Values in Risk Management* (OUP Oxford 1991) 29, 29.

might see diversity in national approaches as inefficient, the WTO system is—subject to its confined harmonisation provisions—built on national regulatory diversity and any attempt to erase national distinctions and homogenise national approaches to regulation should ring alarm bells.[178]

(e) Altering the WTO agenda

In commenting on the American courts' approach to limiting regulators' discretion, Theodore Porter wrote in 1995 that '[p]rocedures have become as important as outcomes.'[179] Procedural review focuses on preventing abuse of discretion. It is not concerned with the *substance* of regulations. As such, procedural review of health regulations relies on procedure and transparency to identify instances of protectionist abuse, or 'sham' health regulations.[180] Procedural review would, as Trebilcock and Soloway promise, eliminate the most egregious protectionist abuses.[181] But, as has been repeatedly emphasised, the SPS Agreement attempts more than this—it attempts to identify SPS measures which are simply not necessary, irrespective of whether they have any protectionist intent. Procedural review necessarily sacrifices this more far-reaching agenda in favour of identifying protectionist abuse. For other WTO Members, this is a poor exchange.

One of the strengths of procedural review is its ability to constrain discretion by ensuring that those whose interests are affected have an opportunity to be heard and by ensuring that all relevant information is considered by decision-makers. In this way, accountability—which is the constant refrain attending executive rule-making[182]—is guaranteed. In essence, procedural guarantees work best within an identifiable political unit. Thus, while its merits are more obvious in domestic review systems, the benefits of procedural review at the international level are questionable. As Joanne Scott notes, an initial problem is that not all WTO Members are liberal democratic states with national regulatory processes that lend

[178] One worthy focus for concern is the nascent set of principles for *national* risk assessment being developed by Codex; work on these principles was initiated in the 17th session of the CCGP (2002) and was still ongoing when the CCGP met in 2003: CCGP *Report* (18th Session 2003 ALINORM 03/33A) para 32ff. While the WTO made it clear (in the 18th session, para 36) that it would welcome a guide on how national governments should undertake risk assessments, there is a risk that, as that statement would carry the imprimatur of Codex, it would be regarded by WTO panels as authoritative, leaving national authorities which do not follow the stated approach struggling to justify measures in the WTO.

[179] TM Porter *Trust in Numbers: The Pursuit of Objectivity in Science and Public Life* (Princeton UP Princeton 1995) 197.

[180] The focus on screening out protectionism is explicitly admitted: Trebilcock and Soloway (n 124) 553, 556.

[181] Trebilcock and Soloway (n 124) 553.

[182] On the theme of accountability, see: C Scott 'Accountability in the Regulatory State' (2000) 27 J Law and Society 38; M Shapiro *Who Guards the Guardians? Judicial Control of Administration* (Georgia University Press Athens 1988) chh 1, 5.

legitimacy to the resulting measures.[183] Some are authoritarian states with opaque regulatory processes. In such circumstances, the democratic legitimacy rationale underpinning procedural review falls down. Even putting aside this limit on the utility of procedure, it is by no means clear that the logic behind procedural review in domestic settings—confining executive decision-makers to their delegated area of authority, and promoting the legitimacy of the regulations through democratised, participatory decision-making[184]—is fully applicable in the WTO. Unlike national regulatory authorities, WTO Members are not acting pursuant to any delegated powers whose borders have to be policed. Rather, they are exercising powers which they have always had to protect health, and the question for WTO panels is whether Member countries are observing the collectively agreed constraints on this power. While, in part, these constraints are procedural (note, for example, the transparency provisions of the SPS Agreement), the most significant constraints are substantive (especially scientific justification)—to turn Porter's remark on its head, 'under the SPS Agreement, outcomes are as, or more, important than procedures'.

When those who promote procedural review at the international level talk of notice and comment procedures and cost–benefit analysis, it is by no means clear who is to be notified, who will have the right to comment, and whose costs and whose benefits are to be weighed in the cost–benefit analysis. For example, where the costs of a measure take the form of lost trade that is to be suffered by the exporters of another WTO Member, will those costs be weighed against the benefits which are purely domestic?[185] It is unlikely that this would be the case because, while the SPS Agreement states the Members should, when determining the appropriate level of protection, 'take into account the objective of minimising negative trade effects', WTO Members are in no way obliged to limit their desired level of protection by reference to the costs which that level of protection would impose on other WTO Members. Unless this state of affairs is radically changed—with quite significant resource implications if meaningful consultation is to occur[186]—it is unlikely that procedural review of

[183] Scott 'On Kith' (n 134) 165.

[184] See, eg, J Black 'Proceduralizing Regulation: Part I' (2000) 20 OJLS 597.

[185] McNelis (n 98) 549.

[186] One should also bear in mind the 'ossification' problem associated with judicial review in the US. Faced with the prospect of regulations being challenged, regulatory agencies are forced to devote enormous resources to assembling copious records that respond to every objection raised. In large part, ossification is a procedural problem; with the focus in review on *how* the regulation was made, regulators must support the regulation on the original administrative record—*post hoc* rationalisations offering explanations not evident in the record are not allowed—and must ensure that all interested parties have been heard. To date, the WTO has avoided these ossification problems because review has been substantive and the focus has been on *current* scientific justifications (*Hormones* AB Report (n 6) paras 189–90). On ossification, see: McGarity 'Some Thoughts' (n 156); M Seidenfeld 'Demystifying Deossificatinon: Rethinking Recent Proposals to Modify Judicial Review of Notice and Comment Rulemaking' (1997) 75 Texas LRev 483; TO McGarity 'The Courts and the

cost–benefit analysis and notice and comment procedures would offer much protection for other WTO Members. Because, in the WTO system, other Members (and, more particularly, the traders in those other countries) are not full members of the community whose interests give them stakeholder status in domestic regulatory decision-making, procedural review would constitute cold comfort. For those whose exports are blocked by scientifically unjustified regulations, the fact that a regulatory authority followed a thorough, deliberative process would be an irrelevant nicety.

Developing countries, in particular, have a lot to lose if the substantive scientific justification criterion is to give way to procedural review. While the scientific justification criterion may present difficulties for developing countries wishing to depart from international standards in their regulations,[187] the value of the scientific justification criterion to developing country interests should not be overlooked.[188] Developing countries rely heavily on agricultural exports[189] and are concerned that some countries put in place unnecessarily strict health regulations which limit the export opportunities of developing countries.[190] There is a growing body of evidence concerning the impact of high SPS standards on developing countries' trading opportunities.[191] Without the substantive scientific

Ossification of Rulemaking: A Response to Professor Seidenfeld' (1997) 75 Texas LRev 525; H Latin 'Good Science, Bad Regulation, and Toxic Risk Assessment' (1988) 5 Yale J on Regulation 89; Mashaw, Merrill and Shane (n 151) 604–10; E Fisher 'Drowning by Numbers: Standard Stting in Risk Regulation and the Pursuit of Accountable Public Administration' (2000) 20 OJLS 109, 128 (procedural review allows generalist decision-makers to scrutinise decisions, but risks ossification).

[187] GE Schuh 'Developing Country Interests in WTO Agricultural Policy' in Kennedy and Southwick (eds) (n 124) 435, 443–44.

[188] For example, a ban by the EC on fish imports which was put in place following a cholera outbreak in Tanzania, Kenya, Uganda and Mozambique severely affected the economies of those countries. The EC was persuaded to drop the ban, following discussion in the SPS Committee (in which a WHO official protested that there was no proven risk of cholera transmission from the foods in question, a statement with which the EU Scientific Committee agreed): WHO and WTO *WTO Agreements and Public Health* (WTO/WHO Geneva 2002) 60–61. Although the case did not reach dispute settlement, it does illustrate the importance of science-based decision-making for developing countries.

[189] T Otsuki, JS Wilson and M Sweadeh *A Race to the Top? A Case Study of Food Safety Standards and African Exports* (Working Paper No 2563 World Bank Washington DC 2001) 2. Note also, the contribution by the same authors, with the same title in K Anderson et al (eds) *The Economics of Quarantine and the SPS Agreement* (Centre for International Economic Studies Adelaide 2001) 287.

[190] SPS Committee *Summary* (n 25) para 10 (Argentina noted that the precautionary principle was of particular concern to developing countries who already face serious problems in complying with SPS measures in export markets, and fear these problems might be exacerbated by the 'blank cheque' of the precautionary principle); V Jha '*Strengthening Developing Countries' Capacities to Respond to Health, Sanitary and Environmental Requirements: A Scoping Paper for Selected Developing Countries* (preliminary draft) (UNCTAD Geneva 2002) (available at <http://www.unctad.org/trade_env/test1/openF1.htm> on 15 May 2002) 7; LA Ruessmann 'Putting the Precautionary Principle in its Place' (2002) 17 AUIntlLRev 905, 908, 940–41.

[191] JS Wilson and T Otsuki *Global Trade and Food Safety: Winners and Losers in a Fragmented System* (Working Paper No 2689 World Bank Washington DC 2001); Otsuki, Wilson and Sweadeh (n 189); WHO and WTO *WTO Agreements and Public Health* (n 188) 68.

discipline of the SPS Agreement, developing countries have little prospect of successfully challenging unnecessarily strict health regulations on procedural grounds. An SPS measure could be put in place that is unnecessarily strict because it is not supported by scientific evidence while observing all applicable procedural requirements. In the WTO, the legitimacy of health regulations is as much concerned with *what* they are, as with *how* they are made.[192] Unless WTO Members whose trading opportunities are curtailed are able to challenge the substantive regulation as scientifically unsupported, the SPS Agreement will achieve a lot less than it set out to. There are, however, some additional difficulties associated with procedural review. As the preceding examination of US judicial review case law showed, procedural review can have negative side-effects and does not necessarily deliver unintrusive review.

C CONCLUSION

The precautionary principle's promise that uncertainty will not be allowed to stand in the way of effective health protection is enticing. This chapter has argued, however, that, while the precautionary principle is not necessarily anti-science, introducing it into the WTO would remove the linchpin of the SPS Agreement: the scientific justification principle. Accordingly, the precautionary principle would need to be accompanied by a complementary basis of review to prevent it being used to justify a proliferation of non-tariff barriers. Two alternatives were critically reviewed—proportionality and procedural review. Strict proportionality review is not well suited to the WTO because, by making the chosen level of protection reviewable, it would take with one hand much of the extra latitude granted to Members by the precautionary principle. Procedural review promises less intrusion, but its guarantees of accountability and transparency are only a partial solution and are, in any case, of limited value to other WTO Members. In addition, procedural review can, through review of methodology and data, become quite intrusive, as the US experience demonstrates. With proportionality rejected and the promise of procedural review tainted, what type of review should WTO panels be exercising? The following chapter takes up this question and suggests that tensions relating to scientific evidence and the role of social and cultural factors in regulation can be eased by employing an appropriate standard of review.

[192] Recall that, in the *Hormones* case, the AB rejected the panel's procedural understanding of the risk assessment discipline in favour of an interpretation which focused on scientific justification at the date of hearing and the relationship between the measure and the risk assessment: *Hormones* AB Report (n 6) paras 189–90.

6

Easing Tensions via the Standard of Review

TWO PARTICULAR CONCERNS underpin the general sense of unease surrounding WTO review of national health regulations. Firstly, there is concern that the WTO regime does not allow sufficient scope for WTO Members to take account of social and cultural preferences when regulating to protect health. Secondly, there is a marked concern that the SPS Agreement's emphasis on scientific justification[1] severely curtails the ability of WTO Members to take protective action in circumstances of scientific uncertainty. It will be recalled that, in Chapter 5, the wisdom of embracing the precautionary principle in the WTO was questioned on the basis that, in order to ensure that the precautionary principle would not open the doors to non-tariff barriers, it would have to be accompanied by strict proportionality review or procedural review. As was discussed, both of those alternatives carry with them undesirable or inappropriate elements.

This chapter pursues another alternative. The precautionary principle promised to ease tensions relating to scientific uncertainty by breaking with the fundamental requirement that regulatory measures be scientifically justified. The alternative being explored here responds to that challenge, not by rejecting the scientific justification discipline, but by focusing attention on the way in which WTO panels should determine whether a scientific justification exists. As we saw in Chapter 4, the relationship between science and regulatory measures is far from straightforward; there is no clear boundary between certain and uncertain science. Moreover, policy enters into science and regulatory processes at a number of stages. By focusing on the standard of review that WTO panels are to apply in determining whether a Member's measure is scientifically justified, we can respond to concerns related to national regulatory autonomy by circumscribing more clearly the role of the international adjudicator. A clearer picture of the standard of review will help us to determine when WTO panels should overrule a national regulator's assessment of

[1] Agreement on the Application of Sanitary and Phytosanitary Measures (SPS Agreement) (Marrakesh, 15 April 1994) Art 2.2.

the sufficiency and significance of scientific evidence, without losing the valuable scientific justification criterion.[2]

This chapter proceeds by taking up the standard of review as it is presently constituted in the WTO, and argues that the 'objective assessment' standard of review is seriously flawed. The standard of review specified for anti-dumping cases[3] is considered, and arguments are then mounted to support a move away from the objective assessment standard of review. It is suggested that the Appellate Body's strong textualist preferences should not mean that the standard of review's development must be regarded as complete. On the contrary, it is suggested that the objective assessment standard has undergone an elaboration in safeguards cases, paving the way for development of the standard of review in other areas.

A THE STANDARD OF REVIEW AND ITS ROLE IN REVIEW

1 The Concept of a Standard of Review and its Value

It might well be asked what exactly a standard of review is, and the question would be well put. The concept of a standard of review is familiar to administrative lawyers from a great many jurisdictions. For English lawyers, the reference to standards of review will evoke *Wednesbury* unreasonableness,[4] the principle whereby a decision is unlawful if it is one to which no reasonable authority could have come. Americans, on the other hand, will be reminded of the various standards provided for by the Administrative Procedure Act,[5] including the arbitrary and capricious standard, the substantial evidence standard and *de novo* review. The immediate point is not what standards of review are applied and how they are expressed in various jurisdictions, but that the term 'standard of review' conceptualises and puts in legal form the level of intensity of the scrutiny that the reviewing body will exert over the decision or regulation being reviewed.

The question of how intense review should be is captured in a number of expressions, such as the 'leeway' or 'room to move' given to decision-makers, different levels of scrutiny, 'deference' and 'restraint'. The intensity of review (and consequently how much regulatory freedom WTO Members have in regulating to protect the health of their people, plants and animals) is the product of a number of factors. The text of the SPS Agreement and

[2] Valuable because it is what takes the SPS Agreement beyond merely identifying disguised protectionism to opening markets which are unnecessarily closed (ie, closed when the health measure is not scientifically justified).

[3] Agreement on the Implementation of Article VI of the General Agreement on Tariffs and Trade 1994 (Anti-Dumping Agreement) (Marrakesh, 15 April 1994) Art 17.6.

[4] The *Wednesbury* standard refers to *Associated Provincial Picture Houses Ltd v Wednesbury Corp* [1948] 1 KB 223 (CA), 229 (Lord Greene).

[5] 5 USCA §§ 551ff, 701–6 (1994).

the TBT Agreement[6] was set by the WTO Members during the Uruguay Round negotiations, and it was their decision to retain the GATT text.[7] The texts do not, however, tell the full story. Those texts are interpreted by WTO panels and the Appellate Body in cases brought before them. In large part, it is how the words of the texts are interpreted that will determine the role of social and cultural factors and how scientific uncertainty is to be treated.[8] Interpretation adds another layer of understanding to the substantive norm—what the SPS Agreement means by 'risk assessment' or 'based on scientific principles'—but there is still another significant factor influencing how intrusive review will be: the standard of review applied in determining whether the Member has fulfilled its WTO obligations. For example, it makes a great deal of difference to the scope of Members' autonomy whether the panel assesses the existence a proper scientific justification *de novo*, or whether it exercises some measure of deference.

In the *Hormones* case, the Appellate Body acknowledged that the promotion of international trade and the protection of health are interests that are shared by the WTO Members, but that it is not always easy to accommodate both objectives.[9] The health protection regulations of one Member can have significant effects on the international trading opportunities of another—trade and health are in tension. In order to manage this tension, a balance needs to be struck between the interests of Members concerned to protect health and the interests of Members to trade. The use of an appropriate standard of review constitutes an important aid to achieving this balance.[10] Of course, the balance is not just one between the rights and obligations of the WTO Members that are parties to a particular dispute. The broader question is where the balance of decision-making authority should be fixed between the national and supra-national participants in the WTO system, between WTO Members individually and panels as the delegates of WTO Members as a self-policing group.[11] As John Jackson put

[6] Agreement on Technical Barriers to Trade (TBT Agreement) (Marrakesh, 15 April 1994).

[7] General Agreement on Tariffs and Trade 1994 (GATT 1994) (Marrakesh, 15 April 1994). GATT 1994 incorporates the provisions of GATT 1947 (Geneva, 30 October 1947; 55 UNTS 194) as amended: GATT 1994 Art 1(a).

[8] On the interpretation of the relevant texts, see Chapters 2 and 3.

[9] *EC Measures Concerning Meat and Meat Products (Hormones)* WT/DS26/AB/R, WT/DS48/AB/R AB Report adopted 13 February 1998 ('*Hormones*') para 177.

[10] On the need for this balance and the role of standard of review, see: JH Jackson 'Dispute Settlement and the WTO: Emerging Problems' in WTO Secretariat *From GATT to the WTO: The Multilateral Trading System in the New Millennium* (Kluwer Law International The Hague 2000) 67, 72; M Wynter 'The Agreement on Sanitary and Phytosanitary Measures in the Light of the WTO Decisions on EC Measures Concerning Meat and Meat Products (Hormones)' in P Mengozzi (ed) *International Trade Law on the 50th Anniversary of the Multilateral Trade System* (A Giuffrè Editore Milano 1999) 471, 494.

[11] On this concern about where power should be allocated, see: JH Jackson 'The Great 1994 Sovereignty Debate: United States Acceptance and Implementation of the Uruguay Round Results' in JH Jackson *The Jurisprudence of GATT and the WTO: Insights on Treaty Law and Economic Relations* (CUP Cambridge UK 2000) 367, 369.

it, the standard of review is 'a critical element of allocating power between an international tribunal and a national government'.[12]

2 Particular Points of Tension in the WTO

There are a number of points at which the balance of authority between the WTO Members individually and the supra-national collective (the WTO) in health cases is particularly contentious. It is at these points that the concerns identified above relating to the role of social and cultural factors and scientific uncertainty are particularly acute. The scientific justification discipline in the SPS Agreement raises questions of what 'sufficient scientific evidence' is, and when a measure is 'based on scientific principles'.[13] Similarly, it is not immediately clear when a measure will be 'based on' a risk assessment.[14] Concerns about what amounts to scientific proof of a hazard may also arise in relation to Article XX(b) of GATT, given the apparent requirement that the health risk be proved.[15] Uncertainty and social and cultural factors are also implicated in what information is taken to be 'pertinent' when provisional measures are taken, and whether the measure is 'based on' that information.[16] A set of questions relating to the use of cultural and social factors arise through the requirement that measures not arbitrarily or unjustifiably discriminate,[17] and when enquiries are made as to whether differences in the chosen level of protection in different situations are arbitrary or unjustifiable,[18] whether the least trade-restrictive measure has been utilised,[19] and even whether a measure is 'based on' international standards.[20]

Three focal points for these tensions can be identified from the foregoing list. Firstly, there are tensions relating to the *characterisation of knowledge and facts*—what does the science say; would a less restrictive measure suffice? Secondly, there are tensions connected with the *evaluation of distinctions*, notably whether particular distinctions that regulators may draw based on national preferences are valid. Finally, there are tensions which arise out of *characterising relationships* between facts and actions, such as

[12] Jackson 'The Great 1994 Sovereignty Debate' (n 11) 389–90; SP Croley and JH Jackson 'WTO Dispute Procedures, Standard of Review, and Deference to National Governments' (1996) AJIL 193, 205.

[13] SPS Agreement Art 2.2.

[14] SPS Agreement Art 5.1.

[15] *EC–Measures Affecting Asbestos and Asbestos-Containing Products* WT/DS135/R modified Panel Report adopted 6 April 2001 para 8.170 ('*Asbestos*').

[16] SPS Agreement Art 5.7.

[17] SPS Agreement Art 2.2; GATT Art XX *chapeau*.

[18] SPS Agreement Art 5.5.

[19] SPS Agreement Art 5.6; GATT Art XX(b) (reference to necessity imports the LTR discipline); TBT Agreement Arts 2.2, 2.3.

[20] SPS Agreement Art 3.1.

whether the measure is 'based on' the risk assessment and whether the provisional measure is 'based on' the pertinent available information. The standard of review can be especially helpful in mediating the first set of tensions by making it clear to what extent the WTO dispute settlement machinery will call into question the way in which national regulators evaluate the evidence before them. While lawyers may look for definitive scientific answers,[21] scientific knowledge continually evolves and does not deliver black and white answers. By using a standard of review in considering the scientific justification discipline, the limitations of scientific information can be accommodated by, for example, focusing on whether the regulatory authorities made a reasonable judgment on the status and relevance of the scientific evidence. The standard of review can also be helpful when the evaluation of regulatory distinctions is at issue, although a greater role in easing tensions will be played by further elaboration (by WTO panels and the Appellate Body) of the role of social and cultural factors in determining whether distinctions are arbitrary or unjustified. In assessing relationship questions, such as whether a measure is 'based on' a risk assessment, utilising an appropriate standard of review can help by articulating the level of deference which will be exercised in determining whether the requisite relationship exists.

It should be emphasised at the outset that the standard of review being examined is that applicable to panel review of national regulations, not the standard of review that governs Appellate Body review of panel determinations. Although a distinct legal question, the standard of review applied by the Appellate Body when reviewing a panel decision does have some impact on the appropriate standard of review to be applied by panels to national decisions. For example, if the Appellate Body is very deferential towards panel findings, there is an added impetus for panels to be more deferential to Members' determinations because the system's inbuilt check (in the form of an appeal process) is limited. Given that the Appellate Body can only hear appeals on questions of law, the standard of review to be applied by panels to questions of fact is doubly important because, provided panels apply the standard of review that the Appellate Body prescribes, their approach to the facts will only rarely generate a reviewable question of law. It is the standard of review that panels will apply in deciding whether national health regulations conform to the SPS and TBT Agreements and GATT 1994 that is important in ensuring that review is effective without being unnecessarily intrusive.

[21] When advising the *Hormones* panel, Dr Ritter referred to the story of the two handed scientists—on the one hand, and on the other—and noted that '[l]awyers are often looking for one-handed scientists': *EC Measures Concerning Meat and Meat Products (Hormones)* WT/DS26/R/USA and WT/DS48/R/CAN modified Panel Reports adopted 13 February 1998 Annex: Joint Meeting with Experts ('*Hormones*') para 799.

B THE STANDARD OF REVIEW IN HEALTH CASES

1 Background

The question of the applicable standard of review is not new to international trade law. As early as the *Fur Felt Hat* case[22] in 1951, GATT Working Parties were grappling with standard of review questions. In that case, the members of the Working Party considered whether, in international review, the opinion of the reviewer (which would be more heavily influenced by international considerations) should take precedence over the views of the national government (which would pay more attention to local factors). It was decided that, unless the regard had by the national authorities to local factors was unreasonable, their decision should not be interfered with.[23] Prior to the Uruguay Round, discussion of the applicable standard of review was sporadic and most prominent in the anti-dumping and countervailing duty cases. Despite having been on the horizon for some 40 years, the proper standard of review was not settled by the time the Uruguay Round commenced with the Ministerial meeting in Punta Del Este in September 1986. During the Uruguay Round negotiations, the question of the applicable standard of review was definitely on the table and, because of US interest in the matter, was a negotiating point of some importance.[24] Ultimately, the negotiators did not stipulate the standard of review to be applied under the Dispute Settlement Understanding (DSU),[25] but provided a specific standard of review only for anti-dumping cases. This left panels and the Appellate Body to arrive at their own conclusions on the proper standard of review, a process which has been troubled and largely unsuccessful. While the Appellate Body has arrived at a standard of review based on Article 11 of the DSU, that standard is unclear, misses the mark conceptually and generates confusion.

[22] *Report on the Withdrawal by the US of a Tariff Concession under Article XIX of the General Agreement on Tariffs and Trade Concerning Women's Fur Felt Hats and Hat Bodies* 27 March 1951 CP/106, GATT/1951–3 ('*Fur Felt Hat*').

[23] *Fur Felt Hat* (n 22) paras 30, 48.

[24] Jackson 'The Great 1994 Sovereignty Debate' (n 11) 389–90; Croley and Jackson (n 12) 194 (noting that, for some negotiators, the standard of review issue was so important that it was listed as a 'deal breaker').

[25] Understanding on Rules and Procedures Governing the Settlement of Disputes (the DSU) (Marrakesh, 15 April 1994). With Members' efforts concentrated on improving the substantive rules on trade and health regulations, insufficient attention was paid to procedural rules: T Christoforou 'Settlement of Science-Based Trade Disputes in the WTO: A Criticial Review of the Developing Case Law in the Face of Scientific Uncertainty' (2000) 8 NYU EnvtlLJ 622, 625–26.

2 Article 11 DSU and the 'Objective Assessment' Standard of Review

The legal texts authorising and guiding WTO review of domestic health regulations do not stipulate the standard of review to be applied. Unlike the Anti-Dumping Agreement, the SPS Agreement, the TBT Agreement and GATT 1994 are silent on this question. To the credit of the Appellate Body, it has not attempted to evade the standard of review question by pretending that panels can assess Members' compliance with the relevant obligations without applying a standard of review. A standard of review is inescapable because adjudicators make choices about how closely to scrutinise the facts, interpretations and conclusions advanced by the responding party. The Appellate Body and panels have acknowledged that, in reviewing for compliance with WTO obligations, it is possible to enquire closely by conducting a *de novo* review in which the panel arrives at its own assessment (in effect a correctness standard), or to exert only the most basic supervisory power by deferring absolutely to the views of the Member except, perhaps, where they are patently untenable or extreme. Not surprisingly, in the *Hormones* case, the Appellate Body endorsed at a standard of review that was somewhere in between these two extremes.

In the *Hormones* case, the EC argued for the adoption of a 'deferential reasonableness standard' on the basis that such a standard was applicable in all highly complex factual situations.[26] The EC regarded this standard as that expressed by Article 17.6(i) of the Anti-Dumping Agreement, which provides, *inter alia*, that, '[i]f the [authorities'] establishment of the facts was proper and the evaluation [of those facts] was unbiased and objective, even though the panel might have reached a different conclusion, the evaluation shall not be overturned.' The Appellate Body rejected the EC's argument, finding instead that the applicable standard of review was the 'objective assessment of the facts'. For the Appellate Body, Article 11 answered the standard of review question:

> In our view, Article 11 of the DSU bears directly on this matter and, in effect, articulates with great succinctness but with sufficient clarity the appropriate standard of review for panels in respect of both the ascertainment of facts and the legal characterization of such facts under the relevant agreements. . . . So far as fact-finding by panels is concerned, their activities are always constrained by the mandate of Article 11 of the DSU: the applicable standard is neither *de novo* review as such, nor 'total deference', but rather the 'objective assessment of the facts'.[27]

The Appellate Body did not, however, go on to elaborate on the meaning of objective assessment and so put in place a standard of review that lacks

[26] *Hormones* AB Report (n 9) paras 112–13, citing paras 128–29 of the EC's Appellant's submission.

[27] *Hormones* AB Report (n 9) paras 116–17.

the clarity one finds in the anti-dumping standard. Article 17.6 of the Anti-Dumping Agreement specifically confines panels to examining the way in which the national authority established the facts and to ensuring that those facts were evaluated in an objective and unbiased manner. In those circumstances, there is no question of the panel establishing for itself the facts underlying the national authority's assessment or the deductions that the national authority drew from those facts. On the other hand, while the Appellate Body has made it clear that it does not regard the objective assessment standard of review as authorising *de novo* review, it is not clear to what extent panels are expected to second-guess the factual assessments of national regulatory authorities under the SPS Agreement or the deductions that those authorities make from the facts.

The Appellate Body's conclusion on the applicable standard of review can be seen to rest on four bases: firstly, the failure of the WTO Agreements to prescribe a particular standard of review (other than for anti-dumping cases);[28] secondly, the perceived need to draw any standard of review from the texts of the applicable Agreements so as not to alter the 'finely drawn balance' of jurisdictional competences reflected in the SPS Agreement;[29] thirdly, the general rejection of *de novo* review by panels, including pre-WTO GATT panels;[30] and fourthly, the previous finding of the panel in the *US–Underwear* case that total deference to the findings of national authorities could not ensure objective assessment as required by Article 11 of the DSU.[31] As the Appellate Body conceded, panels are 'poorly suited' to engage in *de novo* review.[32] The Appellate Body was also correct in rejecting total deference if by that we mean uncritical acceptance of the findings of national authorities. Such extreme deference would fail to ensure that WTO Members are held to their substantive commitments and would disappoint hopes that the scope for health-based non-tariff barriers would be much reduced by the WTO Agreements. It is easy to conclude, as the Appellate Body did, that the proper standard of review lies somewhere between these poles, but it is by no means clear that the objective assessment standard successfully identifies such a standard.[33]

[28] *Hormones* AB Report (n 9) para 114.

[29] *Hormones* AB Report (n 9) para 115.

[30] *Hormones* AB Report (n 9) para 117, citing *US–Restrictions on Imports of Cotton and Man-Made Fibre Underwear* WT/DS24/R modified Panel Report adopted 25 February 1997 ('*US–Underwear*'); *Korea–Anti-Dumping Duties on Imports of Polyacetal Resins from the US* Report adopted 27 April 1993 BISD 40S/205; *US–Imposition of Anti-Dumping Duties on Imports of Fresh and Chilled Atlantic Salmon from Norway* Report adopted 27 April 1994 BISD 41S/229; *US–Initiation of a Countervailing Duty Investigation into Softwood Lumber Products from Canada* Report adopted 3 June 1987 BISD 34S/194.

[31] *US–Underwear* Panel Report (n 30) para 7.10.

[32] *Hormones* AB Report (n 9) para 117.

[33] Note that, in the *Agricultural Products* case, Japan (unsuccessfully) argued that Art 2.2 of the SPS Agreement should only be directly applied when the scientific evidence was 'patently insufficient', otherwise, the case should be dealt with under Arts 5.1 and

3 Problems with the Objective Assessment Standard of Review

(a) Conceptual problems

The essential problem with the objective assessment standard of review established by the Appellate Body is that it is not coherent. The appropriate standard of review is, in large part, to be measured against what the reviewing body is being asked to do or how it is being asked to contribute to achieving the institutional aims of the system in which it plays the adjudicatory role. The function of WTO panels is, according to Article 11, 'to assist the DSB [Dispute Settlement Body] in discharging its responsibilities' under the DSU and the WTO Agreements covered by it. It is, then, not at all surprising that the Appellate Body should turn to this description of how WTO panels are to accomplish this task when striving to identify the applicable standard of review. Article 11 goes on to stipulate that 'a panel should make an objective assessment of the matter before it, including an objective assessment of the facts of the case and the applicability of and conformity with the relevant covered agreements'. It is surprising, however, that the Appellate Body should regard objective assessment as articulating the applicable standard of review with 'great succinctness' and 'sufficient clarity', particularly just two paragraphs after having found that the DSU does *not* prescribe a particular standard of review.

By itself, the expression, 'objective assessment', does not provide the crucial instruction on how intense review is to be. Trebilcock and Howse quite aptly remark that it is 'difficult to see how the AB was able to understand Article 11 as illuminating with respect to where on the spectrum between *de novo* review and total deference the appropriate benchmark is to be found.'[34] Of the available definitions of 'objective' provided by the *Shorter Oxford English Dictionary*, the most helpful in trying to elucidate the meaning of 'objective assessment' as a standard of review is '[d]ealing with or laying stress on what is external to the mind; concerned with outward things or events; presenting facts uncoloured by feelings, opinions, or personal bias; disinterested.'[35] Similarly, 'objectivity' is defined as '[t]he quality or character of being objective; *esp* the ability to present or view facts uncoloured by feelings, opinions, or personal bias.' In its general sense, the word 'assessment' is defined as '[e]valuation, estimation; an

5.2: *Japan–Measures Affecting Agricultural Products* WT/DS76/AB/R AB Report adopted 19 March 1999 paras 7, 23, 82 ('*Agricultural Products*'). Although 'patently insufficient' could be used as a standard of review, Japan's argument was not that this expression should be so utilised, although some commentators do tend to see it as a standard of review argument: DA Farber 'The Case Against Clarity' in DLM Kennedy and JD Southwick (eds) *The Political Economy of International Trade Law* (CUP Cambridge UK 2002) 575, 577.

[34] MJ Trebilcock and R Howse *The Regulation of International Trade* (2nd edn Routledge London 1999) 70.

[35] L Brown (ed) *The New Shorter Oxford English Dictionary* (4th edn OUP Oxford 1993).

the measures in those cases would not have survived even a more deferential standard of review.[54]

The *Apples* case[55] provides further evidence (if further evidence were requried) of the conflation by the Appellate Body of the standard of review it should apply in reviewing panel decisions and the standard of review panels should apply in reviewing Member government measures. In the *Apples* case, Japan appears (quite rightly) to have recognised that appeals for defence articulated in terms of the applicable standard of review would fall on deaf ears. Japan confined its arguments under Article 11 of the DSU (which supposedly embodies the 'objective assessment' standard of review) to alleging: errors in the panel's characterisation of evidence; that evidence regarding mature, symptomless apples could not support conclusions in respect of infected apples; that the panel failed to take into account the precautionary principle or the caution emphasised by the experts; and that the panel's conclusion on the likelihood of completion of the pathway was not consistent with its recognition that the risk was not merely 'theoretical'.[56] Instead, Japan's arguments in favour of deference to its assessments were made under Article 2.2 of the SPS Agreement.

In respect of Article 2.2, Japan argued that the panel should have interepreted that Article in such a way that a 'certain degree of discretion' be accorded to the importing Member as to the manner in which it chooses, weighs and evaluates scientific evidence.[57] In responding to this argument, the Appellate Body referred to the Article 11 of the DSU and found that 'Japan's submission that the Panel was obliged to favour Japan's approach to risk and scientific evidence over the views of the experts conflicts with the Appellate Body's articulation of the standard of "objective assessment of the facts".'[58]

To this extent, the Appellate Body did recognise that Japan's calls for deference raised standard of review issues and connected those issues with Article 11 of the DSU, which is said to embody the applicable standard of review. What the Appellate Body then did, however, was to reject Japan's argument on the basis that requiring panels to accord any precedence to an importing Member's evaluations of scientific evidence and risk

[54] DP Fidler *International Law and Infectious Diseases* (OUP Oxford 1999) 146 also citing S Charnovitz 'The World Trade Organization, Meat Hormones, and Food Safety' (1997) 14 ITR 1781, 1785. For commentary on the intrusive aspects of review in the *Salmon* and *Hormones* cases, also see: Thorn and Carlson (n 47) 845.

[55] *Japan–Measures Affecting the Importation of Apples* WT/DS245/AB/R AB Report adopted 10 December 2003 (*'Apples'*); *Japan–Meausres Affecting the Importation of Apples* WT/DS245/R Panel Report adopted 10 December 2003 (*'Apples'*).

[56] *Apples* AB Report (n 55) para 218.

[57] *Apples* AB Report (n 55) para 150.

[58] *Apples* AB Report (n 55) para 165.

would not be compatible with the well-established margin of discretion panels enjoy in assessing the value of evidence and the weight to be ascribed to it. This margin of discretion refers to the scope of Appellate Body review of panel fact-finding and (as was shown above) is drawn from Article 11's duty of objective assessment. The fact that the Appellate Body is reluctant to review panels' findings of fact does not logically determine the standard of review that panels should apply in reviewing the factual determinations of Members. By referring to its own limited ability to overturn panels' findings of fact as necessitating the rejection of Japan's call for deference by panels, the Appellate Body again failed to recognise that the standard of review to be applied by panels is an entirely distinct legal question which is not answered by reference to the scope of Appellate Body review of panel determinations.

What has happened in these cases is that the original reference to objective assessment as the applicable standard of review to be applied by panels when reviewing Member State measures has been lost in the subsequent focus on the due process—natural justice meaning of objective assessment, breach of which essentially requires abuse of panel discretion. That this should have happened is hardly surprising given that the expression 'objective assessment' naturally raises expectations as to the *quality* of a panel's assessment (objective, not subjective or biased) and does not disclose a comprehensible standard of review that describes the approach panels should take in evaluating Members' measures.

(b) Practical problems

It might be argued that, even if the objective assessment standard is not particularly elegant or conceptually strong, the Appellate Body has, in the *Hormones* and other cases, in fact constructed a workable standard of review. Robert Howse, for example, suggests that the Appellate Body's formulation is not as imprecise as it may appear, but actually points towards 'the more adequate notion that the weight to be given to factual determinations of other institutions will depend on some assessment of the relative competence and credibility of those institutions in the handling of the particular facts at issue.'[59] Insofar as Howse is referring to the Appellate Body's overall approach to institutional sensitivity, his point may well be valid, but, inasmuch as it pertains to the narrower standard of review point, he is overly generous to the Appellate Body. Others agree that the *Hormones* case has not provided definitive guidance on the degree

[59] R Howse 'Adjudicative Legitimacy and Treaty Interpretation in International Trade Law: The Early Years of WTO Jurisprudence' in JHH Weiler (ed) *The EU, the WTO and the NAFTA* (OUP Oxford 2000) 35, 64.

of deference to be given to the findings of national agencies.[60] Other explanations of the meaning of objective assessment, such as that advanced by Gabrielle Marceau—'panels have to examine sufficiently the facts so as to be able to conclude objectively whether the measure of the WTO member is compatible with WTO rules'[61]—tend not to address the basic failing of the expression to describe a proper standard of review. That failure of the objective assessment standard to describe a standard of review is not remedied by its use in practice. An examination of the application of the objective assessment standard in the *Hormones* case does not shed any light on how it is to function as a standard for panel review but, rather, further demonstrates its confused nature. All that can be said is that the Appellate Body appears not to regard the standard of review as particularly deferential.

We know that, according to the Appellate Body in the *Hormones* case, the appropriate standard of review is 'neither *de novo* review as such, nor "total deference", but rather the "objective assessment of the facts"'.[62] While the *Hormones* case itself shed little light on what this means, the approach of the panel in the *Apples* case suggests that the Appellate Body's embargo on *de novo* review is being ignored. In considering the panel's approach to the central question of whether Japan's measure was supported by sufficient scientific evidence, the panel was faced with numerous more specific scientific questions. For example, the panel's approach required it to consider whether mature, symptomless fruit could be infested with endophytic populations of bacteria (ie, whether a mature, symptomless apple could harbour bacteria inside the fruit without itself being infected); whether mature, symptomless fruit could be infested with epiphytic (surface) bacteria; whether mature and apparently symptomless fruit could nevertheless be infected; and whether the bacteria would survive commercial handling, storage and transportation.

It is difficult to discern in the panel's consideration of these and other scientific questions any point at which the panel did *not* conduct a *de novo* assessment. In evaluating these scientific questions, the panel engaged closely with the studies cited (going so far as to point out flaws in a study's methodology), relied heavily on the experts' views, engaged in inter-

[60] R Bhala and DA Gantz 'WTO Case Review 2001' (2002) 19 ArizJIntlCompL 457, 618 (noting that, notwithstanding further AB pronouncements on objective assessment, the precise limits of the doctrine are not clear); JO McGinnis and ML Movsesian, 'The World Trade Constitution' (2000) 114 Harvard LRev 511, 581; AW Shoyer and EM Solovy 'The Process and Procedure of Litigating at the World Trade Organization: A Review of the Work of the Appellate Body Panels' (2000) 31 Law&Pol'yIntlBus 677, 687; Desmedt (n 36) 698.

[61] G Marceau 'The Dispute Settlement Rules of the North American Free Trade Agreement: A Thematic Comparison with the Dispute Settlement Rules of the World Trade Organization' in EU Petersmann (ed) *International Trade Law and the GATT/WTO Dispute Settlement System* (Kluwer Law International London 1997) 487, 513.

[62] *Hormones* AB Report (n 9) para 117.

pretation of the results and implications of studies and arrived at its own conclusions on specific scientific questions.[63] In this respect, the panel's approach in the *Apples* case is not only inconsistent with the Appellate Body's instruction that the applicable standard of review is not *de novo* review, but also stands in marked contrast to the approach of the panel in the *Asbestos* case, in which the panel actively sought to avoid acting as arbiter of scientific controversies.[64]

(c) Application of the same standard of review to questions of law and questions of fact

Common law domestic administrative law systems typically distinguish between the standard of review applicable to review of questions of fact and that applicable to questions of law. Typically, greater deference is accorded to agency assessments of fact than to their legal interpretations. The distinction between facts and law (although often difficult) is well known to the Appellate Body as its own jurisdiction depends on it,[65] and it has evinced greater willingness to review panel determinations of law than of fact.[66] Nevertheless, the Appellate Body does not seem to have regarded the distinction as important when it comes to panel review of domestic measures as it was prepared to find that Article 11 of the DSU prescribes the standard of review for both questions of fact and questions of law. In the *Hormones* case, the Appellate Body, in a rather unclear passage on the standard of review applicable to legal questions, stated that Article 11 was 'directly on point' as it requires a panel to 'make an objective assessment of the matter before it, including an objective assessment of the facts of the case and the applicability of and conformity with the relevant covered agreements'.[67] Although the Appellate Body did not specifically refer to questions of interpretation of the Agreements as falling under this duty of objective assessment, such interpretations must be considered as included in the wider inquiry of the consistency or inconsistency of a Member's actions with the provisions of the applicable agreement, which is undoubtedly a legal question. This interpretation is supported by the Appellate Body's finding in the *Argentina–Footwear* case

[63] See, eg, the panel's approach to the question of whether mature, symptomless apples could harbour endophytic populations of bacteria. The evidence advanced by the US and Japan conflicted and the panel turned to the experts to act as tie-breakers as well as criticise the methodology of and conclusions that could be drawn from the studies cited by Japan: *Apples* Panel Report (n 55) paras 8.123–8.127.

[64] *EC–Measures Affecting Asbestos and Asbestos-Containing Products* WT/DS135/R modified Panel Report adopted 6 April 2001 para 8.181.

[65] Art 17.6 of the DSU limits appeals to issues of law covered by the panel report and legal interpretations developed by a panel.

[66] In particular, see: *Hormones* AB Report (n 9) paras 131–34.

[67] *Hormones* AB Report (n 9) para 118.

where it confirmed that the objective assessment standard of review as articulated in the *Hormones* case was applicable not only to panel review of facts, but also to cases where the panel's assessment of the matter 'more generally' is at issue.[68]

Utilising a single standard of review for questions of fact and questions of law means that panels will not have to be diverted by long arguments about whether a particular question is one of fact or one of law.[69] That is undoubtedly beneficial as far as the speed of proceedings is concerned, but the failure to distinguish between the standard of review applicable to questions of fact and questions of law does have some drawbacks. In particular, panels will obviously be unwilling to accord deference to a Member's interpretation of the textual provisions (clearly a question of law) as the success of the WTO system depends on reciprocity, which demands that the provisions have the same meaning for every Member. With a non-deferential standard applied to these clearly legal questions of interpretation, a panel concerned to observe the Appellate Body's apparent instruction that the same standard of review is to apply to questions of fact and questions of law, may then feel compelled to show little deference on questions of fact.

Were the Appellate Body to distinguish between the appropriate standard of review for factual and legal questions, the standard of review established for factual questions could be explicitly deferential (if that were deemed to be appropriate) without being restrained by the need to at least appear to be the same as the standard applicable to legal questions. Unhitching the two could be useful because much stronger arguments can be made in support of a greater level of deference being accorded to Members' factual determinations than can be mustered in support of deference to their legal interpretations. Although the distinction between questions of fact and questions of law can be difficult, the question of whether a measure is scientifically justified is clearly factual, and the question of whether social factors can be cited to justify a distinction in the levels of protection adopted in different situations (under Article 5.5 of the SPS Agreement) is clearly a question of law.

Support for a greater degree of deference to factual determinations derives from two perspectives: firstly, who is better equipped to make the determination; and secondly, who should be left with decision-making power in order to further the institutional aims and stability of the WTO system. If one considers the factual issues which arise in cases concerning domestic health regulations, it will be apparent that responding Members

[68] *Argentina–Safeguard Measures on Imports of Footwear* WT/DS121/AB/R AB Report adopted 12 January 2000 ('*Argentina–Footwear*') para 120.

[69] On the difficulty of the fact–law distinction, see: P Craig *Administrative Law* (4th edn Sweet & Maxwell London 1999) 474–75.

will be in a better position than panels to make numerous factual determinations as knowledge of local conditions always affects the design and extent of health measures. In such cases, the responding Member is in a better position to make those factual determinations than both the panel and the complaining Member, as well as any third parties. Even for factual questions in respect of which the responding Member is no more expert than the complaining Member (such as abstract scientific questions), panels should carefully consider whether deference to the views of the responding Member might not be appropriate anyway. Such deference might be appropriate because the responding Member is still more expert than the panel, and because deference would avoid overly intrusive review in which the reasonable determinations of national regulators are second-guessed, thus undermining support for WTO review of national health regulations. For questions of law, however, the situation is otherwise and deference does not appear to be in order. As Jackson and Croley remark in their much-cited article, '[t]hat GATT/WTO members have superior information to GATT/WTO panels about the meaning or ultimate aim of the [Anti-Dumping] Agreement's provisions seems implausible. Nor is any particular GATT/WTO member an "expert" relative to any other.'[70] The institutional aims of the WTO are, in general, better served by less deference to national interpretations as multiple interpretations of the legal norms agreed to by WTO Members would undermine the reciprocity of undertakings which underpins the international trading system.[71]

4 Article 11: The End of the Road?

For the Appellate Body, the existence of a specific standard of review for anti-dumping cases constituted an implicit limit on their ability to determine the appropriate standard of review for cases falling outside the Anti-Dumping Agreement. Its reasoning appears to have been that, because Article 17.6 claimed a certain type of review for anti-dumping cases, whatever the standard of review should be for other cases, it could not be the same. What is the anti-dumping standard of review that the EC was so keen to see applied to health cases? Does the existence of that standard really mean that the Appellate Body had to rely on DSU Article 11 to supply the standard of review? These questions are addressed in the following section, which argues that the Appellate Body read too much into the existence of the specific standard of review for anti-dumping cases and so

[70] Croley and Jackson (n 12) 208.

[71] Other commentators also argue against deference on questions of law: eg, D Palmeter and GJ Spak, 'Resolving Antidumping and Countervailing Duty Disputes: Defining GATT's Role in an Era of Increasing Conflict' (1993) 24 Law&Pol'yIntlBus 1145, 1158.

took an unnecessarily narrow view of its options in determining the standard of review to apply to other cases. That said, however, it will be suggested that the anti-dumping standard of review is not necessarily well suited to application in health cases.

(a) The standard of review in anti-dumping cases

Dumping occurs when a product is exported at a lower price than it is sold for in the country of origin or export.[72] When dumping is suspected, the competent authorities of a WTO Member may launch an investigation, in which the normal value (the price of the imported product in the ordinary course of trade in the country of origin or export) is compared with the export price (the price of the product in the country of import) in order to determine whether dumping has occurred. Before anti-dumping measures can be imposed, however, two other substantive requirements must be met: there must be a material injury to the domestic industry, and a causal link between the dumped imports and the injury.[73] The substantive and procedural requirements for national anti-dumping actions are set out in the Anti-Dumping Agreement. An anti-dumping investigation is normally initiated following a request submitted by or on behalf of a domestic industry.[74] Once initiated, the domestic investigation is subject to detailed rules which, *inter alia*, specify that information must be disclosed to interested parties, who must also be provided with adequate opportunity to comment and participate in the investigation.[75] Anti-dumping determinations are subject to domestic judicial review,[76] but may also be challenged in the WTO by an interested WTO Member. Where such a challenge is brought, the WTO panel's review is subject to the standard of review set out in Article 17.6 of the Anti-Dumping Agreement.

Article 17.6 of the Anti-Dumping Agreement specifies the standard of review to be applied by panels. Article 17.6 states that:

> (i) in its assessment of the facts of the matter, the panel shall determine whether the authorities' establishment of the facts was proper and whether their evaluation of those facts was unbiased and objective. If the establishment of the facts was proper and the evaluation was unbiased and objective, even though the panel might have reached a different conclusion, the evaluation shall not be overturned;
> (ii) the panel shall interpret the relevant provisions of the Agreement in accordance with customary rules of interpretation of public international law. Where the panel finds that a relevant provision of the Agreement admits of more than one permissible interpretation, the panel shall find the authorities' measure to

[72] Anti-Dumping Agreement Arts 1, 2.
[73] Anti-Dumping Agreement Arts 1, 3.
[74] Anti-Dumping Agreement Art 5.
[75] Anti-Dumping Agreement Art 6.
[76] Anti-Dumping Agreement Art 13.

be in conformity with the Agreement if it rests upon one of those permissible interpretations.

As is apparent from its text, Article 17.6 prescribes a standard of review to be applied to the establishment and evaluation of factual questions in Article 17.6(i) and a separate standard of review to be applied to the panel's review of questions relating to interpretation in Article 17.6(ii).

The standard of review in Article 17.6(i) stipulates that, if the establishment of the facts was proper,[77] and the evaluation of those facts was unbiased and objective, the panel must not overturn the evaluation of the authorities just because it would have reached a different conclusion. This is an ostensibly deferential standard of review and it is not surprising that the EC sought to have a substantially similar standard applied in the *Hormones* case.[78] The Appellate Body has confirmed the deferential tone of the Article by making it clear that the overarching purpose of this provision is to avoid having panels second-guessing the determinations of the national authorities when the facts have been properly established and subjected to an unbiased and objective evaluation.[79] Cases decided under the Anti-Dumping Agreement confirm its appearance of deference, although the Article 17.6(i) standard of review does still harbour potential for more intrusive review.[80]

The 'unbiased and objective evaluation' criterion has been developed by panels and the Appellate Body in the following way. In applying this provision, panels ask whether an unbiased and objective investigating authority *could properly have reached* the conclusions actually reached by the national authorities.[81] In general, this provision results in fairly

[77] Whether the establishment of facts was proper relates to whether the authority collected relevant and reliable information: *US Anti-Dumping Measures on Hot-Rolled Steel Products from Japan* WT/DS184/R modified Panel Report adopted 23 August 2001 (*'US–Hot-Rolled Steel'*) para 7.26.

[78] *Hormones* AB Report (n 9) paras 112–13, citing paras 128–29 of the EC's Appellant's submission.

[79] *Thailand–Anti-Dumping Duties on Angles, Shapes and Sections of Iron or Non-Alloy Steel and H-Beams from Poland* WT/DS122/AB/R AB Report adopted 5 April 2001 (*'Thailand–Polish Steel'*) para 117.

[80] Bloche goes further and suggests the AB has 'read out' the discretion suggested in the Article: MG Bloche 'WTO Deference to National Health Policy: Toward an Interpretive Principle' (2002) 5 JIEL 825, 831–32.

[81] See, eg: *Mexico–Anti-Dumping Investigation of High Fructose Corn Syrup (HFCS) from the US* WT/DS132/R Panel Report adopted 24 April 2000 para 7.57; *Guatemala–Definitive Anti-Dumping Measures on Grey Portland Cement from Mexico* WT/DS156/R Panel Report adopted 17 November 2000 (*'Portland Cement from Mexico'*) para 8.24; *US–Anti-Dumping Measures on Stainless Steel Plate in Coils and Stainless Steel Sheet and Strip from Korea* WT/DS179/R Panel Report adopted 1 February 2001 (*'US–Stainless Steel Coils'*) para 6.3; *US–Hot-Rolled Steel* Panel Report (n 77) para 7.26; *Thailand–Anti-Dumping Duties on Angles, Shapes and Sections of Iron or Non-Alloy Steel and H-Beams from Poland* WT/DS122/R modified Panel Report adopted 5 April 2001 para 7.51; *Argentina–Definitive Anti-Dumping Measures on Imports of Ceramic Floor Tiles from Italy* WT/DS189/R Panel Report adopted 5 November 2001 (*'Argentina–Italian Tiles'*) para 6.3; *Argentina–Definitive Anti-Dumping Duties on Poultry from Brazil* WT/DS241/R Panel Report adopted 19 May 2003.

deferential review; panels do not overturn simply because they think it would have been preferable for the authorities to have come to a different conclusion.[82] Rather, it is only where things are obviously amiss that the panel will intervene. For example, in *Portland Cement from Mexico* the authorities in Guatemala determined whether the product was being dumped by comparing the price on two Mexican *retail* invoices for a single sack of cement each with the price stipulated in two import certificates for *consignments* of 7,035 and 4,221 bags of cement respectively. As the panel pointed out, there are obvious differences in the quantities and retail stages of the prices being compared, which the Guatemalan Ministry made no attempt to take into account.[83] Accordingly, the panel concluded that 'an unbiased and objective investigating authority could not in our view have concluded that there was sufficient evidence of dumping to justify the initiation of an anti-dumping investigation.'[84] The panel stressed that it was not asking for detailed work on the comparability of prices before an investigation could be launched, but that such glaringly obvious differences could not be overlooked.[85]

Sometimes, the analysis of whether an unbiased and objective investigating authority could have reached the contested conclusions can lead to close review of the underlying facts and what may reasonably be deduced from them. For example, in *US–Stainless Steel Coils*, the panel undertook a detailed review of the actual facts of the case in order to determine whether an unbiased and objective investigating authority could have properly determined (as did the US authorities) that the local sales were made in Korean won rather than in dollars.[86] The proper evaluation of facts also requires that facts which might detract from the decision actually reached must be considered[87]—one-sided explanations which fail to account for such facts will not pass muster. Explanation is, in general, important as not explaining a failure to account for particular information has been held to demonstrate that the evaluation of the facts was not unbiased and objective.[88]

In applying Article 17.6(ii) to interpretations of the Anti-Dumping Agreement, panels adhere to the following procedure. They consider the text according to the principles set out in the Vienna Convention[89] (looking to ordinary meaning in context and in light of the object and purpose,

[82] *US–Hot-Rolled Steel* Panel Report (n 77) para 7.235.
[83] *Portland Cement from Mexico* Panel Report (n 81) paras 8.37–8.39.
[84] *Portland Cement from Mexico* Panel Report (n 81) para 8.39.
[85] *Portland Cement from Mexico* Panel Report (n 81) para 8.40.
[86] *US–Stainless Steel Coils* Panel Report (n 81) para 6.19–6.37 (having reviewed the facts, the panel concluded that, in respect of the steel plate, an unbiased and objective authority could have concluded that the sales were in won, whereas, in respect of steel sheet, it could not).
[87] *US–Hot-Rolled Steel* Panel Report (n 77) para 7.26.
[88] *Argentina–Italian Tiles* Panel Report (n 81) paras 6.24–6.28.
[89] Vienna Convention on the Law of Treaties (Vienna Convention) (Vienna, 23 May 1969).

and looking to the preparatory work if necessary) and then determine whether the interpretation adopted by the Member in question is one that is 'permissible' and, if so, it is allowed to stand.[90] It can happen, however, that, when it comes to Appellate Body review, the fact that the panel did not consider the Member's interpretation to be a 'permissible' one is inferred from the fact of the panel's finding of inconsistency without a reasoned finding to that effect having been provided by the panel.[91]

With the qualifications identified above, Article 17.6 delivers on its promise of deferential review. Panels appear to have taken to heart the message that it is not their prerogative to second-guess the determinations of the national authorities. It is, then, not surprising that the standard holds appeal for a wider audience concerned that review of national regulators' health determinations is unnecessarily intrusive. If a substantively similar standard is to be applied more broadly, it needs to be asked whether the existence of this special provision for anti-dumping cases really does mean that it cannot be applied to health cases.

(b) *Opening-up the standard of review options*

The Appellate Body in the *Hormones* case found that Article 11 of the DSU articulates with great succinctness but with sufficient clarity the appropriate standard of review.[92] In coming to this conclusion, the Appellate Body regarded itself as unable to apply the standard of review set out in Article 17.6 of the Anti-Dumping Agreement and also felt compelled to find the appropriate standard of review clearly rooted in the text of the SPS Agreement.[93] The Appellate Body then latched-on to Article 11's

[90] *US –Hot-Rolled Steel* AB Report (n 37) paras 57–60; *Mexico–Anti-Dumping Investigation of High Fructose Corn Syrup (HFCS) from the US (Recourse to Article 21.5 of the DSU by the US)* WT/DS132/AB/R AB Report adopted 21 November 2001; *EC–Anti-Dumping Duties on Imports of Cotton-Type Bed Linen from India* WT/DS141/R modified Panel Report adopted 12 March 2001 para 6.46. It has, however, been suggested that Art 17.6(ii) is largely ignored by panels and the Appellate Body, which have failed to use the provision to accord the deference its wording suggests: DK Tarullo 'The Hidden Costs of International Dispute Settlement: WTO Review of Domestic Anti-Dumping Decisions' (2002) 34 Law&Pol'yIntlBus 109.

[91] *EC–Anti-Dumping Duties on Imports of Cotton-Type Bed Linen from India* WT/DS141/AB/R AB Report adopted 12 March 2001 para 65. For criticism of Article 17.6(ii) and particularly the possibility of there being other permissible interpretations after the Vienna Convention methods of interpretation have been followed, see: Croley and Jackson (n 12) 200–201 (but cf Tarullo (n 90) 150–51).

[92] *Hormones* AB Report (n 9) paras 116–17.

[93] *Hormones* AB Report (n 9) para 115: 'The standard of review appropriately applicable in proceedings under the *SPS Agreement*, of course, must reflect the balance established in that Agreement between the jurisdictional competences conceded by the Members to the WTO and the jurisdictional competences retained by the Members for themselves. To adopt a standard of review not clearly rooted in the text of the *SPS Agreement* itself, may well amount to changing that finely drawn balance; and neither a panel nor the Appellate Body is authorized to do that.'

objective assessment requirement as accommodating both of these scruples. While the Appellate Body's textualist tendencies are understandable as a valid means to avoid being labelled as activist by going beyond the scope of its authority as set out in the texts, the Appellate Body may have taken too narrow a view of the options available to it. It is true that, to improve on the standard of review, the Appellate Body might *prefer* that the DSU be amended (following a debate on the appropriate standard of review to be applied), but such a change is unlikely in the medium term given the difficulty of securing amendments to the WTO Agreements. The Appellate Body's textualist concerns are, however, not uniform: in some areas, the Appellate Body has shown itself to be less textually constrained.[94] In any event, moving beyond a simple objective assessment standard of review need not even entail too great a sacrifice of textualist caution.

The WTO could open up the standard of review options by adopting a broader view of the ways in which standards of review can be rooted in the text of WTO Agreements. Instead of just looking for a ready-made standard of review in the texts when, really, one does not exist, the Appellate Body could refer to the substantive disciplines and the balance between regulatory autonomy and international supervision that the Agreements seek to implement in order to support a revised standard of review. The Appellate Body's (quite reasonable) concern is to support its chosen standard of review by reference to the WTO texts. Referring to a complete, fully-formulated standard of review in the texts is one way of doing this, but it is not the only way. If no ready-made standard of review is available, a standard can still be supported by the texts if it is based on the nature of the disciplines provided for in the text and the objectives that the text seeks to further. If, as is argued here, objective assessment is not a full, completely formulated standard of review, the Appellate Body could quite legitimately claim to be basing a standard of review on the texts of the relevant Agreements if that standard were based on considerations rooted in the Agreements. For example, regard could be had to: the nature of the substantive disciplines imposed on national health regulations (scientific basis, least trade-restrictive, consistency etc); the aims and objectives of the WTO in that area (minimising the costs to trade of protectionist or unnecessary health measures); the distribution of decision-making authority effected by the WTO Agreements; and the relative strengths and weaknesses of panels and national regulators in answering pertinent questions.

[94] The AB has been more willing to go beyond the narrow confines of its explicitly enumerated powers by filling in the gaps left by panels, an activity which includes making decisions on factual matters: *Salmon* AB Report (n 44) paras 117–19 (citing, *inter alia, US–Standards for Reformulated and Conventional Gasoline* WT/DS2/AB/R AB Report adopted 20 May 1996 pages 19ff). For a criticism of this practice, see: JHJ Bourgeois 'Some Reflections on the WTO Dispute Settlement System from a Practitioner's Perspective' (2001) 4 JIEL 145, 152.

In the *Hormones* case, the Appellate Body made much of the fact that Article 17.6 of the Anti-Dumping Agreement does not apply to disputes not covered by that Agreement.[95] It is quite correct that panels would not be authorised to apply that Article to disputes not covered by the Anti-Dumping Agreement. Panels and the Appellate Body have, however, gone further and seem to regard the fact that Article 17.6 only applies to anti-dumping disputes as precluding the application of substantively similar standards of review in other areas.[96] The existence of a special provision for deference in anti-dumping cases has, at times, even been argued to mean that panels not hearing anti-dumping cases are not authorised to accord any deference at all, although this view has not gained currency.[97]

The fact that Article 17.6 of the Anti-Dumping Agreement applies a specific, deferential standard of review should not be construed as preventing panels according any deference to the decisions of the Members outside that Agreement or that the application of substantively similar standards is necessarily precluded. *Some* standard of review is implicit whether or not it is articulated, and the Appellate Body has recognised that the failure to provide specifically for a standard of review does not mean that one does not apply.[98] Given that *some* standard of review must be applied even though it has not been explicitly stipulated in the texts, there is no basis on which to suppose that panels could not, without authorisation, accord the findings of national authorities any deference. The absence of specification might equally well be argued to mean that panels are not authorised to conduct *de novo* review. In fact, this argument is the more tenable as it is more in keeping with the *in dubio mitius* principle applied by the Appellate Body in the *Hormones* case, on the basis that it is less onerous to the parties.[99] All of which is not to say that the Anti-Dumping Agreement's standard of review *should* be used in health cases—the point is simply that, if a similar standard were justified, based on the applicable texts and the balance of authority between the Member and the WTO that they embody, the mere fact of Article 17.6's existence should not preclude the adoption of that level of deference.

[95] *Hormones* AB Report (n 9) 114.

[96] For a contrary view arguing that panels have not applied the Art 17.6 standards outside the anti-dumping area because they are ambiguous, see: J Gomula 'The Standard of Review of Article 17.6 of the Anti-Dumping Agreement and the Problem of its Extension to other WTO Agreements' in Mengozzi (ed) (n 10) 577, 607–608.

[97] The EC and Brazil (as third party) argued that, because Art 17.6 did not apply, the panel was not authorised to accord *any* deference to the US authorities: *US–Imposition of Countervailing Duties on Certain Hot-Rolled Lead and Bismuth Carbon Steel Products Originating in the UK* WT/DS138/R Panel Report adopted 7 June 2000 para 20 of Second Written Submission of the EC, Panel Report para 4.93 (Brazil).

[98] *Hormones* AB Report (n 9) paras 114, 116.

[99] *Hormones* AB Report (n 9) para 165, n 154.

(c) Development in safeguards cases: using objective assessment as a starting point

The Appellate Body in the *Hormones* case presented the objective assessment standard of review as a general standard of review applicable across the board, with the exception of cases arising under the Anti-Dumping Agreement. It was, in fact, this generality that made that standard of review appealing in the first place; where the Anti-Dumping Agreement provided for a specific standard of review, all other cases were governed simply by the provisions of the DSU which, inasmuch as they spoke to the standard of review, provided for objective assessment. We saw above that the objective assessment standard, as used by the Appellate Body in health-based disputes, has not been a satisfactory guide to the applicable intensity of review. What, then, of its application in other contexts? In the context of safeguard measures,[100] it seems that some content has been built around the objective assessment standard. While not formally a departure from objective assessment as a standard of review, the approach evident in the safeguards cases does move away from the position taken in the *Hormones* case by not treating objective assessment as a complete explanation of the applicable standard of review. What has, in effect, occurred is that the objective assessment standard has been used as a shell into which the appropriate content is fitted. Objective assessment ceases to be *the* standard of review so much as the basis upon which the appropriate standard of review is built.

The safeguards cases do not contest that Article 11 of the DSU sets out the applicable standard of review for all cases except those covered by the Anti-Dumping Agreement.[101] It is agreed that panels must implement the Article 11 objective assessment requirement, but it is not taken for granted, as it was in the *Hormones* case, that this standard is meaningful without further elaboration. What is interesting about the safeguards cases is how the bare objective assessment standard of review has been expanded into a meaningful standard of review, not by attempting to provide a doctrinally more detailed formulation of the objective assessment standard, but by focusing on how the objective assessment standard should be *applied*.[102]

[100] Article XIX of GATT 1994 permits a Member to take a 'safeguard' action to protect a specific domestic industry from an unforeseen increase in imports which is causing or is likely to cause serious injury to the industry. The Safeguards Agreement regulates these actions in greater detail, stipulating certain minimum notice and hearing requirements for the domestic investigation (Art 3): Agreement on Safeguards (Safeguards Agreement) (Marrakesh, 14 April 1994).

[101] *Argentina–Footwear* AB Report (n 68) paras 118, 120; *Korea–Definitive Safeguard Measure on Imports of Certain Dairy Products* WT/DS98/R modified Panel Report adopted 12 January 2000 paras 4.72, 7.26 ('*Korea–Dairy*'); *US–Transitional Safeguard Measure on Combed Cotton Yarn from Pakistan* WT/DS192/AB/R AB Report adopted 5 November 2001 ('*US–Cotton Yarn from Pakistan*') paras 68–69.

[102] The cases describe it as a 'legal test for applying that [the objective assessment] standard to the obligations under Article 4': *US–Definitive Safeguard Measures on Imports of Circular Carbon Quality Line Pipe from Korea* WT/DS202/R modified Panel Report adopted 8 March 2002 ('*US–Line Pipe from Korea*') para 4.291.

This is done by laying down what is, in effect, a roadmap of the questions a panel is to ask. This roadmap provides practical instructions to panellists rather than developing the standard of review through more abstract means. In the safeguards cases, objective assessment has been taken to mean that the panel should objectively assess the review conducted by the national investigating authority by determining whether the national authority examined all the relevant facts and provided an adequate explanation of how the facts as a whole supported the determination made.[103] This standard of review can be traced back to the influential *US–Underwear* case and, although that case predates the *Hormones* case's pronouncement that objective assessment is *the* standard of review, the panel in the *US–Underwear* case did see its formulation as fulfilling its duty to make an objective assessment.[104] Moreover, subsequent cases have brought the safeguards standard of review under the *Hormones* case banner.[105]

The approach taken in the safeguards cases stems from the structure and content of the Safeguards Agreement. In the *Argentina–Footwear* case, the Appellate Body found that the panel had not conducted a *de novo* review or substituted its analysis and judgment for that of the Argentine authorities but, rather, had fulfilled its responsibility under Article 11 of the DSU by examining, *as the very terms of Article 4 required it to do*,[106] whether the Argentine authorities had considered all the relevant facts and had adequately explained how the facts supported the determinations that were made. In approving the panel's application of the objective assessment standard of review, the Appellate Body approved what amounts to a procedurally focused review in which the panel is to ask whether all relevant facts have been considered and whether an adequate explanation of the connection between the facts and the decision has been provided. This procedural approach is one way of finding a workable balance between *de novo* review and complete deference, but relies on being able to refine the standard of review by means of practical guidance rather than abstract elaboration.

[103] *US–Underwear* Panel Report (n 30) para 7.13; *Korea–Dairy* Panel Report (n 101) para 7.30; *Argentina–Safeguard Measures on Imports of Footwear* WT/DS121/R modified Panel Report adopted 12 January 2000 para 8.124 (affirmed and reiterated in *Argentina–Footwear* AB Report (n 68) para 121).

[104] *US–Underwear* Panel Report (n 30) para 7.13.

[105] *Korea–Dairy* Panel Report (n 101) paras 7.26, 7.30 and *Argentina–Footwear* AB Report (n 68) paras 117, 121 (The panel in the *Argentina–Footwear* case adopted the *US–Underwear* approach without reference to the *Hormones* case, but the AB found that that the panel had correctly stated the applicable standard of review as set out by the *Hormones* case (even though it had referred to different cases) and approved its application of that standard.)

[106] *Argentina–Footwear* AB Report (n 68) para 121. Safeguards Agreement Art 4, which governs the determination of serious injury or threat thereof to the domestic industry and provides that the national authorities must evaluate all relevant factors including those listed, requires a causal link between increased imports and the injury or threat thereof, and requires that the authorities publish a detailed analysis.

Procedurally focused review can provide a means by which to deliver review which safeguards interests by ensuring transparency and that rights to make representations are respected. Because procedurally focused review is concerned with *how* a decision was reached, it tends to stray beyond purely procedural concerns (such as whether relevant notices were provided, whether consultation obligations were met etc) to the methodology employed by decision-makers. Methodology differs from procedure because it refers to the intellectual framework for decision-making—what makes a conclusion valid. As was shown in relation to judicial review in the US, review which promises to avoid substituting the adjudicator's analysis for that of the original decision-maker can easily become intrusive when the decision-maker's methodology is scrutinised. Similarly, in safeguards cases, one can find close scrutiny of the methodology of the authorities in safeguards investigations.[107] For example, in *US–Line Pipe from Korea*, the panel examined whether the US International Trade Commission's methodology in determining whether there were increased imports was 'appropriate'.[108] Moreover, the formulation of safeguards review set out above (which asks whether relevant facts have been considered and a reasonable explanation provided) has been explicitly elaborated on in a way that makes intrusive review a quite real possibility. Substantive conclusions are not insulated from review: avoiding *de novo* review 'does not mean that panels must simply accept the conclusions of the competent authorities.'[109] Rather:

> a panel can assess whether the competent authorities' explanation for its determination is reasoned and adequate *only* if the panel critically examines that explanation, in depth, and in the light of the facts before the panel. Panels must, therefore, review whether the competent authorities' explanation fully addresses the nature, and, especially, the complexities, of the data, and responds to other plausible interpretations of that data. A panel must find, in particular, that an explanation is not reasoned, or is not adequate, if some *alternative explanation* of the facts is plausible, and if the competent authorities' explanation does not seem adequate in the light of that alternative explanation.[110]

It can be seen, then, that a high bar has been set for the quality and comprehensiveness of reasoning that will be required of national authorities. Again, procedural review can ultimately show itself to be quite demanding.

[107] Tarullo suggests that panels and the AB exercise close scrutiny when reviewing the anti-dumping, safeguards and countervailing duty determinations of domestic trade administrations, perhaps because national authorities are thought to favour domestic interests and because foreign producers are not properly represented: Tarullo (n 90) 154–56.

[108] *US–Line Pipe from Korea* Panel Report (n 102) paras 7.192–7.203.

[109] *US–Safeguard Measures on Imports of Fresh, Chilled or Frozen Lamb Meat From New Zealand and Australia* WT/DS177/AB/R AB Report adopted 16 May 2001 para 106. See also: *US–Cotton Yarn from Pakistan* AB Report (n 101) para 69.

[110] *US–Lamb* AB Report (n 109) para 106 (emphasis in original). See also: *US–Cotton Yarn from Pakistan* AB Report (n 101) para 69; *US–Line Pipe from Korea* Panel Report (n 102) para 7.216.

C CONCLUSION

The Appellate Body's 'objective assessment' standard of review is flawed. It does not act as a coherent standard of review because it does not instruct panels on how to conduct their review of domestic health measures. The Appellate Body has reasoned itself into a corner by regarding itself as unable to move beyond the terms of Article 11 of the DSU in discussing the standard of review. The Appellate Body could, however, take a broader view of the standard of review options open to it by discussing deference openly and re-examining its approach to textual support and the significance of Article 17.6 of the Anti-Dumping Agreement. The approach taken in the safeguards cases of building a standard of review suited to the particular area and presenting it as a fulfilment of the Article 11 duty of objective assessment shows that 'objective assessment' need not be the end of the story. In the safeguards cases, the Appellate Body has taken the objective assessment standard of review forward and implicitly recognised that, while succinct, a bare reference to objective assessment does not constitute a useful standard of review. Might it not be possible to move beyond objective assessment in health cases as well? The following chapter considers how the standard of review might be developed in order to strike the right balance between intrusiveness and ineffectiveness when reviewing health cases.

Conclusion

[illegible]

7

Developing the WTO's Standard of Review in Health Cases

IF THE STANDARD of review is to help mediate points of tension, it is necessary to have some idea of where the balance in authority between the WTO and the Member States individually is to rest. The Appellate Body has referred to the need to preserve the delicately negotiated balance between promoting trade and protecting health,[1] but has not taken the next step of developing the standard of review in a way that connects that balance with a legally comprehensible doctrine. Instead, objective assessment has been allowed to retain its place as the applicable standard of review notwithstanding the doctrine's shortcomings. This failure to develop the standard of review in health cases reflects a kind of stasis in which the stakes are so high and feelings so strong that there has been little open discussion of the role of WTO panels vis-à-vis that of the Members individually. Without a clear idea of how the institutional balance of authority should rest,[2] it is hard to develop a useful standard of review. There needs to be a candid discussion about just how much deference, if any, should be accorded to the Members when they regulate to protect health. This is the *what* question—what level of deference will best accommodate both the needs of the WTO system and the needs of national regulators? Following the *what* question, comes the *how* question—how can we structure the standard of review so that it helps to achieve the desired intensity of review?

In addressing the appropriate level of deference, it is instructive to look beyond the confines of the WTO to other legal systems that have grappled with analogous questions. To this end, this chapter revisits the judicial review case law of the US (which was introduced in Chapter 5), takes up the US commerce clause jurisprudence and expands on the way in which

[1] *EC Measures Concerning Meat and Meat Products (Hormones)* WT/DS26/AB/R, WT/DS48/AB/R AB Report adopted 13 February 1998 ('*Hormones*') para 177.

[2] Note that the balance of authority on health questions has both horizontal (judicialised dispute settlement or executive rule-making) and vertical components (international or national): JH Jackson 'Sovereignty, Subsidiarity, and Separation of Powers: the High-Wire Balancing Act of Globalization' in DLM Kennedy and JD Southwick (eds) *The Political Economy of International Trade Law* (CUP Cambridge UK 2002) 13, 18–24.

the ECJ has handled challenges to both Community and Member State health regulations. These bodies of law are useful as they show how different legal systems have chosen to distribute authority over health regulations when rights to trade cross the territorial boundaries of different regulatory regimes. It is by looking at underlying reasons why close scrutiny or deference is considered appropriate that we can start thinking about whether those arguments carry any weight in the WTO.

Similarly, in developing the WTO's standard of review, it is helpful to look at how a standard of review is actually expressed and structured in other jurisdictions. Given that the objective assessment standard appears (for better or worse) to be entrenched in the WTO, development of the standard of review will most probably have to occur within a framework that continues (at least formally) to identify objective assessment as the applicable standard of review.

A WHAT LEVEL OF DEFERENCE IS DESIRABLE? US AND EU PERSPECTIVES

1 Scrutiny of Regulatory Decisions in US Judicial Review

In Chapter 5, the basic framework of judicial review of health and safety regulations in the US was set out. It will be recalled that, under the APA,[3] two standards of review are provided for: the substantial evidence standard, which applies to formal rule-making (rule-making with quasi-judicial hearings) and the arbitrary and capricious standard, which applies to informal rule-making.[4] In both cases, there is an outward show of deference—courts are not to substitute their views for those of the regulators—but, as was shown in Chapter 5, intense scrutiny of data and methodology means that deference in judicial review comes with heavy qualifications.

(a) Lessons from review under the APA

The constitutional structure of the US produces a tension between deference and close scrutiny. On the one hand, rigorous review is required to ensure that federal regulatory agencies remain within the limits of their *delegated* powers.[5] On the other hand, deference to the will of Congress in making that delegation, and recognition of the legitimate role of expert

[3] Administrative Procedure Act 5 USC § 551 ff (1994) ('APA').

[4] APA § 706(2)(A) (arbitrary and capricious), § 706(2)(E) (substantial evidence).

[5] JL Mashaw, RA Merrill and PM Shane *Administrative Law: The American Public Law System: Cases and Materials* (4th edn West Group St Paul 1998) 802; AC Aman and WT Mayton *Administrative Law* (West Publishing Co St Paul 1993) 435; RS Melnick *Regulation and the Courts: The Case of the Clean Air Act* (Brookings Institution Washington DC 1983) 67.

regulatory agencies, demand that some deference be given to the expertise of agencies, at least on factual questions within the scope of their expertise and responsibility. As was pointed out in the *Benzene* case (in which the Secretary of Labor's newly promulgated exposure limits were challenged), courts are not supposed to pass judgment on the wisdom of specific regulations; it is assumed that ill-considered or unwise regulations will be corrected through the democratic process.[6] The applicable standard of review is supposed to help manage this constitutional tension, but deference has been undermined by the focus on methodology and data. On many occasions, the courts have seen fit to reject agency rule-making because they have found fault with the way in which studies underpinning regulations were conducted or data were gathered, or with the model used in processing data.[7]

When it comes to the WTO, there is a different matrix of factors. The regulations being reviewed come, not from agencies exercising delegated authority, but from independent sovereign members of an international organisation exercising their inherent rights to protect public health[8] in circumstances where those rights are expressly preserved.[9] Where a US court has to police the boundaries of *delegated* powers, a WTO panel is faced with the exercise of an inherent power to protect health that was never relinquished. It is true that, while not given up, the sovereign right of WTO Members to protect health has been subjected to various disciplines, but the existence of those agreed disciplines—significant as they are—does not change the essential fact that, when WTO Members act to protect health, they are not acting pursuant to a delegation of power. In view of this distinction, WTO panels cannot justify close scrutiny (as do their American counterparts) by pointing to the need to ensure that the limits of delegated powers are respected. Given the absence of this justification for close scrutiny, greater deference to the regulatory decisions of WTO Members may be in order.

[6] *Industrial Union Department, AFL-CIO v American Petroleum Institute* 448 US 607, 688 (Justice Marshall dissenting), 100 S Ct 2844 (1980) ('*Benzene*').

[7] See, eg: *International Harvester Co v Ruckelshaus* 478 F 2d 615 (US Ct of Apps (DC Cir), 1973); *Motor Vehicle Manufacturers Association of the US Inc v State Farm Mutual Automobile Insurance Co* 463 US 29, 103 S Ct 2865 (1983); *Ohio v EPA* 784 F 2d 224, 230 (US Ct of Apps (6th Cir), 1986); *AFL-CIO v OSHA* 965 F 2d 962 (US Ct of Apps (11th Cir), 1992).

[8] For a similar view on deference to GATT Members' interpretations, see: JR Cannon and KL Bland 'GATT Panels Need Restraining Principles' (1993) 24 Law&Pol'yIntlBus 1167, 1168–69.

[9] Agreement on the Application of Sanitary and Phytosanitary Measures (the SPS Agreement) (Marrakesh, 15 April 1994) Preamble, Art 2.1; General Agreement on Tariffs and Trade (GATT) (Geneva, 30 October 1947; 55 UNTS 194) Art XX(b); Agreement on Technical Barriers to Trade (the TBT Agreement) (Marrakesh, 15 April 1994) Preamble, Art 2.2.

(b) *The* Chevron *doctrine and the WTO*

In Chapter 6, the Appellate Body's suggestion that the standard of review must be the same for legal and factual questions was criticised. It should be recalled that that position arose only because the Appellate Body identified Article 11 of the DSU (which refers to factual *and* legal issues) as articulating the standard of review, and not because of any considered decision that the standard of review should be the same in each case. In the US, judicial review doctrines do distinguish between factual and legal questions, applying a distinct standard of review to the legal interpretations of regulatory agencies. In *Chevron USA Inc v NRDC*, the Supreme Court set out a two part test for review of legal questions: if Congress has spoken on 'the precise question at issue', its clear intent must be respected; but if the statute is silent or ambiguous with respect to the specific issue, the court must uphold an agency's permissible or reasonable interpretation.[10] Not surprisingly, the apparent simplicity of the test masks a number of questions, the answers to which have the potential to affect markedly the degree of deference that a test like that in the *Chevron* case actually delivers.[11] Firstly, any simple discussion of 'questions of law' conceals the fact that it is notoriously difficult to draw clear lines between questions of law and questions of fact.[12] Secondly, the *Chevron* test leaves open wide scope for disagreement about whether Congress has in fact spoken to the issue in question.[13] Differing degrees of enthusiasm for textualism and the different levels of generality with which the 'precise question at issue' can be framed[14] have led some commentators to declare that courts are free to find ambiguities under the first step of *Chevron*, or not, as they please.[15] Finally, the lengths to which the court should go to find out

[10] 467 US 837, 842–43, 104 S Ct 2778 (1984).

[11] Note the intrusive review effected by taking an activist approach to interpretation in the following cases: *Benzene* (n 6) 639 (where the Supreme Court read into the statute a requirement that OSHA prove the existence of a 'significant risk' at the current level of exposure); and *AFL-CIO v OSHA* 965 F 2d 962 (US Ct of Apps (11th Cir), 1992) (where the Eleventh Circuit was not prepared to allow OSHA to regulate chemicals by categories, but insisted that each of the 400 chemicals had to be individually assessed).

[12] Attorney General's Committee on Administrative Procedure *Final Report* (1941) 88–90 (on the difficulties with the traditional distinction between questions of law and fact).

[13] Shapiro and Buzbee note that the rise of textualism in the Supreme Court means that some justices very rarely find any ambiguity triggering *Chevron* stage two: RA Shapiro and WW Buzbee 'Unidimensional Federalism: Power and Perspective in Commerce Clause Adjudication' (2003) 88 Cornell LRev 1199, 1261–62.

[14] PM Wald 'Judicial Review in Midpassage: The Uneasy Partnership Between Courts and Agencies Plays On' (1996) 32 Tulsa LJ 221, 227; Mashaw, Merrill and Shane (n 5) 774–75 (citing Wald).

[15] SB Zellmer 'The Devil, the Details, and the Dawn of the 21st Century Administrative State: Beyond the New Deal' (2000) 32 ArizStLJ 941, 1013; SP Croley and JH Jackson 'WTO Dispute Procedures, Standard of Review, and Deference to National Governments' (1996) 90 AJIL 193, 203.

whether Congress has spoken on the issue is another contentious question.[16] The problems with the functioning of the doctrine are, however, not of concern here; the point of interest is why the legal opinions of regulatory agencies should be deferred to and whether those reasons suggest any call for deference to the legal interpretations of the WTO Members.

In an article that has attracted attention in the WTO,[17] Croley and Jackson present three rationales for *Chevron*-style deference to agencies' legal interpretations: agency expertise, democratic accountability and efficiency or co-ordination.[18] The expertise rationale argues that agencies' expertise extends to the legal aspects of their task and respects the fact that agencies' interpretations are informed by policy.[19] The democracy rationale is based on the fact that, whereas the courts are not democratically accountable, in the US, agencies enjoy delegated powers and are at least indirectly accountable to Congress and the President. The efficiency justification stems from the fact that, unless there is a degree of deference to agency interpretations, the many different federal courts could arrive at different interpretations of the same statute, placing the agency in an invidious position.

As Croley and Jackson argue, a comparison with the nature of the WTO system suggests that the rationales which support deference to the legal interpretations of domestic regulatory agencies in the US do not retain their vigour when applied to the WTO. Croley and Jackson refute the argument that agency expertise justifies deference by pointing out that no WTO Member has greater expertise when it comes to the meaning or ultimate aim of the WTO Agreements and that WTO Members are not charged with implementing WTO Agreements in the same way as an American agency is charged with implementing its statute.[20] The democracy argument (according to which agencies should be held accountable to Congress and the President rather than the courts) is rejected in the WTO because it is the panels who are the membership's delegates and there is no analogous democratically legitimate focus for accountability.[21] Finally, the efficiency argument is dismissed because deference to WTO Members would ensure that variable interpretations proliferate when part

[16] *Immigration and Naturalization Service v Cardoza-Fonseca* 480 US 421, 107 S Ct 1207 (1987) (where the Supreme Court was prepared to exhaust its tools of interpretation before finding that Congress had not expressed its intent on the matter); Aman and Mayton (n 5) 474–75.

[17] *US–Imposition of Countervailing Duties on Certain Hot-Rolled Lead and Bismuth Carbon Steel Products Originating in the UK* WT/DS138/R Panel Report adopted 7 June 2000, Second Written Submission of the EC para 20, n 163, para 27, n 178; *US–Anti-Dumping Duty on Dynamic Random Access Memory Semiconductors (DRAMS) of One Megabit or Above from Korea* WT/DS99/R Panel Report adopted 19 March 1999 paras 4.66–4.70 (cited by Korea).

[18] Croley and Jackson (n 15) 206–7.

[19] Aman and Mayton (n 5) 467; cf The Hon A Scalia 'Judicial Deference to Administrative Interpretations of Law' [1989] Duke LJ 511, 514–15.

[20] Croley and Jackson (n 15) 208–9.

[21] Croley and Jackson (n 15) 209.

of the point of the WTO's dispute resolution system is to avoid such a multiplicity of interpretations.[22] On the whole, the US experience of deference to agency interpretations suggests that deference to national interpretations of the WTO Agreements would not be appropriate.

2 Review of State Health and Safety Regulations under the Commerce Clause

In both the US federal system and the WTO, regulations that adversely affect trade can, broadly speaking, survive challenge if they exist to promote health and safety. In any system attempting to accommodate trade and health values, questions will arise as to how reviewers are to approach health justifications advanced by state or national regulators. Under the US Commerce Clause, close scrutiny of the health and safety assertions advanced by the states (to justify trade-limiting laws and practices) is tied to the operation of representative democracy and the historical legacy of federalism.[23] In making this connection, the US jurisprudence encourages us to think about the competing claims of deference and scrutiny in the WTO in terms of the nature of the WTO system and the interests it promotes.

(a) The commerce clause

The commerce clause gives Congress the power '[t]o regulate commerce with foreign nations, and among the several States, and with the Indian Tribes'.[24] Although expressed as a grant of power to Congress, the commerce clause has been construed to include an implicit limit on the ability of the states to regulate in a manner that affects commerce between the states[25] because state health and safety laws often have an adverse impact on inter-state trade. In order to appreciate the role of health justifications

[22] Croley and Jackson (n 15) 210. Palmeter and Spak offered a similar view in relation to interpretation of the old GATT: D Palmeter and GJ Spak 'Resolving Antidumping and Countervailing Duty Disputes: Defining GATT's Role in an Era of Increasing Conflict' (1993) 24 Law&Pol'yIntlBus 1145, 1157–58.

[23] Not all commentators recognise this close scrutiny. Eg, Howse sees the US courts as quite deferential to the needs of the regulatory state under the commerce clause: R Howse 'Managing the Interface Between International Trade Law and the Regulatory State: What Lessons Should (and Should Not) be Drawn from the Jurisprudence of the United States Dormant Commerce Clause' in T Cottier and PC Mavroidis (eds) *Regulatory Barriers and the Principles of Non-Discrimination in World Trade Law* (U Michigan P Ann Arbor 2000) 139, 141–42.

[24] Art I §8 cl 3 US Constitution ('commerce clause').

[25] *Cooley v Board of Wardens of the Port of Philadelphia* 53 US (12 How) 299, 318, 13 L Ed 996 (1851) ('*Cooley*'); LH Tribe *American Constitutional Law* (Vol 1, 3rd edn Foundation Press New York 2000) 7, 1021, 1030.

in the commerce clause, a brief statement of the applicable tests is necessary.[26] The first question to be addressed is whether inter-state commerce is affected. If it is, the next question is whether the measure discriminates against inter-state commerce. If it is overtly discriminatory, then the measure is virtually always invalid and can only be saved if it can be shown that the measure is justified by a valid factor unrelated to economic protectionism (such as health and safety) and that that valid local objective cannot be achieved by non-discriminatory means.[27] The existence of valid local benefits and the non-availability of alternatives is subjected to the 'strictest scrutiny'.[28] If, on the other hand, the measure is apparently neutral, it will only be overturned if the burden imposed on commerce is 'clearly excessive' when compared with local benefits relating to a legitimate local public interest (such as health and safety).[29]

(b) Close scrutiny of asserted health and safety benefits

Even in the early days of the old quarantine cases, the courts showed that they were not prepared to accept any glib assertion of a health justification.[30] Subject to a set of constraining principles,[31] the courts have continued (under the modern commerce clause jurisprudence) to show themselves to be willing to enquire very closely into asserted health and

[26] The following tests were affirmed by the SC in *Carbone v Clarkstown* 511 US 383, 390, 114 S Ct 1677, 128 L Ed 2d 399 (1994) ('*Carbone*') but note that, as the SC has been developing its approach to the affirmative commerce clause (in *US v Lopez* 514 US 549, 115 S Ct 1624 (1995) and *US v Morrison* 529 US 598, 120 S Ct 1740 (2000)), some spill-over into the dormant commerce clause is likely.

[27] *Hughes v Oklahoma* 441 US 322, 336, 99 S Ct 1727 (1979) ('*Hughes*').

[28] *Hughes* (n 27) 337; *Carbone* (n 26) 392.

[29] *Pike v Bruce Church Inc* 397 US 137, 142, 90 S Ct 844 (1970). Note, however, that it has been argued that no 'balancing' actually occurs under the dormant commerce clause. Regan argues that an enquiry into whether the measure in question is the result of purposeful protectionism is in fact the focus of analysis in dormant commerce clause cases: DH Regan 'The Dormant Commerce Clause and the *Hormones* Problem' in T Cottier and PC Mavroidis *The Role of the Judge in International Trade Regulation: Experience and Lessons for the WTO* (U Mich P Ann Arbor 2003) 91, 94ff.

[30] Eg *Hannibal and St Joseph Railroad Co v Husen* 95 US (5 Otto) 465, 470–71, 24 L Ed 527 (1878) ('*Husen*') (a law failed to distinguish between healthy and diseased cattle); *Bowman v Chicago and Northwestern Railway Co* 125 US 465, 488, 8 S Ct 689 (1888) (a law prohibiting the import of liquor not a quarantine or inspection law at all).

[31] Those principles are: safety measures are to be accorded a 'strong presumption of validity' (*Bibb v Navajo Freight Lines* 359 US 520, 524, 79 S Ct 962 (1959) ('*Bibb*'); *Raymond Motor Transportation v Rice* 434 US 429, 443, 98 S Ct 787 (1978) ('*Raymond Motor Transportation*'); *Proctor & Gamble v Chicago* 509 F 2d 69 (US Ct of Apps (7th Cir), 1975)); courts should not decide between alternative ways of solving safety problems; policy decisions are the province of state legislatures (*Bibb* (above in this note) 524); and states have 'a legitimate interest in guarding against imperfectly understood environmental risks despite the possibility that they may ultimately prove to be negligible' (*Maine v Taylor* 477 US 131, 148, 106 S Ct 2440 (1986)).

safety benefits and whether or not non-discriminatory means might achieve those objectives.[32]

The Supreme Court has been quick to dismiss patently disingenuous or distinctly dubious health-based justifications, sending a strong signal that asserting a health or environmental justification is not a short-cut to successfully defending a commerce clause challenge.[33] Even when the *bona fides* of the stated health and safety motive are not questioned, the precise nature and basis of the problem and the regulatory solution have been subjected to intensive scrutiny. For example, in *Southern Pacific Co v Arizona*,[34] the Supreme Court was asked to review an Arizona law making it unlawful to operate a railroad train of more than 14 passenger cars or 70 freight cars. The court recognised that state and national claims to power were to be reconciled by appraisal and accommodation of the competing demands of state and national interests.[35] In effecting this accommodation, the court determined that the question to ask was whether, in the circumstances, the 'total effect of the law as a safety measure in reducing accidents and casualties is so slight or problematical as not to outweigh the national interest in keeping interstate commerce free from interferences which seriously impede it'.[36] The court then had no hesitation in analysing for itself the problem of 'slack action' in trains and drew fresh conclusions from empirical figures on accident rates. The court found (following the trial court's findings) that the Arizona law afforded only a 'slight and dubious' advantage over unregulated train lengths because it would cause the number of trains and train operations to increase, leading to an overall increase in accidents of a more severe character.[37] In that case, the court came very close to engaging in *de novo* review by drawing fresh conclusions from the empirical evidence.

[32] While there has been close scrutiny of alleged health-based justifications, it seems environmental measures come in for even rougher treatment; Christine Klein has shown that the Supreme Court has been confining both the affirmative and dormant aspects of the commerce clause by emphasising the natural, non-commercial nature of the environment to invalidate federal environmental measures taken under the affirmative commerce clause while also emphasising the the market-related aspects of natural resources in order to invalidate state environental measures as unduly interfering with interstate commerce: C Klein 'The Environmental Commerce Clause' (2003) Harvard Environmental Law Review 1. See also Shapiro and Buzbee (n 13).

[33] Eg *Baldwin v GAF Seelig Inc* 294 US 511, 55 S Ct 497 (1935) ('*Baldwin*') (the SC rejected the argument that prohibiting the sale of out-of-state milk unless the provider had been paid the in-state minimum rate was necessary to ensure milk was wholesome); *Dean Milk Co v Madison* 340 US 349, 354–55, 71 S Ct 295 (1951) (Madison's law requiring that milk not be sold as pasteurised unless it had been pasteurised and bottled within five miles of Madison's central square was overturned).

[34] 325 US 761, 65 S Ct 1515 (1945) ('*Southern Pacific*').

[35] *Southern Pacific* (n 34) 768–71.

[36] *Southern Pacific* (n 34) 776.

[37] *Southern Pacific* (n 34) 779. For concern that this level of intrusive review takes judges beyond their proper constitutional role: see, eg: *Southern Pacific* (n 34) 789 (Justice Black) and *Kassel v Consolidated Freightways Corp of Delaware* 450 US 662, 680–81 (Justice Brennan), 692 (Justice Rehnquist), 101 S Ct 1309 (1981) ('*Kassel*').

(c) Justifications for close scrutiny: federalism and democratic representation

Reviewing local health and safety regulations which impinge upon free movement of commerce has involved American courts in close scrutiny of the precise basis and extent of the claimed health and safety benefits. In exercising their constitutional power to review state regulations under the commerce clause, US courts have referred to the functioning of democratic representation and the values secured by federalism in order to justify the intensity of their scrutiny. Observing that state decision-makers (whether legislatures or regulatory bodies exercising delegated powers) are susceptible to lobbying pressure and are, in fact, charged with the task of protecting their local constituents, the courts have shown themselves to be concerned to protect out-of-state interests that are not represented in the state's democratic processes.[38] In *Kassel v Consolidated Freightways*, Justice Powell spoke for the majority in saying that the customary deference to state highway safety regulations derived, in part, from the assumption that the burden of such regulations falls on local interests as well as out-of-state interests, thus ensuring that the state's political process will 'serve as a check against unduly burdensome regulations.'[39] However, when those affected do not have the power to vote those who impose burdens on them out of office, that power is open to abuse and is unaccountable in political terms, thus justifying probing judicial intervention.[40] On the other hand, where the affected out-of-state interests have in-state equivalents that are also affected, it is assumed that their interests are protected through the ability of their in-state counterparts to pursue normal political remedies.[41]

The perceived need for courts to engage in close scrutiny to protect out-of-state interests rests, of course, on the notion that out-of-state enterprises have interests that warrant protection under the Constitution. This is where the theme of federalism comes in. Not only do out-of-state enterprises have a direct interest in the free flow of commerce, they also have broader interests in political integration and mutual security.[42] As Justice Cardozo stated in *Baldwin v GAF Seelig*, the US Constitution was 'framed

[38] Tribe (n 25) 1051–58 (citing a footnote in *Southern Pacific* (n 34) 767, which in turn cites *Cooley* (n 25)).

[39] *Kassel* (n 37) 675 (quoting *Raymond Motor Transportation* (n 31) 444).

[40] Tribe (n 25) 1053. Cf DH Regan 'The Supreme Court and State Protectionism: Making Sense of the Dormant Commerce Clause' (1986) 84 MichLRev 1091, 1162.

[41] Eg, *South Carolina State Highway Department v Barnwell Bros* 303 US 177, 58 S Ct 510 (1938) and *Minnesota v Clover Leaf Creamery Co* 449 US 456, 101 S Ct 715 (1981) (with a strained search for an in-state surrogate) cited in Tribe (n 25) 1053–54. Note also *Cloverland-Green Spring Dairies v Pennsylvania* 298 F 3d 201, 215–16 (US Ct of Apps (3rd Cir), 2002) where the court found that in-state milk dealers were not proper substitutes for the interests of out-of-state dealers.

[42] RB Stewart 'International Trade and Environment: Lessons from the Federal Experience' (1992) 49 Wash&LeeLRev 1329, 1330.

upon the theory that the peoples of the several states must sink or swim together, and that in the long run prosperity and salvation are in union and not division.'[43] Non-isolationism has been a core concern of the Supreme Court, leading to any perceived attempts by a state to shut itself off from national problems such as waste disposal,[44] or to shift hazards to other states,[45] being subjected to fierce scrutiny.

(i) Federalism and democratic representation: WTO analogies? If federalism justifies close scrutiny in the US, what does that suggest about scrutiny of health claims in the WTO? The WTO is clearly not a federation in the sense that the US is. Nevertheless, there are two questions that are central to the relationship between the constituent parts of a federation that can be usefully asked of the WTO.[46] The first question concerns how powers are to be divided between the levels of government. The second question concerns when the interests of the smaller unit should give way to the interests of the collective. The answers to these two questions in the US take us back to the nature and purpose of US federation. In the US, the independence of the states is recognised by the fact that they continue to enjoy regulatory powers, but the needs of the federal system mean that state powers must be limited. Accordingly, the states are only deprived of their residual police powers[47] to protect local health and safety to the extent that the federal government has acted or to the extent that the exercise of those powers burdens inter-state commerce to such an extent as to be inconsistent with the underlying basis of the Constitution. The Constitution is based on the existence of shared problems and a shared future, and the conviction that out-of-state economic actors have legitimate interests which should be protected. Where states seek to isolate themselves, intrusive review is justified by the need to secure the aims of the Constitution.

In asking how authority over health questions should be shared between the WTO and the Members individually, and in assessing when one Member's preference should give way to the interests of others, we need to look at what common interests and goals form the bedrock of the WTO's control of domestic health regulations. Where a Member is concerned about a health threat but the scientific evidence is equivocal, it is

43 *Baldwin* (n 33) 523.

44 *Philadelphia v New Jersey* 437 US 617, 628, 98 S Ct 2531 (1978).

45 In *Kassel* the majority suspected Wisconsin of trying to shift the burden of road accidents to neighbouring states by banning the use of trucks longer than 55 feet and double trailer trucks on its roads: *Kassel* (n 37) 678, 685.

46 S Charnovitz 'Environment and Health Under WTO Dispute Settlement' (1998) 32 The Intl Lawyer 901, 901 (applying federal analysis to the WTO). For an analysis of federalism and regulation, see: GA Bermann 'Regulatory Federalism: European Union and United States' (1997) 263 Recueil des Cours 9.

47 The term 'police power' refers to the power to protect the health, safety, welfare and morals of those within the state's jurisdiction: *Husen* (n 30) 530.

necessary to address two questions: firstly, whether that Member's desire to 'play it safe' should take precedence over the interests of other Members in being able to continue to export the suspected products; and secondly, whether the decision-maker (the panel) should seek to re-examine the scientific case for regulatory protection. In some respects, WTO review of health regulation begins from similar starting points as does review under the commerce clause. WTO Members, like the American states, have (and have always had) the power to protect the health and safety of their populations. There is no question of WTO Members exercising powers *granted* to them by a body of a higher constitutional order.[48] Similarly, WTO Members enjoy something akin to the US presumption of validity in the requirement that challengers raise a *prima facie* case of breach before the responding state is called to account for its health measures.[49] There are, however, notable points of departure. Most obviously, there is no international equivalent of the US federal government. Although there are various international bodies which cooperate to develop health standards (eg, Codex), those standards are not backed by coersive powers. That means that, whether or not health standards are developed at an international level, health protection as such remains a national concern. Whatever cooperative international efforts may be taken on health, WTO Members remain free to protect health irrespective of the trade costs that their measures impose on others. Where close scrutiny of health and safety claims is justified in the US on the basis of: (i) the need for national solutions to national problems; (ii) an abhorrence of isolationism; and (iii) a concern to protect out-of-jurisdiction interests, those arguments have only limited resonance in the WTO. In the health area in the WTO, there is no real notion of shared problems: by proceeding from the recognition that states may protect themselves irrespective of the trade costs to others, isolationism is the norm, not the exception. Historically, countries have always had to bear the costs stemming from indigenous diseases but have been free to refuse to take on any of the costs of foreign diseases.[50] Isolationism is nothing new and, while addressing problems through mutual cooperation is encouraged (for example by the use of common international standards and sharing information), the presumption in the WTO is that health problems are fundamentally local, or at least that it is entirely proper that they be responded to locally. The basic vision of the

[48] Cf McNelis who, in comparing AB review of one of a number of WTO Members with ECJ review of 'sister institutions', appears to regard WTO Members as subordinate: N McNelis 'The Role of the Judge in the EU and WTO: Lessons from the *BSE* and *Hormones* Cases' (2001) 4 JIEL 189, 200. Verhoosel also conceives of the WTO as a 'higher legal order': G Verhoosel *National Treatment and WTO Dispute Settlement: Adjudicating the Boundaries of Regulatory Autonomy* (Hart Publishing Oxford 2002) 1, 4.

[49] *Hormones* AB Report (n 1) para 108.

[50] JA Kellar 'The Application of Risk Analysis to International Trade in Animals and Animal Products' (1993) 12 SciTechRev (OIE) 1023, 1024.

WTO as a system of trade concessions requires only that, in determining the appropriate level of protection, WTO Members 'take into account' the objective of minimising negative trade effects; there is no obligation to actually weigh the trade costs that health measures will impose on other Members in national regulatory decision-making.[51] In the WTO, ignoring the interests of one's neighbours is not a failure of democracy in the same way as it is in the US. There, the exclusion of out-of-state interests from state political processes exposes the failure of *sub-federal* democracy to protect interests which, by virtue of the *federal* structure, *do* warrant consideration.[52] In the US, this failure constitutes the major justification for close scrutiny of health and safety claims by counterbalancing the presumption of validity that flows from the exercise of state regulatory powers. In WTO review of domestic health regulations, there is no analogous failure to consider out-of-jurisdiction interests that would justify heightened scrutiny.[53]

3 ECJ Review of Community and Member State Health Regulations

Like WTO panels and the US courts, the ECJ has to address the legitimacy of health regulations that hamper cross-border trade. Those familiar with both GATT and the EC cannot fail to be struck by the similarity of the wording of GATT Article XX(b) (including the *chapeau*) and Article 30 (ex 36) of the EC Treaty. Article 30 permits the European Member States to take trade-limiting regulatory action, *inter alia*, for the 'protection of health and life of humans, animals or plants', provided that the prohibition or restriction does not 'constitute a means of arbitrary discrimination or a disguised restriction on trade'. When one compares the ECJ's approach to Member State health regulations with its approach when reviewing the health claims of the Community institutions, one sees that the ECJ's review of Member State health claims is much more demanding. The reasons for this distinction are explored in order to focus, once again, on whether the reasons for deference or scrutiny that prevail in the EC are transferable to the WTO. In this way, the following section complements the analysis of the level of deference in the US by viewing the WTO challenge against the backdrop of the EC.

[51] Cf DA Farber and RE Hudec 'Free Trade and the Regulatory State: A GATT's-Eye View of the Dormant Commerce Clause' (1994) 47 VandLRev 1401, 1405.

[52] Cf Regan (n 40) 1164–65.

[53] Note, though, Tarullo suggests that there may be such a justification for close scrutiny in respect of the national administration of trade remedies (specifically, the imposition of anti-dumping and countervailing duties, and safeguard measures) because foreign producers are either unrepresented or underrepresented in the political systems of the states imposing these duties and measures: DK Tarullo 'The Hidden Costs of International Dispute Settlement: WTO Review of Domestic Anti-Dumping Decisions' (2002) 34 Law&Pol'yIntlBus 109, 154–56.

(a) ECJ review of Member State health claims

(i) Review of health claims The health claims of the European Member States come before the ECJ when a Member State's regulation is challenged as inconsistent with Article 28 of the EC Treaty[54] (which guarantees free movement of goods between the Member States) and the Member State defends the regulation as a health measure under Article 30. Article 30 states that restrictions or prohibitions on imports are not precluded by Articles 28 and 29, if they are justified, *inter alia*, on the grounds of protection of the health and life of humans, animals and plants. The second sentence of Article 30 qualifies the first sentence by providing that the prohibition or restriction must not be a means of arbitrary discrimination or a disguised restriction on trade between the Member States. In order to take advantage of Article 30, the Member State must show that the measure in question is a health measure. This means that the existence of a threat to health must be shown. Sometimes the ECJ has faulted a Member State for simply failing to prove the threat. At other times, however, the ECJ has hardly troubled to consider scientific evidence on the existence of a risk, either because it has been prepared to assume the existence of a threat, or because it has been prepared to dismiss the measure on pragmatic grounds.

Pragmatism and common-sense reasoning form a prominent part of the ECJ's approach to health claims. Where the ECJ suspects that the asserted health justification is simply a ruse, it will dismiss the health justification on common-sense grounds even if some supporting evidence is submitted. For example, in *UK Poultry I*, when the UK submitted scientific evidence on the risk of vaccination masking infection to support its import restrictions on poultry, the ECJ did not consider this evidence, but dismissed the health justification because the circumstances in which the import restrictions were adopted—in time to prevent the import of French Christmas turkeys—smacked of protectionism and not health policy.[55] The ECJ has similarly focused on pragmatic considerations of *consistency* in dismissing health justifications even where the Member State has made an effort to present a credible basis for its health claims. For example, in the *German Beer* and *Greek Beer* cases, the ECJ showed its concern for con-

[54] Consolidated Version of the Treaty Establishing the European Community (available at <http://europa.eu.int/eur-lex/en/treaties/dat/ec_cons_treaty_en.pdf>) (the EC Treaty). The consolidated version incorporates amendments since the treaty was originally signed (Treaty Establishing the European Economic Community (Treaty of Rome) (25 March 1957)).

[55] Case 40/82 *Commission v UK* [1982] ECR 2793 ('*UK Poultry I*') paras 22–24, 37–39. Note also *Cassis de Dijon* where a health argument to support a German law restricting the marketing of low alcohol spirits was dismissed on common sense grounds: Case 120/78 *Rewe-Zentral AG v Bundesmonopolverwaltung für Branntwein* [1979] ECR 649 ('*Cassis de Dijon*') paras 10–11.

sistency by pointing out that the additives banned in beer by Germany and Greece were permitted in other products.[56]

In the above cases, there was little concern with the scientific basis of the alleged health threats because the ECJ has been prepared to dismiss the health claim as a protectionist cover (as in the *UK Poultry I* case) or as undermined by inconsistent application (as in the *German Beer* and *Greek Beer* cases). There is another category of cases where there is little concern with scientific evidence establishing the existence of a risk: cases where the risk is already recognised at the European level. This is one of the most notable features of review of health measures in the ECJ. Where the measure relates to a class of substances that are known to be dangerous to health, such as vitamins,[57] pesticides,[58] colourants,[59] additives[60] and certain chemicals and biocidal products,[61] the ECJ does not require even an attempt to prove the harm unless the Member State's approach shows the type of inconsistencies referred to above.[62] Where, however, the product in question does not fall within one of these notorious categories, the Member State will have to prove harm by reference to credible evidence.[63] For example, in a case concerning a Belgian law limiting the maximum salt content in bread to 2 per cent, the ECJ stressed the need to measure the risk to human health on the basis of 'relevant scientific research', and not 'according to the yardstick of general conjecture'.[64] In that case, the ECJ

[56] Case 178/84 *Commission v Germany* [1987] ECR 1227 ('*German Beer*') paras 48–49; Case 176/84 *Commission v Greece* [1987] ECR 1193 ('*Greek Beer*') para 42. Note also Case 216/84 where the ECJ noted France's inconsistent approach to low nutrition foods when rejecting its nutrition-based arguments advanced to support its ban on substitute milk powers: Case 216/84 *Commission v France* [1988] ECR 793 para 15.

[57] Case 174/82 *Criminal Proceedings against Sandoz BV* [1983] ECR 2445 ('*Sandoz*') para 11; Case 227/82 *Criminal Proceedings against van Bennekom* [1983] ECR 3883 ('*van Bennekom*') para 36. Compare Case C–192/01 *Commission v Denmark* (ECJ 23 September 2003) where the ECJ appeared to qualify its earlier position on vitamins by finding that a 'detailed assessment of the risk alleged' is required even in respect of nutitional supplements: para 47.

[58] Case 94/83 *Criminal Proceedings against Albert Heijn BV* [1984] ECR 3263 para 13 ('*Heijn*'); Case 54/85 *Ministère Public v Xavier Mirepoix* [1986] ECR 1067 ('*Mirepoix*') para 13.

[59] Case 274/84 *The State v Leon Motte* [1985] ECR 3887 ('*Motte*') para 12 (the Commission did not contest the absolute harmfulness of colourants, but argued that there was no uncertainty surrounding the ADI figure).

[60] *German Beer* (n 56) para 44; *Greek Beer* (n 56) para 36; Case C–42/90 *Criminal Proceedings against Jean-Claude Bellon* [1990] ECR I–4863 ('*Bellon*') para 12; Case C–344/90 *Commission v France* [1992] ECR I–4719 ('*Nitrate in Cheese*') paras 8–10.

[61] Case C–293/94 *Criminal Proceedings against Jacqueline Bradsma* [1996] All ER (EC) 837 para 11 ('*Bradsma*') (biocidal product to prevent algae); Case C–473/98 *Kemikalieinspektionen v Toolex Alpha AB* [2000] ECR I–5681 ('*Toolex*') para 39 (the case concerned the use of tricholorethylene in industrial processes).

[62] See, eg: *German Beer* (n 56) para 49; *Greek Beer* (n 56) para 42.

[63] See, eg Case 51/83 *Commission v Italy* [1986] 2 CMLR 274 para 17 (failure to substantiate alleged health threat posed by gelatin); Case 205/89 *Commission v Greece* [1991] ECR I–1361 ('*Greek Butter*') para 12 (Greece failed to substantiate claimed risks).

[64] Case C-17/93 *Criminal Proceedings against JJJ Van der Veldt* [1994] ECR I-3537 ('*Van der Veldt*') para 17. See also Case 123/00 *Criminal Proceedings against Christina Bellamy and English Shop Wholesale* [2001] ECR I-2795 para 12.

found that the Belgian authorities had not advanced scientific data demonstrating the alleged risk to public health and, moreover, could have protected public health by requiring that consumers be informed about the salt content of bread by prescribing suitable labelling.[65]

According to established case law, where there are uncertainties in the present state of scientific research, it is for the Member States, in the absence of harmonisation, to decide what degree of protection of health they intend to assure, having regard to the requirements of free movement of goods.[66] While still subject to the proportionality doctrine (the 'requirement of free movement of goods') the ECJ gives the Member States a great deal of leeway where it is generally agreed that the scientific evidence is uncertain.[67] Of course, there is room for argument about whether the scientific evidence is, indeed uncertain. By whose yardstick should uncertainty be gauged? In *Motte* (which concerned the import of lumpfish roe prepared with colourants banned in Belgium but permitted in the state of export), the Commission tried to persuade the ECJ that there was no uncertainty regarding the harmfulness of those colourants because the Community's Scientific Committee for Food had provided ADI (acceptable daily intake) figures.[68] Even though the colourants in question were not the subject of a harmonised regime, meaning that Belgium was still free to regulate in that area, the Commission still sought to establish the Community's scientific opinion as decisive. Notwithstanding its favourable predisposition towards the scientific opinions of the Community, the ECJ rejected this attempt to completely oust the ability of Member States to make their own assessment of the risks posed by colourants. The court said that the Member States must 'take into account' the results of international scientific research, especially that of the Scientific Committee for Food, but noted that 'it must be emphasized that the Opinions of the Committee do not have binding force'.[69] Just because an ADI figure has been established or the substance has been authorised by another Member State does not mean that all uncertainty, particularly

[65] *Van der Veldt* (n 64) paras 18–19.

[66] Case 53/80 *Officier van Justitie v Koninklijke Kassfabriek Eyssen BV* [1981] ECR 409 paras 14, 16; *Sandoz* (n 57) para 16; *van Bennekom* (n 57) paras 37–38; Case 97/83 *Criminal Proceedings against CMC Melkunie BV* [1984] ECR 2367 (*'Melkunie'*) para 18; *Motte* (n 59) para 19; Case 304/84 *Ministère Public v Claude Müller* [1986] ECR 1511 paras 20–21; *German Beer* (n 56) para 41; *Greek Beer* (n 56) para 35; *Bellon* (n 60) para 12; *Bradsma* (n 60) 845 (AG Fennelly); *Toolex* (n 61) para 45.

[67] See, eg, *van Bennekom* (n 57) para 38 (the uncertainties in scientific assessment of vitamins helped to justify the national measure even though other Member States had adopted different solutions) and Case C-121/00 *Criminal Proceedings against Walter Hahn* (ECJ 24 October 2002) paras 38–45 (the court relied on the report of the Scientific Committee on Veterinary Measures Relating to Public Health (which stressed the uncertainties relating to the risks associated with *listeria monocytogenes*) to find that Austria's zero-tolerance for lysteria was not disproportionate).

[68] *Motte* (n 59) para 12.

[69] *Motte* (n 59) para 20.

that arising from differences in eating habits, has been removed. Accordingly, the responsibility of the national authorities to protect health in the absence of harmonised rules was not abrogated.[70]

In sum, the ECJ's review of the veracity of the health claims of the Member States is marked by pragmatism. While the ECJ does not seek to engage in in-depth analyses of the data and methodology underlying scientific studies (as US courts might), its attitude to Member States' health claims is by no means deferential. It seems that the degree of scrutiny that the ECJ will exert depends on: (i) the context of the measure (do the circumstances suggest that health is being argued to cover-up protectionism?); (ii) whether the substance falls into a recognised category (such as pesticides); and (iii) whether the scientific evidence regarding a substance is acknowledged to be uncertain. As such, there is no single answer to the question of what degree of deference the ECJ accords to the health claims of the Member States—the answer is that it depends. Nevertheless, the ECJ's attitude to the question of deference more clearly emerges from its exercise of proportionality review.

(ii) Proportionality review When Member State action is reviewed for proportionality, the focus is on whether the measure adopted was the least trade-restrictive alternative (LTA). Wherever one finds a least trade restrictive alternative discipline, the potential for intrusive review is immediately apparent. When considering the application of this discipline in the WTO, attention was drawn to the use of consistency analysis—what do other states do?—and the question of how sensitive panels should be to local peculiarities and resource allocations, as well as the question of who should determine whether the proposed alternative would be effective in the state in question.

One striking feature of the ECJ's case law on the LTA test is the court's willingness to use the test to effectively reorientate a Member State's approach to a particular regulatory problem; very little deference is accorded the regulatory preferences of the Member States. In applying the test, the ECJ has not hesitated to tell a Member State which regulatory techniques are preferable, to pass judgment on the effectiveness of regulatory techniques and to reject in principle arguments relating to the cost-effectiveness of regulatory and administrative measures.[71]

In order for a restriction to be proportionate, the ECJ has consistently required that the Member State provide traders with the opportunity to apply for permission to use the product. In these cases, the trader's tech-

[70] *Motte* (n 59) para 20.

[71] Case 104/75 *Adriann de Peijper, managing director of Centrafarm BV* [1976] ECR 613 (*'de Peijper'*) para 18; Case 251/78 *Denkavit Futtermittel GmbH v Landes Nordrhein–Westfalen* [1979] ECR 3369 (*'Denkavit I'*) para 23; Case C–128/89 *Commission v Italy* [1990] I ECR 3239 (*'Italy–Grapefruit'*) para 22.

nical need must be balanced against the risks to health in the light of national dietary habits and international scientific research.[72] In requiring the Member States to put in place these application schemes, the court has not explicitly told them that they must sacrifice absolute health protection in the name of free movement, but, in emphasising the importance of traders' technical needs, the court has not only mandated the use of a particular regulatory technique (restriction tempered by application processes) and administrative machinery, but has also effectively put in place an approach which gives traders' interests an importance that Member States might not otherwise afford them. The court has also sought to reduce the impact of trade barriers which, pursuant to Article 30, remain in place by promoting strategies involving information provision and regulatory cooperation in preference to product bans and establishment requirements.[73] What is notable about these cases is the confidence with which the ECJ purports to grasp the full extent of regulatory problems and assess the efficacy of regulatory solutions, as well as its willingness to posit alternatives with little examination (at least in the judgment) of whether those alternatives are actually suitable for the Member State in question and will actually achieve the desired level of health protection. For example, can the ECJ really be confident that labelling will be as effective in protecting health as a maximum salt content in bread?[74]

The latitude that Article 30 affords the Member States is heavily qualified because the ECJ is using the proportionality principle to promote free movement of goods. This is not to say that the court's changes are bad—facilitation of regulatory cooperation and the replacing of product bans with information and evidence requirements makes sense—but the court is promoting a set of regulatory priorities and techniques (particularly labelling and information-based requirements) in a situation where, according to Article 30, the Member States are still entitled to act independently. In essence, as judicial guardian of the fundamental freedoms, including free movement of goods, the ECJ is promoting that value at every turn.

[72] *Sandoz* (n 57) para 19.

[73] See, eg: Case 153/78 *Commission v Germany* [1979] ECR 2555 ('*German Pork*') para 10 (promotion of evidence of the place of slaughter and processing to combat trichinae in pork); *de Peijper* (n 71) paras 23–27 (promotion of parallel importing by requiring the Member States to use their powers to compel the provision of information and urging cooperation); see also: *Denkavit I* (n 71) para 23 (reciting *de Peijper*); Case 124/81 *Commission v UK* [1983] ECR 203 ('*UK UHT I*') para 18 (the import licensing procedure for UHT milk could be replaced, without prejudice to health protection, by information requirements); Case 261/85 *Commission v UK* [1988] ECR 547 ('*UK UHT II*') paras 15, 17 (it was for the UK to establish a system allowing importers to prove compliance with UK health standards); Case 247/81 *Commission v Germany* [1984] ECR 1111 paras 11–12 (in place of establishment requirements for marketing pharmaceuticals, reliance on authorisation procedures, cooperation and publicity).

[74] Eg, *Van der Veldt* (n 64).

(b) Review of Community action

The main points pertaining to ECJ review of Community action to protect health have already been emphasised in Chapter 5: the Community's broad discretion leads to very light review, especially in circumstances of uncertainty. According to the ECJ's formula, 'the Community judicature must, when reviewing such measures, restrict itself to examining whether the exercise of such discretion is vitiated by a *manifest error* or a *misuse of power* or whether the Commission did not *clearly exceed* the bounds of its discretion'.[75] This 'manifestly inappropriate' formula constitutes the ECJ's understanding of its task in reviewing the proportionality of Community action. As shown in Chapter 5, when it comes to reviewing the health claims of the Community institutions, the 'manifestly inappropriate' threshold will rarely be crossed. For example, in the *Fedesa* case, Fedesa challenged legislation partly implementing a directive banning certain hormones. Fedesa put forward evidence demonstrating that the hormones were safe, but the court did not find it necessary to even address that evidence because, 'when faced with divergent appraisals by the national authorities . . . the Council remained within the limits of its discretionary power in deciding to adopt the solution of prohibiting the hormones in question.'[76] The court was also reluctant to enquire very thoroughly into the applicant's proportionality arguments, but dismissed them rather quickly, emphasising instead the absence of manifest error.[77] In sum, when the ECJ considers the basis of Community measures, it seems to be more concerned to verify that the measure was arrived at in a considered way[78] than to address the scientific basis of the measure. Moreover, the ECJ's interpretation of the requirements of proportionality (whether Community action is manifestly inappropriate) means that the proportionality principle will only rarely be breached.

(c) Looking to the WTO's desirable level of deference

The ECJ case law reveals an approach to review that focuses explicitly on what type of review will best promote the objectives of the EU. As one of the

[75] Case C–180/96 *UK v Commission* [1998] 4 ECR I–2265 ('*UK BSE*') para 60 (emphasis added). See also: Case 138/79 *SA Roquette Frères v Council* [1980] ECR 3333 para 25; Case C–331/88 *R v The Minister for Agriculture, Fisheries and Food and the Secretary of State for Health, ex p Fedesa* [1990] ECR I–4023 ('*Fedesa*') para 16; Case C–84/94 *UK v Council* [1996] ECR I–5755 ('*UK–Working Time Directive*') para 58; Case C–120/97 *Upjohn Ltd v The Licensing Authority* [1999] ECR I–223 para 34; Case C–189/2001 *Jippes v Minister van Landbouw, Natuurbeheer en Visserij* [2001] ECR I–5689 ('*Jippes*') para 80.

[76] *Fedesa* (n 75) para 9.

[77] *Fedesa* (n 75) para 15 (dismissing the argument that the outright prohibition was inappropriate as it promoted a dangerous black market) and para 16 (dismissing the argument that consumer fears could be allayed by less restrictive alternatives).

[78] Note, eg, the concern with process in *Jippes* (n 75) para 95.

four fundamental freedoms,[79] free movement of goods constitutes a critical part of the bedrock on which the EU enterprise is built. If goods cannot move freely, the EU simply cannot exist in the form that inspired its inception.[80] It is because Member State limitations on free movement of goods strike at the foundations of the EU that they attract such close scrutiny by the ECJ. When the Community institutions act, almost by definition, they contribute to the realisation of the single market—their actions build the union—and the ECJ has been loath to curtail their discretion. It is this regime-building analysis (which underpins the ECJ's vastly different attitude to the health claims of the Member States and the Community) that the WTO should take note of. Emulating the ECJ's approach would force the WTO Membership to tackle fundamental questions about what type of group the WTO is and what it wants to achieve. What the EU has that the WTO does not is a clear picture of the extent to which the Members are to adopt a common approach to health. According to that vision, the needs of the EU venture drive the ECJ to promote Community action on health by exercising light review over the Community institutions, and to discourage Member State individualism by exercising more stringent control over their actions when those actions hamper free movement.[81]

The relationship between the WTO Members falls far short of the commitment to 'sink or swim together' that marks American federalism. It also falls short of the mutual trust and confidence required of the European Member States by the common market. That said, it is surprisingly difficult to pin down exactly how loose the relationship between the WTO Members is, and, in light of the character of that relationship, what level of intensity of review is appropriate? One way to address the question is to consider the relative emphasis on trading rights vis-à-vis rights to regulatory self-determination. Trade liberalisation is the raison d'être of the WTO, but it is just that—trade liberalisation—not *free* trade[82] and, more importantly,

[79] The others are: free movement of persons, freedom to provide services, and freedom of establishment.

[80] On the importance of the common market in goods in European constitutionalism, see: JHH Weiler 'The Constitution of the Common Market Place: Text and Context in the Evolution of the Free Movement of Goods' in P Craig and G de Búrca (eds) *The Evolution of EU Law* (OUP Oxford 1999) 349; G Slynn 'The Concept of the Free Movement of Goods and the Reservation for National Action under Article 36 EEC Treaty' in J Schwarze (ed) *Discretionary Powers of the Member States in the Field of Economic Policies and Their Limits under the EEC Treaty* (Nomos Baden-Baden 1988) 17, 17.

[81] Note, in particular, the principle of mutual recognition, according to which goods lawfully marketed in one Member State should, in principle, be admitted to the market of the other Member States: Communication from the Commission concerning the consequences of the judgments given by the Court of Justice on 20 February 1979 in Case 120/78 ('Cassis de Dijon') [1980] OJ C256/2.

[82] As emphasised by an AB Member (J Bacchus 'Table Talk: Around the Table of the Appellate Body of the World Trade Organization' (2002) 35 VandJTransL 1021, 1031) and commentators (Verhoosel (n 48) ch 1; T Cottier and PC Mavroidis 'Regulatory Barriers and the Principle of Non-Discrimination in WTO Law: An Overview' in Cottier and Mavroidis (eds) *Regulatory Barriers* (n 23) 3, 4).

not the building of a community which demands commonality and trust. In the WTO, trade is an economic end unto itself, and not the means to achieve some other, greater end. It is true that the WTO encourages cooperative approaches in health protection by promoting international harmonisation. But, in the WTO, cooperation has to be legislated for; in the absence of specific provisions requiring cooperation, Members are free to chart their own course on health. This fundamental distinction in the role of trade and the extent of cooperative obligations in the WTO and EU suggests that the WTO Members are entitled to more deference than has been accorded to the European Member States. When the WTO Members regulate to protect health, they may limit the trading opportunities of other Members, but trading opportunities have, since the earliest days of GATT, been qualified by the possibility of health measures. Individual health measures in the WTO may not *contribute* to building anything, but they do not undermine a larger project either.

B HOW CAN OBJECTIVE ASSESSMENT BE DEVELOPED?

1 Standard of Review Models

Having considered the appropriate level of deference in the WTO, it remains to address the second question posed at the start of this chapter: how should the standard of review be developed? In developing the standard of review, one very important matter is whether the applicable standard of review is to be the same across the whole spectrum of cases covered by the DSU. The Appellate Body's position on whether the standard of review is to be the same in all cases is not clear. On the one hand, the Appellate Body did identify the reference to objective assessment in Article 11 of the DSU as encapsulating the standard of review applicable in *all* cases not covered by the Anti-Dumping Agreement.[83] On the other hand, in arriving at that conclusion, the Appellate Body specifically referred (in the *Hormones* case) to the need for the standard of review to reflect the balance established in the SPS Agreement and to find a standard of review rooted in the text of that Agreement.[84] These comments suggest that the Appellate Body was at least open to establishing a standard of review on an Agreement-by-Agreement basis. Moreover, as was shown in Chapter 6, the Appellate Body has taken the objective assessment standard of review and elaborated on it in the safeguards cases in a way that is

[83] Understanding on Rules and Procedures Governing the Settlement of Disputes (the DSU) (Marrakesh, 15 April 1994); Agreement on the Implementation of Article VI of the General Agreement on Tariffs and Trade 1994 (the Anti-Dumping Agreement) (Marrakesh, 15 April 1994).

[84] *Hormones* AB Report (n 1) para 115.

unique to those cases. With these indications from the Appellate Body, it seems that the standard of review need not to be identical in every circumstance. Still, deciding that the applicable standard of review will not be identical in every case before an adjudicative body is only the first step. There are a number of questions which follow from that preliminary conclusion, including the important question of how that variation is to be structured.

There are two principal ways in which a dispute resolution system can adopt a variable standard of review. Firstly, it can articulate formally distinct standards of review that are applied by reference to the type of question at hand or the specific Agreement or Act being considered without there being any overarching connection between the standards. Secondly, the dispute resolution system can deploy a *single* standard of review that is articulated at a high degree of generality, with more detailed elaboration on that single standard's operation in respect of a type of question, a specific Agreement or a specific Act. The choice between these two approaches need not affect the *substantive* level of deference accorded to national decision-makers, but that choice may affect the legal coherence of the standard of review doctrine adopted.

If we could wind the clock back to the Uruguay Round negotiations, we might well advise the negotiators to pay more attention to the detailed legal machinery supporting the dispute resolution system. In this context, it may well have been preferable to develop a number of formally distinct standards of review tailored to the needs of specific areas of the WTO's broad jurisdiction.[85] The standard of review developed for health cases could, then, have been entirely different from the standard of review applied, for example, to safeguards cases. Of course, we cannot turn back time and proposals for the development of the standard of review in health cases must take into account that the Appellate Body has committed itself to the objective assessment standard of review. While the Appellate Body might in principle prefer to develop distinct and unconnected standards of review (the first approach), its textualist conservatism means that it is highly unlikely that the Appellate Body would be prepared to develop multiple standards that are wholly divorced from the objective assessment standard. It is, however, also unlikely that the WTO Membership at large will develop explicit standards of review in future negotiating rounds because the legislative process of the WTO is notoriously difficult and slow, and there is no guarantee that the issue of standards of review would make it on to the limited agenda. Given these

[85] The number need not have been large: a few broad distinctions—for example between areas of the WTO's remit where procedurally focused review is appropriate and those where it is not, between legal and factual questions, and between groups of factual questions where some deference is appropriate and those where it is not—may well have sufficed.

constraints, the standard of review must be developed by working with the objective assessment standard to develop settled approaches to its meaning and method of application in different settings.

2 Working with the Objective Assessment Standard

If, as appears to be the case, objective assessment is here to stay, how might the objective assessment standard be developed in health cases? We have already seen that, in the safeguards cases, the Appellate Body developed a roadmap providing practical instructions to panels on how the objective assessment standard should be applied in those cases. By referring to the terms of Article 4 of the Safeguards Agreement, the Appellate Body has instructed panels that they must ask whether all relevant facts were considered by the national authorities and whether the authorities have given an adequate explanation of the connection between those facts and their decision. Might a similar approach be taken in health cases as well?

(a) Prospects of the safeguards approach in cases reviewing health regulations

The success of the safeguards cases lies in treating Article 11 of the DSU as a starting point in the formulation of the standard of review and being willing openly to adapt the standard of review to new situations.[86] The safeguards cases did not suggest, in the way that the Appellate Body did in the *Hormones* case, that objective assessment is a complete standard of review, rather than merely a starting point. If this fundamental distinction is borne in mind, the safeguards approach has the potential to extricate the WTO from the doctrinal confusion generated by the *Hormones* case. The safeguards cases confirm that the Appellate Body is not hidebound by the narrow terms of Article 11, but is able to develop workable standards of review by drawing on the specific disciplines being adjudicated. Treating objective assessment as merely a starting point is one way of doing this. It is in confirming that the development of the standard of review in health cases need not come to a complete halt in the face of the words of Article 11 that the real value of the safeguards cases lies. Whether

[86] Eg, in one case, the panel found that it was necessary to expand on the standard of review formulated in the *US–Definitive Safeguard Measures on Imports of Wheat Gluten from the EC* WT/DS166/AB/R AB Report adopted 19 January 2001 paras 147–63 because it had focused on review of factual rather than methodological issues: *US–Definitive Safeguard Measures on Imports of Circular Carbon Quality Line Pipe from Korea* WT/DS202/R modified Panel Report adopted 8 March 2002 para 7.1974. The approach has also been adapted for use in cases relating to the Agreement on Textiles and Clothing: *US–Transitional Safeguard Measure on Combed Cotton Yarn from Pakistan* WT/DS192/AB/R AB Report adopted 5 November 2001 para 76.

or not the particular development of the objective assessment standard in the safeguard cases might be emulated in health cases is another matter. The suitability for deployment in health cases of the procedurally focused elaboration of objective assessment is, however, questionable.

Practical difficulties would confront any attempt to apply the safeguards approach to review of health regulations. In the *Argentina–Footwear* case, the panel and Appellate Body were able to support the expanded content of objective assessment by reference to the terms of Article 4 of the Safeguards Agreement. Article 4 stipulates how, in the domestic investigation, the competent authorities are to determine whether increased imports have caused (or threaten to cause) injury. The focus, within the Safeguards Agreement, is on the investigation conducted by the national authorities, and it is not surprising, then, that the content built into the objective standard of review should take a procedural direction. We can see that the safeguards approach works by focusing on the measure being reviewed as a completed deliberative process. This is apparent when the panel in *Korea–Dairy* said, 'we consider that the Panel's function is to assess objectively the *review conducted by the national investigating authority*'.[87] This approach generates a standard of review which tends to deliver procedurally focused review. As such, it echoes the emphasis that Article 17.6(i) of the Anti-Dumping Agreement puts on the panel examining the national authorities' approach to the facts and not examining the facts *per se*.

The specific development of the objective assessment standard of review utilised in the safeguards cases is a specifically procedural standard that focuses on whether the national authorities considered all the relevant facts and explained how the facts supported the conclusion. Accordingly, in safeguards cases, when panels apply this expanded version of the objective assessment standard of review, they are not focusing on the correctness of the national authority's decision. Health cases are, however, less suited to such a procedural approach because, at present, the SPS Agreement and GATT Article XX(b) focus on the substantive measure—is there a real threat to health? would a less restrictive measure suffice?—and are only concerned with how the regulatory authority reached its decision as a secondary matter. Although Annex B of the SPS Agreement provides for publication and notification of regulations, there is nothing akin to the national investigation provided for in the Safeguard Agreement, in which importers, exporters, producers and other interested parties have the right to present their views and to respond to the views of others.[88] Rather, the provisions of the SPS Agreement do not lend

[87] *Korea–Definitive Safeguard Measure on Imports of Certain Dairy Products* WT/DS98/R modified Panel Report adopted 12 January 2000 Panel Report (n) para 7.30 (emphasis added).

[88] Safeguards Agreement Art 3.1. Note that the Anti-Dumping Agreement provides even more protection for interested parties, providing for notice, disclosure and hearing rights, as well as judicial review: Anti-Dumping Agreement Arts 6, 13.

themselves to any particular standard of review in the same way.[89] Some disciplines in the SPS Agreement, such as the requirement in Article 5.2 to 'take into account' various factors in assessing risks, are well suited to this approach, but the core discipline, scientific justification, is not. Far from assisting panels to apply the objective assessment standard, the scientific justification requirement presents a particularly difficult discipline to which the standard of review must be fitted. The scientific questions which arise in SPS cases are enormously complicated and the scientific justification discipline does not assist panels in determining where on the spectrum from *de novo* review to total deference it should conduct its review of the scientific justification advanced by the responding Member. Other applicable disciplines such as the requirement that the measure be the least trade-restrictive possible to achieve the Member's appropriate level of protection[90] also fail to assist in directing the panel whether an objective assessment of this discipline requires some deference to the responding Member's views on whether alternative measures are practical. It can, then, be seen that the safeguards procedural elaboration of the objective assessment standard cannot be easily transferred to health cases. In addition, it should be recalled that procedural review is not *necessarily* deferential, as the anti-dumping cases, the safeguards cases and the US experience have all shown. Procedural review emphasises the national authorities' approach to the facts, and so discourages *de novo* review, but it does not actually prevent panels from undertaking an independent consideration of the facts.[91]

In sum, utilising the insight of the safeguards approach that objective assessment can be treated as a *framework* rather than a *complete statement* of the standard of review would allow panels and the Appellate Body to develop the standard of review in other areas, such as health, with tact and a firm legal basis. The way could, thereby, be opened for considering what objective assessment means for panel review of health regulations. In this process, there would be no need to follow the safeguards approach further by taking on its procedural orientation—the shell of objective assessment could be filled by other means in other areas.

[89] Note that the procedural focus of the TBT Agreement might make a procedural approach more suitable for use in review of cases falling under it.

[90] SPS Agreement Art 5.6; TBT Agreement Art 2.2; GATT 1994 Art XX(b) as interpreted in *Thailand–Restrictions on Importation of and Internal Taxes on Cigarettes* Report adopted 7 November 1990 BISD 37S/200 paras 74–75.

[91] J Gomula 'The Standard of Review of Article 17.6 of the Anti-Dumping Agreement and the Problem of its Extension to other WTO Agreements' in P Mengozzi (ed) *International Trade Law on the 50th Anniversary of the Multilateral Trade System* (Giuffré Editore Milano 1999) 577, 595.

(b) The 'reasonable regulator' approach

The question of the applicable standard of review is particularly keenly contested in relation to the scientific discipline imposed by the SPS Agreement. If health measures are to stand or fall based on whether they are scientifically justified, how panels approach scientific justifications advanced by responding Members is enormously important. If the parties advance conflicting scientific evidence, will panels enter the scientific fray and come to their own conclusions about whether a particular substance is dangerous to health, or will they exert less intense scrutiny by assessing whether the scientific justification advanced by the responding Member is tenable? Unlike the panels which heard the *Hormones*, *Salmon* and *Agricultural Products* cases[92] (which were able to avoid directly deciding on the standard of review applicable to scientific evidence because the defending Members' cases were lacking in other respects), the panel in the *Asbestos* case was faced with this kind of scientific contest. Interestingly, in deciding how it would handle itself in reviewing this evidence, the panel did not find its answer in the objective assessment standard of review set out in the *Hormones* case. Although the panel did refer to the *Hormones* case and the Appellate Body's concern to find the applicable standard of review in the texts,[93] the panel in the *Asbestos* case proceeded as follows:

> [I]n relation to the scientific information submitted by the parties and the experts, the Panel feels bound to point out that it is not its function to settle a scientific debate, not being composed of experts in the field of the possible human health risks posed by asbestos. Consequently, the Panel does not intend to set itself up as an arbiter of the opinions expressed by the scientific community.[94]
>
> . . .
>
> Its [the panel's] role, taking into account the burden of proof, is to determine whether there is sufficient scientific evidence to conclude that there exists a risk for human life or health and that the measures taken by France are necessary in relation to the objectives pursued.[95]

Most crucially, the panel decided that it would have to proceed by making 'a pragmatic assessment of the scientific situation and the measures available, *as would the decision-makers responsible* for the adoption of a health policy.'[96] Thus, the panel repeatedly expressed its conclusions in

[92] *EC–Measures Concerning Meat and Meat Products (Hormones)* WT/DS26/R/USA and WT/DS48/R/CAN modified Panel Reports adopted 13 February 1998; *Australia–Measures Affecting Importation of Salmon* WT/DS18/R modified Panel Report adopted 6 November 1998; *Japan–Measures Affecting Agricultural Products* WT/DS76/R modified Panel Report adopted 19 March 1999.

[93] *EC–Measures Affecting Asbestos and Asbestos-Containing Products* WT/DS135/R modified Panel Report adopted 6 April 2001 ('*Asbestos*') para 8.180, n 128.

[94] *Asbestos* Panel Report (n 93) para 8.181.

[95] *Asbestos* Panel Report (n 93) para 8.182.

[96] *Asbestos* Panel Report (n 93) para 8.183 (emphasis added).

terms of what a decision-maker responsible for health measures might reasonably conclude. Two statements by the panel will illustrate the point. Firstly, in relation to crysotile-cement products, the panel said that 'a decision-maker responsible for taking public health measures might *reasonably conclude* that the presence of chrysotile-cement products posed a risk because of the risks involved in working with those products'.[97] Secondly, in relation to the viability of regulatory alternatives, the panel found that 'in view of the difficulties of application of controlled use, an official in charge of public health policy might *reasonably consider* that controlled use did not provide protection that was adequate'.[98]

Unlike the objective assessment standard of review, the standard applied by the panel in the *Asbestos* case, which might be dubbed the 'reasonable regulator' standard of review, provides clear guidance on how intense scrutiny is to be, at least as regards scientific issues.[99] In systems of judicial review, the very essence of a standard of review is that it indicates how far the reviewer should go, how intrusive it should be, in delving into the decision made by the primary decision-maker. The 'objective assessment' standard of review simply does not do this. It provides minimum standards for review, which are undoubtedly useful in their own right,[100] but it does not provide any maximum standards that set a ceiling on how intrusive panel review should be. The 'reasonable regulator' standard, on the other hand, at least has the basic virtue of being a standard of review in the sense that it sets a ceiling on how intrusive review should be. For example, if a reasonable regulator might conclude that there is a scientific basis for an impugned measure, then the panel should not overturn it.

There are some signs that an approach emphasising reasonableness is growing in popularity. In a countervailing duty case—*US–Preliminary Determinations on Softwood Lumber*—the US argued that if there was a 'reasonable basis' for the US authorities' preliminary countervailing duty determination, there could be no breach of the relevant Agreement.[101]

97 *Asbestos* Panel Report (n 93) paras 8.193 (emphasis added).

98 *Asbestos* Panel Report (n 93) para 8.209 (emphasis added). For further examples of similar analysis see: paras 8.211, 8.214, 8.217.

99 It should, however, be noted that the panel's approach has not received the imprimatur of the Appellate Body as Canada did not raise the panel's approach directly on appeal. Although Canada argued that the panel had failed to make an objective assessment of scientific data by not assessing it in accordance with the principle of the balance of probabilities, the Appellate Body treated this as an argument about the credibility and weight ascribed to the evidence by the panel, and so subjected it to the abuse of discretion test: *EC–Measures Affecting Asbestos and Asbestos-Containing Products* WT/DS135/AB/R AB Report adopted 6 April 2001 paras 176–77.

100 For example, a Member may appeal a panel decision to the AB if the panel does not exercise its powers with good faith and deliberately disregards or refuses to consider evidence: *Hormones* AB Report (n 1) para 133.

101 *US–Preliminary Determinations with respect to Certain Softwood Lumber from Canada* WT/DS236/R Panel Report adopted 1 November 2002 ('*US–Preliminary Determinations on Softwood Lumber*').

Although the panel did not specifically address the standard of review, the submission is interesting because it highlights a common desire on the part of the Member States to have their reasonable domestic determinations respected in the WTO. Respect for the reasonable determinations of the Members is also a position that has attracted some academic support.[102] If one were to just read the *Asbestos* and *US–Preliminary Determinations on Softwood Lumber* panel reports, one might be tempted to suggest that, whatever the merits of reasonableness review, it is a new concept without a respectable pedigree in GATT/WTO law, but an examination of earlier cases suggests that this may not be the case.

While the identification of the 'reasonable regulator' approach as a standard of review is new—even the panel in the *Asbestos* case did not explicitly *identify* it as such, although they did use it as a standard of review—reasonableness review is not new to GATT. Even in the very early days of GATT, references to reasonableness review can be found. The most notable case is the *Fur Felt Hat* case.[103] In that case, Czechoslovakia challenged the US's withdrawal of a tariff concession, which the US defended as justified under GATT Article XIX.[104] In detailing its conclusions, the panel emphasised the fact that the US authorities had conducted a thorough investigation and had 'reached in good faith the conclusion that the proposed action fell within the terms of Article XIX'.[105] Although good faith is a distinct concept in international law, it is certainly true that it stands in a close relationship to reasonableness by protecting against unnecessary interference with national processes or second-guessing of national decisions.[106] Moreover, in the *Fur Felt Hat* case, the panel went on to explicitly refer to reasonableness: according to the panel, it is only natural that national authorities would, on occasion, be 'greatly influenced by social factors, such as local employment problems' but that the consequent withdrawal of a tariff concession should not be regarded as contrary to Article XIX 'unless the weight attached by the government concerned to such factors was clearly *unreasonably* great.'[107]

[102] J Trebilcock and R Howse *The Regulation of International Trade* (2nd edn Routledge London 1999) 165 (advocating reasonableness review); DC Esty *Greening the GATT: Trade, Environment, and the Future* (Institute for International Economics Washington DC 1994) 129 (proposing a 'clearly disproportionate' test which is similar to reasonableness review in avoiding second-guessing of decisions which are not obviously 'off base').

[103] *Report on the Withdrawal by the US of a Tariff Concession under Article XIX of the General Agreement on Tariffs and Trade Concerning Women's Fur Felt Hats and Hat Bodies* 27 March 1951 CP/106, GATT/1951–3 (*'Fur Felt Hat'*).

[104] Article XIX requires that there be an unforseen increase in imports causing or threatening serious injury to domestic producers.

[105] *Fur Felt Hat* (n 103) para 48.

[106] *US–Restrictions on Imports of* Tuna DS29/R, 16 June 1994 (unadopted) (reprinted in (1994) 33 ILM 839) para 3.73 (EEC and the Netherlands).

[107] *Fur Felt Hat* (n 103) para 48 (emphasis added).

Reasonableness also recommends itself as a standard of review because the concept is familiar to panels and the WTO. Firstly, the SPS Agreement, the TBT Agreement and GATT are all littered with references to obligations that are expressly qualified by the concept of reasonableness. For example, one of the most important provisions of the SPS Agreement, Article 5.7, provides that provisional measures must be reviewed within a *reasonable* period of time. Moreover, Panels and the Appellate Body have frequently turned to reasonableness when interpreting the Agreements. For example, under GATT Article XX(b), a health measure will not be 'necessary' only if it is not the least trade-restrictive measure *reasonably* available.[108] Another example is also apt: under the SPS Agreement, the results of a risk assessment must 'reasonably support' the SPS measure.[109] In short, the concept of reasonableness is not out of keeping with GATT/WTO review.

Whether the panel's approach in the *Asbestos* case represents an advance that should be applied more widely depends on a number of factors and, in particular, on how intense one believes scrutiny should be. This is, in itself, a question whose answer will reflect a particular conception of the relationship between trade and health and what type of control an international organisation like the WTO should be exerting. Weighing the conclusions of national authorities against whether a reasonable regulator might have come to the same conclusion constitutes a moderate form of review. Such reasonableness review is appealing because it protects the ability of WTO Members to regulate to protect the health of their citizens provided that regulators act reasonably. In this respect, the 'reasonable regulator' standard: (i) would uphold the Uruguay Round bargain pursuant to which WTO Members retained the right to take trade-limiting action to protect health;[110] (ii) would prevent the scientific justification discipline from authorising wholesale interference by the WTO; and (iii) would more easily accommodate scientific uncertainty. Some might object that such an approach would fail to secure a trading world in which health regulations are limited to those that are strictly necessary in the sense of being based on 'correct' science rather than merely reasonably supported scientific conclusions. While greater leeway would undoubtedly be afforded the Members in their assessments of science under such a reasonableness standard, it is important to bear in mind that panels do not

[108] *US–Section 337 of the Tariff Act of 1930* Report adopted 7 November 1989 BISD 36S/345 para 5.26.

[109] *EC–Measures Concerning Meat and Meat Products (Hormones)* WT/DS26/AB/R, WT/DS48/AB/R AB Report adopted 13 February 1998 para 193. Note that McNelis argues that the standard of review in the *Hormones* case was substantively close to reasonableness review: N McNelis 'The Role of the Judge in the EU and WTO: Lessons From the *BSE* and *Hormones* Cases' (2001) 4 JIEL 189, 198.

[110] SPS Agreement Preamble, Art 2.1; TBT Agreement Preamble; GATT 1994 Art XX(b).

enjoy a monopoly on scientific truth. They rely heavily on the evidence presented by the parties and the advice of the experts they appoint. As Chapter 4 explained, scientific knowledge is negotiated in that it is the product of an ongoing dialogue between scientists; there is always a zone for argument.[111] There is no single, neatly-packaged 'truth' to which panels can refer. In this context, where scientific knowledge is the product of interpretation and evaluation, it may well be appropriate to judge the Members on whether their interpretation and evaluation of the scientific evidence is reasonable. Perhaps the 'reasonable regulator' standard's most valuable contribution would be concentrating the panel's mind on the fact that it is reviewing a regulatory action and not a disembodied set of facts. One of the risks associated with review under the SPS Agreement in particular is that the model of regulation-making that it puts in place simply does not reflect the incremental, ad hoc reality of the accumulation of national regulations over time. In fixing the mind of the reviewer firmly on the pragmatic assessments that a reasonable regulator might make, this standard of review helps to reduce the risk that reviewers will hold Members to unrealistic standards of coherence and consistency.

With its focus on evaluating measures as the outcomes of the evaluations and actions of regulators, the reasonable regulator approach also shows that it is also possible to avoid the all or nothing trap identified by the Appellate Body in the *Apples* case. It will be recalled that Japan had argued that, in evaluating the scientific evidence before it, the panel should have accorded some deference to the views and approach of Japan in evaluating the scientific evidence. According to the Appellate Body, Japan's submission required the panel to 'favour' Japan's approach to risk and scientific evidence over the views of the experts.[112] Whether or not this is what Japan argued, the point is that a standard of review entailing some deference to the evaluations and approach of the defending Member does not necessarily entail 'preferring' the views of the Member over those of the experts (or the panel or complaining Member for that matter). What a standard of review like the resonable regulator standard does do is at least have the adjudicator *begin* with the Member's evaluations and proceed by asking whether they are reasonable. Deference of this kind does not require the panel to prefer the defending Member's approach come what may; it simply requires the panel to take a more contextualised proceed to review and to refrain from overturning the Member's measure unless the evaluations and approach that support the measure do not achieve the minimum standards expected of reasonable regulators.

[111] DA Wirth 'The Rule of Science in the Uruguay Round and NAFTA Trade Disciplines' (1994) 27 Cornell ILJ 817, 841–42.

[112] *Japan–Measures Affecting the Importation of Apples* WT/DS245/AB/R AB Report adopted 10 December 2003 ('*Apples*') para 165.

It is important that the 'reasonable regulator' standard (or any other, for that matter) not be seen in isolation. Standards of review work *within* systems of review and their content and efficacy is partly dictated by those contextual factors, as well as the substantive norms being applied. With respect to health cases, it has been suggested that there is significant scope for the Appellate Body to develop interpretations of some of the more contested SPS disciplines that would go some way to easing the two major sources of tension surrounding review of health regulations—regulation in circumstances of scientific uncertainty and the role of social and cultural factors. For example, it was suggested in Chapter 4 that the Appellate Body should develop the interpretation of Article 5.5's consistency discipline so that it permits some distinctions to be justified based on public perceptions and cultural traditions. Similarly, in explaining the requirements for reliance on Article 5.7 (provisional measures), further scope may be given to Members, for example, by adopting a generous interpretation of what information might be regarded as 'pertinent' when the question is whether provisional measures were based on pertinent information. The 'reasonable regulator' standard of review would not resolve these tensions alone, but would work alongside doctrinal developments to ease those tensions. The interaction between doctrinal developments and the standard of review would also also serve to prevent the 'reasonable regulator' standard from being too deferential.[113] By explicitly developing the interpretation of contentious disciplines, the Appellate Body would be able to craft constraints that strike the best balance between the individual Member's desire for regulatory autonomy and the Members' collective need for a disciplined, science-based approach to health regulation. The 'reasonable regulator' standard would be prevented from becoming too deferential because it would have to function within the field circumscribed by these interpretations.[114] In this way, the standard of review would temper the potentially intrusive effects of the otherwise unqualified requirement that SPS measures have a scientific justification, without undermining the mutual commitments of the Members with unconstrained deference.

C CONCLUSION

The two questions which must guide development of the standard of review in the WTO are the *what* question, and the *how* question. In

[113] English lawyers in particular may have this concern as they will doubtless be reminded of the highly deferential *Wednesbury* unreasonableness standard of review.

[114] For example, if the Appellate Body determined that public fear is not a sufficient basis for provisional measures under Art 5.7 of the SPS Agreement, the panel would not be able to circumvent that restriction and defer to the Member by using the 'reasonable regulator' standard.

addressing the first question—what level of deference is appropriate—a comparison with US and ECJ case law suggests that a greater level of deference than is accorded in those jurisdictions is appropriate. In the US, the need to ensure that agencies stay within the bounds of their delegated powers justifies intrusive judicial review of agencies' methodology, data and models, notwithstanding formal deference to agency expertise. Cases decided under the Commerce Clause show that the US courts will exercise intrusive review when states attempt to isolate themselves, export problems to neighbouring states, or ignore the interests of out-of-state actors who are excluded from the state level political remedies against unpopular regulations. In the EU, free movement of goods is fundamental. The crucial role of free movement of goods to the development of the EU has meant that health measures taken by the Member States which interfere with free movement of goods warrant much closer scrutiny than do Community-wide measures put in place by the Community institutions.

When one views WTO review of national health measures against this backdrop, it is hard to escape the conclusion that a greater degree of deference is required. The disciplines WTO Members took on represent the limit of their commitment to one another—they did not take on any comparable community-building undertaking. Moreover, no ready replacement justifying intense review can be found. In an effort to prevent protectionism and ensure that markets are not restricted through unnecessary health measures, the SPS Agreement puts in place significant substantive and procedural commitments. Those commitments are far-reaching. WTO Members have promised to base their SPS measures on scientific principles, including the risk assessments. Of course it is necessary to ensure that WTO Members abide by their commitments, but that can be done while according a degree of deference to the Members. For example, the value of the scientific justification discipline can be assured without panels determining whether they would characterise the risk in the same way as the Member did—it should be enough to ensure that health measures are based on a *reasonable* reading of the scientific evidence and that the scientific evidence was arrived at by studies meeting the minimum requirements of scientific method.[115] By limiting review in this way, the points of tension relating to uncertainty and social and cultural factors can be significantly eased.

As was stressed in Chapter 4, scientific evidence is constituted as a spectrum in which uncertainty is always present, at greater or lesser levels. The

[115] [D Crawford-Brown] J Pauwelyn and K Smith 'Environmental Risk, Precaution and Scientific Rationality in the Context of WTO/NAFTA Trade Rules' (forthcoming in Risk Analysis, draft on file) 16 (risk estimates must have some minimal epistemic status to be labelled 'scientific'); DA Wirth 'The Role of Science in the Uruguay Round and NAFTA Trade Disciplines' (1994) 27 Cornell IntlLJ 817, 845 (any domestic scientific determination that has withstood peer review should satisfy Uruguay Round requirements).

point on the spectrum at which a scientific justification no longer exists cannot be fixed in the abstract. If panels focus on whether the regulators made a reasonable judgment about the sufficiency of the evidence and recognise that a certain amount of uncertainty does not mean that the evidence is not properly scientific, significant progress will have been made in easing tensions relating to uncertainty. Further progress could be made if a deferential standard of review were applied in determining whether a provisional measure under Article 5.7 was based on pertinent information and reviewed within a reasonable period of time—recall that Article 5.7 stipulates that, 'where relevant scientific evidence is insufficient', a Member may adopt provisional measures on the basis of 'available pertinent information' provided that the Member seeks to obtain the 'additional information necessary for a more objective assessment of risk' and reviews the measure within a 'reasonable period of time'. Article 5.7 does have shortcomings, but an interpretation of that provision which overcomes the impression that all uncertainty is remediable by further work and which clarifies the meaning of review within a reasonable period of time should, when complemented by a deferential standard of review, largely ameliorate concerns that WTO rules prevent Members from acting to protect their citizens when threats are not scientifically substantiated.

When it comes to social and cultural factors, a deferential standard of review again has a role to play. In assessing whether a measure is based on scientific evidence or whether a less-restrictive measure would suffice, a deferential standard of review can provide a certain amount of space for social and cultural factors in regulation. Of course, some Appellate Body clarification is needed on whether such factors are relevant to assessing whether differences in the levels of protection chosen are arbitrary or unjustifiable. However, a deferential standard of review could also help by making it clear that panellists are not to see themselves as regulators determining anew whether two situations are sufficiently comparable that the level of protection chosen ought to be the same. By adopting a deferential standard of review which focuses on reasonableness, the WTO could accommodate the imperfections inherent in regulation as a human activity.

In achieving the desired intensity of review, the standard of review intersects with the disciplines stipulated in the agreements and their interpretation in cases. As such, the particular disciplines applicable to health cases and their interpretation by the Appellate Body provides the raw material with which a standard of review works to deliver the intensity of review which will best balance both the needs of WTO Members and the demands of meaningful review. Not only will the level of deference considered appropriate in the wide range of areas covered by the DSU differ, but the fact that panels consider such a wide range of agreements with a multitude of substantive commitments means that, in order to ensure that the desired intensity of review is achieved, the standard of review must vary. How it might do this is a significant challenge given the Appellate Body's fixation upon objective assessment. Realism dictates that suggestions for developing the standard of review in the WTO work with the objective assessment standard, but the approach taken in the safeguards cases shows that the standard of review can be developed without jettisoning the 'objective assessment' framework.

In safeguards cases, the WTO has taken the objective assessment shell and constructed a distinct standard of review within it. One possibility is that the 'reasonable regulator' approach, as hinted at in the *Asbestos* case, could be brought under the objective assessment banner as an articulation of how objective assessment is to be applied to the factual assessments of the national authorities in health cases. Reasonableness answers the *what* question—*what* level of deference?—by capturing the notion that unnecessary interferences with national judgments should be avoided. It also answers the *how* question—*how* can the desired level of deference be achieved?—by offering itself for incorporation under the objective assessment standard of review. An added benefit of the 'reasonable regulator' approach is that reasonableness review even has a respectable history in GATT. This would allow panels and the Appellate Body to embrace it without standing accused of judicial legislation. Although not a purist's ideal, development of the objective assessment standard of review along the lines of the second standard of review model represents a pragmatic but worthwhile alternative. Using the reasonable regualtor as an elaboration of the objective assessment standard in health cases would deliver review which ensures that protectionism does not proliferate and that clearly unnecessary health regulations are not allowed to limit trade, while not interfering with the reasonable assessments of national regulators.

8

Conclusion

WE LIVE IN a world in which trade and health regulation must co-exist. This reality is not new: people have engaged in trade ever since they developed the means to transport their goods to distant places for sale or exchange. Similarly, human societies have long been concerned to protect themselves from threats to their health. The relationship between trade and health has never been easy but the passage of time has, if anything, served to complicate rather than simplify that relationship. As the importance of international trade has grown, so too has the pressure to find a way to manage the impact of health regulation on trade without compromising health protection standards. When co-ordinated international efforts were first made to control the negative trade-effects of health in the mid-19th century, those efforts were primarily diplomatic.[1] With the advent of GATT in 1947, however, the trade–health interface moved into the realm of law notwithstanding the widely recognised problems with GATT's dispute settlement system. With the WTO now well established, Member countries are undoubtedly legally accountable to each other for their decisions on health in a way that they have not been before.

Both the desire to trade and the desire to protect health are immutable. Both objectives are important for societies and are legitimate—one simply cannot triumph over the other. Rather, the challenge is to work out how the difficult interface between these two basic objectives can be managed. Since the middle of the 20th century, the international community has agreed a set of rules to manage that interface. Initially, these rules were somewhat crude. We saw in Chapter 2 that GATT qualified its promise of non-discrimination and its ban on quantitative restrictions to trade by providing that measures necessary to protect health would still be permitted. Although an appreciable legal edifice was built on the slim provisions of Article XX(b) and the terms of the *chapeau*—recall in particular the interpretation that, for a measure to be 'necessary', it must constitute the least trade-restrictive alternative, and the development of a balancing approach

[1] DP Fidler *International Law and Infectious Diseases* (OUP Oxford 1999) 21 (measures taken to combat infectious diseases had a sizeable impact on shipping, leading to international co-operative efforts, beginning with the first international sanitary conference in 1851).

to the *chapeau*—GATT proved ineffective in giving proper structure to the trade–health interface. With the Uruguay Round, however, came a new principle by which to manage trade and health. That principle was scientific justification. The resort, in the Uruguay Round, to science needs to be seen in its historical context. In the past, trade-limiting action to protect health was based on an amalgam of fact, suspicion and educated hunches.[2] With the growth of scientific methods of analysing risks came the promise of more fact-driven decision-making. By relying primarily on science to manage the trade–health relationship, the Uruguay Round negotiators embraced this vision of science. With science as the organising principle, trade would no longer have to give way to health assertions that had no scientific justification. In this way, science promised more than non-discrimination: trade barriers based on fears and assumptions about health risks—rather than facts—would have to be dismantled. In short, science allowed the Uruguay Round to adopt a significant, if limited, market-opening agenda.

This faith in the rational power of science underpins the Uruguay Round's response to the question of how the interface between health and trade is to be managed. Although the SPS Agreement retains the disciplines familiar from GATT—SPS measures must not be discriminatory or more trade-restrictive than necessary and must not be applied so as to constitute a disguised restriction on trade—its centrepiece is undoubtedly the requirement that SPS measures must have a scientific justification. More than any other provision, the scientific justification provision of Article 2.2 (which is backed up by the risk assessment discipline of Article 5) defines the SPS Agreement's approach to trade and health. The SPS Agreement does not, of course, cover the whole spectrum of health regulations. Health regulations not directed specifically at pests, diseases, toxins, contaminants and additives may well come under the TBT Agreement if they lay down product characteristics. Some health regulations may not even fall within the TBT Agreement, whereupon their survival will depend on GATT alone. Like the SPS Agreement, the TBT Agreement retains the disciplines familiar from GATT but it, like GATT, does not contain an explicit reference to risk assessment and scientific justification. In short, depending on their focus and characteristics, health regulations may be considered under the SPS Agreement, under the TBT Agreement or under GATT alone. In each case, a different set of disciplines applies.

The fact that the WTO does not have a unified approach to health regulations is unfortunate. The disciplines provided for in the SPS Agreement are more onerous than those provided for in the TBT Agreement and

[2] JA Kellar 'The Application of Risk Analysis to International Trade in Animals and Animal Products' (1993) 12 SciTechRev (OIE) 1023, 1030–31 (on this approach to regulation and the promise of science-based decision-making).

GATT, meaning that the scope of the Agreements will continue to attract attention as disputing WTO Members argue over which Agreement will apply (or, indeed, if more than one Agreement will apply). The difficult relationship between the three Agreements applying to health regulations is particularly prominent when one considers the latest frontier of the contested trade–health relationship: genetically modified organisms (GMOs). Opposition to GMOs has a number of fronts. GMOs are said to threaten sustainable development, biodiversity and public health. In addition, opposition to GMOs can derive from a philosophical or moral objection to the very activity of genetic modification. As such, any GMO ban or mandatory labelling scheme will, in all likelihood, have public health, environmental and moral dimensions. Which Agreement or Agreements would apply in the WTO?[3] The anwer to that question is particularly important given the striking differences between the disciplines imposed by the three Agreements considered here: GATT, the SPS Agreement and the TBT Agreement.

In many ways, the broader GMO example (as opposed to the particular dispute brought by the US, Canada and Argentina) serves to illustrate the difficulties with which this study has been concerned. As Chapter 4 showed, science's promise of value-neutrality has, in some respects, turned out to be illusory. Perhaps science never really promised to be entirely value-free; when international trade negotiators chose science as the benchmark of legitimate health regulation, they probably imputed to science a greater degree of value-neutrality and a greater degree of certainty than science would have claimed for itself. Time, and the experience of decisions being made under the SPS Agreement, have shown that science is not entirely value-free and that uncertainty is a feature of scientific risk assessment, not anathema to it. While this dose of reality does mean that science can no longer be regarded as an *uncomplicated* and *uncontroversial* means by which to determine when trade must give way to health, its value as an organising principle survives. Although its image is a little tarnished, science continues to constitute the primary organising principle

[3] In their requests for consultations with the EC, Argentina, Canada and the US have alleged breaches of the SPS Agreement, GATT, the TBT Agreement and the Agreement on Agriculture: *EC–Measures Affecting the Approval and Marketing of Biotech Products* WT/DS291/1 (US request for consultations dated 20 May 2003), WT/DS292/1 (Canada's request for consultations dated 20 May 2003), WT/DS293/1 (Argentina's request for consultations dated 21 May 2003). For views on which Agreements would apply, see: J Scott 'European Regulation of GMOs and the WTO' (2003) 9 Columbia JEurL 213, 228; S Safrin 'Treaties in Collision? The Biosafety Protocol and the World Trade Organization Agreements' (2002) 96 AJIL 606, 610; AH Qureshi 'The Cartagena Protocol on Biosafety and the WTO—Co-existence or Incoherence?' (2000) 49 ICLQ 835, 848–50; F MacMillan and M Blakeney 'Regulating GMOs: Is the WTO Agreement on Sanitary and Phytosanitary Measures Hormonally Challenged?' (Part I) (2000) 6 IntlTradeL&Reg 131, 133; S Shaw and R Schwartz 'Trade and Environment in the WTO: State of Play' (2000) 36 JWT 129, 143–44; M Stilwell and B van Dyke 'An Activist's Handbook on Genetically Modified Organisms and the WTO' 7–8 (the TBT Agreement should apply to GMO labelling).

applicable to the trade–health interface. That is not to say that it is always easy to identify when a scientific justification exists, or what should happen when the scientific evidence to support a politically popular measure is rather thin. For example, if considered under the SPS Agreement, would a GMO ban be 'based on' a risk assessment if any risk assessment constituted only a minor motivating factor that was in fact dwarfed by the importance of public objections? What would happen if a Member were unable even to complete a risk assessment due to scientific uncertainty?

Herein lie the two points of tension that make it so difficult to establish a satisfactory balance between national regulatory autonomy and international supervision. The nature of scientific justification—specifically, the sufficiency of scientific evidence and the treatment of scientific uncertainty—is one significant point of tension. The other point of tension relates to the role of social and cultural factors in science-driven regulation. Social and cultural factors can enter into the regulatory process in a number of ways. Firstly, they may motivate the instigation of a regulatory investigation by influencing the choice of perceived hazards that are thought important enough to warrant the dedication of resources sufficient to gather and, if necessary, generate further scientific information, analyse it and conduct a risk assessment. Social and cultural factors will clearly be implicated in a range of risk management decisions from the choice of the science policies for use in scientific risk assessments to the choice of the appropriate level of protection, and from a choice between alternative regulatory techniques to decisions about how risk should be distributed across social groups. In the highly rational, science-focused world of the SPS Agreement (and to a lesser extent, of GATT) how reference to such factors is treated will have a significant impact on the nature of the retained national right to take trade-limiting measures to protect health.

The treatment of social and cultural factors in the WTO is complicated by the fact that it will often be difficult to isolate those factors. For example, concern over GMOs has both health and ethical dimensions. These sources of concern are likely to be intermingled in any regulatory action relating to the access of GMO products to a particular market. For example, ethical discomfort at the very nature of genetic modification may well influence the *way* in which the particular health risks feared to be associated with GMOs are identified and investigated. The sense that some frontier in human existence is being crossed by GMOs may also influence what deductions are made based on the available scientific evidence and the significance accorded to any points of uncertainty. In this way, one can see how the two points tension—social and cultural factors and the treatment of uncertainty—can be interrelated.

If the existence of a risk must be shown to be supported by 'sufficient scientific evidence', then the question of what amounts to scientific evidence and what sufficiency refers to becomes crucial. In this respect, the structure of the SPS Agreement raises some problems as it posits a clear line between circumstances in which there is a scientific justification and circumstances in which there is not. This binary division is problematic because scientific evidence is constituted as a spectrum, with greater or lesser degrees of uncertainty. Who is to say at what point the uncertainties are so pervasive or so significant that a scientific justification for regulatory action does not exist? The Appellate Body has sought, through its analysis of the risk assessment discipline, to avoid imposing quantitative requirements on scientific evidence; rather, it has sought to emphasise the relationship between the risk assessment and the measure. That said, however, the Appellate Body has not really addressed the question of the significance of varying degrees of scientific uncertainty and what regard should be had to the opinions and deductions of national regulators. When it comes to the role of social and cultural factors, the waters are even muddier. The Appellate Body refused to draw a firm distinction between risk assessment and risk management under the SPS Agreement. This decision exacerbated the confusion already surrounding the question of whether such factors have a legitimate role in risk assessment, and continues to undermine the emerging international consensus on this question—the Codex Alimentarius Commission adopted a statement identifying reference to 'other legitimate factors' as part of the risk management process. The Appellate Body has also not made clear its attitude to whether social and cultural factors may be cited to justify the adoption of different levels of protection in apparently comparable situations when the adoption of different levels of protection would otherwise contravene the consistency discipline of Article 5.5 of the SPS Agreement. In particular, a specific cultural fear or ethical position may mean that, for the regulating Member, the two situations are not comparable whereas, for the exporting Member, the distinction appears arbitrary.

The question of how scientific uncertainty is handled within a fact-driven trade regime is particularly contentious. With spectacular failures such as the BSE crisis being blamed on an unwillingness to act in circumstances of scientific uncertainty, the fear is that the scientific justification discipline puts at risk the ability of governments to take protective action before the scientific jury is in. This concern is prominent in the discussion of GMOs and has led many commentators to suggest that the future of GMO regulation depends in large part on whether the precautionary principle is accepted in the WTO.[4] In some respects, the precautionary

[4] D Smits and S Zabroski 'Trade and Genetically Modified Foods: GMOs: Chumps or Champs of International Trade?' (2001) 1 Asper Rev Intl Bus & Trade 111, 138; Shaw and Schwartz (n 3) 140; F MacMillan and M Blakeney 'Regulating GMOs: Is the WTO Agreement on Sanitary and Phytosanitary Measures Hormonally Challenged?'(Part II) 2000 6 IntlTradeL&Reg 161, 162.

principle is seductive. It short-circuits the SPS Agreement's problematic distinction between sufficient and insufficient scientific evidence by doing away with the basic requirement that regulatory action be supported by positive evidence of a risk. If regulatory action can be taken without such proof, the question of whether the scientific evidence justifies the action taken becomes moot. While avoiding the SPS Agreement's problematic bifurcation of scientific sufficiency in favour of a recognition that scientific certainty constitutes a continuum, the full implications of adopting the precautionary principle need to be considered. To this end, Chapter 5 took up the European Commission's Communication on the Precautionary Principle. Although the Commission's version of the precautionary principle is not 'anti-science', it does ultimately reject the fundamental basis of the SPS Agreement—the requirement that regulatory measures be based on scientific evidence of harm. Therefore, in order to salvage the Agreement's benefits to trade and prevent the proliferation of health-based non-tariff barriers, some additional bases of review would be needed.

One way in which the precautionary principle could be implemented is if it were accompanied by strict proportionality review. In the trade context, strict proportionality review refers to the type of review in which the adjudicator is authorised to determine whether the regulatory measure constitutes a disproportionate response given the magnitude of the risk or because of the costs imposed on other participants in the trade system.[5] If WTO panels were authorised to engage in such strict proportionality review, recognition of the precautionary principle would not permit the Members to engage in disguised protectionism or to adopt an unreasonably conservative attitude to domestic health protection. Under the current system, WTO panels are not empowered to engage in this kind of strict proportionality review. If implemented together with strict proportionality review, the adoption of the precautionary principle in the WTO would, in fact, *extend* the scope of international review and establish a platform for much more intrusive review than is currently provided for. When accompanied by strict proportionality review, the precautionary principle actually results in *more* review of national action and preferences, not less. This alone might cause one to question the value of such an implementation of the precautionary principle. Such concerns are reinforced when one observes the weak application of strict proportionality review in the much closer-knit EU; if the ECJ is reluctant to engage in strict proportionality review, is it really appropriate in the WTO?

Another alternative for implementing the precautionary principle is to focus on the procedural aspects of regulation-making. There has, of late,

[5] Strict proportionality review is to be distinguished from the weaker form of proportionality review in which the adjudicator asks whether a less-restrictive alternative could have secured the regulatory objective.

been a general move to embrace procedural review. Several academics have proposed procedural models for WTO review, and it can be seen in cases like *Pfizer* that there is an increasingly procedural approach to keeping the precautionary principle within bounds in the EU.[6] By focusing on the *way* in which decisions are reached rather than their substantive aspects, procedural review promises a less-intrusive review which respects national democratic preferences and processes. There are two fundamental problems with this view, when applied to the WTO. The first problem is that procedural review is not as unintrusive as it may at first appear. A review of the US approach to judicial review of health and safety regulation-making shows that procedural review can become very substantive and very intrusive. The second problem is that it is by no means clear that, in the WTO setting, the validity of process is a sufficient reason to respect national regulatory decisions. By focusing on the democratic legitimacy of regulatory trade-offs, the frame of reference is necessarily national. Accordingly, the interests of other WTO Members are likely to be excluded. While one may embrace or bemoan such a development, it must at least be acknowledged that the basic bargain negotiated in the Uruguay Round would be altered by a switch to procedurally-focused review.

There may, however, be another way in which tensions relating to scientific uncertainty and the role of social and cultural factors could be eased. At base, these concerns relate to the degree of international intrusion on national decisions and preferences. When one talks of intrusive and deferential approaches to review, one is concerned, at least in part, with the standard of review. In the WTO, the question of the standard of review applicable in health cases has been neglected. The standard of review concept has been fully recognised in the WTO, but it is regrettable that the Appellate Body decided that a reference in the DSU to panels making an 'objective assessment' of the matter constitutes the applicable standard of review. Given the shortcomings of the objective assessment standard—its conceptual confusion and failure to articulate a clear standard of review—it would greatly benefit from development.

If the standard of review is to contribute as much as it can to the easing of tensions in the WTO, it must be substantially developed. To this end, a comparative study of the standard of review chosen in other systems is appropriate. Chapter 7 contributes to the process of developing the WTO's standard of review by addressing two questions: what level of deference is desirable, and how might the objective assessment standard of review be developed? As it is unlikely that the WTO Members will negotiate a totally new standard of review in the short to medium term, and the Appellate Body's emphasis on textualism suggests that it will be reluctant

[6] Case T-13/99 *Pfizer Animal Health v Council* [2002] ECR-II 3305.

to jettison the objective assessment standard altogether, attempts to develop the standard of review must build on that standard of review. The most that can be hoped for is that the objective assessment standard of review will undergo further development by an articulation of its meaning or method of application in various circumstances. Such a development of the WTO's standard of review should proceed from a clear understanding of the level of deference to be applied. When one considers the approach taken in the US, both in judicial review cases and under the commerce clause, as well as the ECJ's different approach to review of the health claims of the Member States and the Community institutions, it seems appropriate to accord a greater level of deference to the factual aspects of WTO Members' health measures. The WTO Members are not exercising any delegated powers and their actions, in protecting health, do not undermine any overarching community-building agenda, as was the case in the US and EU.

The second question addressed in Chapter 7 is how the objective assessment standard of review might be developed. It was argued in Chapter 6 that, by itself, objective assessment does not constitute a useful standard of review. It is only when it is complemented by an elaboration of its application in specific circumstances—as occurred in the safeguards cases—that the objective assessment standard of review comes to function as a useful adjudicatory tool in managing the tension between national prerogatives and international review. There has been no equivalent explanation of how objective assessment is to be applied in health cases generally, or under the SPS Agreement, TBT Agreement or Article XX(b) of GATT specifically.

Signs of an articulation of objective assessment for health cases may, however, be beginning to appear. In the *Asbestos* case, the panel effectively chose to determine the intensity of its review by reference to what a reasonable regulator would have deduced from the evidence or would have done in the circumstances in which the French regulator was working. This raises the possibility that a 'reasonable regulator' approach may come to be developed in the WTO.

It has been argued here that the 'reasonable regulator' approach should be developed as an articulation of the objective assessment standard of review suitable for application in health cases. By adopting a 'reasonable regulator' articulation of the objective assessment standard of review, a number of challenges can be successfully met. Firstly, by retaining the objective assessment umbrella, the Appellate Body's textualist scruples can be respected as the 'reasonable regulator' approach would simply be an articulation of the objective assessment standard. In the safeguards cases, the Appellate Body showed itself to be willing to adopt a variable articulation of the application of the objective assessment standard and there is no reason to presume that it would not similarly be willing to develop an application of the objective assessment standard for health cases. Secondly, the 'reasonable regulator' standard of review delivers a level of deference that ensures that the needs of the WTO trading system are met while respecting, to the greatest degree consistent with the needs of the WTO compact, the rights and prerogatives of national governments. A standard of review hinging on reasonableness would allow a WTO panel to ensure that a defending Member is meeting its substantive commitment only to take regulatory action where there is a scientific justification without unnecessarily intruding into the national regulator's assessment of the significance of various pieces of scientific evidence or its integration of social and cultural factors into the regulatory process.

It should not be supposed that taking up such a reasonableness standard of review would instantly resolve tensions relating to international supervision of national health regulation. It is likely that some measure of tension is inevitable, given that the integration of health and trade concerns is inherently difficult. It is also the case that the scope of national regulatory autonomy is determined by the substantive disciplines negotiated, their interpretation and application, as well as the standard of review applied. Taking the existing disciplines as a basis, there is still room for the Appellate Body to adopt interpretations that would contribute to the overall effort to structure a system of review that balances international supervision and national prerogatives. In particular, the Appellate Body has yet to offer full interpretations of Articles 5.5 and 5.7 of the SPS Agreement. How the Appellate Body interprets these provisions will, in large part, determine whether Article 5.7 will afford the flexibility necessary to accommodate reasonable regulatory action in circumstances of uncertainty, and whether social and cultural factors will be deemed relevant to consistency analysis under Article 5.5. The development of interpretations that further the aims of the WTO system without needlessly intruding into national decision-making is one important task in managing the trade–health relationship. With that task in mind, it is clear that applying a proper standard of review to help resolve tensions relating to scientific uncertainty and social and cultural preferences is not the whole answer. That said, developing the standard of review is a start, and a promising one at that. The discussion of what level of deference is appropriate must begin in earnest. It will require a searching examination of the nature of the WTO system and, in particular, the level of integration and mutual consideration it requires. Non-discrimination is no longer a complete statement of one Member's obligations to another. As Members, we owe each other more, but we don't seem quite sure how much more—this is what we need to work out.

Bibliography

AMAN AC and WT MAYTON *Administrative Law* (West Publishing Co St Paul 1993).

ANGELL M *Science on Trial: The Clash of Medical Evidence and the Law in the Breast Implant Case* (WW Norton & Co New York 1996).

ATIK J 'Science and International Regulatory Convergence' (1996–7) 17 Northwestern Journal of International Law and Business 736.

BACCHUS J 'Table Talk: Around the Table of the Appellate Body of the World Trade Organization' (2002) 35 Vanderbilt Journal of Transnational Law 1021.

BALDWIN R et al *A Reader on Regulation* (OUP Oxford 1998).

BALDWIN R and M CAVE *Understanding Regulation: Theory, Strategy and Practice* (OUP Oxford 1999).

BALZANO Q and AR SHEPPARD 'The Influence of the Precautionary Principle on Science-Based Decision-Making: Questionable Applications to Risks of Radiofrequency Fields' (2002) 5 J Risk Research 351.

BARFIELD CE *Free Trade, Sovereignty, Democracy: The Future of the World Trade Organization* (AEI Press Washington DC 2001).

BARRETT K and C RAFFENSPERGER 'Precautionary Science' in C Raffensperger and JA Tickner (eds) *Protecting Public Health and the Environment: Implementing the Precautionary Principle* (Island Press Washington DC 1999) 105.

BECK U *Risk Society: Towards a New Modernity* (M Ritter (trans) Sage Publications London 1992).

BENTLEY P 'A Re-Assessment of Article XX, Paragraphs (b) and (g), of GATT 1994 in the Light of Growing Consumer and Environmental Concern about Biotechnology' (2000) 24 Fordham International Law Journal 107.

BERMANN GA 'Regulatory Federalism: European Union and United States' (1997) 263 Recueil des Cours 9.

BHALA R and DA GANTZ 'WTO Case Review 2001' (2002) 19 Arizona Journal of International and Comparative Law 457.

BLACK J 'Proceduralizing Regulation: Part I' (2000) 20 Oxford Journal of Legal Studies 597.

BLOCHE MG 'WTO Deference to National Health Policy: Toward an Interpretive Principle' (2002) 5 Journal of International Economic Law 825.

BODANSKY D 'The Precautionary Principle in US Environmental Law' in T O'Riordan and J Cameron (eds) *Interpreting the Precautionary Principle* (Cameron May London 1994) 203.

BOEHMER-CHRISTIANSEN S 'The Precautionary Principle in Germany—Enabling Government' in T O'Riordan and J Cameron (eds) *Interpreting the Precautionary Principle* (Cameron May London 1994) 31.

BOHANES J 'Risk Regulation in WTO Law: A Procedure-Based Approach to the Precautionary Principle' (2002) 40 Columbia Journal of Transnational Law 323.

BOURGEOIS JHJ 'Some Reflections on the WTO Dispute Settlement System from a Practitioner's Perspective' (2001) 4 Journal of International Economic Law 145.

BRAITHWAITE J and P DRAHOS *Global Business Regulation* (CUP Cambridge UK 2000) 401.

BREYER S *Breaking the Vicious Circle: Toward Effective Risk Regulation* (Harvard UP Cambridge MA 1993).

BROWN L (ed) *The New Shorter Oxford English Dictionary* (4th edn OUP Oxford 1993).

DE BURCA G 'The Principle of Proportionality and its Application in EC Law' (1993) 13 Yearbook of European Law 105.

CAMERON J 'The Precautionary Principle' in G Sampson and WB Chambers (eds) *Trade, Environment and the Millennium* (UN UP Tokyo 1999) 239.

CAMERON J 'The Precautionary Principle in International Law' in T O'Riordan, A Jordan and J Cameron (eds) *Reinterpreting the Precautionary Principle* (Cameron May London 2002) 113.

CANNON JR and KL BLAND 'GATT Panels Need Restraining Principles' (1993) 24 Law and Policy in International Business 1167.

CASS RA and JR HARING 'Domestic Regulation and International Trade: Where's the Race?' in DLM Kennedy and JD Southwick (eds) *The Political Economy of International Trade Law* (CUP Cambridge UK 2002) 111.

CHALMERS D ' "Food for Thought": Reconciling European Risks and Traditional Ways of Life' (2003) 66 Modern Law Review 532.

CHANG SW 'GATTing a Green Trade Barrier: Eco-Labelling and the WTO Agreement on Technical Barriers to Trade' (1997) 31(1) Journal of World Trade 137.

CHARNOVITZ S 'The World Trade Organization, Meat Hormones, and Food Safety' (1997) 14 International Trade Reporter 1781.

CHARNOVITZ S 'Environment and Health Under WTO Dispute Settlement' (1998) 32 The International Lawyer 901.

CHARNOVITZ S 'Improving the Agreement on Sanitary and Phytosanitary Standards' in GP Sampson and WB Chambers *Trade, Environment and the Millennium* (UN UP Tokyo 1999) 171.

CHARNOVITZ S 'The Supervision of Health and Biosafety Regulation by the World Trade Rules' (2000) Tulane Environmental Law Journal 271.

CHOI WON-MOG *'Like Products' in International Trade Law: Towards a Consistent GATT/WTO Jurisprudence* (OUP Oxford 2003).

CHRISTOFOROU T 'Settlement of Science-Based Trade Disputes in the WTO: A Critical Review of the Developing Case Law in the Face of Scientific Uncertainty' (2000) 8 New York University Environmental Law Journal 622.

CODEX ALIMENTARIUS COMMISSION *Statements of Principle Concerning the Role of Science in the Codex Decision-Making Process and the Extent to Which Other Factors Are Taken into Account* (Decision of the 21st Session of the Commission 1995 ALINORM 95/37).

CODEX ALIMENTARIUS COMMISSION *Statements of Principle Relating to the Role of Food Safety Risk Assessment* (Decision of the 22nd Session of the Commission 1997 ALINORM 97/37).

CODEX ALIMENTARIUS COMMISSION *US Government Submission to the Committee on General Principles of the CAC for the Committee's April 10–14, 2000 meeting* (available at <http://www.fsis.usda.gov/OA/codex/confpaper.htm>).

CODEX ALIMENTARIUS COMMISSION *Criteria for the Consideration of the Other Factors Referred to in the Second Statement of Principle* (Decision of the 24th Session of the Commission 2001 ALINORM 01/41).

Codex Alimentarius Commission *Report* (24th Session 2001 ALINORM 01/41).

Codex Alimentarius Commission *Procedural Manual* (13th edn FAO/WHO Rome 2003).

Codex Alimentarius Commission *Working Principles for Risk Analysis in the Framework of the Codex Alimentarius (36th Session 2003 ALINORM 03/041).*

Codex Committee on General Principles *Proposed Draft Working Principles for Risk Analysis* (Report of the 17th Session 2002 ALINORM 03/33).

Codex Committee on General Principles *Report* (17th Session 2002 ALINORM 03/33).

Codex Committee on General Principles *Report* (18th Session 2003 ALINORM 03/33A).

Cottier T and PC Mavroidis 'Regulatory Barriers and the Principle of Non-Discrimination in WTO Law: An Overview' in T Cottier and PC Mavroidis (eds) *Regulatory Barriers and the Principles of Non-Discrimination in World Trade Law* (U Michigan P Ann Arbor 2000) 3.

Covello VT et al 'Guidelines for Communicating Information about Chemical Risks Effectively and Responsibly' in DG Mayo and RD Hollander (eds) *Acceptable Evidence: Science and Risk Values in Risk Management* (OUP Oxford 1991) 66.

Craig P *Administrative Law* (4th edn Sweet & Maxwell London 1999).

Crawford-Brown D, J Pauwelyn and K Smith 'Environmental Risk, Precaution and Scientific Rationality in the Context of WTO/NAFTA Trade Rules' (forthcoming in Risk Analysis, draft on file).

Croley SP and JH Jackson 'WTO Dispute Procedures, Standard of Review, and Deference to National Governments' (1996) American Journal of International Law 193.

Cromer J 'Sanitary and Phytosanitary Measures: What They Could Mean for Health and Safety Regulations Under GATT' (1995) 36 Harvard International Law Review 557.

Croome J *Reshaping the World Trading System: A History of the Uruguay Round* (2nd edn WTO Geneva 1999).

Cross FB 'Paradoxical Perils of the Precautionary Principle' (1996) 53 Washington and Lee Law Review 851.

Davey WJ ' "Has the WTO Dispute Settlement System Exceeded Its Authority"' in T Cottier and PC Mavroidis *The Role of the Judge in International Trade Regulation: Experience and Lessons for the WTO* (U Mich P Ann Arbor 2003) 43.

Desmedt GA 'Hormones: "Objective Assessment" and (or as) Standard of Review' (1998) 1 Journal of International Economic Law 695.

Desmedt A 'Proportionality in WTO Law' (2001) 4 Journal of International Economic Law 441.

van Dijk P and GJH van Hoof *Theory and Practice of the European Convention on Human Rights* (3rd edn Kluwer Law International The Hague 1998).

Durodié B 'Plastic Panics: European Risk Regulation in the Aftermath of BSE' in J Morris (ed) *Rethinking Risk and the Precautionary Principle* (Butterworth-Heinemann Oxford 2000) 140.

Echols M *Food Safety and the WTO: The Interplay of Culture, Science and Technology* (Kluwer Law International The Hague 2001).

Ely JH *Democracy and Distrust: A Theory of Judicial Review* (Harvard UP Cambridge MA 1980).

Esty DC *Greening the GATT: Trade, Environment, and the Future* (Institute for International Economics Washington DC 1994).

EC—*Comments from the European Commission Services to the Codex Secretariat* (available at 'europa.int/comm/food/fs/ifsi/eupositions/ccgp/ccgp01_en.html').

EC—*Response from the European Commission to Comments Submitted by WTO Members under Either or Both G/TBT/N/EEC/6 and G/SPS/N/EEC/149* (G/SPS/GEN/337, G/TBT/W/179 26 July 2002).

European Commission *Communication from the Commission on the Precautionary Principle* (G/SPS/GEN/168 14 March 2000) (COM/2000/0001).

European Commission *Final Report on Setting the Scientific Framework for the Inclusion of New Quality of Life Concerns in the Risk Assessment Process* (adopted by the Scientific Steering Committee 10–11 April 2003).

European Commission *The Future of Risk Assessment in the European Union: Second Report on the Harmonisation of Risk Assessment Procedures* (adopted by the Scientific Steering Committee 10–11 April 2003).

European Commission *White Paper on Food Safety* COM (1999) 719 final.

European Council *Presidency Conclusions: Nice European Council Meeting* (SN 400/00 December 2000).

European Parliament *Resolution on the Commission Communication on the Precautionary Principle* (A5–0352/2000 December 2000).

Joint FAO/WHO Expert Consultation *Application of Risk Analysis to Food Standards Issues* (WHO/FNU/FOS/95.3 Geneva 1995).

Joint FAO/WHO Consultation *Risk Management and Food Safety* (FAO Food and Nutrition Paper 65 Rome 1997).

Farber DA 'The Case Against Clarity' in DLM Kennedy and JD Southwick (eds) *The Political Economy of International Trade Law* (CUP Cambridge UK 2002) 575.

Farber DA and RE Hudec 'Free Trade and the Regulatory State: A GATT's-Eye View of the Dormant Commerce Clause' (1994) 47 Vanderbilt Law Review 1401.

Farber DA and RE Hudec 'GATT Legal Restraints on Domestic Environmental Regulations' in J Bhagwati and RE Hudec (eds) *Fair Trade and Harmonization* (Vol 2 MIT Press Cambridge MA 1996) 59.

Fidler DP *International Law and Infectious Diseases* (OUP Oxford 1999).

Fisher E 'Drowning by Numbers: Standard Setting in Risk Regulation and the Pursuit of Accountable Public Administration' (2000) 20 Oxford Journal of Legal Studies 109.

Fisher E 'Is the Precautionary Principle Justiciable?' (2001) 13 Journal of Environmental Law 315.

Fisher E and R Harding 'The Precautionary Principle in Australia: From Aspiration to Practice?' in T O'Riordan, A Jordan and J Cameron (eds) *Reinterpreting the Precautionary Principle* (Cameron May London 2002) 215.

Fraiberg JD and MJ Trebilcock 'Risk Regulation: Technocratic and Democratic Tools for Regulatory Reform' (1998) 43 McGill Law Journal 835.

Franck TM *Fairness in International Law* (Clarendon Press Oxford 1995).

Garvey JH and TA Aleinikoff *Modern Constitutional Theory: A Reader* (3rd edn West Publishing St Paul 1994).

GATT *Analytical Index: Guide to GATT Law and Practice* (6th edn GATT Geneva 1994).

GOMULA J 'The Standard of Review of Article 17.6 of the Anti-Dumping Agreement and the Problem of its Extension to other WTO Agreements' in P Mengozzi (ed) *International Trade Law on the 50th Anniversary of the Multilateral Trade System* (A Giuffrè Editore Milano 1999) 577.

GRAHAM JD and S HSIA 'Europe's Precautionary Principle: Promise and Pitfalls' (2002) 5 Journal of Risk Research 371.

HELFER LR 'Consensus, Coherence and the European Convention on Human Rights' (1993) 26 Cornell International Law Journal 133.

HELFER LR and AM SLAUGHTER 'Toward a Theory of Effective Supranational Adjudication' (1997) 107 Yale Law Journal 273.

HENKEL C 'The Allocation of Powers in the EU: A Closer Look at the Principle of Subsidiarity' (2002) 20 Berkeley Journal of International Law 359.

HORLICK GN and PA CLARKE 'Standards for Panels Reviewing Anti-Dumping Determinations under the GATT and WTO' in EU Petersmann (ed) *International Trade Law and the GATT/WTO Dispute Settlement System* (Kluwer London 1997) 318.

VAN HOUTTE H 'Health and Safety Regulations in International Trade' in P Sarcevic and H van Houtte (eds) *Legal Issues in International Trade* (Graham & Trotman London 1990) 128.

HOWSE R 'Adjudicative Legitimacy and Treaty Interpretation in International Trade Law: The Early Years of WTO Jurisprudence' in JHH Weiler (ed) *The EU, the WTO and the NAFTA* (OUP Oxford 2000) 35.

HOWSE R 'Democracy, Science, and Free Trade: Risk Regulation on Trial at the World Trade Organization' (2000) 98 Michigan Law Review 2329.

HOWSE R 'Managing the Interface Between International Trade Law and the Regulatory State: What Lessons Should (and Should Not) be Drawn from the Jurisprudence of the United States Dormant Commerce Clause' in T Cottier and PC Mavroidis (eds) *Regulatory Barriers and the Principles of Non-Discrimination in World Trade Law* (U Michigan P Ann Arbor 2000) 139.

HOWSE R and D REGAN 'The Product/Process Distinction—An Illusory Basis for Disciplining "Unilateralism" in Trade Policy' (2000) 11 European Journal of International Law 249.

HOWSE R and E TUERK 'The WTO Impact on Internal Regulations—A Case Study of the Canada–EC Asbestos Dispute' in G de Búrca and J Scott (eds) *The EU and the WTO: Legal and Constitutional Issues* (Hart Publishing Oxford 2001) 283.

HUDEC RE *Adjudication of International Trade Disputes* (Trade Policy Research Centre London 1978).

HUDEC RE '"Like Product": The Differences in GATT Articles I and III' in T Cottier and PC Mavroidis (eds) *Regulatory Barriers and the Principles of Non-Discrimination in World Trade Law* (U Michigan P Ann Arbor 2000) 101.

HUDEC R 'GATT/WTO Constraints on Natinoal Regulation: Requiem for an "Aim and Effects" Test' (1998) 32 International Lawyer 619.

HUNT J 'The Social Construction of Precaution' in T O'Riordan and J Cameron (eds) *Interpreting the Precautionary Principle* (Cameron May London 1994) 117.

JACKSON JH *The World Trading System: Law and Policy of International Economic Relations* (2nd edn MIT Press Cambridge MA 1997).

JACKSON JH 'The Birth of the GATT–MTN System: A Constitutional Appraisal' in JH Jackson *The Jurisprudence of GATT and the WTO* (CUP Cambridge UK 2000) 34.

JACKSON JH 'Dispute Settlement and the WTO: Emerging Problems' in WTO Secretariat *From GATT to the WTO: The Multilateral Trading System in the New Millennium* (Kluwer Law International The Hague 2000) 67.

JACKSON JH 'The Great 1994 Sovereignty Debate: United States Acceptance and Implementation of the Uruguay Round Results' in JH Jackson *The Jurisprudence of GATT and the WTO* (CUP Cambridge UK 2000) 367.

JACKSON JH 'The Legal Meaning of a GATT Dispute Settlement Report: Some Reflections' in JH Jackson *The Jurisprudence of GATT and the WTO* (CUP Cambridge UK 2000) 118.

JACKSON JH 'World Trade Rules and Environmental Policies: Congruence or Conflict?' in JH Jackson *The Jurisprudence of GATT and the WTO* (CUP Cambridge UK 2000) 414.

JACKSON JH 'Sovereignty, Subsidiarity, and Separation of Powers: the High-Wire Balancing Act of Globalization' in DLM Kennedy and JD Southwick (eds) *The Political Economy of International Trade Law* (CUP Cambridge UK 2002) 13.

JASANOF S 'Acceptable Evidence in a Pluralistic Society' in the DG Mayo and RD Hollander (eds) *Acceptable Evidence: Science and Risk Values in Risk Management* (OUP Oxford 1991) 29.

JHA V *'Strengthening Developing Countries' Capacities to Respond to Health, Sanitary and Environmental Requirements: A Scoping Paper for Selected Developing Countries* (preliminary draft) (UNCTAD Geneva 2002) (available at <http://www.unctad.org/trade_env/test1/openF1.htm>).

JOERGENS KJ 'True Appellate Review Or Only A Two-Stage Process? A Comparative View of the Appellate Body Under the WTO Dispute Settlement Understanding' (1999) 30 Law and Policy in International Business 193.

JORDAN A 'The Precautionary Principle in the European Union' T O'Riordan, A Jordan and J Cameron (eds) *Reinterpreting the Precautionary Principle* (Cameron May London 2002) 143.

JORDAN A and T O'RIORDAN 'The Precautionary Principle in Contemporary Environmental Policy and Politics' in C Raffensperger and JA Tickner (eds) *Protecting Public Health and the Environment: Implementing the Precautionary Principle* (Island Press Washington DC 1999) 15.

KASPERSON R and JX 'Hidden Hazards' in DG Mayo and RD Hollander (eds) *Acceptable Evidence: Science and Risk Values in Risk Management* (OUP Oxford 1991) 9.

KATES RW 'Managing Technological Hazards: Success, Strain, and Surprise' in National Academy of Engineering *Hazards: Technology and Fairness* (National Academy Press Washington DC 1985) 206.

KELLAR JA 'The Application of Risk Analysis to International Trade in Animals and Animal Products' (1993) 12 Scientific and Technical Review (OIE) 1023.

KENNEDY D *A Critique of Adjudication* (Harvard UP Cambridge MA 1997).

KLEIN C 'The Environmental Commerce Clause' (2003) Harvard Environmental Law Review 1.

KURAN T and CR SUNSTEIN 'Availability Cascades and Risk Regulation' (1999) Stanford Law Review 683.

LATIN H 'Good Science, Bad Regulation, and Toxic Risk Assessment' (1988) 5 Yale Journal on Regulation 89.

LITTLE G 'BSE and the Regulation of Risks' (2001) 64 Modern Law Review 730.

LÖFSTEDT RE and D VOGEL 'The Changing Character of Regulation: A Comparison of Europe and the United States' (2001) 21 Risk Analysis 399.

LONGINO HE *Science as Social Knowledge* (Princeton UP Princeton 1990).

LUCY W *Understanding and Explaining Adjudication* (OUP Oxford 1999).

MACMILLAN F and M BLAKENEY 'Regulating GMOs: Is the WTO Agreement on Sanitary and Phytosanitary Measures Hormonally Challenged?' (Part I) (2000) 6 International Trade Law Regulation 131.

MACMILLAN F and M BLAKENEY 'Regulating GMOs: Is the WTO Agreement on Sanitary and Phytosanitary Measures Hormonally Challenged?' (Part II) (2000) 6 International Trade Law and Regulation 161.

MADURO MP *We, the Court: The European Court of Justice & the European Economic Constitution* (Hart Publishing Oxford 1998).

MADURO MP 'Is There Any Such Thing As Free or Fair Trade? A Constitutional Analysis of the Impact of International Trade on the European Social Model' in G de Búrca and J Scott (eds) *The EU and the WTO: Legal and Constitutional Issues* (Hart Publishing Oxford 2001) 257.

MAHONEY P 'Universality versus Subsidiarity in the Strasbourg Case Law on Free Speech: Explaining Some Recent Judgments' [1997] European Human Rights Law Review 364.

MAHONEY P 'Marvellous Richness of Diversity or Invidious Cultural Relativism?' (1998) 19 Human Rights Law Journal 1

MARCEAU G, 'The Dispute Settlement Rules of the North American Free Trade Agreement: A Thematic Comparison with the Dispute Settlement Rules of the World Trade Organization' in EU Petersmann (ed) *International Trade Law and the GATT/WTO Dispute Settlement System* (Kluwer London 1997) 487.

MARKS MJ and HB MALMGREN 'Negotiating Nontariff Distortions to Trade' (1975) 7 Law and Policy in International Business 327.

MASHAW JL, RA MERRILL and PM SHANE *Administrative Law: The American Public Law System: Cases and Materials* (4th edn West Group St Paul 1998).

MATHIS JH 'Mutual Recognition Agreements: Transatlantic Parties and the Limits to Non-tariff Barrier Regionalism in the WTO' (1998) 32(6) Journal of World Trade 5.

MCGARITY TO 'Some Thoughts on "Deossifying" the Rulemaking Process' (1992) 41 Duke Law Journal 1385.

MCGARITY TO 'The Courts and the Ossification of Rulemaking: A Response to Professor Seidenfeld' (1997) 75 Texas Law Review 525.

MCGARVIN M 'Science, Precaution, Facts and Values' in T O'Riordan, J Cameron and A Jordan (eds) *Reinterpreting the Precautionary Principle* (Cameron May London 2002) 35.

MCNELIS N 'EU Communication on the Precautionary Principle' (2000) 13 Journal of International Economic Law 545.

MCNELIS N 'The Role of the Judge in the EU and WTO: Lessons From the *BSE* and *Hormones* Cases' (2001) 4 Journal of International Economic Law 189.

MCRAE DM 'The Contribution of International Trade Law to the Development of International Law' (1996) 260 Recueil Des Cours 99.

MCRAE DM 'The Emerging Appellate Jurisdiction in International Trade Law' in J Cameron and K Campbell (eds) *Dispute Resolution in the World Trade Organisation* (Cameron May London 1998) 98.

McGinnis JO and ML Movsesian 'The World Trade Constitution' (2000) 114 Harvard Law Review 511.

Melnick RS *Regulation and the Courts: The Case of the Clean Air Act* (Brookings Institution Washington DC 1983).

Morris J 'Defining the Precautionary Principle' in J Morris (ed) *Rethinking Risk and the Precautionary Principle* (Butterworth-Heinemann Oxford 2000) 1.

Morrison ER 'Judicial Review of Discount Rates Used in Regulatory Cost-Benefit Analysis' (1998) 65 University of Chicago Law Review 1333.

National Research Council *Risk Assessment in the Federal Government: Managing the Process* (National Academy Press Washington DC 1983).

National Research Council *Science and Judgment in Risk Assessment* (National Academy Press Washington DC 1994).

National Research Council *Understanding Risk: Informing Decisions in a Democratic Society* (National Academy Press Washington DC 1996).

Neugebauer R 'Fine-Tuning WTO Jurisprudence and the SPS Agreement: Lessons From the Beef Hormones Case' (2000) 31 Law and Policy in International Business 1255.

OECD *Overview of National Food Safety Systems and Activities* (SG/ADHOC/FS(2000)5/FINAL).

Ogus A *Regulation: Legal Form and Economic Theory* (OUP Oxford 1994).

O'Riordan T and J Cameron 'Editorial Introduction' in T O'Riordan and J Cameron (eds) *Interpreting the Precautionary Principle* (Cameron May London 1994) 62.

O'Riordan T, J Cameron and A Jordan 'The Evolution of the Precautionary Principle' in T O'Riordan, J Cameron and A Jordan (eds) *Reinterpreting the Precautionary Principle* (Cameron May London 2002) 9.

Otsuki T, JS Wilson and M Sweadeh *A Race to the Top? A Case Study of Food Safety Standards and African Exports* (Working Paper no 2563 World Bank Washington DC 2001).

Otsuki T, JS Wilson and M Sweadeh *A Race to the Top? A Case Study of Food Safety Standards and African Exports* in K Anderson et al (eds) *The Economics of Quarantine and the SPS Agreement* (Centre for International Economic Studies Adelaide 2001) 287.

Palmeter D 'International Trade Law in the Twenty-First Century' (1995) 18 Fordham International Law Journal 1653.

Palmeter D and GJ Spak 'Resolving Antidumping and Countervailing Duty Disputes: Defining GATT's Role in an Era of Increasing Conflict' (1993) 24 Law and Policy in International Business 1145.

Pauwelyn J 'Does the WTO Stand for "Deference to" or "Interference with" National Health Authorities When Applying the Agreement on Santiary and Phytosanitary Measures (SPS Agreement)?' in T Cottier and PC Mavroidis *The Role of the Judge in International Trade Regulation: Experience and Lessons for the WTO* (U Mich P Ann Arbor 2003) 175.

Pauwelyn J 'Evidence Proof and Persuasion in WTO Dispute Settlement: Who Bears the Burden?' (1998) 1 Journal of International Economic Law 227.

Pauwelyn J 'The Use of Experts in WTO Dispute Settlement' (2002) 51 International and Comparative Law Quarterly 325.

PETERSMANN EU *The GATT/WTO Dispute Settlement System: International Law, International Organizations and Dispute Settlement* (Kluwer London 1997).

PETZOLD H 'The Convention and the Principle of Subsidiarity' in RStJ Macdonald, F Matscher and H Petzold (eds) *The European System for the Protection of Human Rights* (Martinus Nijhoff Publishers Dordrecht 1993) 41.

PIERCE RJ 'Judicial Review: Rulemaking and the Administrative Procedure Act' (1996) 32 Tulsa Law Journal 185.

PORTER TM *Trust in the Numbers: The Pursuit of Objectivity in Science and Public Life* (Princeton UP Princeton 1995).

QUICK R and C LAU 'Environmentally Motivated Tax Distinctions and WTO Law' (2003) 6 Journal of International Economic Law 419.

QURESHI AH 'The Cartagena Protocol on Biosafety and the WTO—Co-existence or Incoherence?' (2000) 49 International and Comparative Law Quarterly 835.

RAY EJ 'The Political Economy of International Trade Law and Policy: Changing Patterns of Protectionism: The Fall in Tariffs and the Rise in Non-Tariff Barriers' (1987) 8 Journal of International Law and Business 285.

REGAN DH 'The Supreme Court and State Protectionism: Making Sense of the Dormant Commerce Clause' (1986) 84 Michigan Law Review 1091.

REGAN DH 'Judicial Review and Member-State Regulation of Trade within a Federal or Quasi-Federal System: Protectionism and Balancing, Da Capo' (2001) 99 Michigan Law Review 1853.

REGAN DH 'Regulatory Purpose and "Like Products" in Article III:4 of GATT (With Additional Remarks on Article III:2' (2002) 36 Journal of World Trade 443.

REGAN DH 'The Dormant Commerce Clause and the *Hormones* Problem' in T Cottier and PC Mavroidis *The Role of the Judge in International Trade Regulation: Experience and Lessons for the WTO* (U Mich P Ann Arbor 2003) 91.

REID TR 'What's Eating the Europeans? Killer Cornflakes' *International Herald Tribune* (London) 2 March 2001, 1.

RUESSMANN LA 'Putting the Precautionary Principle in its Place' (2002) 17 American University International Law Review 905.

SAFRIN S 'Treaties in Collision? The Biosafety Protocol and the World Trade Organization Agreements' (2002) 96 American Journal of International Law 606.

SALMON N 'A European Perspective on the Precautionary Principle, Food Safety and the Free Trade Imperative of the WTO' (2002) 27 European Law Review 138.

SANTILLO D et al 'The Precautionary Principle in Practice: A Mandate for Anticipatory Preventative Action' in C Raffensperger and JA Tickner (eds) *Protecting Public Health and the Environment: Implementing the Precautionary Principle* (Island Press Washington DC 1999) 36.

SASSEN S *Losing Control? Sovereignty in an Age of Globalization* (Columbia UP New York 1996).

SCALIA A 'Judicial Deference to Administrative Interpretations of Law' [1989] Duke Law Journal 511.

SCHOKKENBROEK J 'The Basis, Nature and Application of the Margin-of-Appreciation Doctrine in the Case-Law of the European Court of Human Rights' (1998) 19 Human Rights Law Journal 30.

SCHUH GE 'Developing Country Interests in WTO Agricultural Policy' in DLM Kennedy and JD Southwick *The Political Economy of International Trade Law* (CUP Cambridge UK 2002) 435.

SCHWARZE J *European Administrative Law* (Sweet & Maxwell London 1992).

SCOTT C 'Accountability in the Regulatory State' (2000) 27 Journal of Law and Society 38.

SCOTT J 'On Kith, Kine (and Crustaceans): Trade and Environment in the EU and WTO' in JHH Weiler *The EU, the WTO, and the NAFTA: Towards a Common Law of International Trade?* (OUP Oxford 2000) 125.

SCOTT J 'European Regulation of GMOs in the WTO' (2003) 9 Columbia Journal of European Law 213.

SCOTT J and E VOS 'The Juridification of Uncertainty: Observations on the Ambivalence of the Precautionary Principle within the EU and the WTO' in C Joerges and R Dehousse *Good Governance in Europe's Integrated Market* (OUP Oxford 2002) 25.

SEIDENFELD M 'Demystifying Deossification: Rethinking Recent Proposals to Modify Judicial Review of Notice and Comment Rulemaking' (1997) 75 Texas Law Review 483.

SHAFFER GC '"If Only We Were Elephants": The Political Economy of the WTO's Treatment of Trade and Environment Matters' in DLM Kennedy and JD Southwick (eds) *The Political Economy of International Trade Law* (CUP Cambridge UK 2002) 349.

SHAPIRO M *Integrating Scientific Expertise into Regulatory Decision-Making: The Frontiers of Science Doctrine: American Experiences with the Judicial Control of Science-Based Decision-Making* (EUI Working Paper No 96/11 EUI Florence 1996).

SHAPIRO M *Who Guards the Guardians? Judicial Control of Administration* (Georgia University Press Athens 1988).

SHAPIRO RA and WW BUZBEE 'Unidimensional Federalism: Power and Perspective in Commerce Clause Adjudication' (2003) 88 Cornell Law Review 1199.

SHAPIRO SA and RE LEVIN 'Judicial Incentives and Indeterminacy in Substantive Review of Administrative Decisions' (1995) 44 Duke Law Journal 1051.

SHAW S and R SCHWARTZ 'Trade and Environment in the WTO: State of Play' (2000) 36 Journal of World Trade 129.

SHOYER AW and EM SOLOVY 'The Process and Procedure of Litigating at the World Trade Organization: A Review of the Work of the Appellate Body Panels' (2000) 31 Law and Policy in International Business 677.

SHRADER-FRECHETTE KS *Risk and Rationality: Philosophical Foundations for Populist Reforms* (U California Press Berkeley 1991).

SLOVIC P 'Beyond Numbers: A Broader Perspective on Risk Perception and Risk Communication' in DG Mayo and RD Hollander (eds) *Acceptable Evidence: Science and Risk Values in Risk Management* (OUP Oxford 1991) 48.

SLYNN G 'The Concept of the Free Movement of Goods and the Reservation for National Action under Article 36 EEC Treaty' in J Schwarze (ed) *Discretionary Powers of the Member States in the Field of Economic Policies and Their Limits under the EEC Treaty* (Nomos Baden-Baden 1988) 17.

SMITS D and S ZABROSKI 'Trade and Genetically Modified Foods: GMOs: Chumps or Champs of International Trade?' (2001) 1 Asper Review of International Business & Trade 111.

SOUTH CENTRE *WTO Agreement on Sanitary and Phytosanitary Measures: Issues for Developing Countries* (South Centre Geneva 1999).

STEWART TP and AA KARPEL 'Review of the Dispute Settlement Understanding: Operation of Panels' (2000) 31 Law and Policy in International Business 593.

STEWART RB 'International Trade and Environment: Lessons from the Federal Experience' (1992) 49 Washington and Lee Law Review 1329.

STEWART RB 'Environmental Regulatory Decisionmaking under Uncertainty' (preliminary discussion draft) (UCL Symposium on the Law & Economics of Environmental Policy 2001) (available at <http://www.cserge.ucl.ac.uk/Stewart.pdf> on 16August 2002).

STILWELL M and B VAN DYKE 'An Activist's Handbook on Genetically Modified Organisms and the WTO' (Consumer's Choice Council 1999, available at <http://www.consumerscouncil.org/policy/handbk799.htm>.

STIRLING A *On Science and Precaution in the Management of Technological Risk* (Institute for Prospective Technological Studies Seville 1999).

STIRLING A 'The Precautionary Principle in Science and Technology' in T O'Riordan, J Cameron and A Jordan (eds) *Reinterpreting the Precautionary Principle* (Cameron May London 2002) 61.

SUNSTEIN C *After the Rights Revolution: Reconceiving the Regulatory State* (Harvard UP Cambridge MA 1990).

SUNSTEIN CR 'Beyond the Precautionary Principle' (preliminary draft) (John M Olin Law & Economics Working Paper No 149 Chicago 2002).

SUNSTEIN CR and R PILDES 'Experts, Economists, and Democrats' in CR Sunstein *Free Markets and Social Justice* (OUP New York 1997) 128.

SUPPERSTONE M QC and J COPPEL 'Judicial Review after the Human Rights Act' [1999] European Human Rights Law Review 301.

SYKES AO *Product Standards for Internationally Integrated Goods Markets* (Brookings Institution Washington DC 1995).

SYKES AO 'Regulatory Protectionism and the Law of International Trade' (1999) 66 University of Chicago Law Review 1.

SYKES AO 'Exploring the Need for International Harmonization: Domestic Regulation, Sovereignty, and Scientific Evidence Requirements: A Pessimistic View' (2002) 3 Chicago Journal of International Law 353.

TARULLO DK 'The Hidden Costs of International Dispute Settlement: WTO Review of Domestic Anti-Dumping Decisions' (2002) 34 Law & Policy in International Business 109.

THORN C and M CARLSON 'The Agreement on the Application of Sanitary and Phytosanitary Measures and the Agreement on Technical Barriers to Trade' (2000) 31 Law and Policy in International Business 841.

THOMAS RD 'Where's the Beef? Mad Cows and the Blight of the SPS Agreement' (1999) Vanderbilt Journal of Transnational Law 487.

TICKNER J and C RAFFENSPERGER 'The American View on the Precautionary Principle' in T O'Riordan, A Jordan and J Cameron (eds) *Reinterpreting the Precautionary Principle* (Cameron May London 2002) 183.

TREBILCOCK MJ and R HOWSE *The Regulation of International Trade* (2nd edn Routledge London 1999).

TREBILCOCK M and J SOLOWAY 'International Trade Policy and Domestic Food Safety Regulation: The Case for Substantial Deference by the WTO Dispute Settlement Body under the SPS Agreement' in DLM Kennedy and JD Southwick (eds) *The Political Economy of International Trade Law* (CUP Cambridge UK 2002) 537.

TRIBE LH *American Constitutional Law* (Vol 1, 3rd edn Foundation Press New York 2000).

TRIDIMAS T *The General Principles of EC Law* (OUP Oxford 1999).

UNITED STATES (1994) 6 US Code Congressional and Administrative News 4040.

UNITED STATES ATTORNEY GENERAL'S COMMITTEE ON ADMINISTRATIVE PROCEDURE *Final Report* (1941).

US FOOD AND DRUG ADMINISTRATION *Precaution in US Food Safety Decisionmaking* (Annex II to the US's National Food Safety System Paper submitted to the OECD, SG/ADHOC/FS(2002)5/ANN/FINAL).

VERHOOSEL G *National Treatment and WTO Dispute Settlement: Adjudicating the Boundaries of Regulatory Autonomy* (Hart Publishing Oxford 2002).

VOGEL D *Ships Passing in the Night: The Changing Politics of Risk Regulation in Europe and the United States* (EUI Working Paper 2001/16 Florence 2001).

WAGNER JM 'The WTO's Interpretation of the SPS Agreement has Undermined the Right of Governments to Establish Appropriate Levels of Protection Against Risk' (2000) 31 Law and Policy in International Business 855.

WALD PM 'Judicial Review in Midpassage: The Uneasy Partnership Between Courts and Agencies Plays On' (1996) 32 Tulsa Law Journal 221.

WALKER VR 'Keeping the WTO from Becoming the "World Trans-science Organization": Scientific Uncertainty, Science Policy, and Factfinding in the Growth Hormones Dispute' (1998) 31 Cornell International Law Journal 251.

WARD H 'Trade and Environmental Issues in Voluntary Eco-Labelling and Life Cycle Analysis' (1997) 6(2) Review of European Community and International Environmental Law 139.

WEILER JHH 'The Constitution of the Common Market Place: Text and Context in the Evolution of the Free Movement of Goods' in P Craig and G de Búrca (eds) *The Evolution of EU Law* (OUP Oxford 1999) 349.

WEILER JHH 'The Rule of Lawyers and the Ethos of Diplomats: Reflections on WTO Dispute Settlement' in RB Porter et al (eds) *Efficiency, Equity, and Legitimacy: The Multilateral System at the Millennium* (Brookings Institution Washington DC 2001) 334.

WHO and WTO *WTO Agreements and Public Health* (WTO/WHO Geneva 2002).

WIENER JB and MD ROGERS 'Comparing Precaution in the United States and Europe' (2002) 5 Journal of Risk Research 317.

WIENER JB 'Whose Precaution After All? A Comment on the Comparison and Evolution of Risk Regulatory Systems' (2003) 13 Duke Journal of Comparative & International Law 207.

WILSON JS and T OTSUKI *Global Trade and Food Safety: Winners and Losers in a Fragmented System* (Working Paper No 2689 World Bank Washington DC 2001).

WIRTH DA 'The Role of Science in the Uruguay Round and NAFTA Trade Disciplines' (1994) 27 Cornell International Law Journal 817.

WIRTH DA 'European Communities–Measures Concerning Meat and Meat Products' (1998) 92 American Journal of International Law 755.

WTO COMMITTEE ON SANITARY AND PHYTOSANITARY MEASURES *Summary of the Meeting Held on 15–16 March 2000* (G/SPS/R/18 18 April 2000).

WTO SECRETARIAT *Trade Policy Review: Australia* (WT/TPR/S/104 26 August 2002).

WTO Secretariat *Implementation of the Provisions for Review, Future Work or Negotiations in the WTO Agreement and Related Decisions and Declarations* (WT/L/271 7 May 1998).

Wynne B 'Uncertainty and Environmental Learning: Reconceiving Science and Policy in the Preventative Paradigm' (2000) Global Environmental Change 111.

Wynter M 'The Agreement on Sanitary and Phytosanitary Measures in the Light of the WTO Decisions on EC Measures Concerning Meat and Meat Products (Hormones)' in P Mengozzi (ed) *International Trade Law on the 50th Anniversary of the Multilateral Trade System* (A Giuffrè Editore Milano 1999) 471.

Zampetti AB and P Sauvé 'New Dimensions of Market Access: An Overview' in OECD *New Dimensions of Market Access in a Globalising World Economy* (OECD Paris 1995) 13.

Zedalis RJ 'The Environment and the Technical Barriers to Trade Agreement: Did the *Reformulated Gasoline* Panel Miss a Golden Opportunity?' (1997) 44 Netherlands International Law Review 186.

Zellmer SB 'The Devil, the Details, and the Dawn of the 21st Century Administrative State: Beyond the New Deal' (2000) 32 Arizona State Law Journal 941.

Ziegler AR 'WTO Rules Supporting Environmental Protection' in F Weiss, E Denters and P de Waart (eds) *International Economic Law with a Human Face* (Kluwer Law International The Hague 1998) 203.

Zleptnig S 'The Standard of Review in WTO Law: An Analysis of Law, Legitimacy and the Distribution of Legal and Political Authority' (2002) 13 European Business Law Review 427.

Index